The Psychology of Counseling

The Psychology
of Counseling

Edwin C. Lewis
Iowa State University

HOLT, RINEHART AND WINSTON, INC.

New York   Chicago   San Francisco   Atlanta
Dallas   Montreal   Toronto   London   Sydney

Copyright © 1970 by Holt, Rinehart and Winston, Inc.
All rights reserved
Library of Congress Catalog Card Number: 79–118724
SBN: 03–078270–8
Printed in the United States of America
1 2 3 4 5 6 7 8 9

To Jonathan

Preface

For about twelve years I have been teaching a course, primarily for first-year graduate students, in the psychology of counseling. Like many other teachers, I began this course with the assurance that I knew a great deal about the subject, only to discover that the communication of one's own concepts is much more difficult than it first appears. Over the years, therefore, my view of counseling has evolved, through my experience both as a counselor and as a teacher, to the point where I believe I can now take the step of venturing beyond the confines of my own classroom. This book represents that step.

I have aimed this book at persons who know little about counseling and who want to learn about it. It is, as the title indicates, a psychological view of counseling, but it attempts to provide a broad survey of the field, as a psychologist sees it. In one sense it is by no means a novel effort: much of the ground has already been covered by other writers, although I hope that my organization of it will be helpful to the novice. Yet this book is not meant to be an encyclopedia of counseling; it presents counseling as I see it, with an emphasis on its psychological nature. It presents a view of counseling derived both from my own experience as a counselor and from my study of the relevant psychological literature. Thus the organization of the book is in some respects quite traditional, but the content in some areas is not, although I hope it is defensible.

There is no room here to enumerate all of the persons who have influenced the development of my view of counseling—my teachers, my colleagues, my students, and of course my clients. Specifically, though, I must mention my colleagues who have read and reacted to parts of this manuscript: Fred Brown, Roy Warman, Ron Baker, Dave Mills, Russ Canute, and Charles Poe. These persons, as well as Clyde Parker and Harold Pepinsky, have supplied many helpful criticisms and, although I have not written the book each of them would have written, their help has been invaluable. I am greatly indebted also to Becky Smaha who typed the manuscript. Finally, I cannot adequately acknowledge the contribution of my wife, Nancy, and my children, without whom this book might have been completed with greater dispatch, but certainly with much less humanity.

Edwin C. Lewis

Ames, Iowa
February 1970

Contents

The Psychology
of Counseling

PART I
The Nature
of Counseling

1

The Development
and Present Status
of Counseling

This could be called the age of confusion. Modern man is pictured as a bewildered organism, buffeted this way and that by the cyclonic pressures of life. In his search for help he is offered aid by many persons who call themselves "counselors": vocational counselors, investment counselors, burial counselors, and even used-car counselors. The addition of the word "counselor" to one's title gives him increased status and respectability, in a society which has come to revere labels.

Who, then, is this ubiquitous and omniscient counselor? What miracles does he perform, and in what manner? The answer is simple: he is not omniscient and he does not perform miracles. The sad fact is that the term "counseling" has been distorted far out of its original meaning. Most so-called "counselors" do no counseling whatsoever; in truth, their goals and methods are quite dissimilar to those of professional counselors. The result is that, although counseling is a term which most persons will instantly recognize, their conception of its meaning will probably be confused at best and in many cases downright wrong.

Perhaps those concerned with counseling in its professional sense should abandon the term entirely. It is obvious, however, that any book which has the word "counseling" in its title is not about to discard the term on the first page. Instead, one purpose of this book is to rescue counseling from its public image, by developing a meaning for the term which can serve as a communications anchor for persons concerned with counseling in its basic, helping sense.

In a way, counseling is the victim of its own popularity. We therefore must ask how this popularity has come about, in order to find our way back to a meaningful, coherent concept.

THE SOCIAL CONTEXT

Social movements grow out of social needs, and the growth of counseling is no exception. Modern life is complex, and problems abound. This in itself is not a new phenomenon. People have always had to deal with problems, but those of today are of a different nature. There was a time when most problems which confronted an individual in his lifetime were not "new." The world changed slowly, so that most of the difficulties that arose had been encountered before. If a man hadn't previously experienced a specific problem himself, he could turn for help to someone who had. Life was by no means better or easier than it is today, but it was simpler and more predictable.

The man of yesterday had another advantage when he hit snags in his life. The chances were good that he would be surrounded by friends and relatives who had known him for many years and who could provide him with the kind of help he needed. As will be emphasized throughout this book, the key to any problem is the man in the middle, the person who must in some way cope with it. Any help from an outside source is useful only to the extent that it takes into consideration who this person is and how he can best be helped. In the days when families and communities were stable, relatives and friends knew each other well enough to be able to help one another.

Modern life, by contrast, is characterized by instability: one-fifth of the population changes their homes each year, and many others move socially if not geographically away from their former relationships. The individual in our society has been encouraged, and even forced, to be independent of others. In doing so, he may have gained an increased personal identity, but often at the expense of long-standing personal relationships which he could use constructively in time of trouble.

A third characteristic of modern life which has had an important influence on the counseling movement is that the nature of man's personal struggles has changed. Not too long ago man fought his greatest battles with his environment. He was threatened by diseases and hostile forces which he had difficulty in controlling, and his greatest accomplishments were the imposition of his will on his environment and on his society.

Many of these threats still exist, but they are decreasing rapidly as man has begun to look elsewhere for challenges. In many cases he has found them within himself. He has become more aware of himself as a person, and he has raised his sights as to his own way of living. He is asking questions about himself which at one time would have been buried by the pressures of an untamed environment. Now these questions sound with intense clarity. They may be expressed in many ways: questions about choice of a career, about relationships with the opposite sex, about child-raising, about how to handle fears and anxieties, and a myriad others. But running through most of them there seems to be a basic theme: "Who am I?" "Where do I want to go?" "How can I get there?" For help in finding answers, he turns to the counselor.

Professional counseling has thus developed as a response to a strong social need. It has long been recognized that a person confused about himself and his future may be helped by discussing his problems with another person, but only in this century has this helping process become formalized. As professionals in various areas have developed increased understanding of the nature of the human condition, they have used this knowledge to help persons deal more effectively with their problems. Educators, for example, recognizing the need of young persons to make wise decisions about their educational and vocational futures, instituted counseling services in the public schools. Social workers provided counseling for families with problems in marital relationships or questions about child-raising. Psychiatrists and clinical psychologists, concerned originally with the diagnosis and treatment of mental disorders, gradually moved in the direction of helping persons with "normal" adjustment problems, partly as a means of preventing the development of more serious difficulties.

This description implies, deliberately, that the development of counseling has not been monolithic nor even well coordinated. As we will see, many professions make use of counseling in their service roles in helping persons in trouble. Nor is there an agreement on a single definition of counseling. Since counseling has developed via a number of diverse routes, it has been molded in different forms. Nonetheless, there appear to be some basic elements which do delineate it from other helping processes. We will return to these shortly.

THE PSYCHOLOGICAL CONTEXT

From the viewpoint of society, counseling is a process by which one person helps another to deal more effectively with himself and the stresses imposed by his environment. In this sense, persons from a variety of professions may engage in counseling and be vitally concerned with understanding its nature.

But counseling can also be viewed as a process which results in *behavior change*. The outcome of counseling is some change on the part of the individual who sought help (the client) and this change can be defined and demonstrated in behavioral terms. When conceptualized in this manner, counseling becomes a topic for the study of the *psychologist,* whose goal is the advancement of knowledge concerning human behavior.

The psychologist, therefore, is interested in counseling as a tool by which to effect positive change in persons who are dissatisfied with their present behavior. He may express this interest in a dual role: by being of direct help to troubled persons, as are members of several other professions, and by studying the counseling process to gain insight into the nature of behavior change which it produces. It is in the latter role that the psychologist makes his unique contribution to the advancement of counseling as a helping process. Members of many professions engage in counseling as a professional activity, but the psychologist is also interested in studying the counseling process scientifically. This does not necessarily make him a better counselor, but it has resulted in an increased understanding of the nature of counseling and the development of tools and techniques to make counseling more effective.

The focus of this book, then, will be on counseling as viewed from the standpoint of a psychologist. It will deal with counseling in breadth, to provide a conceptual framework for the beginning counselor, but it will try to emphasize those aspects which are of particular interest to psychologists and to which psychologists have made important contributions. A few of these will be noted here briefly, and some will be discussed in detail later.

Psychological Measurement

One of the early concerns of counseling, especially to educators, was helping young people make decisions about education and jobs. To do so counselors needed information about the person that would be relevant to these decisions. It is much more than coincidence that the development of vocational counseling closely paralleled the growth of psychological testing, especially the development of group tests. Counselors found that knowledge about abilities and interests gained from standardized tests aided greatly in the decisions which their clients made about future academic plans and the choice of an occupation.

Psychological tests thus became a basic tool of the counselor, so much so that the early approach to counseling, popular during the 1920s and 1930s, is known as the "trait-and-factor" approach. Counselors during this period believed that educational and vocational decisions could best be made by matching relevant client characteristics, as specified by psychological tests, with corresponding job variables. As the testing movement grew more sophisticated, it became evident that matching in this manner was naive and unwise, and some counselors subsequently became disillusioned with tests altogether. But most counselors continue to include psychological tests as a basic tool in their repertoire, to the extent that two chapters later in this book will be devoted to their use in counseling.

Learning Theory

Counseling can be viewed as a learning process, in which the client learns more effective and satisfying modes of behavior as well as changes in attitudes, feelings, and so forth. The study of the learning process has long been of central concern to psychologists, both in the laboratory and in real-life situations. Numerous theories of learning have been developed and tested in experimental situations, and the results of this research have increased our understanding of the learning process. This knowledge is being applied to the study of the counseling process and has generated a major approach known as "behavioral counseling," which will be described in greater detail in the next chapter.

The application of principles of learning to the counseling situation has the virtue of allowing for a more systematic study of the nature of counseling, with the inclusion of verifiable theoretical constructs and the development of a comprehensive body of knowledge concerning counseling. As additional knowledge concerning the learning process is gained by psychologists, it should help to clarify those aspects of counseling still not well understood.

The Role of Client Attitude

A more recent movement in the study of counseling has been the application of principles of interpersonal interaction, derived from social psychology, to the counseling relationship (see, for example, Goldstein, 1966; Goldstein, Heller, and Sechrest, 1966; Strong, 1968). The characteristics of the typical client as he enters counseling—anxious, insecure, in need of help—coupled with the aura of competence and authority which surround the counselor combine to produce a situation which maximizes the probability that change in the client's behaviors, attitudes, and feelings will occur. The exact nature of this influence is not yet well understood, but the research paradigms of the social psychologists offer promise of leading to greater understanding of it.

The counselor-client interaction is a powerful social dyad, and the intensity of the relationship, coupled with the client's feelings of anxiety and insecurity when he enters counseling, conspire to make a profound impression on the client and thereby to influence his behavior. The counselor, then, must recognize that he can and does exert on his clients important indirect influences, as well as those which are more deliberate on his part, and that the effect of a given counseling experience may depend as much on the atmosphere and relationship between client and counselor as upon the techniques which the counselor employs.

Study of Human Development

Counseling has typically been made available to persons who are at crucial points in their development and may therefore be experiencing "developmental crises." It has been especially helpful to young persons making the transition from adolescence to adulthood and is therefore most commonly found in high schools and colleges. Gradually, however, counseling services have been extended in both directions, so that counselors are now available in many elementary schools as well as in agencies dealing with the problems of adults.

Counseling within a developmental framework requires an understanding of the nature of human development and, as psychologists have gained in knowledge about development, counseling has likewise become more sophisticated. The needs of persons at various stages of development are better understood, as are their cognitive and emotional status which may influence the type of counseling from which they can benefit most. Several theoretical approaches to counseling, to be described in the following chapter, concern themselves directly with the nature of human development and aim at promoting positive growth in the client. Knowledge about the process of development is thus of great importance if such approaches are to accomplish their goals.

Since one of the original sources of impetus for the counseling movement was concern with effective vocational planning and since vocational choice continues to be a major reason for persons to seek counseling, psychologists have been especially interested in the process of career development. This has led to the creation of several theories of vocational development which in turn have generated considerable research.[1] The result is a better understanding of the process by which persons come to make vocational decisions and the role which the counselor can effectively play in this process.

Theoretical Conceptions of Counseling

Psychology is a science, and one of the major tools of science is theory. A theory allows the scientist to fit a series of events into a coherent pattern and to systematically extend his knowledge about the relationships among

[1] Among those investigators whose work has had an important impact have been Ginzberg (Ginzberg and others, 1951), Super (1953; Super and others, 1963), Tiedeman (1961; Tiedeman and O'Hara, 1963), and Holland (1959). For reviews of the literature and summaries of the theories see Borow (1961), Hewer (1963), Holland (1964), Holland and Whitney (1969), and Whiteley (1969).

these events by testing predictions generated by the theory. Psychologists interested in the counseling process have attempted, therefore, to create theories to explain the events which take place in counseling, often borrowing from the more basic experimental areas of psychology as a starting point. The practicing counselor, while familiar with some of the leading theories, probably has little time or inclination to build and test a theory for himself. He must rely on the theories and research of the behavioral scientists interested in counseling, most of whom are either psychologists or have had psychological training.

DEFINITIONS OF COUNSELING

In order to discuss counseling meaningfully, we must first attempt to define it. This should not, however, mislead the reader into believing that memorizing a formal definition is essential to becoming a counselor. In actuality the working counselor operates, not on the basis of a static definition, but from his personal concept of the goals of counseling and the best means of reaching these goals. Insofar as counselors differ in their beliefs as to the most appropriate goals and means, it follows that they will also differ in their formal definitions of counseling. It is thus not surprising to find that there is no generally accepted definition of counseling. Although the differences among the definitions which have been propounded are not great, they are varied enough to suggest that each writer is operating from a unique point of view.

Some Representative Definitions

Despite their diversity, most definitions of counseling include at least three elements: (a) a troubled person (the client), (b) a person whose role is to help the client (the counselor), and (c) an interaction between the counselor and client which results in some change in the client. It is in describing this interaction, however, that definitions differ: some emphasize the *relationship* between the client and counselor, while others stress the *process* by which client change takes place.

Either of these emphases is defensible, but they produce somewhat different definitions of counseling. The definitions which emphasize the *relationship* tend to follow that proposed by Rogers almost three decades ago (Rogers, 1942):

> Effective counseling consists of a definitely structured permissive relationship which allows the client to gain an understanding of himself to a degree which enables him to take positive steps in the light of his new orientation [p. 18].

A more recent definition emphasizing the relationship aspect of counseling has been proposed by Stefflre (1965a):

> Counseling denotes a professional relationship between a trained counselor and a client. This relationship is usually person-to-person, although it may sometimes involve more than two people, and it is designed to help the client understand and clarify his view of his life space so that he may make meaningful and informed choices consonant with his essential nature in those areas where choices are available to him [p. 15].

Other writers, however, have chosen to emphasize counseling as a *process* in their definitions. Of these, Gustad (1953) has produced the most comprehensive definition, based on a thorough survey of previous attempts to define counseling:

> Counseling is a learning-oriented process, carried on in a simple, one-to-one social environment, in which a counselor, professionally competent in relevant psychological skills and knowledge, seeks to assist the client, by methods appropriate to the latter's needs and within the context of the total personnel program, to learn how to put such understanding into effect in relation to more clearly perceived, realistically defined goals to the end that the client may become a happier and more productive member of society [p. 17].

Since no single definition has proved to be a rallying point for a majority of counselors,[2] it may be futile to propose another. No two persons see exactly the same sunset, nor do two different counselors perceive counseling in exactly the same way. Yet there is sufficient communality among the views of most counselors that a definition can be ventured. Furthermore the reader is entitled to know where this writer stands and to understand the framework within which the remainder of the presentation will be set. It is hoped that the definition presented here will serve as a stimulus to the reader's thinking and aid him in reaching his own personal definition of counseling.

The approach favored by this writer is to emphasize the counseling process rather than the relationship in a definition, primarily because the process seems more amenable to behavioral description and psychological analysis. To describe the counseling process requires, however, a consideration of two aspects: the goal of the counseling, and the procedure by which the goal is to be attained.

The counseling goal is determined by both the client and counselor: the client comes to counseling with a specific need, and the counselor has a

---

[2] The inability of counselors to agree on a single definition has plagued efforts to control the terms "counselor" and "counseling" by legislation. It is very difficult to define counseling so as to include persons with certain professional qualifications and to exclude persons less well qualified.

conception of how counseling may help this person meet his need. Whatever his specific concern may be, however, the typical client enters counseling seeking a way of dealing more effectively with himself or with his environment. He is puzzled, indecisive, worried, or in some way not coping satisfactorily with some kind of personal stress or environmental demand, and he believes that the counselor can help him handle things more effectively. The counselor, in turn, perceives the potential contribution which counseling can make to the development of this individual, perhaps going beyond the specific presented need. In combination, the two enter into a relationship designed to produce an outcome with which both can be satisfied.

A Definition of Counseling

On this basis, the following definition of counseling is proposed: *Counseling is a process by which a troubled person (the client) is helped to feel and behave in a more personally satisfying manner through interaction with an uninvolved person (the counselor) who provides information and reactions which stimulate the client to develop behaviors which enable him to deal more effectively with himself and his environment.*

This definition assigns a rather specific role to both the client and the counselor, yet it allows for a wide range of counseling goals and of counselor techniques. Its intent is to emphasize that the purpose of counseling is to produce sufficient change in the client to enable him to accomplish what he was formerly not able to accomplish. It is implied that the client's development as a person is enhanced by the counseling experience: he has become "more" rather than "different."

Establishing the Concept

A concept is more than a definition. Since one purpose of this chapter is to develop a concept of counseling, the definition proposed above requires discussion and amplification. The following propositions follow from the proposed definition, and extend it.

1. Counseling is an activity, not a profession. Any activity which satisfies the proposed definition is "counseling," which means that counseling is not defined by the professional qualifications of the practitioner. The counseling process is the cornerstone of several professions, although the specific approach may differ from one to another. The term "counselor" will be used here to denote a professional counselor regardless of his specific professional identification.

2. Counseling deals with normal problems of development. Persons are most likely to seek a professional counselor when they are having difficulty in some aspect of personal development. Thus counseling can be viewed as an opportunity for the client to enhance his own development, through the use of a special relationship in which he can learn techniques for coping with the demands of his life. In doing so, he becomes a more fully functioning person, more secure in his control of himself and of his environment.

Counseling is therefore aimed at "developmental facilitation," as a tool which a person can use to help himself overcome difficulties in the developmental process. It is important to bear in mind that these difficulties are *normal;* that is, they may be experienced by many persons, although each in his unique manner. Some may choose to use professional counselors as a means of facilitating the resolution of such difficulties, and others may not. The latter may obtain counseling from nonprofessional sources, perhaps as a byproduct of other relationships. Presumably, everyone can benefit from counseling at some point in his life, but some people are reluctant to seek professional help. While counselors are committed to the belief that counseling is a useful tool, they must respect the individual's right to decide which sources of help are most appropriate for him.

The developmental nature of counseling is evident in the fact that professional counselors are most available to persons who are at a crucial stage in their development: students in high school and college. Persons at this age are assuming greater responsibility for their own lives and are faced with the necessity for making decisions which will restrict their later opportunities for choice: choice of school, choice of job, choice of marriage partner, choice of values, and so on. In addition, young people have considerable growth potential: they are encountering new situations to which they must respond, and they have a wider repertoire of possible responses than does an older person who has established a rather consistent and restricted response pattern.

In recent years, however, psychologists have widened their concept of human development to include the entire life span. They recognize that development is a continuous process and that a person's exposure to new experience and new kinds of stress does not disappear simply because he has reached the age of thirty or forty. As one grows older, his life changes as his children grow up and leave home, job requirements and opportunities vary, and social interactions are reduced. This is part of the developmental process, and counseling can be useful to persons in the later stages of life in the same way as it is useful to those who are young: by providing an opportunity for them to learn to cope more effectively with their behavior, their feelings, and the stresses of their environment.

3. *The counseling relationship is unique.* A key element in counseling is the relationship between the counselor and the client. This relationship is unique because the focus is entirely on the client. It is structured by the counselor so as to provide a situation which the client can use to facilitate

some aspect of his personal development, by becoming more aware of himself as a person and acquiring a view of himself and his world which enables him to behave in a manner more satisfying to him.

A special relationship is necessary because the typical kind of relationship is not designed to promote the development of one of the parties in a systematic, constructive manner. In the typical relationship between strangers, both parties are guarded. As they become better acquainted, emotional attachments tend to develop, so that neither party can remain objective enough to provide maximum help to the other. Thus there are few relationships in everyday life in which a person can express himself freely and honestly to another person with whom he does not already have some other relationship. Such an opportunity is necessary if the client is to become more fully aware of himself and able to view himself and his difficulties calmy and constructively.

The counselor tries to provide such a relationship, by indicating to the client that the usual threats do not exist in the counseling setting. He does this by reacting calmly to whatever the client expresses, by not passing judgment on the client or his behavior, and in general by encouraging the client to be as completely himself as possible. This is often referred to as an *acceptance* attitude. Although techniques to communicate this attitude to the client can be learned, the basic attitude itself must be genuine. The counselor cannot, and should not try to, fake an attitude of acceptance which he does not truly feel. If the counselor expects to encourage the client to be truly himself in the counseling setting, he too must present an honest picture of his own feelings and attitudes toward the client. The skillful counselor is able to react openly to the client in a nonthreatening manner, thereby providing an atmosphere in which a free interchange of ideas and feelings is possible.

Counseling, then, can be distinguished from other relationships by this attitude and behavior on the part of the counselor, which in turn can be a means of determining whether a given activity is in fact counseling. This implies, however, that other relationships may at times have counseling components, which in turn leads to our fourth principle.

4. The counseling relationship need not necessarily involve a professional counselor. It is often assumed that counseling occurs only when one of the participants is a professionally trained counselor, but such a requirement seems both untenable and unnecessary. Counseling is better defined in terms of the activity and operations involved than by the titles of the participants. Thus a person who has completed a training program in counseling is not automatically a counselor, while a counseling relationship may be established between two persons, neither of whom is professionally trained as a counselor.

This proposition is rather risky, because it seems to undermine the growing insistence that persons who get involved with other people's problems should be professionally trained. Its purpose, however, is to emphasize that the value of a professional training program for counselors lies not in the fact that a person has completed it, but instead in the changes that it has made in him during his progress through it. Presumably a training program of high quality will evaluate its students frequently for evidence of personal growth, but it is important to emphasize that a counselor must be judged by what he can *do* rather than by the amount of training he has had.

Although this proposition does allow for the possibility that two persons, neither of whom has been trained as a counselor, can establish an effective counseling relationship for the benefit of one of them, in practice the likelihood of this occurring is slight. It is difficult to conceive of a situation in which such a relationship could be maintained, let alone established, without being diluted by the other relationships between the two persons involved. What is more probable is that certain relationships, established on other bases, may for a short time become quasi-counseling relationships, as for example when a student discusses his future plans with a teacher. However, the overtones of the other relationship between the two persons will tend to reduce its counseling value.

This leaves the professional counselor with two advantages: (a) His clients have sought him out in order to establish a counseling relationship, so that their use of this relationship is not encumbered by other relationships with him. (b) By virtue of his training and experience, the professional counselor is more likely to be able to establish an effective counseling relationship than is the layman. Although it can be argued that counseling is an art, the skills of most artists are enhanced by training and experience. In almost any area of life, the professional's training and experience give him a considerable advantage over the gifted amateur. A person who desires a counseling relationship in which to deal with some aspect of his life will therefore maximize his chances of finding a beneficial relationship by seeking out a professional counselor.

5. *The counselor is a disinterested person who is used by the client to achieve his counseling goal.* The counselor's job is to help the client make the most effective possible use of him (the counselor). The counselor is a tool which the client uses to move toward his goal.

At the same time that the counselor is promoting the client's effective *use* of him, he must guard against being *misused*. The latter occurs when the counselor accepts the client's request that he do something, such as giving advice, which would be in violation of the basic counseling relationship which he is attempting to promote.[3] Since it is part of the counselor's

---

[3] As with all principles, the experienced counselor will occasionally violate this, as we shall discuss later. It is valid as a guide, however, to those who are learning about counseling.

responsibility to help the client learn how to use the counseling relationship most effectively, he should resist the client's attempts to misuse him.

The term "disinterested" may also need clarification. This is not meant to imply that the counselor doesn't care one way or the other what happens to the client. On the contrary, the counselor is vitally concerned with the client's needs, in the sense that he communicates to the client that he wants to do what he can to help him, consistent with his conception of counseling. Few clients would feel comfortable talking to a brick wall.

Disinterest on the part of the counselor primarily means that he does not directly experience the feelings of the client, so that he is not personally confused or upset by them as the client is. This is necessary not only because the counselor could not be expected to share the emotional burdens of a series of clients, but also because the client needs the security of a situation in which he knows that the other person will not react emotionally to problems and questions which are disturbing him. A common characteristic of quasi-counseling relationships, such as some aspects of parent-child relationships, is that *both* parties tend to become emotionally involved in the topic under discussion.

The counselor's disinterest also means that *he does not feel responsible* for the client's behavior or feelings or for the outcome of the counseling. The competent counselor makes every effort to promote a helpful relationship with each client and to be as useful as possible, but he does not berate himself for those relationships which do not reach a satisfactory conclusion. The blame for an unsuccessful counseling experience can probably be assigned to several factors, one of which may well be the counselor himself. But if the counselor believes he was striving to do a good job, even though he fell short of his goal, he need not bear the entire responsibility for the outcome. By the same token, neither may he take full credit for his successes. Both success and failure must be shared with the client, and in most cases the client can claim the greatest share of both.

A common error of inexperienced counselors is their tendency to assume too much responsibility for their client's behavior and for the counseling outcome. If the beginning counselor is to weather the stresses and strains of counseling, he must learn that he cannot shoulder the burdens of his clients. Not only is this emotionally impossible, but it encourages a dependency relationship which is likely to have undesirable results.

6. Counselor and client share a cooperative relationship. The success of a counseling experience depends a great deal on the extent to which the counselor and client are able to work together. To this end, the counselor must try to avoid being an authority figure to the client. The counselor's major role as an expert is that he has a clearer concept than does the client of an effective counseling relationship, and he has learned some techniques for producing behavior change. The client, on the other hand, supplies the *raison d'être* for the existence of the counseling relationship. Through teamwork with the counselor, the client is able to accomplish what was formerly difficult, if not impossible, by himself.

Clients' Views of Counseling

It may help to clarify the concept of counseling just described by quoting from two successfully counseled clients. The counselors involved were not of the same theoretical orientation, as is evident from the statements of the clients, yet in each case the client was able to achieve, with the help of the counselor, a level of personal self-understanding and environmental control sufficient to meet his needs.

The first statement is from a woman counseled by a nondirective counselor (quoted by Arbuckle, 1961a):

> Through the help given me in these sessions . . . I have been able to get on an even keel again. The permissive atmosphere which was established allowed for an outpouring of feelings and emotions from the past and present such as I had never experienced before. This left me free to concentrate on regaining control of myself, and I learned how to help myself over any bad spots which came along. I don't know what the future will bring, but in the past three weeks I have succeeded in throwing off a life which I had grown to hate but had allowed to become a habit which could not be shaken. I know I have many more problems to face and temptations to resist, but somehow I feel I have gained the strength to face life squarely and accept what it has to offer [p. 22].

The second statement was written by a college student who had been counseled in a university counseling service. Although his problem was more specific than that of the woman quoted above, his counseling experience seems to have had a no less important effect on him:

> I entered Iowa State University as a freshman in the Fall Quarter of 19— as a physics major. Looking back I think my choice of major was based largely on a romantic view of the career of a physicist gleaned from the post-Sputnik pro-science propaganda. My achievements in science on the high school level had been good but not spectacular. Again in retrospect, I can see various facts which should have provided some warning that I was not suited for a career in science, and at the end of the quarter I possessed a 2.76 grade point [out of a possible 4.00] and a very discouraged attitude because my preliminary test scores had led me to anticipate much greater success. In addition I had a General Motors scholarship and felt that I had failed both them and myself.
>
> During Freshman Orientation I had heard about the Student Counseling Service and, when matters grew no better, I made an appointment for a preliminary interview with a staff counselor. After the general nature of

the problem had been ascertained, I was assigned and completed a battery of aptitude and interest tests. For a variety of reasons my attitude in taking the tests was antipathetic toward science and certainly this was reflected to some degree in the results. While the aptitude tests suggested that my chances for success in science were fairly good, they gave stronger indications in the humanities, and the interest tests gave me no better than an average interest in science.

Thus far matters were simple, but then followed the task of evaluating the results. I realized at the time that my views were strongly colored both by my recent scholastic experiences and by a friend who had similar problems and changed to Modern Languages. In addition the humanities seemed a stagnant backwater so far as any connection with "significant" ideas was concerned. It was here that my counselor was of great assistance. While carefully stipulating that the decision must be a personal one, he helped me to achieve perspective in the matter and finally, after a good deal of procrastination, I switched to an English major.

In the meantime an adjustment to school had apparently been made, for my grade point for Winter Quarter was over 3.5 and included an "A" in physics. However, I still had no love for the subject and today have no regrets that I changed. I have found myself much happier with the subject matter and, perhaps more important, with the people in the English Department. My grades have been consistently higher (including a 4.00 for one quarter), and I am involved in the creative writing program and was recently elected editor of [the student magazine]. Thus, the predictions made in the tests given by the Counseling Service have by and large proved accurate.

It is difficult to assess the precise role that counseling has played in my college career to date, but it is certain that it provided the impetus for change, and in a greater sense it helped me to become acclimated to the university by graphically demonstrating that others had similar problems and that there were people willing to try to help us to solve them. [My counselor] also helped me to see that the stigma attached to "giving up" was far less important than the need to find a curriculum commensurate with my skills and interests.[4]

RELATED TERMS

It may help to clarify the concept of counseling by differentiating it from two terms with which it is frequently confused. Part of this confusion comes from a tendency among writers to use these terms interchangeably,

[4] I am grateful to Mr. Homer Smothers, formerly a member of the staff of the Iowa State University Student Counseling Service, for permission to quote from a letter written by one of his clients. The client also graciously consented to being quoted.

as though they had the same meanings. Communication is improved, however, when a term is restricted to a single meaning and is used to denote a specific concept.

Guidance

The phrase "guidance and counseling" is frequently heard, especially in reference to high school counseling services. At that level, the two terms have become nearly synonymous, as evidenced by the title "guidance counselor" which is applied to many high school counselors. It is possible, however, to distinguish between guidance and counseling, and for the purposes of this book it is important that this distinction be made.

Earlier we presented a definition of counseling, stressing that it is a person-to-person interaction for the purpose of helping one of the individuals to achieve a personal goal or to resolve some personal dilemma. Guidance, on the other hand, can be applied to a variety of services performed within the school which aid students in self-development and in making the most of their present and future (Stewart and Warnath, 1965). Counseling is one of these services, and many believe it is the most important, but others are also included, such as career programs, occupational files, and testing programs. Thus the typical "guidance counselor" has many responsibilities in addition to that of counseling. It may be argued that his basic skill should nonetheless be in counseling, but he cannot expect to spend a large part of his time counseling with individual students. (See the more detailed discussion in Chapter 11.)

Psychotherapy

A greater degree of confusion exists between the terms "counseling" and "psychotherapy." Most writers feel called upon to discuss their relationship, and few have emerged unscathed from the effort. Although there seems to be general agreement that a distinction should be made between these terms, most attempts to draw a distinction have floundered in inconsistencies.

It may help to first examine the problem historically, to understand why this confusion now exists.

Thirty years ago things were much simpler. Psychotherapy was the province of psychiatrists and other professional persons, such as clinical psychologists and psychiatric social workers, who worked with psychiatrists, and as the term implies it was based on a medical model. In addition, psychotherapy was equated in the layman's mind with psychoanalysis, which had had a remarkable amount of publicity. Even those practitioners who did not consider themselves to be true analysts nevertheless gave lip service to many of its concepts and did not object to being identified with such a highly prestigious profession.

Counselors also had their place, but at some distance removed from therapists. Counselors worked with persons planning their future (vocational counseling) or with persons having marital difficulties (marriage counseling). In either case the focus was on a specific problem, and the techniques were generally concentrated on finding ways to solve the problem. Counselors were assumed not to be trained to do psychotherapy, and no one expected them to engage in it.

As counselors became better educated and more proficient, however, some became frustrated. They began to realize that a problem which seemed superficially simple might, on closer examination, not be amenable to traditional counseling techniques. Thus the boy who was having difficulty in choosing a vocation might not be aided much by interest and aptitude tests; it might, instead, become obvious that his problem had a more deep-rooted cause, perhaps lack of self-confidence or friction with his parents.

What was the counselor to do at this point? His first reaction would probably be to make a referral to a psychotherapist, but this may have been impractical on at least two grounds: (a) there were not enough therapists to handle such problems, especially in small towns and rural areas; and (b) many analytically oriented therapists were not interested in such mundane patients. Thus, the counselor was faced with a dilemma: in order to do an adequate job of counseling with his clients, he found it necessary to go beyond the traditional bounds of his profession and engage in an activity for which he was not well trained and in which he did not feel confident.

Part of the counselor's discomfort arose because he was acutely conscious of the gap between himself and the psychotherapist, as it was then drawn. Psychotherapists had propagated the doctrine, accepted by society, that psychotherapy was a very complicated and difficult process, requiring many years of training, preferably of a medical nature, to master. This view of psychotherapy as an esoteric activity, practiced competently only by persons of high intelligence and lengthy training, was further promoted by the public image of the psychoanalyst as a rather eccentric individual who practiced a mysterious form of treatment that helped persons who were emotionally disturbed.

The typical counselor, with little more than a master's degree in education or psychology, was thus made to feel that any technique which went beyond the traditional bounds of counseling was encroaching on psychotherapy, which he was eminently unqualified to practice. The gap between his skills (counseling) and psychotherapy seemed insurmountable, and he was unable to identify with the medically trained therapists with their beards, couches, and Viennese accents. Yet the counselor had the nagging feeling that he should be doing something more for his clients than administering and interpreting tests and providing information; they needed other kinds of help, and there was no one to whom he could refer them.

At this point Carl Rogers arrived on the scene, with the publication of *Counseling and Psychotherapy* (1942). Few books in this area have had such an impact, and in retrospect the reasons seem clear. Rogers was a psychotherapist, but without a medical background. Instead, he was a clinical psychologist, with whom counselors could achieve some degree of identification. Above all Rogers presented a doctrine which was music to the ears of the frustrated counselor: *he destroyed the gap between counseling and psychotherapy by denying that any difference existed.* To him, counseling and psychotherapy were one and the same. Therefore, if there was no difference between them, counselors could engage in activities which seemed to encroach on the domain of the therapists without fear of attack. They could point to Rogers's book as evidence that the distinction which had frustrated them for so long was actually a myth.

Not only did Rogers destroy the psychotherapy-counseling distinction, but he made a further contribution: *he described a technique of counseling (or psychotherapy) which could be easily grasped by the typical counselor.* He effectively undermined the concept, so long nurtured by traditional psychotherapists, that psychotherapy, as best exemplified by psychoanalysis, required many years of intensive training to master. Rogers counteracted this by presenting an approach which anyone could aspire to learn. Thus it can be seen that the success of Rogers's approach lay not in its "validity," but in the scope which it provided for counselors to enter into areas where they had formerly feared to tread.

Perhaps this was necessary at the time, to free counselors from the bondage of their limited techniques. Certainly many of the results have been desirable. Many people have been helped by counselors who would not have been helped before Rogers. But in correcting one evil, Rogers created another. By asserting that counseling and psychotherapy were synonymous terms, he instigated a confusion which persists to this day. If they were in fact synonymous, why have both continued to exist, and why are they still the subject of so much heated discussion? Some residual distinction evidently remains, and it is necessary to delineate this distinction in order to sharpen our concept of counseling.

With the exception of Rogers and some of his followers, most authorities agree that a differentiation between counseling and psychotherapy is desirable, although their reasons differ. Some, such as Patterson (1959) and Stefflre (1965a), urge a distinction because of differences between training levels of counselors and psychotherapists. This argument may have some validity, in that Rogers's views have encouraged some high school counselors to attempt to work with problems they are not equipped to handle, but it has the disadvantage of implying a hierarchical distinction which contributed to the original problem.

A better argument for establishing a distinction between counseling and psychotherapy is that they are actually different, but equally important, activities. A major reason for the original blurring of the distinction was to thwart the notion, prevalent at that time, that counseling was a "poor man's psychotherapy." Unfortunately this attitude still exists, as evident in the arguments noted above concerning differences in training *levels*. If counseling is to survive and grow as a professional activity, it must be valued in its own right rather than riding the coattails of the more glamorous psychotherapy. One result of the current confusion is that proposals are periodically raised for the merger of counseling and clinical psychology, which would have the effect of destroying counseling psychology as a profession. If counseling and psychotherapy are synonymous, this makes sense; but if they are not the same, any such merger would be to the detriment of counseling because of the larger number and greater prestige of clinical psychologists. Thus it becomes necessary to determine whether a reasonable difference exists, and to attempt to describe this difference in terms which will enhance the uniqueness of each concept.

To begin, we need a definition of psychotherapy to compare with our earlier definition of counseling. Wolberg's (1967) definition seems useful:

> Psychotherapy is the treatment, by psychological means, of problems of an emotional nature in which a trained person deliberately establishes a professional relationship with the patient with the object of removing, modifying or retarding existing symptoms, of mediating disturbed patterns of behavior, and of promoting positive personality growth and development [p. 3].

A number of differences suggest themselves, and we shall examine these to determine which distinctions are legitimate and which are not.

Unreliable Distinctions.   Some writers have attempted to distinguish between counseling and psychotherapy along dimensions which seem either superficial or unreliable, in that they do not provide a consistent basis for distinguishing one activity from the other.

1. Client differences. It is commonly asserted that counseling clients are "normal," whereas psychotherapeutic patients are "disturbed." Psychologists, however, have long agreed that normality is an extremely difficult term to define, partly because it has several meanings. Thus, although it may be obvious that a high school boy who has a problem of vocational choice is normal and in need of counseling, whereas a psychotic inmate of a mental institution is abnormal and needs psychotherapy, there is a wide no-man's land between these extremes within which it is difficult to distinguish "clients" from "patients" on the basis of the individual alone.

An additional complication is that the same person may receive both psychotherapy and counseling concurrently. The most likely instance is the patient who is about to be released from a mental hospital. He may be continuing to receive psychotherapy in connection with the difficulty which brought him to the hospital in the first place, but he may also be discussing with a rehabilitation counselor his work plans after he is released. (See the discussion of rehabilitation counseling in Chapter 11.)

2. Practitioner differences. It has also been suggested that counseling can be distinguished from psychotherapy in terms of the person who is conducting the activity. Here again, the extremes are easily separated: the high school counselor engages in counseling, while the psychiatrist practices psychotherapy. Yet there are many practitioners who may move back and forth between counseling and psychotherapy, not wanting to limit themselves to one activity or the other.

It is unfortunate that some writers have chosen to differentiate counseling from psychotherapy in terms of the level of training of the practitioner. They suggest that psychotherapy requires more training and skill, so that a person with a master's degree is limited to "counseling," while an individual with a doctorate may call his activity "psychotherapy." The obvious drawback to this view is that it downgrades counseling, implying that it is simpler and requires less training and may only be second-rate psychotherapy. This in turn underlines the need for the development of a concept of counseling which can stand on its own feet, without having to cling to psychotherapy for status.

3. Settings. The setting in which the activity is conducted does not differentiate, either. As noted above, both counseling and psychotherapy may be conducted in a mental hospital, and they likewise may both be available in a university counseling service. The tendency to equate psychotherapy with a medical setting is one that few nonmedical authorities would attempt to defend.

4. Severity of the problem. This is a variation on the theme of client differences and is no more reliable. Severity is no more useful as a differentiating concept than is normality. The student who is flunking out of school believes that his problem is very serious, while the schizophrenic may be oblivious to his difficulty. Even to an outsider, it may be difficult to decide which of these two persons is in greater need of help, since several conflicting values are involved. The most reasonable conclusion is that both persons have something to be concerned about, and both might benefit from professional help.

Reliable Distinctions.   Having rejected several possible bases on which to differentiate between counseling and psychotherapy, we can now examine three criteria which appear to allow reasonably reliable distinctions to be made.

1. Goals. Numerous writers agree that the goals of counseling are somewhat different from those of psychotherapy. In general terms, psychotherapy aims at personality change, while counseling tends to focus on more specific problems and to emphasize making fuller use of the individual's present resources (Wolberg, 1954; Tyler, 1961; Vance and Volsky, 1962; Stefflre, 1965a; Stewart and Warnath, 1965). Anastasi (1964, pp. 431–432) has expressed the distinction as one of changing "basic personality structure and personal constructs [versus enabling] the individual to utilize his present resources more effectively in solving problems; [psychotherapy] focuses on weaknesses to be overcome, [while counseling] focuses on positive strengths to be developed." Counseling builds on a person as he is now, recognizing that this person is a product of past experiences, but deemphasizing his past in favor of his present and future. The psychotherapist, on the other hand, attempts to help the client remake himself, by concentrating on understanding and eliminating or minimizing his shortcomings.

2. Techniques. It seems logical that if the goals of counseling and psychotherapy are somewhat different, the techniques involved must differ too. Earlier it was pointed out that techniques in counseling are a function of the goals to be achieved; thus if counseling and psychotherapy are intending to arrive at different destinations they must be traveling somewhat different routes. Although it is probably not possible to draw any clear-cut distinctions between the techniques of the two activities, differences are generally evident in duration of the process, frequency of contacts, the extent to which past experiences are emphasized, and the use made of the relationship.

3. Training requirements. If the techniques involved in counseling and psychotherapy are somewhat different, then it should also be possible to differentiate the activities on the basis of the training required to perform them. Training in counseling does not qualify a person to engage in psychotherapy, nor does training as a psychotherapist concurrently produce a competent counselor. Both counseling and psychotherapy involve a unique body of knowledge and skills, although there are obviously some areas in which they overlap. An individual may, however, be trained in both areas so that, as noted earlier, it is not possible to distinguish the two activities in terms of the persons performing them.

General Conclusions. Counseling can thus be differentiated from psychotherapy in terms of three highly interrelated criteria: goals, techniques, and training. This description does not, however, provide a foolproof method for categorizing any helping activity as either counseling or psychotherapy. All of these criteria are continua, not discrete categories, which enable us to make a reasonably accurate estimate of an activity which lies at some distance from the center but which allow for activities near the middle which cannot be neatly classified under either label.

This sort of blurring is characteristic of most psychological traits, and many physical ones as well. Although we assume, for example, that the male-female distinction is highly reliable, an occasional hermaphrodite comes along to confuse us. Therefore simply because some helping activities are not easily labeled as counseling or psychotherapy is no reason to eliminate the distinction. It is a useful distinction, and attempts to do away with it have only created unnecessary difficulties for both fields.

Differentiation is further complicated by the fact that for purposes of discussion it is often difficult to separate counseling from psychotherapy, since many of the same principles apply to both. Thus, although this book concerns counseling, not psychotherapy, many of the principles, concepts, and techniques discussed in its pages apply equally well to psychotherapy. On the other hand, much of the content of this book is *not* relevant to psychotherapy, and the content of a text on psychotherapy would contain much that is not relevant to counseling. (See, for example, Wolberg's *The Technique of Psychotherapy,* 1967.) Books which attempt to combine both into one concept must omit a great deal of material important to one or the other alone, which is further evidence that a real distinction exists between them.

The identity of many of the techniques used in both counseling and psychotherapy has undoubtedly created much of the confusion between the terms. Techniques such as reflection and interpretation (to be discussed in Chapter 4) are utilized by both counselors and psychotherapists, but for somewhat different purposes. Other techniques, however, are more specific to one or the other approach by virtue of furthering its goals. Psychotherapists, for example, may utilize techniques such as psychodrama with clients who have difficulty in verbalizing their feelings; few counselors would accept this as a counseling technique. On the other hand, the interpretation of psychological tests, such as aptitude and interest measures, in terms of future planning is a counseling technique and would have no place in psychotherapy *per se*.

As a final point we may note that counseling is probably appropriate for more persons than is psychotherapy, since the goals of the former have greater relevance for more people. This is consistent with the ratio of professional persons who specialize in counseling to those who specialize in psychotherapy.

TOWARD A THEORY OF COUNSELING

The bulk of this chapter has been devoted to setting the stage for the reader by presenting the writer's concept of counseling. But this is only a starting point, a prelude to the main theme. The process by which counseling, as it has been conceptualized here, effects change in the client has not been described or explained. The following two chapters will be concerned, therefore, with analyzing more systematically the nature of the counseling process, within the framework already presented. Several of the leading theories will be described, followed by the presentation of a theoretical model which attempts to incorporate the contributions of psychological research in a variety of areas.

2

Theoretical Bases
of Counseling

THE ROLE OF THEORY IN COUNSELING

To the uninitiated, the counseling process resembles the world of William James's baby: a great blooming, buzzing confusion. The client talks, the counselor talks, physical actions and expressions take place, and somehow out of this something important happens: the client accomplishes something he had been unable to accomplish before. But how does this come about?

Many answers are given, but no one knows for certain the process by which the client attains his counseling goal. The events of counseling can be observed, but the relationship among these events remains to be discovered. And because the counselor must understand the nature of the process in which he is involved, he strives to put the events of counseling together into some coherent pattern, in order to explain the relationships among the events and thereby to gain greater control over them. In doing so, he is developing a *theory* of counseling.

Man abhors isolated events; he must fit them together into a pattern in order to understand and control them. If the pattern is obvious in the juxtaposition of the events themselves, there is agreement and a "fact" is established. If, however, the pattern is not obvious, but must instead be inferred from the events, then each person who observes them is entitled to formulate his own explanation, and these observers often come into conflict over the relative merits of the various explanations advanced. This is the situation in counseling, as it is in many areas involving the study of complex interactions among behaviors, whether human or otherwise.

A theory, then, is simply a hypothetical explanation for observed events, a model which imposes some sort of order on these events. It is, at first, no more than a guess which seems to make sense, at least to the person who devised it. But a useful theory goes beyond an *explanation* of events which have already taken place. It should lead to the *prediction* of future events which involve the same sorts of behaviors. A theory of counseling, then, should conform to events already observed, and it should enable its user to predict the effects of varying certain elements in the counseling situation. If the prediction proves correct, the validity of the theory has been strengthened, and its user has gained some control over the counseling process.

One of the tasks then of the beginning counselor is to develop a theoretical conception of counseling which will enable him to function effectively as a counselor. There are many ways he can operate in a counseling relationship with another person. How he chooses to behave will depend on his concept of the optimum goals of counseling and his theory as to how he can most effectively help his clients achieve these goals. One of the major reasons for the development of conflicting, and sometimes widely differing, theoretical approaches to counseling and psychotherapy is that different counselors begin with different concepts of optimum goals. These differences in goals are, however, based on philosophical differences—differences in concepts of the nature of man, or of the good life—and as such are not truly theories since they cannot be scientifically validated. Once a goal is selected, however, the process by which movement toward that goal is achieved *can* be studied scientifically, and the counselor's conception of that process can therefore be considered as a theory.

In a sense each counselor develops his own personal theory of counseling, out of his own experiences and his imagination. But knowledge about counseling can be systematically advanced only by the development of theories acceptable to a number of counselors. A few persons have been especially adept in devising theoretical formulations which appeal to many practitioners. Therefore, even though a counselor's theory is ultimately his own individual formulation, most counselors have drawn upon the ideas of a relatively few writers who have dared to advance broader and more complex theories than most counselors would have devised for themselves. As a result, it is possible to consider a rather small number of systematic theoretical approaches to counseling. Adherents of a certain approach will, of course, vary among themselves in their day-to-day application of that approach, but they will share a number of common concepts and techniques which will differentiate them from the adherents of another approach.

Because of these different approaches, the beginning counselor is faced with the dilemma of choice. How can he decide which theory will be most useful to him? Should he learn as much as possible about each, or should he concentrate on one approach and learn it well? The broader his knowledge about theoretical approaches to counseling, the more flexible should be his own ability to deal with his clients. On the other hand, the skillful use of any approach requires intensive experience, and it may be more reasonable to advise the new counselor to learn one approach well and later broaden it as seems appropriate. As Frank (1961) has pointed out, one of the major values of a theoretical approach for a beginning counselor is that it bolsters his confidence. He has some idea as to how he will handle the demands of the counseling situation, and this confidence generally enables him to do a better job than he would have done without it.

Theories of Personality
versus Theories of Counseling

Strictly speaking, a theory of counseling deals with the events of the counseling process. It attempts to organize these events into a meaningful pattern, so that the role of various counselor behaviors becomes more evident. A good theory should enable the counselor to gain increased control over the counseling process, to use himself more effectively to produce in his clients the kinds of changes he believes are desirable.

There is, however, another set of behaviors which also cries out for an explanation: the behavior of the client as an individual, both within and outside of the counseling situation. For centuries, mankind has devised theories to account for the vicissitudes of human behavior. The need to "understand" oneself and other people is apparently endless, and man has long searched for elegant explanations of personality development to make it easier for him to live with himself. These explanations are termed *theories of personality,* and many have become a basic part of the vocabulary and thought of psychologists. Presumably those which have survived and have grown over the years have proved especially useful and stimulating, and have fulfilled at least some of their promise for bringing order into the chaotic events of life.

This need to understand the client is of great importance to many counselors, and of course to their clients as well. Most counselors make some theoretical assumptions about the nature of personality development and the probable source of the difficulties which their clients bring to counseling. Some approaches to counseling stress the counselor's understanding of the client as an essential element, while others deem it to be of less importance, but few counselors can feel comfortable with a client without some framework which allows them to "explain" his behavior.

A theory of personality is not, however, a theory of counseling, although many writers have failed to make this distinction and have repeatedly confused the two. A theory of personality attempts to explain the client as a person, accounting for his behavior in a wide variety of situations. A theory of counseling, on the other hand, is concerned *only* with the on-going events of the counseling situation. It is concerned with the process of counseling, not the product.

In practice, personality theories and counseling theories are usually intimately related. Often they develop together, as a practitioner finds that certain techniques produce desirable results and attempts to explain this by devising an elaborate model of the *client* rather than of the *process*. The result is a sophisticated picture of the development of the human being but with little gained in an understanding of the counseling process as a vehicle for producing behavior change.

It is possible, therefore, to consider a theory of the counseling process apart from a theory of personality, although many counselors may feel uncomfortable doing so. But if we are truly to understand the nature of counseling, as it applies to counselors operating from within the frameworks of different personality theories, greater emphasis must be placed on understanding the counseling process itself.

An additional reason for maintaining a distinction between theories of counseling and theories of personality lies in their implications for the role of the counselor as scientist. A theory of personality meets the traditional requirements of a theory: the scientist studies his subject objectively, forming hypotheses and collecting data to test these hypotheses in as objective a manner as possible. The counselor, by contrast, cannot subject his theory of counseling to a similar analysis, since he is intimately involved in the process itself. He is in the unique position of being both the experimenter and an independent variable. Contrary to experimenters in other areas of research, the counselor must generate his own data. Many writers fail to recognize this crucial distinction and urge the neophyte counselor to develop a theory of counseling and improve his counseling by the scientific method. In effect he is being asked to study himself as a variable.

The counseling process can, of course, be studied objectively but not by someone in the center of it. The counselor *as scientist* can make important contributions to the objective study of counseling, but the counselor *as counselor* must recognize that he himself is a unique variable in the counseling situation and that this places severe limitations on his ability to analyze it objectively.

To summarize, the counselor's behavior in counseling is dictated by his theoretical model of the nature of counseling and the process by which counseling produces behavior change. This model may include a theory of how personality develops and why problems arise, but this is not a necessary component. What is necessary is that the model explain with reasonable accuracy the relationships among counselor behaviors, client behaviors, and other significant aspects of the counseling situation. On the basis of this model, the counselor should be able to use himself more effectively to produce the kinds of client behavior he believes are desirable, and he should be able to observe interactions of other counselors with their clients to locate those elements which are not peculiar to himself as an individual but which can be generalized to other counselors.

SYSTEMATIC APPROACHES TO COUNSELING

No two counselors hold exactly the same theoretical orientation, because no two counselors are exactly alike as persons. A counselor's theoretical approach to counseling is governed in part by his individual characteristics. His goal is to use himself effectively as a counselor, which means that he must adapt whatever approach he selects to fit himself.

Counselors, however, do tend to draw upon more highly developed systematic approaches to counseling, and groups of counselors who share certain basic beliefs and who behave in much the same manner can be identified. Each group tends to align itself with a rather formal theoretical position, usually one which has a fairly sophisticated theoretical structure and which has proved useful in helping counselors to develop their own personal approach. It is therefore possible to consider each of these formal approaches as providing a nucleus of concepts and techniques on which individual counselors have drawn to aid in the development of their personal approaches to counseling.

The existence of these formal theories is vital to counseling. They provide a structure by which the experience of many counselors can be synthesized and transmitted to those new to the field, to give them a basis on which to operate until they gain experience; and they stimulate the growth of knowledge about the counseling process by generating research by a variety of counselors in a variety of settings. Although a counselor is wise not to align himself too rigidly with a single formal theoretical approach, the sophisticated counselor should be aware of the basic concepts underlying the major approaches as well as those aspects of each which have been subjected to scientific validation. The counselor who is unaware of developments in formal theories is locked in a world of his own.

The existence of a variety of theoretical approaches to counseling makes many people uneasy. The wide diversity among the models implies a wide diversity in counselor behaviors, depending on one's theoretical orientation, which suggests that a client may expect to encounter widely different kinds of counseling, depending on what kind of counselor he happens to select. Perhaps even more upsetting is the assumption that eventually one approach will be proved correct, through research, and the others will then fall aside, with their adherents clutching the remnants of a few tattered and discredited constructs. For those persons who want to be on the winning side, a dilemma is apparent.

In reality, neither concern is worth worrying about. Evidence indicates that experienced counselors of different theoretical persuasions do not actually behave a great deal differently in counseling itself (Fiedler, 1950a, 1950b; Strupp, 1958). They may use different constructs in their vocabulary and may structure the role of client and counselor a little differently, but their behaviors are not dramatically dissimilar. Inexperienced counselors, attached more rigidly to a formal system, tend to be further apart from one another, a distinction which diminishes as they gain in experience and flexibility.

Nor is there much danger that one theoretical approach will vanquish the others, at least not in the foreseeable future. A counselor usually adopts a theoretical position not so much because the evidence for its effectiveness is overwhelming—as will be discussed in a later chapter, the evidence for the effectiveness of any form of counseling is not overwhelming—but primarily because it is philosophically congenial to him. Since different approaches are based on different philosophical values and assumptions, it is hard to see how any can actually be disproved. A theory may lose its sparkle because of social changes which make it less relevant to contemporary life, but adherence to a theory of counseling is much like adherence to a religion: it is based on faith and on one's view of one's place in the universe, not on scientifically established facts.

To attempt to describe in depth the various formal theoretical approaches to counseling which are currently in vogue would be an impossible undertaking in these pages. Entire books have been devoted to this topic, and the interested reader is referred to these.[1] The most sensible approach at this point seems to be to survey briefly a few of the most influential and representative theories, with the understanding that these by no means exhaust the current state of counseling theory.

It is evident, when counseling theories are examined, that they can be grouped into a few general categories. The problem is to determine which groupings are the most meaningful, and how these groups are to be labeled. Most writers group the theories, but no two writers agree on their groupings or the labels applied to the groups. The organization presented here is one

---

[1] The most useful for counselors are *Theories of Counseling and Psychotherapy,* by Patterson (1966), and *Theories of Counseling,* edited by Stefflre (1965c).

which is meaningful to the writer and seems to be as defensible as any other.

Theories of counseling can be organized into two general categories. One group includes those which are closely related to a theory of personality development. Bordin (1968) calls these "dynamic" theories, because they are concerned with the development of the individual and view the counseling process as facilitating this development. These theories present a model of the client in terms of the structure of his personality and his reactions to various forms of stress. They attempt to explain why he is having difficulty in coping effectively with his environment, and they indicate what changes should be expected in order that he become a more mature and fully functioning individual.

Theories of this sort have developed primarily within psychotherapy rather than counseling, as is evident in their emphasis on a disturbed client and the assumption that his personality structure must be altered in some respect if he is to function effectively. They do, however, have useful applications to counseling, by providing a framework which explains how problems arise and how they can be solved. In either case, the counselor's (or therapist's) behavior is oriented toward producing changes in the client in terms of the personality model on which the theory is based, and the counselor's techniques are consistent with this framework.

Of the many theoretical approaches which are based on a view of client personality development, the two which have most influenced counseling are the psychoanalytic and phenomenological approaches, and the individuals most closely identified with each are Sigmund Freud and Carl Rogers. The approach of each will be discussed below, with the caution that they are only representative and should not be assumed to cover the entire field.

The second major approach to counseling theory is represented by theories based on behavior modification, or what Bordin (1968) calls the "instrumental" approach. These theories are concerned primarily with the nature of the counseling process itself. They make only minimal assumptions about the nature of the client, but instead focus on the behavior to be changed and the process by which this change can be effected. In general, they assume counseling to be a learning situation in which the basic principles of learning theory can be applied to produce behavior change. The counselor thereby becomes an instrument for effecting change in the client.

The learning-theory approach is the more recent, and as yet no individual has emerged clearly as its spokesman. There are, however, several approaches within this general framework which will be discussed. As is the case with the personality-oriented approaches, those based on learning theory have developed primarily from research in psychotherapy, and formal applications to counseling have only recently been devised.

PSYCHOANALYSIS AND ITS INFLUENCE ON COUNSELING

Freud's theory and technique of psychoanalytic therapy ushered in a new era in the treatment of emotional disturbance. In an age when emotional disorders were assumed to be caused by mysterious forces which no one could fathom, Freud provided a complex model of the development of personality within which such disorders were comprehensible, and an approach to their treatment more successful than any which had preceded it. Psychoanalytic theory and practice has evolved greatly since Freud's time and has split into many conflicting schools, but the basic principles which Freud introduced and popularized have had a profound effect on modern-day approaches to helping people deal with their problems.

Over a period of forty years, beginning late in the nineteenth century, Freud refined and elaborated his theory of personality into a complex integration of constructs and models. It is impossible in a few pages to deal adequately with even its principal concepts.[2]

But much of Freud's theory has little direct relevance for counseling anyway. The purpose of this discussion is to highlight those aspects of psychoanalytic theory and technique which have most directly influenced modern approaches to counseling and to describe the approach which an analytically-oriented counselor would most likely take.

Background

Sigmund Freud was trained as a physician, but he soon became interested in treating what at the time were known as "nervous disorders," especially the psychoneuroses which had no evident physical basis. After several false starts, Freud was attracted to an approach developed by Joseph Breuer, which involved helping the patient to overcome his difficulty by talking with him about it. Freud and Breuer first worked together but soon parted company, primarily over Freud's insistence on emphasizing the sexual basis of neurotic disorders.

For a number of years Freud worked alone, seeing patients and putting his ideas into writing. His first major publication, *The Interpretation of Dreams,* appeared in 1900, and numerous others followed. Freud was no overnight success, but gradually he attracted followers who extended and publicized his work, until he became the acknowledged leader in the field of psychotherapy. Although Freudian psychoanalysis, in its strictest sense, is

---

[2] Useful summaries of Freudian theory are found in the writings of Hall (1954), Patterson (1966), and Ross and Abrahms (1965).

now practiced by only a handful of psychotherapists, Freud's influence on the development of psychotherapy can hardly be overestimated. Much of the modern layman's concepts of the nature of personality development and of emotional disturbance can be traced to views which Freud either originated or popularized.

To understand Freudian psychoanalysis, it is necessary to recognize several characteristics of Freud and of the time in which his views developed. To begin with, Freud was a physician, so it is hardly remarkable that his approach to psychotherapy relies very strongly on a medical model and that it is aimed at "treatment" of disorders. Although Freud later abandoned his earlier insistence that to become a psychoanalyst one must first be a physician, it is evident that his thinking throughout his life was colored by his early training and experience in medicine.

Freud's theory of personality development has its roots in his experiences in treating patients who were emotionally disturbed. In other words, it is based primarily on the personality patterns of *abnormal* persons, and therefore not surprisingly accounts for abnormal behaviors more readily than for normal behavior. For this reason, it is rather difficult to adapt psychoanalytic theory directly to counseling, since counseling deals for the most part with normal problems of normal people.

Finally, Freud did his early work during an era of rather severe emotional repression. Given the character of the times, it is reasonable that many of Freud's patients exhibited neurotic symptoms produced by repressed emotions and that, especially among the women, these repressions were often associated with sex. The mores of the times made it difficult for upper- and middle-class women to acknowledge and satisfy their sexual needs without arousing guilt feelings. Freud had the insight to recognize this connection, but he assumed that it had a biological rather than a cultural basis. As times have changed and repressions have been reduced, other forms of treatment of emotional disturbances have replaced Freudian psychoanalysis in popularity.

One of Freud's major achievements was his ability to stimulate the thinking of others, although he was unhappy when this produced views with which he was in disagreement. Freudian psychoanalysis has continued to maintain its importance in psychotherapy not so much because Freud's approach itself has remained popular but because it spawned a variety of approaches, each with its own theory and adherents. Among these are the approaches of Freud's immediate colleagues, Alfred Adler, Carl Jung, Otto Rank, and those of a later generation, Karen Horney, Erich Fromm, Harry Stack Sullivan, and Franz Alexander. Few of these persons have contributed directly to counseling, as contrasted with psychotherapy, but all have made indirect impact by their modifications of Freud's theory and techniques.

Where there is controversy, there is life. There are many quarrels which can be raised with Freudian psychoanalysis, but it must be acknowledged that it is not a sterile approach. It can be said of Freud, as of few men, that after him the world was no longer the same. This is surely a mark of genius.

Psychoanalytic Theory of Personality

The techniques of psychoanalysis are closely tied to Freud's theory of the nature and development of personality. To understand the techniques, therefore, one must be acquainted with the theory.

In simple terms, Freudian theory begins with the assumption that all behavior has some logical cause, a principle called *psychic determinism*. This assumption is basic to most approaches to counseling and psychotherapy, but Freudian psychoanalysis was the first treatment approach in which it was a central tenet.

A difficulty arises, however, when one attempts to explain behavior which does not on the surface seem logical. To do this, Freud postulated that much of human behavior is the product of certain innate *basic instincts,* some of which cause the individual to behave in a socially unacceptable manner and must therefore be subdued. The major type of instinct which causes trouble and which must not be allowed to assert itself is the sexual instinct (libido), with which all children are born and which they first demonstrate through physical contact with adults and through manipulation of their genital organs. Because sexual behaviors are strictly controlled in our society, the child is taught from a very early age that responding to these instincts will produce unpleasant reactions from those with power over him, primarily his parents. Not wanting to gain his parents' disfavor, the child learns to control these unacceptable impulses by repressing them.

These instincts, however, do not simply disappear. Instead, they retreat into the *unconscious,* where they lie uneasily in wait of an opportunity to assert themselves when the person's conscious controls weaken, most likely when he is asleep or under stress. Because the person cannot acknowledge the existence of these irrational, unacceptable impulses, he cannot satisfactorily explain his irrational behavior under stress and cannot, therefore, gain control of it.

Freudian theory also conceptualizes the personality as being composed of three divisions: the id, the ego, and the superego. The *id* is the source of the basic instincts and operates according to the *pleasure principle.* As he matures, the person must bring this aspect of his personality under control. The *ego* represents the unique aspect of the individual and his means of controlling the id. The ego operates according to the *reality principle,* as the person learns that it is not always wise to succumb to the desire for immediate gratification and as he is rewarded by those around him for becoming socialized. The *superego* represents the internalization of the controls imposed from outside; in general terms, it corresponds to conscience. The individual whose behavior is too strongly governed by either the id or the superego is not a fully functioning person. In Freudian theory, the development of a well-rounded ego, with realistic control over the id impulses but not slavishly bound by the wishes of others, is the ultimate goal in personality development.

In Freudian theory, then, emotional disturbances arise because of conflicts between the individual's unconscious, unacceptable impulses and social restrictions which do not allow these impulses direct expression. Somehow in his development the person has not come to terms with these "unacceptable" aspects of himself but instead has been forced to deny their existence and therefore has lost the opportunity to develop conscious control of them.

Because these impulses begin to affect the individual quite early in his life, Freudian theory puts a strong emphasis on the importance of *early learning experiences* and assumes that the basis of all personality disturbance can be traced back to early traumatic experiences in the patient's life. And because most of these early experiences occur within the family setting, psychoanalysis puts great stress on the importance of the *parent-child relationship,* assuming that most of the essential learning of social restrictions is taught by the parents and that the nature of the relationship between the child and his parents determines in large part how the child will adjust to these restrictions.

There are many aspects of psychoanalytic theory, as propounded by Freud and others, which have been neglected in this brief summary, but the elements presented here are those which seem to have had the greatest impact on the development of counseling and psychotherapy.

Technique of Psychoanalysis

The goal of psychoanalysis is to uncover the repressed motives and, by exposing them, enable the patient to assume conscious control over them. Psychoanalysts believe that only by perceiving and understanding all aspects of himself, both conscious and unconscious, can a person truly become a fully functioning individual.

The techniques of psychoanalysis then are aimed primarily at locating the repressed motives and bringing them to the surface. To do this, the patient is helped to probe into his unconscious and to dredge up feelings and urges of which he may be only dimly aware. This requires that the repression of these feelings must be minimized, by the creation of an atmosphere as relaxed and as free from distraction as possible. It is for this reason that the analytic session is often arranged so that the patient reclines on a couch in a dim light with the analyst seated behind him, out of his line of vision.

Since it is assumed that the patient does not have direct access to his unconscious mind, its contents must be tapped through indirect methods. A few analysts make use of hypnosis for this purpose, but most have found, as did Freud, that the results are incomplete and often unsatisfactory. The method most commonly used, at least in the early stages, is *free association*. The patient is instructed to let his mind wander freely and to describe whatever comes into his mind under these conditions. It is assumed that eventually the content of the unconscious will begin to filter through, although in a disguised form. It is then the analyst's responsibility to help the patient see the true meaning of this material by interpreting (analyzing) it in terms of basic analytic concepts. Doctrinaire psychoanalysts make use of elaborate constructs and analogies in this interpretation, and the patient in time learns this vocabulary and gradually becomes able to take on more responsibility for the analysis himself.

Much is also made of *dream analysis*, again on the assumption that during sleep the conscious mind is less watchful and the unconscious impulses are freer to expose themselves, albeit still in disguised form. A significant portion of a psychoanalysis is usually spent in the recounting and analysis of the patient's dreams. Over the years, certain recurring themes have come to be assumed to stand for certain kinds of motives, and the analyst provides this interpretation for the patient.

It became evident rather early to Freud that some patients did not readily accept the wisdom of the analyst's interpretations, especially if it was emphasized that the patient was repressing certain socially unacceptable motives. Freud explained this reluctance to accept a "valid" interpretation as *resistance* on the part of the patient: the conscious mind is still struggling to repress the unacceptable motives by its unwillingness to acknowledge their existence. Some patients are able eventually to overcome their resistance and accept the view propounded by the analyst, while others terminate the analysis, the ultimate act of a resistant patient.

The repressed motives typically have strong emotional content, and it is therefore to be expected that the exposure and examination of these motives will be emotionally traumatic for the patient. The psychoanalytic view is that only by experiencing the true emotional content of the unconscious can the patient come to grips with himself. Therefore a simple intellectual understanding of one's personality dynamics is not sufficient. The patient must "work through" the emotional components of the original situations which produced the repression. Usually this has involved the patient's relationship with his parents, so that the emotional elements stressed in analysis are those basic to the parent-child relationship.

As the patient's latent feelings toward his parents are uncovered and exposed during analysis, they may initially be directed toward the therapist. This is the phenomenon known as *transference*. If, for example, the patient becomes angry with his analyst, this will probably be interpreted as indicating that angry feelings toward the patient's father have been exposed which the patient has not yet been able to acknowledge directly. There may also, of course, be positive transference, as happens when the patient falls in love with or becomes overly dependent on the therapist, as would a child in relation to a parent. The analyst must recognize that these feelings are not directed at him as a person but rather that he serves as a surrogate for the true object of the feelings, and it is his responsibility to interpret this to the patient so that the true source of the feelings is clarified.

A complete psychoanalysis takes a very long time; it is not uncommon for a patient to be seen several times a week for a period of several years. To explore completely one's psyche is a long and arduous process. One never knows when another unconscious motive may be lurking around the next corner of one's mind, ready to exert its baneful influence over one's behavior if it is not exposed. In a sense, a psychoanalysis never comes to an end. Eventually, if it is successful, the patient finds that he is behaving more satisfactorily than before and is content to terminate, perhaps having gained enough insight into the process to be able to carry it on for himself.

Psychoanalytic Training

Despite the popularity of psychoanalysis, there are few genuine psychoanalysts in existence, as compared with the number of psychotherapists in general. The reason is evident when the training program is examined. Most analytic training programs accept only persons who have a professional degree, usually in medicine, although a few programs accept non-medical persons such as psychologists. This means that the individual has already invested a substantial portion of his life in obtaining an advanced education. If he is fortunate enough to be accepted by one of the few psychoanalytic training institutions in the country, he must undergo a rigorous program. Included as a basic part of this program is a personal analysis, lasting perhaps several years, for which he will be charged a fee. It is little wonder that most psychoanalysts, once trained, enter private practice and charge substantial fees for their services. In the little time left to them, they must recoup the expenses they have incurred in attaining this position.

Critique

The picture of the psychoanalyst as an elderly, distinguished gentleman with a beard, couch, and Viennese accent is no longer typical, if indeed it ever was. Although some psychoanalysts have a tendency to engage in rather convoluted explanations of human behavior which make their colleagues wince, the modern analyst is in close touch with the modern world. He has adapted his basic theoretical approach, whether Freudian or otherwise, to the needs of his patients, and his behavior as a therapist is unlikely to be markedly different from that of therapists of other persuasions.

Psychoanalysis has been legitimately criticized for being quite lengthy and concomitantly expensive. The analyst will retort that anything worth doing is worth doing well, and that the depths of the unconscious do not respond to a crash dive and quick surfacing. To the analyst the time required for complete treatment may be disappointing, but seldom discouraging. Basically, though, psychoanalysis is a terribly inefficient process. Whether it actually works is debatable. Obviously enough people believe in it to have kept it alive and flourishing for many years. But even if it were proved to be the most effective form of psychotherapy ever discovered, it could help only a small fraction of people with problems. There are too few analysts and the process takes too long to be of value to a significant part of the population.

But what of its efficacy? Does psychoanalysis work? As we noted earlier, the question of which approach works best is pointless. The fact is that many persons believe they have been helped by psychoanalysis, while others believe it to be quackery. The truth probably lies somewhere in between.[3]

One of the difficulties in evaluating the effectiveness of psychoanalysis is that it is not, strictly speaking, a theory at all. It is an elegant philosophy, but it does not permit the generation of testable hypotheses as a good theory should. To put it another way, as a theory it is not predictive. It provides elaborate explanations for what has already occurred in a person's life, but it offers little help in predicting where he will go from here. This difficulty is inherent in the nature of the theory itself: by postulating an active, seething unconscious and the existence of a wide variety of motives, both acceptable and unacceptable, it allows for the individual to behave in almost any manner at any given time. This sort of loose construction is anathema to scientists, but it seems to provide a feast of thought-provoking ideas for persons more philosophically inclined.

The fairest evaluation at this point is that few psychoanalytic concepts have been scientifically verified. Until this has been done, we must conclude that psychoanalysis is an interesting, but unproven, technique.

---

[3] For an interesting set of criticisms of psychoanalysis, see the volume edited by Rachman (1963a), especially the descriptions of personal psychoanalyses therein by Landis and Boring. Both authors were evidently disappointed with their experiences, although it can be argued that they approached it with overmuch skepticism.

Influence on Counseling

More important for our purposes, however, is the influence of psychoanalysis on counseling. Psychoanalysis deals with emotional disturbances and aims to produce rather extensive personality change, so that it is not directly applicable to counseling. Few counselors would consider themselves to be psychoanalytically oriented, although this is certainly not beyond conception, as King (1965) has demonstrated. But the impact of Freudian analysis on concepts of personal problems and how they can best be helped has been powerful. Many of the assumptions made in counseling have been derived from psychoanalysis. Among these are the view that behavior is caused, that unconscious motives and feelings may influence behavior, that a person's past experiences may be relevant to his present condition, and that the child-parent relationship plays a critical role in the individual's development. All of these assumptions, and many more, owe their popularity to psychoanalysis. The same is true for many counseling techniques—the insistence on providing a relaxed atmosphere for the client, encouraging the client to express his thoughts and feelings, interpretations made by the counselor to help the client better understand his behavior all are direct outgrowths of psychoanalysis. This is not to say that these ideas would never have developed except for Freud, but he did bring them together into a coherent system. Few modern counselors consider themselves to be psychoanalytically oriented, but most owe more to Freud and his followers than they can ever hope to repay.

ROGERS'S CLIENT-CENTERED COUNSELING

A second major group of theoretical approaches to counseling and psychotherapy have emerged from the *phenomenological* theories of personality. Their major difference from the analytic approaches is that they de-emphasize the causal element in personality development. Phenomenology emphasizes the individual as an *experiencing* organism and stresses the importance of understanding him as he presently is and as the person which he is becoming. The emotional, rather than the intellectual, aspects are of concern, and emphasis is placed on the normal course of development rather than the abnormal.

The treatment approaches consistent with phenomenology are little concerned with determining the origins of the client's difficulties. The therapist is concerned with the client as he is now, not as he was in the past. Historical material is not ignored, but it is utilized to understand the person now, rather than to search for the origins of his problems. Considerable emphasis is placed, too, on the therapeutic relationship. Since the therapist is concerned with the client as he currently is, the relationship between the client and therapist is viewed as a major arena for the development of the client's personal strengths and in which he can learn to cope with his difficulties. The therapist, then, becomes an important part of the client's world and must be acutely aware of his personal impact on the client. The phenomenologically oriented therapist would never remove himself from the patient's sight, as might the psychoanalyst. Instead he would do everything possible to remove any barriers to a close relationship between himself and the client.

There are several approaches to counseling and psychotherapy which can be classified as phenomenological. We will consider here only the approach of Carl Rogers, best known as "nondirective" or "client-centered" counseling. Rogers will be presented in some detail because his views have had a tremendous impact on the practice of counseling and psychotherapy in this country.

Background

Freud originally studied to be a physician, while Rogers studied to be a minister, and therein lies a clue to their diverse views of the nature of man and of the helping relationship. Rogers did not complete his theological studies; becoming dissatisfied with them, he shifted to psychology and obtained a Ph.D. in clinical psychology from Teachers College, Columbia University, in 1928. For the next twelve years he worked as a staff psychologist in a community child guidance center, where he has described himself as being in "professional isolation" (Rogers, 1961). Out of his experience in working with children and their parents he developed his own approach, which was published in *Counseling and Psychotherapy* (1942) after he had moved into the academic world. This book is one of the milestones in the history of counseling and has had a strong impact on the subsequent development of the field.[4]

Rogers's approach to counseling did not, of course, emerge full-blown with no antecedents. Despite its contrasts with traditional psychoanalytic theory, Rogers's client-centered counseling has direct historical ties to Freud. One of Freud's followers, Otto Rank, developed a form of psychotherapy which he called "will therapy," emphasizing the view that the therapeutic relationship involves a contest of wills between therapist and patient and that, for his own personal development, the patient's will should be allowed to prevail. An American social worker, Jessie Taft, translated Rank's writings into English and propagated "relationship therapy," which

---

[4] See Chapter 1 of this book for a discussion of Rogers's impact on counseling.

placed even more stress on the importance of the patient-therapist relationship and on the freedom of the patient to control the relationship. Rogers drew many of his ideas from Taft, adapting and extending them to develop a model of the kind of client-therapist relationship which he believed would produce maximum client growth.

Although Rogers has been active in psychological research, his early views developed before his research involvement, so that the nature of his research and the questions it seeks to answer have been dictated by his previously developed philosophy of counseling and psychotherapy. Rogers's views have been modified since his original publications, partly as a result of his research studies, but a basic humanistic element continues to be central to his approach. Rogers has tremendous faith in the goodness of man and in man's potential for positive growth, given the right kind of nurturing conditions. Despite his rejection of the ministry as a profession, Rogers's philosophy of therapy and of life has spiritual overtones of a humanistic if not a sectarian nature. Anyone who reads or hears Rogers must be convinced that had he chosen to become a minister he would have been quite successful. The number and fervor of the disciples of client-centered counseling attest to Rogers's ability to inspire love and loyalty in his followers.

Theory of Personality

Like most phenomenologists, Rogers has never been greatly interested in personality theory for its own sake. His original writing dealt primarily with therapeutic techniques, and only gradually has he developed a theory of personality as a basis for these techniques. In some respects, this sequence of development is similar to Freud's, but whereas Freud eventually spent the greater part of his energies in refining his theory of personality, Rogers has continued to concern himself primarily with techniques of psychotherapy. Although Rogers made his first extensive statement of his approach to psychotherapy in 1942, it was not until 1959 that he presented a reasonably complete theory of personality (see Rogers, 1959).

Rogers's theory of personality does not strike one as very complex or profound. Compared with Freud's theory, it seems a little mundane and borrows freely from other self-theorists. It goes about as far as is absolutely necessary to provide underpinnings for client-centered therapy, but in itself it would hardly have gained Rogers the reputation he holds.

The basic constructs of Rogerian personality theory are the *self* and the *experienced world*. The self develops through the person's interactions with his environment, and these interactions are in turn influenced by the developing self. The person perceives his world in accordance with his developing self-concept, so that his interactions with his environment become highly personalized. His experience of reality becomes colored by his concept of himself, and he in turn tends to behave in a manner consistent with his self-concept. The person becomes an individual, defining himself to others through his behavior in interpersonal situations, and reinforcing or modifying his self-concept through his perception of the actions of others.

This describes the development of a healthy personality, providing that the self-concept is reasonably consistent—or "congruent"—with reality. A realistic self-concept enables the individual to perceive his environment realistically and to acknowledge his experiences. He can therefore remain in close touch with reality with a minimum of difficulty and is in a good position to adapt to changes in his world.

If, however, the individual's self-concept is *incongruent* with reality, difficulties may arise. Incongruence generally comes about when the person is attempting to protect an unrealistic self-concept. To do so, he must distort reality by denying an aspect of his self which he is incapable of accepting. For example, the perfectionist who cannot allow himself to make a mistake may deny evidence that at times he does make mistakes. Or, if unable to do this, he may insist that he *always* makes mistakes. Both perceptions reflect his inability to accept that part of himself which sometimes makes mistakes, and both result in the distortion of reality.

The distortion of reality and denial of part of oneself in order to resolve incongruence between self and reality has two unfortunate outcomes: the continual effort causes anxiety, and the distortion and denial make it quite difficult for the person to deal directly with the cause of his anxiety. Thus he is anxious and unhappy, but he doesn't understand why because he can't acknowledge the feelings which underlie his unhappiness.

At this point we must introduce another construct basic to Rogerian theory: the *drive to self-actualization*. Despite the distortions and denials to which the unhealthy self is subjected, there are underlying positive elements waiting to assert themselves, given the proper conditions. Rogers believes that each person possesses a drive to become his true self, and that this true self will include positive self-regard. The true, positive self is waiting to emerge, whenever the individual can allow himself to experience his true feelings openly and honestly and can accept himself with both his negative and positive characteristics. Client-centered psychotherapy provides a situation and techniques in which the true self is able to flourish.

Technique of Client-Centered Psychotherapy

The heart of the Rogerian approach is a technique of psychotherapy which emphasizes the self-actualization potential of the client and provides a relationship in which this potential can be activated. Rogers originally called his technique "nondirective" counseling, meaning that the therapist does not lead the client in a direction chosen by the therapist. Some non-

Rogerian therapists objected, however, to the implication that they were being directive; moreover, research studies soon established that even the so-called nondirective techniques actually do have some elements of directive influence. Subsequently, therefore, Rogers began to use the term "client-centered," which has continued up to the present time. The intent here seems to have been to emphasize that his approach focused on the client as a person. Other therapists were still not mollified, however, since now it was implied that they were "counselor-centered," a highly objectionable accusation.

Whatever the terminology, however, Rogers does stress the importance of orienting the therapy session around the client's perceptions of himself and of his world, with the therapist's function being to provide a setting in which the client can become acutely aware of his feelings toward himself and toward other people. Rogers (1959) has best expressed his view of client-centered psychotherapy. by reference to the six "conditions of the therapeutic process" which he believes are essential if therapy is to succeed:

1. Two persons (the client and the therapist) are in *contact.*
2. The client is in a state of *incongruence,* which makes him vulnerable to the world and probably anxious as well.
3. The therapist is *congruent* in the *relationship.*
4. The therapist is experiencing *unconditional positive regard* toward the client.
5. The therapist is experiencing an empathic understanding of the client's *internal frame of reference.*
6. The client *perceives* the therapist's regard for him and the therapist's understanding of his frame of reference.

It is evident that Rogers puts considerable emphasis on the client-therapist relationship, with the therapist's role being to establish contact with the client, to develop a genuine regard for the client, and to attempt to understand the client's feelings about himself and his environment. The client, in turn, can lower his self-defenses and begin to experience those aspects of himself which he previously denied. Although this experiencing is likely to be painful—since the denied elements generally have strong emotional implications for the client—the therapeutic relationship provides the support he needs to view himself openly and honestly and thereby begin to incorporate his feelings into his true self-concept.

Rogers does not discuss in detail the techniques by which the therapist establishes this relationship and provides this atmosphere. To him, the crucial element is the therapist's participation in the relationship as a genuine person. Techniques *per se* are rejected, since they imply that the therapist is operating as a machine rather than a person. Nevertheless, client-centered therapists can be seen to emphasize certain behaviors and to avoid others which therapists of other persuasions might draw upon.[5]

The client-centered therapist relies primarily on techniques which encourage the client to express his thoughts and feelings and which help the client to clarify their meaning. The actual verbalizations of the therapist are minimal; often he relies a great deal on nodding his head and saying "uh-huh," and from time to time making comments to reflect the client's feelings. He avoids statements which would imply that he is taking some responsibility for the direction of the session, such as by asking a question or making an interpretation. This approach puts a good deal of responsibility on the client to set his own goals and to initiate movement toward them. Some clients respond favorably while others, who expect the therapist to take a more active part in the discussion, are disappointed. The client-centered counselor, however, feels strongly that if he became more verbally active his verbalization would be a barrier to the client's personal growth. Further, the counselor holds that the client needs to learn that he can trust his own resources and does not have to rely on others to do his thinking for him.

Critique

The strengths of the client-centered approach lie in its emphasis on the positive development of the individual through a therapeutic technique which does not involve mystical constructs and years of intensive training to master. This is not to imply that client-centered therapy is simple; although the basic concepts are easily understood, the true client-centered therapist must be acutely self-aware and must be capable of forming relationships of a nature not usually experienced. In this respect much is required of the therapist as a person, rather than as a therapist *per se*.

Optimum use of the client-centered approach by the client seems to require certain characteristics: rationality, intelligence, self-insight, verbal ability, and the potential for control over one's destiny. Some critics have therefore argued that it is most appropriate for late adolescents or young adults who are bright and verbal, a description which fits college students best. Rogers himself, despite his start in a child guidance center, has spent most of his productive career in university settings, and it is therefore not surprising that his techniques have proved successful with the typical clients in these settings. He and his students have made some attempts to apply his approach to the treatment of schizophrenics (see, for example, Wharton, 1963), but the results have not been as positive. A nondirective form of play therapy has been developed, which seems only tangentially related

---

[5] For examples of Rogerian-oriented therapists in action, see the *Casebook of Non-Directive Counseling,* edited by Snyder (1947).

to the bulk of Rogers's work. Whether the client-centered approach would prove successful with older clients or with those from lower social class levels, whose problems are largely environmental, has not been adequately demonstrated. In any event, the client-centered approach has found its most fervent advocates in university counseling services and clinics, where the population of clients is ideally suited to it.

The brief description of the behavior of a client-centered counselor provided earlier suggests that his approach is quite permissive, with the client free to control the therapy session with a minimum of interference by the therapist. In actuality, however, the client-centered therapist does set stringent boundaries by reacting to certain client behaviors and ignoring others, and by refusing to take a more directive role despite the client's entreaties that he do so. Haley (1963) has pointed out that the client-centered approach enables the therapist to exercise a subtle yet powerful control of the therapeutic relationship, since by refusing to assume the role of authority he gives the client no opportunity to challenge his authority. Despite his seemingly permissive aura, the therapist makes it clear that he expects the client to behave in certain ways if the relationship is to continue, yet since he does not directly tell the client how to behave, the client must "voluntarily" adopt the proper role. The typical client, having nothing to fight against, submits peaceably and commits himself to a productive use of the relationship.

One of the major contributions which Rogers has made to the advancement of psychotherapy is his concern with the scientific study of the therapy process. A concomitant of his residence in university settings has been his work with graduate students and their research which his theories have generated. Although many persons remain unconvinced that Rogers has proved the validity of the client-centered approach to the exclusion of all others, his insistence that his theories be empirically tested has gained him the respect of the psychological community at large. Reports of this research (see Rogers and Dymond, 1954) have demonstrated that many of his concepts can be empirically validated, although as will be discussed in a later chapter, the results of research in this area are dependent on the kinds of questions which are originally asked. Nevertheless, Rogers has had a positive influence on the development of counseling and psychotherapy by his insistence on the support of research evidence for his views. In this respect, he has certainly moved beyond the philosophical boundaries of Freud and his followers.

Applications to Counseling

It may seem incongruous to consider the application of Rogers's work to counseling as a separate topic, since Rogers himself and most of his followers would insist that he has been talking about counseling all along. As discussed in Chapter 1, Rogers has argued since the publication of his first major work, *Counseling and Psychotherapy,* that the two terms refer to the same process and that no distinction should be made between them. This writer, however, believes that a distinction is of value, and that, despite his denials, Rogers has concentrated almost exclusively on personality change and psychotherapy and has largely ignored traditional counseling.

Nevertheless, Rogers's work has had some important implications for the development of counseling. Certainly it has called attention to the importance of considering the individual as a whole in any discussion of plans to be made and conflicts to be resolved. Prior to the appearance of Rogers's writings, counselors had tended to restrict their activities to narrow areas of human life, often relying rigidly on psychological tests and occupational information and little on themselves and their counseling skills. By emphasizing the importance of the counseling relationship itself, Rogers put the tools of counseling in a more appropriate perspective.

Similarly, Rogers's emphasis on the emotional aspects of the individual has provided a necessary balance for those counselors who might otherwise view counseling as strictly a cognitive process. Although some client-centered counselors can be accused of overemphasizing feelings and ignoring the client's cognitions, the recognition of the importance of the client's experiencing all aspects of himself, including his emotional reactions, has contributed to a clearer understanding of the counseling process. The constructs of acceptance and empathy have consistently been stressed by Rogers as basic conditions for counseling, and most modern counselors would accept the view that a foundation of acceptance and empathy must first be established before the more directive techniques have any real value for the client.

Perhaps the greatest drawback to Rogers's approach is that, like all great men, he has tended to attract followers with less vision and insight than he, who have slavishly seized his pronouncements and attempted to propagate them in a rather heavy-handed manner. The result has been that many individuals with a minimum of training have been encouraged to mechanically adopt client-centered techniques, with little understanding of the circumstances under which they are appropriate nor of the basic qualities of a counselor which are required for their meaningful use. As a consequence, many clients have suffered through interminable sessions with counselors who seem incapable of doing more than nodding their heads or offering occasional grunts. While such behaviors may approximate the letter of client-centered law, they certainly ignore its spirit.

The true client-centered counselor, who prizes the integrity of the individual, should recognize that counselors as well as clients have individual selves which must be honestly expressed. This means that all forms of counseling, if presented as a sincere attempt to help another person, must be valued as the expression of a concerned individual. There is no one true religion in counseling.

APPROACHES BASED ON THEORIES OF BEHAVIOR MODIFICATION

The theories of counseling previously described have been closely related to theories of personality. In each case, it is assumed that the counselor's prime concern is with understanding the dynamics of the client and with providing a relationship which will enhance the development of the client as a person. The counselor's theoretical orientation provides a model of the client and dictates how the counselor should behave in accordance with this model.

It is possible, however, to view the counseling situation strictly in terms of its own dynamics, concentrating on the *process* by which the client changes, rather than on the internal dynamics of the change. Counseling can be viewed as basically a learning situation, in which the client learns more appropriate and satisfying behaviors, and counselors who take this approach rely heavily on theories of learning to guide their counseling behavior. To them, the counseling situation represents an opportunity to apply the principles of learning derived from experimental psychology. The dynamics of the client as a person are of secondary importance. What is most important is structuring the counseling situation so as to optimize changes in client behavior, once the desired behaviors have been specified.

Just as there are several theories of learning, there are also several learning approaches to counseling. We will mention each briefly, trusting that the reader will go to a primary source to pursue further those which intrigue him.[6]

Most of the behavior modification approaches have been developed by persons interested in psychotherapy rather than counseling. Therefore it will be necessary to describe the approaches primarily in terms of psychotherapy, since that is mostly where they have been applied. When possible, applications to counseling will be indicated, and the work of those individuals who have expressly concerned themselves with counseling will be described.

Psychodynamic Approaches

Early attempts to apply learning theory to psychotherapy operated within the framework of the traditional model of psychotherapy. It was as-

[6] General descriptions which the reader may find useful include those by Rachman (1963b), Grossberg (1964), Kalish (1965), Bachrach and Quigley (1966), and Bandura (1967).

sumed that the traditional model could be explained by principles of learning, but that the model itself must be retained. Only recently have psychologists begun to question the model itself and to apply learning principles more directly to the alteration of client behavior.

The development of learning-oriented theories of psychotherapy was strongly influenced by John Dollard and Neal Miller, social and experimental psychologists respectively, who combined their talents in a 1950 publication, *Personality and Psychotherapy*. Like Rogers's *Counseling and Psychotherapy*, Dollard and Miller's treatise had a profound impact on psychotherapy, although in a rather different manner. Dollard and Miller contended that the process of psychotherapy could be explained by a stimulus-response model of learning derived primarily from the work of Clark Hull and relying on basic learning constructs such as drive, cue, response, and reinforcement. They postulated that disordered behavior develops out of conflict and fear, which lead to the suppression and repression of relevant stimuli. The goals of treatment, therefore, are to help the client reduce these conflicts by gaining conscious control of his behavior and by acquiring more appropriate responses. They explained in learning terms the procedure by which traditional psychotherapy produces this change, and they described how the traditional approach could be improved by paying greater attention to responses and reinforcements.

Despite their emphasis on psychotherapy as a learning situation, Dollard and Miller accepted the assumption that an understanding of the personality dynamics of the client is essential to psychotherapy. It was their purpose to explain these dynamics in learning-theory terms and then to indicate how psychotherapy should be structured to promote optimum personality development on the part of the client. In this respect, therefore, they had much in common with both Freud and Rogers. The notion that the psychotherapy situation itself could be viewed solely in terms of learning principles was still to come.

The attempt by Dollard and Miller to amalgamate Hullian learning theory and psychotherapy has been viewed with awe and wonder by psychologists on both sides of the applied-experimental fence, but it cannot be said to have had much direct effect on psychotherapy itself. They did not found a school of psychotherapy or begin a cult. Their techniques are frequently discussed but seldom directly employed. Perhaps because neither Dollard nor Miller was a practicing psychotherapist, they have not actually caused any major changes in therapeutic approaches. They have influenced the vocabulary of psychotherapists, but not their behavior.

And yet their influence should not be underestimated. Since the publication of their book, psychotherapists and counselors have become increasingly aware that basic experimental psychology has something worthwhile to offer practitioners of behavior change. Dollard and Miller paved the way for the acceptance of the more radical techniques of behavior modification to be described next.

Behavior Shaping

The next step was the recognition that, if counseling is truly a learning situation, the constructs and hypotheses involved in devising a model of the client's personality structure may not be necessary. If behavioral goals can be specified, then the counseling situation can be structured on the basis of learning principles to produce those changes. The personality dynamics of the client are considered an unnecessary encumbrance: the counselor's role is to help the client change his behavior, not to understand him.

Verbal Conditioning. Some of the early attempts to structure the counseling situation in this manner dealt primarily with the client's verbal behavior. It readily became apparent that client verbalizations could be manipulated by following simple reinforcement procedures (Krasner, 1958, 1965; Strong, 1964; and Williams, 1964). It was evident that counselor behaviors such as a nod or an "uh-huh," which many had assumed to be "nondirective," could in fact operate as powerful reinforcers. Clients could be conditioned to talk more about certain topics, to use the first person more frequently, or to produce verbalizations of just about any sort that seemed potentially useful in counseling.

But what did this mean? Research on verbal conditioning has, of course, demonstrated that client behavior can be manipulated within the counseling situation, but of what value are such changes in terms of the needs which caused the client to seek counseling in the first place? In some respects, probably very little. As Grossberg (1964) has pointed out, the verbal conditioning investigators seem to have proceeded on the assumption that verbal behavior is a central part of the counseling process, and that effecting changes in verbalizations must therefore produce concomitant changes in feelings and behaviors outside of counseling. In actuality, this correspondence has generally not been demonstrated, and much of the research on verbal conditioning appears to have been an interesting sort of experimental game, but without much direct relevance to behavior change itself. Verbalizations are only one facet of behavior, and the study of their modification outside of the total context of counseling or psychotherapy has proved of only peripheral value to the understanding of the counseling process itself.

From verbal conditioning, however, it is only a short step to a much more fundamental approach to counseling and psychotherapy: the conditioning of the maladaptive behavior itself. This step, however, has proved to be one of the most significant in the history of counseling and psychotherapy and has produced some of the most exciting and controversial techniques yet developed.

Approaches Based on Classical Conditioning.   Perhaps the simplest place to begin is with those techniques designed to eliminate specific undesirable behaviors through the application of classical conditioning principles.[7] The general approach is to weaken the current stimulus-response connection and to substitute a more desirable response to the crucial stimulus. One method is *aversion therapy*, in which the therapist attempts to interrupt an undesirable stimulus-response connection by substituting a highly unpleasant reinforcement whenever the stimulus occurs. Aversion therapy has been most successful in the treatment of sexual deviations, such as homosexuality (Feldman, 1966). A variety of negative reinforcements have proved effective, the most common being electric shock and drugs which produce a strong, unpleasant physiological reaction. By introducing the aversive stimulus at the same time as the stimulus which produces the undesirable response—in the case of a male homosexual, for example, the stimulus might be pictures of naked men—the client develops a conditioned negative reaction to the previously positive stimulus.

Aversion therapy concentrates on elimination of an undesirable response on the apparent assumption that desirable responses will naturally follow; once homosexual behaviors have been reduced, for example, normal heterosexual behavior should develop without further therapeutic intervention. In other instances, however, it is important that a specific desirable response also be established. For such cases, a more appropriate technique is *counterconditioning,* in which the goal is to establish a specific response to a specific stimulus. A typical example is in the treatment of enuresis (bedwetting), in which the goal is to cause the individual to establish a subconscious conditioned response between bladder pressure and contracting the sphincter muscles long enough to awaken and go to the bathroom. Conditioning approaches have proved quite successful in the treatment of enuresis, generally much more so than attempts to reason with the child or punishing him for being wet at night (Werry, 1966).

Perhaps the most highly developed approach to the elimination of undesirable behaviors is *desensitization,* which has proved especially useful in the treatment of phobias. The technique of desensitization was developed by Joseph Wolpe (1958), who based it on a Hullian learning model and referred to it more technically as "reciprocal inhibition"; it has subsequently

[7] There is some disagreement in the literature as to the theoretical basis for the various techniques of behavior modification. Those discussed in this section seem most closely aligned to classical conditioning, but some authorities (for example, Rachman, 1967) would argue that other theoretical models should also be considered.

been utilized in the research and treatment procedures developed by Lang (1965) and by Eysenck and Rachman (1965).

The basic principle involved in desensitization is to establish an incompatible situation in which the undesirable response which is normally aroused by a certain stimulus cannot occur. Typically this incompatibility is induced by training the client to relax completely, so that the phobic stimulus can be gently introduced without arousing anxiety. To do this, the therapist assumes a rather directive role, questioning the client to establish the exact nature of the difficulty and the stimuli which arouse the anxiety, and instructing the client as to the procedure to be followed (Rachman, 1967). If, for example, the client has a fear of snakes, the therapist would first determine the exact nature of this fear, the circumstances under which it arises, and the levels of anxiety produced by various stimuli. In this way, he would establish a *hierarchy* of stimuli, ranging from those which arouse a slight degree of anxiety in the client to those which arouse very strong anxiety. The client would then be instructed to relax as completely as possible, and a fear-inducing stimulus from the low-anxiety end of the hierarchy would be introduced. The stimulus may be introduced in its concrete form, but more often the client is simply instructed to imagine the stimulus. In this example, the first stimulus would probably be something that looked only vaguely like a snake, perhaps a shoestring or something equally innocuous. If the client experienced some anxiety at this stage, the stimulus would be removed or he would be instructed to put it out of his mind, and further relaxation would be stressed. After a few trials, the client should be able to relax to the point where the introduction (or imagining) of a low-level, fear-inducing stimulus arouses no anxiety. From then on, the therapist guides the client in moving up the hierarchy of fear-inducing stimuli, in each case concentrating on further relaxation whenever the client experiences anxiety. Eventually, the client should become able to approach the strongest stimulus—in this case, a live snake—with no anxiety reaction.

Desensitization can be employed with behaviors other than phobias, providing that the difficulty is basically a neurosis rather than a psychosis and providing that a rather specific source of anxiety can be located (see, for example, Patterson, 1966; Geer and Katkin, 1966). Success rates with the procedure are quite high compared with the more traditional forms of psychotherapy, although Wolpe begins by screening his clients carefully and selects only those who he believes have the proper "temperament" to use the procedure constructively.

Operant Conditioning. If the goal of counseling and psychotherapy is defined as a change in some aspect of the client's behavior, then conditioning techniques can be employed to "shape" the behavior in the desired form. The basic model usually employed is operant (instrumental) conditioning, in which the subject must make the desired response in order to receive the reinforcement. In this approach, the desired behavior is specified, a setting is established in which the behavior can be emitted, and reinforcement is provided when the desired behavior occurs. Eventually the desired behavior becomes a normal part of the client's repertoire, and the special reinforcement situation is no longer needed. If undesirable behaviors are also present, care is taken to ensure that they are not reinforced and thus are extinguished. Behavior shaping relies primarily on a Skinnerian model of learning; in effect, the client's behavior is "programmed" much as a learning situation is programmed by the Skinnerian approach. (For further descriptions of operant conditioning as applied to psychotherapy see Bachrach, 1965, and Bachrach and Quigley, 1966.)

A therapist who relies primarily on operant conditioning begins by establishing, with the client, the behavior to be changed. They will attempt to determine what is reinforcing the client's undesirable behavior and will select appropriate reinforcements for the behavior to be learned. At first the reinforcement may be supplied primarily by the therapist within the therapy situation itself, but eventually the client should learn to apply his own reinforcement outside of therapy. In a sense, the client learns how to program his own behavior, so that further help from the therapist becomes unnecessary.

Goldiamond (1965) has described this procedure as a learning of self-control: "If you want a specified behavior from yourself, set up the conditions which you know will control it [p.853]." He describes several cases in which this approach proved successful, involving compulsive eating, inability to study, and marital discord. In each case, the client was helped to determine the stimulus conditions which produced the undesirable behavior and then helped to control these conditions so that the behavior was reduced. Potential reinforcements were located, and those which produced desirable effects were stressed. In the marital problem, for example, each member was helped to recognize how his own behavior elicited undesirable behaviors from his spouse and to learn to provide reinforcements to obtain the behaviors from his spouse which he wanted.

Therapists who rely primarily on behavior shaping techniques do not concern themselves much with the causes of the undesirable behavior. The important considerations are to specify the desired change and to establish a sequence of steps by which this change can be accomplished, with emphasis on the client acquiring control of the stimulus and reinforcement conditions himself.

Behavior Modeling.   Behavior change through conditioning can be criticized on the grounds that the client must first produce the desired behavior in order that it can be reinforced, which may be an inefficient and inexact process. It is also argued that conditioning techniques, being based originally on research with lower animals, do not make use of those cognitive qualities of the human being which permit more complex forms of learning. On the basis of these arguments, Albert Bandura (1965) has developed an approach to behavior modification in which the subject first observes another person performing the desired behavior, which the subject subsequently attempts to perform for himself. In Bandura's procedure, the client is generally not instructed to copy the model's behavior, but given certain environmental demands it is assumed that he will make use of the examples he has observed. Bandura has worked primarily with children, but his techniques appear to be adaptable to counseling and psychotherapy with adolescents and adults. A modeling approach would require that the client have the opportunity to observe other persons engaging in the kind of behavior he would like to develop; he would then be positively reinforced for performing similar behaviors. Although the evidence is inconclusive, it seems desirable that the model be similar to the client in age and setting, so that identification is facilitated, and that the situation produce anxiety in the client. Such an approach should expedite behavior therapy by narrowing the range of client responses to those most likely to achieve success.

Models for a given client may be located in real-life situations, or they may be presented by film or by television tape. For example, a young man too shy to ask a girl for a date might be shown a film of a young man asking several different girls for dates and obtaining various reactions from them. By observing how the man in the film responds, the client may be able to develop some behaviors that he can employ in his own situation. Persons are often frightened when approaching a situation which they don't know how to handle. A modeling technique can help them develop behaviors to deal effectively with the common contingencies in that situation. In this respect, modeling seems potentially more valuable than simple instruction, by putting more responsibility on the client to think through the situation he is observing and to select those behaviors which may be useful to him.

Critique

Whatever behavior therapy may or may not be, it is certainly controversial. Perhaps no other series of techniques in the history of psychotherapy has sparked so many publications, both attacking and defending learning-theory approaches. Some of the criticisms are primarily philosophical: learning-theory approaches are condemned for being concerned only with symptom removal rather than with the underlying dynamics of the individual's problem, for being too manipulative, and (worst of all) for dehumanizing the client by turning him into some sort of robot.

These arguments are difficult to counter directly, since their basis is more emotional than rational. However, it can be pointed out that removal of "symptoms" is often what the client hopes to attain, and that symptom removal need not necessarily imply that another symptom will emerge to take its place (Cahoon, 1968). The manipulation argument can be countered by pointing to evidence that all forms of psychotherapy are in some respects manipulative (see Grossberg, 1964; Truax, 1966a, 1966b) and that behavior therapy is perhaps more honest than most by making the manipulation obvious so that the client is more directly aware of what is happening to him.

The concern with dehumanization of the client assumes that the goal of behavior therapy is to establish a fixed stimulus-response connection of a reflex nature, when in actuality most such approaches are concerned with broadening the client's response repertoire by freeing him from the constraints of a previously limited and maladaptive stimulus-response bond. Clients treated by behavior therapy do not seem to have been turned into machines in the process. Generally they are satisfied with the experience, having obtained relief from the undesirable behavior which brought them to the therapist originally, and are functioning more adequately as persons than before.

More cogent criticisms, however, may be lodged against behavior therapy. A critical evaluation of behavior therapy has been made by Breger and McGaugh (1965), who dispute the claims of behavior therapists on several grounds. Their primary objection is that, whatever the effectiveness of the techniques themselves, their theoretical basis is questionable. According to the writers, behavior therapists have misconstrued the constructs of traditional learning theory to fit their techniques and have thereby forfeited their claim to be direct descendants of experimental psychologists. Breger and McGaugh argue that the behavior therapists have naively applied principles of conditioning derived from laboratory research with little appreciation for the complexities of the conditioning paradigm. In other words, they believe that behavior therapy does not have the sound theoretical basis which its proponents claim for it.

There seems some merit in this criticism, although as Bachrach and Quigley (1966) have pointed out, Breger and McGaugh have been guilty of some of the same overgeneralization of which they accuse the behavior therapists. For our purposes, however, evidence of effectiveness would seem to be a telling point, and the evidence for the effectiveness of behavior therapy is impressive. Dealing with rather specific behaviors and often with a select group of clients, behavior therapists have demonstrated an improvement rate considerably higher than that of traditional forms of psychotherapy (see, for example, the research summaries by Grossberg, 1964; Eysenck and Rachman, 1965; Rachman, 1967; and Gelfand and Hartmann,

1968). Breger and McGaugh have also taken behavior therapists to task for claiming success on the basis of case studies, biased sampling, and lack of controls, although subsequent controlled studies utilizing more sophisticated samples and controls (for example, Paul, 1966, 1967) have demonstrated the superiority of behavior therapy techniques.

One must bear in mind, however, that behavior therapy is most effec- ✓ tive when applied to specific behavior disorders—most notably phobic re- actions and enuresis—treated within specified environmental conditions. Grossberg (1964) seems to have drawn a fair conclusion: "Behavior therapies have been most successful when applied to neurotic disorders with specific behavioral manifestations [p. 81]." Behavior therapy is not a pan- acea for all neurotic disorders, let alone for adjustment problems of a less specific nature. But it has demonstrated its value for the treatment of specific disorders, especially those which are typically resistant to treatment by more conventional techniques.

At the bottom of the controversy surrounding behavior therapy are basic differences in concepts of the human personality. As noted earlier, the techniques which a given psychotherapist will use depends on their com- patibility with his theory of personality, and many therapists therefore reject behavioristic approaches primarily because they cannot accommodate them to their personality theory. To some psychotherapists, therefore, behavior therapy is not really psychotherapy, since it does not produce personality change within the framework of the traditional theories of personality. But this is a philosophical rather than a scientific dispute. To the client who has been relieved by a behavioristic approach of an anxiety or a behavior which has been a source of considerable personal discomfort, the validity of behavior therapy is evident, and he is understandably not ✓ greatly concerned with philosophical debates as to its effectiveness.

Applications to Counseling

The techniques based on learning theory described up to this point would more likely qualify as psychotherapy than as counseling. Generally they are designed to eliminate or modify some form of behavior which is causing the client discomfort, a behavior which might be termed "neurotic." The development of psychotherapeutic approaches based on principles of learning has, however, had an impact on counseling techniques, and in- novations have been devised in counseling to take advantage of this new perspective.

Following the lead of Dollard and Miller, the earliest emphasis was on recognizing the counseling relationship as a learning situation, but retaining a concern for the dynamics of the client. Examples of this view can be found in the writings of Combs (1954), Shoben (1954), and the Pepinskys

(1954), all of whom attempted to explain the counseling process in terms of learning-theory principles but who had not yet taken the step of applying these principles to effect changes in specific behaviors.

At the time of this writing, the development of counseling techniques based directly on learning-theory principles is in its early stages. Counselors have been slow to respond to the challenge presented in 1962 by Michael and Meyerson in their article, "A Behavioral Approach to Counseling and Guidance": "Observable behavior is the only variable of importance in the counseling and guidance process, and it is the only criterion against which the outcome of the process can be evaluated [p. 395]." They go on to point out that ". . . behavior is controlled by its environmental consequences and an effective procedure for producing behavioral change is the manipulation of the environment so as to create consequences that will produce the desired behavior [p. 396]." They did not, however, specify the techniques by which this approach was to be implemented. In spirit, they obviously have much in common with the behavior therapists, but inasmuch as counseling is not generally directed toward the elimination or modification of specific undesirable behaviors, behavior therapy techniques must be adapted rather than applied directly in counseling situations.

The person most responsible for the development of behavioral counseling is John Krumboltz of Stanford University. According to Krumboltz (1966a), client problems are seen primarily as learning problems, and the counselor ". . . should see his job as arranging conditions so that his client will learn more adaptive ways of coping with difficulties [p. 5]." Or, as Bijou (1966) has put it, the counselor becomes a "behavioral engineer." Krumboltz believes that a learning approach encourages clients to take more responsibility for their own actions by specifying the behaviors that must be changed or developed and expecting the client to be an active participant in this process.

Krumboltz relies on no single approach, but has borrowed from several behavior therapy techniques. His studies have included the use of operant learning procedures, with reinforcement provided both within and outside of counseling; imitative learning through the use of models, both live and on film; relaxation training in situations involving high anxiety, such as the taking of tests; and cognitive learning, which includes role playing and the establishment of "behavior contracts," by which the client develops better conscious controls of his behavior.

Krumboltz and his students have studied behavioral approaches in a variety of settings and have found them to be effective for many purposes. Among those behaviors which have been successfully altered or developed through behavioral techniques are information-seeking activities (by reinforcement and by modeling), test-taking skills, acceptance of test information, maladaptive behaviors such as shyness and aggression, and decision-making behavior. (See Krumboltz, 1965 and 1966a, for references to specific studies.)

Behavioral counseling will certainly not replace other forms of counseling, but it should provide a useful supplement to the more traditional techniques. Much controversy could be avoided if proponents of various theoretical approaches to counseling would bear in mind that counseling can be useful for a wide variety of clients. Within this range, certain approaches are more apt to produce certain outcomes than are other approaches, provided that both the counselor and client can accept the approach as being potentially useful. The sophisticated counselor should be familiar with new techniques and should recognize situations in which they may be of value. To ignore new developments is just as foolish as to jump blindly on every bandwagon that comes along.

3

A Cognitive-Behavioral
View of Counseling

The preceding chapter has presented a smorgasbord of counseling approaches. No counselor can be expected to become skilled in all of them, nor indeed would it be possible to do so, since some make opposing assumptions. Ultimately, therefore, the individual counselor must adopt his own approach, drawing from those which are most congenial to him and integrating them into a conceptualization which he is able to use effectively.

In order that the remainder of this book communicate as well as possible to the reader, I must therefore undertake to describe my own view of counseling. I have tried as far as possible to incorporate relevant principles derived from the psychological study of the learning process and of the process of social interaction, as described in Chapter 1, but the end product must of necessity be a highly personal one. It is offered here as a framework within which to view the material in the succeeding chapters and with the hope that it will be of help to persons seeking to understand the nature of the counseling process.

My own view of the counseling process accepts an emphasis on a change in behavior as the primary goal of counseling, but it is not restricted to a stimulus-response model of behavior change. I believe that behavior can be self-directed and that a person can learn to take responsibility for his behavior and to control it consciously. Counseling, then, is a process by which the client learns how to control and change his behavior so that it becomes more satisfying to him and produces outcomes which he desires.

I believe that this change in the client comes about through a complex interaction between the counselor and the client, and that certain character-istics of each are especially relevant to an understanding of the nature of this process. The process of counseling itself will be described in detail in the following chapter. The purpose of the present discussion is to establish a psychological basis for this process and to try to explain the cause and nature of the effects of a counseling experience on the client.

BASIC ELEMENTS

The key to the understanding and improvement of counseling lies, I believe, in an analysis of the interaction between the client and counselor, given the circumstances of a typical counseling experience. I have therefore abstracted from this interaction certain elements which seem to me to be basic to the nature of this relationship. Other writers might prefer to focus on other elements instead, but I suggest the following as being of major importance to a cognitive-behavioral view of counseling.

The Person Who Seeks Counseling

People seek counseling for many different reasons, but they would seem to have at least three characteristics in common:

1. The person is experiencing some sort of personal dissatisfaction. He is unable to behave in such a way as to reduce this dissatisfaction suffi-ciently. He thus perceives a *need* to change his behavior without knowing how to go about it. He may recognize that certain behaviors are producing dissatisfying results but be unable to control them, or he may simply have a vague sense of disquiet without being able to specify clearly its cause. In any case, the person who seeks counseling is not entirely satisfied with his current method of coping with a situation and seeks help in doing better.

It is unnecessary at this point to speculate as to the possible causes of a breakdown in the person's previously adequate modes of behavior. Per-haps he has actually been coping poorly for some time but has only now become aware of his limitations. More likely, though, he has reached a developmental stage at which his previous coping behaviors are no longer adequate. As noted earlier, persons are most likely to seek counseling at times of "developmental crisis," when their normally adequate coping mech-anisms no longer produce satisfactory results.

2. The person approaches counseling with a substantial amount of anxiety and uncertainty. Not only is he troubled by some aspect of his life which he is handling inadequately, but he is taking a step into a strange and foreboding land: the counselor's office. The fact that he is probably not entirely clear as to the nature of that on which he is embarking tends to heighten the anxiety which he is already experiencing.

3. The person who seeks counseling expects that the counselor will be able to help him. Many people who might be good candidates for counseling, and to whom it is recommended, do not take advantage of it, in many cases because they do not actually believe it will do them any good. Persons in difficulty have a variety of possible resources: the church, their doctor, a friend, an astrologer, and so forth. Some get help from sources of which other persons would be highly dubious. Yet it seems unlikely that a person who did not have at least a slight expectation that a counselor could help him would seek counseling in the first place. He may have no specific expectation as to what counseling will be, but he at least enters counseling hoping and expecting that it will do him some good.

The research of social psychologists leads to the conclusion that the client's expectation that counseling will help him contributes to its effectiveness. Rosenthal (1966) has demonstrated in a series of studies that a person's expectation that a certain outcome will occur increases the likelihood that he will behave in such a way as to produce the desired outcome, even though he himself may have made no deliberate effort to do so. In counseling research itself, a number of investigators (Goldstein, 1962; Strupp, Wallach, and Wogan, 1964; Clemes and D'Andrea, 1965) have demonstrated a relationship between a client's expectations that a given counselor will be able to help him, and the actual benefit which the client believes he obtained from the counseling.

The typical client, then, enters counseling with an expectation that the counselor will help him deal more effectively with whatever is troubling him, but with no clear idea as to just what will occur. He must rely on the counselor to define the nature of their interaction and the role to be played by the client in this interaction. The naive client, therefore, immediately puts the counselor in an authority role, as he has been encouraged to do by his past experiences with other professional persons. Much as the counselor may try to deny the role of an authority, in this sense he *is* an authority whether he likes it or not: it is he, not the client, who knows how counseling operates. And his initial role as the authority in the relationship gives him the status from which to exercise a strong influence on the client.

To summarize, the person entering counseling for the first time does so because he senses that his present behaviors are not coping adequately with some demand being made by himself or his environment. This situation itself makes him anxious, and the approach to the counselor's office increases his feelings of insecurity and anxiety. He expects that the counselor may be able to help him, but he doesn't know the process by which this help will be obtained, so he is dependent on the counselor to define the nature of counseling and the respective roles of each participant. Looked at another way, the client enters counseling in a state which makes him highly susceptible to the suggestions of a person whom he respects and holds in high esteem, and his expectations of the counselor are such that the counselor will probably fill this role.

The Counselor's Position

The counselor also enters into a new counseling relationship with the expectation that its outcome will be successful. He cannot, of course, guarantee success, but on the basis of his experience he knows that the probabilities of success are high enough to warrant the investment of his time and effort in helping this client. Just as the client's expectation that counseling will be helpful is an important step on the road to success, so is the counselor's expectation of success an important contributing factor. It has been demonstrated, for example, that counselors are less successful with clients whom they believe they will be unable to help (Strupp and Wallach, 1965). In the latter situation, the counselor will probably refer the client elsewhere, to someone who he judges is likely to be more successful

One of the major reasons for the counselor's positive expectations with a new client is his faith in the theoretical approach which he employs. Faced with an insecure, confused, and probably anxious client, the counselor reacts by behaving in a way consistent with his theoretical framework, thereby providing an initial structure to the relationship. His own belief in the eventual effectiveness of this approach enables him to maintain a calmness and assurance in the face of the client's confusion and provides a stable basis for the initiation of the counseling experience.

The counselor's theoretical base thus plays a very important role in the initial stages of counseling, by bolstering his own confidence and by helping him chart a course with the client. This implies that the counselor's selection of a particular theoretical orientation is of crucial importance, and indeed it is. Given the variety of available theories, however, how does he know which is best? This question plagues beginning counselors, as they seek to learn as much as possible about the different theories and to decide which is most valid.

The counselor's choice of a theory, however, cannot be entirely objective. It must take into account his own personality and philosophy of life, as well as the available evidence as to the validity of the various approaches. Since the counselor as a person is a basic element in the counseling relationship, he can more effectively use a theoretical approach which is consistent with his own personality. The counselor's behavior must be natural and spontaneous, not mechanical and contrived, if he is to achieve an effective relationship with his clients. The theoretical framework which he chooses should lead him to emphasize certain aspects of his personality in his role as a counselor, but it should not force him to try to become a radically different kind of person.[1]

The importance of consistency between the counselor's personality and his behavior as a counselor is evident in the fact that different counselors, using different approaches, can be equally successful, although not necessarily with the same clients. The experienced counselor has made his approach a part of himself and he can therefore present it honestly and convincingly to his clients. Counselors may continue to debate the validity of their differing approaches, but each will probably remain convinced that his is superior because it achieves the desired results. And the personal strength which that belief provides makes him a strong figure in the counseling relationship.

The Development of the Relationship

Counseling begins, therefore, with the juxtaposition of a person who is dissatisfied with the way he is coping with some aspect of his life, and who is probably confused and anxious, with a person who is experienced in helping persons in similar difficulties and who has evolved an approach which generally seems to be effective. *The counselor, then, initially communicates to the client a feeling of strength and calmness in opposition to the client's confusion and anxiety.* This has at least two important immediate effects: (1) it meets the client's expectation that the counselor will know what to do and thereby increases the client's faith in the counselor; and (2) it reduces the client's anxiety, which in turn reinforces his positive attraction to the counselor and the counseling situation.

It is generally accepted by psychologists that the reduction of anxiety can be a powerful reinforcement, and several writers (for example, Pepinsky and Pepinsky, 1954) have suggested that this may account for much of the learning which takes place in counseling. In the early stages of counseling, when not much in the way of objective change has yet taken place, this anxiety reduction encourages the client to continue the counseling process. But anxiety reduction alone is probably not a sufficient basis for the necessary behavior change and may in fact interfere with substantial client improvement. The client who becomes anxious and upset when things go badly for him, and who learns that a counseling session will make him "feel better," may be encouraged to use counseling simply as a means of gaining temporary relief from his anxiety rather than working to change the behavior which is producing it. Anxiety reduction, then, may help to get the client involved in the counseling process, but further steps must be taken to insure that something worthwhile develops.

---

[1] The relationship between the counselor's personal values and his adoption of a particular theoretical approach has been explored at length by Glad (1959).

One of the first tasks of the counselor is to present the approach which he will take. He seldom does this directly, but instead relies on his own behavior to define to the client the role which is expected of him. If the counselor asks many questions, for example, the client's role is defined as that of passively responding to the counselor's inquiries; whereas if the counselor does little talking but reacts only to what the client says, the client's role is defined as that of taking the lead in producing material to be discussed. Although the client may at first be unsure of what is expected of him, the counselor, by playing a consistent role himself, indicates rather forcefully what the client is expected to do.

With a few exceptions, most counselors do not define the roles openly. Instead, the counselor communicates the expected roles by his own behavior and relies on the client to "catch on" to his role. Although this method may be less efficient than that of simply explaining the approach directly to the client, it is psychologically more powerful and more persuasive. By not explaining his approach directly, the counselor does not provide the client with a basis for argument or disagreement. Moreover, the client seldom realizes that he has been subtly manipulated into assuming the role which the counselor thinks best for him; he believes he adopted it "voluntarily" and therefore accepts it more wholeheartedly than would probably be the case if he felt coerced into it. The subtle counselor thus produces a strong commitment on the part of the client by avoiding a direct explanation of the approach he is following, although he is clear in his own mind as to the direction that the counseling should be taking.

Clients are, however, by no means entirely pliable, and some resist adopting the counselor's approach and playing the role which he expects. Some are simply unable to do so: the expected role is too foreign to them and they cannot adopt it. Others have strong doubts as to the validity of the approach which the counselor is offering. They decide that it will not be helpful to them to proceed in this manner and they terminate counseling. The number of clients who terminate counseling prematurely and who subsequently express dissatisfaction with their counseling experience attests to the fact that not all clients are easily won over to the counselor's approach.

The circumstances of the situation, however, favor the client's acceptance of the counselor's approach: the client is confused, uncertain, and anxious, while the counselor is confident and hopeful, with the status of an authority figure. It is hardly surprising that most clients will accept the counselor's approach as at least worth a try.

The client generally, however, goes further than merely agreeing to go along with the counselor's method. In most cases, he also adopts the counselor's *faith* in the approach they will take. In so doing, he commits himself to make it work, which is an important step in the direction of constructive use of the approach.

The acceptance by the client of the approach presented by the counselor may not come easily. Much depends on the extent to which this approach meets the client's initial expectations. If the counselor behaves as the client had expected, and his own role is defined in accordance with these expectations, acceptance is easily obtained. But if there is an initial discrepancy between the client's expectations and the approach presented by the counselor, a period of accommodation may be necessary.

It is during this period that the client must decide whether to accept the approach offered by the counselor and to play the role which it requires of him. One factor contributing to this decision is the *persuasiveness* of the counselor. Although there is no evidence to support this contention directly, it seems likely that successful counselors are more persuasive than those who are less successful. The counselor's persuasion must of course be subtle, since the client must feel that he has decided for himself to adopt the offered approach. If he feels he was coerced into it against his will, he has no obligation to make it work and an important aspect of the counseling relationship would therefore be missing.

Some clients, however, will reject the counselor's subtle techniques, perhaps because their expectations are quite different from those of the counselor and they simply don't understand what he is trying to communicate. When this occurs, the counselor may be forced to fall back on a more formal "structuring" of the situation, explaining more explicitly to the client the nature of the approach he wants to use. Lennard and Bernstein (1966), for example, suggest that structuring in counseling is simply role definition and cite evidence that counselors spend more time in references to the interaction system with clients whose expectations are at odds with theirs. Most counselors, however, prefer to minimize the amount of structuring in the early part of counseling, believing that the client should adopt a role with which he feels comfortable within the framework of the general approach which the counselor wants to take.

It is important to recall at this point that the counselor is presumably operating out of a theoretical framework in which he personally believes very strongly. The strength of this belief is communicated to the client by the intensity with which the counselor plays his own role, especially in the face of hints from the client that he should do otherwise, and by his obvious faith in his approach. This consistency and faith on the part of the counselor has a powerful impact on the typical client and helps to persuade him that the counselor's approach is worthy of trial.[2]

No counselor will be able to persuade all clients to accept his approach

[2] For a more extensive discussion of the role of faith and persuasion in the effectiveness of counseling and psychotherapy, see *Persuasion and Healing* by Jerome Frank (1961).

and to play the role he expects. For some, the gap between their expectations and the counselor's method is too great, while for others the counselor's personality may itself present a barrier. Under such conditions, the counselor has several alternatives. The most obvious would seem to be that he should alter his approach to one closer to the client's expectations and which the client would more likely find acceptable. Although the skilled counselor may be able to make some modifications in this direction, he will be restricted by the limitations of his own personality. As noted earlier, the counselor is most effective with an approach with which he personally feels comfortable and which "fits" him as a person. A counselor cannot be expected to run the gamut of techniques and be equally effective with all of them.

A better alternative, therefore, may be to refer the client to a counselor who makes use of an approach which the client is more likely to accept. Given the immediate circumstances this is not always possible, but the counselor who is unable to develop an effective working relationship with a given client should always consider the possibility that another counselor, using a different approach, might be more successful.

In order for counseling to proceed, therefore, the counselor and client must agree on the procedure to be followed and the role which each will play in this procedure. This relationship is continually being refined and modified as they progress, but the basic approach generally remains consistent.

The major value of the approach, from the client's point of view, is that it provides a means of conceptualizing his problem and of mounting an attack on it. As he interacts with the counselor and adopts the counselor's approach, the client also adopts his way of viewing the problem. The client, we must recall, enters counseling in a confused state of mind, trying to cope with some sort of stress which makes little sense to him. One of the early values of the counselor's approach, therefore, is that it provides a framework by which both the counselor and the client together can impose a kind of order on the client's difficulties. By adopting the counselor's way of looking at the situation, the client finds it begins to make sense to him and thereby becomes more amenable to a rational attack. The first step, therefore, is to organize the client's thoughts and feelings into some comprehensible framework, followed by a decision to deal with some limited aspect of the problem in a systematic way.

The counselor, then, provides an approach to the problem which (1) organizes it so that it makes some sense to the client, and (2) suggests something that the client can do which may have a positive effect. In other words, the client's behavior change begins to occur within a cognitive framework which he adopts from the counselor; he can now direct his energies in a productive manner in terms of the relationships which he sees among the thoughts and feelings that were formerly jumbled in his mind.

It must be recognized that the client does not simply transpose a framework from the counselor's mind into his own. Each is a unique individual, and neither therefore would be expected to view the same situation in exactly the same way. The client, instead, adapts those aspects of the counselor's framework which make sense to him and, in effect, creates a unique framework of his own. The client's framework will probably be much like that of the counselor, but with its own unique features.

The psychological concept of "modeling," described in the previous chapter, would seem to explain some aspects of this transposition. The client begins by modeling his thinking and behavior on that of the counselor, within the limitations of the counseling situation itself, but as he extends this approach to behavior occurring outside of the counseling situation he finds that he can no longer model solely on the counselor. He then looks for other examples of behaviors which he might add to his repertoire and tries them out, retaining those which achieve the desired results and fitting them into the framework he has already begun to build.

This concept of counseling would seem to apply regardless of the specific approach which the counselor espouses: psychoanalytic, Rogerian, behavior modification, or any other. All make certain assumptions about the nature of man and of the causes of human problems, which both the counselor and client must share; all require intimate interaction between the counselor and the client; and all require the client to produce changes in his behavior. The explanations which account for this behavior change may vary among these approaches, but behavior change is the ultimate goal of each.

As the client develops a framework within which he and his environment can be viewed in a rational, coherent form, and as he isolates certain aspects of his behavior to be changed, he begins to gain control over himself and his world. His anxiety is reduced, which in itself is reinforcing, and he gains in the ability to handle situations which formerly caused him difficulty. He becomes able to act in ways which are more personally satisfying to him and to guide his behavior so as to reach important goals. In so doing, he becomes a more fully-functioning individual, with greater control over himself and his environment. This control in turn frees him from his prior anxieties and insecurities to develop new behaviors as well as to modify old ones.

It is far from unimportant that the client's progress in gaining control over his behavior and in progressing toward the counseling goal is pleasing to the counselor as well. His pleasure is communicated to the client, who is further reinforced by it. The client and counselor have met a common challenge, and both are entitled to gain satisfaction from a successful outcome.

IMPLICATIONS FOR COUNSELING

The view of counseling presented here has a number of implications for the practice of counseling.

Counseling is designed to achieve a goal of behavior change, as agreed upon by both the client and the counselor. Counseling must be goal-directed, and the counselor and client must work together to reach this goal. This means that the counselor must initially help the client to explain and clarify his reason for seeking counseling, so that they both understand and accept a common goal. This goal may, of course, be altered as the counseling proceeds, but counseling cannot progress while either the client or the counselor is in the dark as to its destination.

Most clients come to counseling with problems of a rather restricted nature, and counselors agree that these problems can be clustered into three general areas: vocational, educational, and "personal" (Warman, 1960). The first two represent fairly specific and well-defined constellations of difficulties and compose the bulk of problems with which most high school and college counselors deal, while the third is an ill-defined category which accounts for those not readily classified as vocational or educational. The first two are the traditional areas of counseling, growing out of its vocational guidance antecedents, while the third probably represents the need of traditionally oriented counselors to differentiate their area of interest from that of their more therapeutically oriented colleagues. In a sense, the noncategory of "personal" problems is what the counselors of a generation ago would have considered to be the province of psychotherapy. Likewise, it is now in this area that the distinctions between counseling and psychotherapy become blurred and in which techniques from both may often be appropriate.

In defining the counseling goal, the counselor should bear in mind that the problem initially presented by the client may not actually indicate his true counseling need. Some clients begin by presenting a *facade* problem —a blind to cover their true purpose for coming until they can assess the counseling situation. The counselor who is too eager to pick up the first ball he sees and run with it may find after it is too late that he is out of the game and cannot get back in.

There is some question as to whether a facade problem necessarily represents a deliberate attempt by the client to deceive the counselor. In some cases this is probably true; the client misrepresents his reason for coming to counseling in order to try counseling in a "safe" area before opening up an area in which he is less sure of himself. More frequently, however, the client honestly believes in his initial problem, and it is only as the counseling relationship develops and he comes to understand the nature of counseling that he finds more meaningful ways in which to use it.

This is not meant to imply that the counselor should play the role of detective, doubting each new client until he has established, by clever questions and deductions, that the presented need for counseling is or is not the truth. Instead, the counselor should accept the presented need as the true need *for the present,* but he should not limit the discussion so that the client has no opportunity to raise other areas as the counseling progresses.

It is in the setting of a goal that the various approaches to counseling differ most importantly. Since the counselor must acquiesce in the goal, this means that the counselor's concept of counseling and his belief as to the most valuable outcomes of counseling will have a strong influence on the goal which is finally agreed upon. In this way it can be seen that brief approaches, which aim primarily at symptom removal, have something worthwhile to offer. Not all counselors would accept this as a worthwhile goal, nor for that matter would all clients. It is only necessary, however, that the counselor and client agree on what they are trying to accomplish and how they will go about it.

It is of basic importance that the counselor develop a firm theoretical orientation, consistent with his own personality. If the counselor has anything of value to offer a troubled person, it is a theoretical framework within which this person can learn to deal more effectively with himself and his world. Neophyte counselors should therefore be encouraged to develop a theoretical framework for their counseling and be guided in learning to handle it with skill. Frank (1961) has pointed out that an important product of a therapist's experience and training in a specific orientation is that his self-confidence as a therapist is strengthened, which in turn encourages his clients to believe that the therapist knows what he is doing and can help them. Perhaps more important, however, is that a counselor with a consistent theoretical framework has something to offer his clients in the way of a structure which will enable them to assume control of themselves and of their environment.

This means that programs of counselor training should provide a variety of models for the beginning counselor, so that he can be guided skillfully in selecting that which is most congenial to him. Many programs, unfortunately, are restricted in the approaches which they teach, and the trainee who is not able to adopt the approach being taught may be lost from the profession. Since the instructors themselves are committed to their individual approaches, it is hardly surprising that they try to persuade their students to imitate them, but in the long run they would be doing their students a greater service by allowing for greater flexibility and by encouraging each to develop an approach consistent with his own personality.

The assignment of a new client to a counselor within a counseling agency should be made on the basis of compatibility of expectations. At the present time, such assignment is usually made unsystematically, determined primarily by the corresponding free hours of the client and counselor. If the client requests a certain counselor his request will probably be honored, if the counselor's schedule permits. Such a request is usually based on some previous knowledge about that counselor and his approach, probably gained from a current or former client, so that in this case the client-counselor expectations are more apt to be similar. But the view presented here suggests that counseling agencies might reduce their proportion of premature terminations if they were to arrange to match clients and counselors on a more systematic basis. More research, however, is needed to determine the variables which are relevant to such a matching and to develop instruments to measure these variables.

The physical setting for counseling should be arranged so as to maximize its persuasive elements. This does not mean that the counselor's office should resemble that of a witch doctor, but it does mean that its professional elements should be accentuated. This principle may be especially important for counselors-in-training, who are likely to be assigned to the most sparsely furnished and unkempt offices in the agency. Coupled with their lower degree of self-confidence, such an arrangement decreases the probability that their counseling experience will be optimally successful. Of all counselors, these probably need more rather than less help from the physical setting to establish an appropriate relationship with their clients.

A corollary of the previous suggestion is that the professional counselor has an advantage over the amateur because of the setting in which he works. Earlier it was noted that counseling need not necessarily involve a professionally trained person, although the latter had certain advantages. The persuasive aspects of his professional qualifications and setting are an additional advantage.

The resistant client, and the client who terminates too early, can be explained as a failure by the client to accept the approach offered by the counselor. Perhaps this counselor was not a very good persuader and therefore failed to convince the client that his approach would be helpful. More likely, however, there was a basic incompatibility of counselor and client belief systems. A prospective client probably has a limited range of approaches to which he can accommodate, so that if he draws a counselor whose orientation is outside of these limits it is unlikely that a counseling relationship will ever develop. When this occurs, the client will resist committing himself to counseling and will probably terminate rather quickly.

This implies that no counselor can expect all prospective clients to accept his approach, but that the more flexible his theoretical orientation, within the limits of his personality, the wider the range of clients with whom he can develop a counseling relationship.

The counselor has an obligation to refer elsewhere those clients who are unable to accept his approach or to use it effectively. Since counseling approaches vary widely, it is quite possible that a resistant client may be helped by another counselor, using a different approach. The counselor should accept the limitations of his approach and should be aware of other sources of help for those clients with whom he is ineffective.

PART II

The Counseling Process

4

The Counseling Process

Having considered the purpose of counseling as well as its psychological basis, we can now examine the interaction between the counselor and client in some detail. The purpose of this chapter is to describe the process of counseling itself; subsequent chapters in this section will consider variables which influence this process as well as some specialized aspects of counseling.

PHASES OF COUNSELING

Casual observation of a series of counseling interviews may suggest that the process is disorganized and haphazard. To be sure, any activity involving subtle interplay between two individuals who are dealing with bits and pieces of personal experience does not lend itself to a neatly organized pattern. It seems to be generally accepted, however, that a close examination of the counseling process shows it to have a reasonably consistent internal structure (see, for example, Robinson, 1950; Buchheimer and Balogh, 1961), although different writers emphasize different aspects of the structure, according to their theoretical orientation.

For purposes of description and clarification, we will consider the counseling process in five phases. This is, of course, only one way of conceptualizing counseling; any organizational scheme must be to some extent arbitrary.

Phase 1. Establishment of the Purpose

To begin with, the client must state his reason for seeking counseling. This may be a very brief phase, if he can verbalize his need easily. Some clients, however, require some time in order to do this, either because their ability to put their thoughts into words is poor, or because they are reluctant to be frank about their reason for coming until they have made an initial assessment of the counselor and the counseling situation. Nevertheless, the counseling process *per se* cannot begin until the client indicates his reason for wanting counseling and both he and the counselor have a goal toward which to work.

The importance of a goal in counseling cannot be overemphasized. Counseling must be goal-directed, and the goal must be set by the counselor and client together. It may happen that the purpose originally stated by the client will be subsequently modified, but a purpose of some sort must be established in order that a counseling experience can be inaugurated. A common error of beginning counselors is a reluctance to press a new client to commit himself to a counseling goal; they may instead try to wait him out, hoping that eventually he will come up with a good reason for being there. The danger of such an attitude is that counseling may quickly degenerate into little more than casual conversation which, while perhaps rewarding in some respects to the client, is not meeting the need which brought him to the counselor.

The counselor's role during this phase is that of an active listener. With a client who expresses himself easily and who can state his reason for coming openly and frankly, the counselor needs only to ask him his purpose and listen to his response. Other clients, however, may not express their needs so easily. With these, the counselor must work to create an atmosphere in which the client will feel freer to discuss his reason for seeking counseling. It is in this respect that the *acceptance attitude*, stressed by many writers, becomes especially important. The counselor attempts to communicate to the client his interest in him as a person, trying to help him reduce his defenses and fears sufficiently to enable counseling to proceed. As with all basic counseling attitudes, the acceptance attitude is maintained throughout the counseling process, but it seems to play an especially important role during the initial phase.

The acceptance attitude is essentially one in which the counselor attempts to communicate to the client that he values him as a person and that the client can feel free to express himself as fully as possible. The counselor attempts to present himself as a nonpunitive person, encouraging the client to express concerns and fears which he would not acknowledge in a more typical interpersonal situation. This attitude must, however, be genuine on the counselor's part. An acceptance attitude cannot be faked, at least not for long, and most counselors find it difficult to develop a satisfactory counseling relationship with persons toward whom they feel some personal antipathy.

If such an attitude can be established and communicated to the client, he will typically reveal his reason for seeking counseling as soon as the threat of counseling has diminished sufficiently. Once this purpose is established, the counseling can move into the second phase.

Phase 2. Definition of the Counseling Process

Having determined the purpose for which a counseling relationship is to be established, the counselor and client must then agree as to how this goal will be achieved. This requires that the client, who is likely to be unsophisticated about counseling, develop some idea of the nature of the counseling relationship and its legitimate uses. It is the counselor's job to help him do this, and the counselor accomplishes this through a variety of techniques. He may, of course, simply make a statement concerning the purpose and procedures of counseling, but in few instances will this be sufficient. Instead, the counselor communicates to the client in a variety of ways —words, attitudes, manner—how the counseling process operates and what role is expected of both parties. As the client acquires a concept of what counseling is all about, he is able to make more effective use of it to reach his counseling goal.

Few clients enter counseling without some preconceptions about its nature. If these conceptions are reasonably accurate, the client and counselor can quickly reach agreement as to how they will operate. Sometimes, however, the client enters with a misconception: he may expect, for example, that the counselor will play a medical role, asking questions and prescribing a treatment. The client may be reluctant to abandon his concept of counseling, and there may be a definite disagreement, overt or covert, between client and counselor as to how they will proceed. This disagreement must be resolved before counseling can continue, and it must be resolved in favor of the counselor. Although the counselor tries to adapt his approach to meet the needs of individual clients, he cannot allow the client to dictate the nature of the counseling. The counselor should know how he can be most effective, and it is his responsibility to persuade the client that this approach will be helpful to him.

In one way or another, then, the counselor and client must reach a mutual agreement as to the way in which their counseling relationship is to operate, so that a working relationship can be established. The development of this working relationship is generally referred to as *rapport,* which means not only that there is close communication of thoughts and feelings between client and counselor, but in addition that each is meeting the role expectations of the other.

In most cases, the two phases just described will both take place during the first interview. Thus the first interview is likely to be concerned primarily with establishing the counseling goal and agreeing on the nature of the counseling relationship. If this can be completed in a rather short time, the counseling may move into the next phase during the first interview also; if not, the third phase will begin with the second interview.

Phase 3. Clarification and Understanding of the Client's Needs

The client has stated his purpose, and he and the counselor have agreed as to how they will proceed. Their next step is to clarify the nature of the client's difficulty and to gain some understanding of its dynamics. This includes a consideration not only of the problem itself, but also of the client as a person in relation to the problem. Thus the counselor is concerned with clarifying both the client's perception of his difficulties and his feelings concerning them. Essentially this is an exploration phase, but not random exploration. The counselor and client, working together, attempt to expose and examine as many facets of the problem as necessary in order that an appropriate attack can be made on it.

Counselors employing different approaches vary in the amount of exploration they desire, and the areas which they want to explore. The exploration activities of a psychoanalytically oriented counselor would be rather different, for example, from one who emphasized a behavior modification approach. But all approaches require a certain amount of clarification and understanding of the client's needs, within the framework appropriate to the approach itself.

In this phase the construct of *empathy* assumes special importance. Most writers stress the role of empathy in counseling, and much has been written about it (see, for example, Buchheimer, 1963, and Katz, 1963). Empathy refers to the counselor's ability to perceive the client's thoughts and feelings and to communicate this perception to the client. The counselor himself does not experience the feelings directly, which differentiates empathy from sympathy, a quite different behavior. If the client becomes tearful, for example, the counselor doesn't cry along with him. Instead, the counselor attempts to perceive the feeling underlying the tears and to articulate this feeling, helping the client to acknowledge and accept his feelings and thus sharpen his perception and understanding of himself. Much of this phase of counseling is a cyclical process: the client communicates a thought or a feeling to the counselor who focuses on the essence of the expression and reflects it back to the client in such a way as to sharpen it for him, thus helping him to explore it further.

Much has been speculated concerning the qualities which promote empathy in a counselor, or why some counselors are better empathizers than others. Although much remains to be learned about empathy as a skill, it would seem that in order to empathize with a client a counselor must not stand aloof and above the client. It seems evident that in order to be sincerely empathic, the counselor must be able to feel that, although he is not himself experiencing the client's emotion, given the proper circumstances he *could* experience it. The counselor who feels superior to his clients, believing that he could never get himself into a position in which he would have to turn to someone else for help, will probably find it difficult to empathize effectively with his clients.

Phase 4. Progress toward the Goal

As the client's thoughts and feelings about his difficulties become clarified and better understood, he begins to move toward his counseling goal. Part of this movement may, in the beginning, simply be the result of this clarification; as the client begins to understand the nature of his difficulty and to express his feelings about it, he begins to learn to handle these feelings. He becomes able to look squarely at himself and his concerns without feeling overwhelmed by them. In addition, as the problem is clarified it becomes more amenable to attack. Based on their tentative understanding of the problem, the counselor and client try various approaches to it. Those which seem to work are pursued, and progress is made in a consistent direction.

Again it is important to stress that this progress is directed toward a goal. This need not necessarily be the goal which the client originally set; during the clarification phase the counselor and client may have agreed that another goal would be more appropriate. In any case, however, the counselor and client are progressing toward a goal upon which both have agreed.

The progress phase of counseling continues until the client and counselor agree that counseling can be terminated. This is usually an indication that the goal has been reached, or at least that the client feels capable of continuing his progress by himself. The counselor accompanies the client along the road only as far as he is needed; when the decision is made that the client can continue alone, the counselor can drop out of the picture.

Ideally, the decision to terminate counseling should be mutual, although either party may raise the possibility at any time. In any case, however, the client should have a major responsibility for this decision as he should for all of his decisions.

Phase 5. Consolidation and Planning

Before counseling is terminated, a brief period of consolidation and planning is generally advisable. The counselor encourages the client to consider his counseling experiences in the light of probable future developments. The client tries to draw from his counseling experience some insights about himself and his approach to personal difficulties and to apply these to his future. As noted earlier, the outcome of counseling should be not only an increased ability to deal with the difficulty which brought the person to counseling in the first place, but also a general improvement in the client's ability to cope with himself and his world. This is not to say that a person may not seek further counseling later, but it is hoped that the effects of a counseling experience will continue beyond the termination of the counseling itself.

The phases of counseling as described here are not discrete. They shade over into one another, and a specific point in the counseling process may not lie clearly in any one phase. Similarly, the counselor's attitudes and techniques do not vary greatly from one phase to another; the acceptance attitude, for example, is important during the entire counseling process, although it may be relatively more important during some phases than others.

VERBAL TECHNIQUES IN COUNSELING

The goals of counseling are achieved primarily through verbal interactions between the counselor and client. In one sense, then, the verbal techniques which the counselor employs are the heart of counseling. The techniques themselves, however, are of secondary importance in comparison with the purpose which they are designed to achieve. They are a means to an end, the end being the counseling outcome toward which both the counselor and client are striving.

The counselor helps the client to achieve his goal primarily through the techniques at his disposal, but the techniques should never become an end in themselves. It is for this reason that techniques *per se* are not a major part of this book. It is much more important that the beginning counselor first understand what he is trying to do before he becomes too concerned with how it is to be done. Otherwise, he might find himself in the position of a person who has expended a great deal of time and effort in learning to drive a car, only to find when he has mastered the machine that there is really no place he wants to go in it.

The reader should bear in mind throughout the following discussion that the value of any technique depends primarily on the extent to which it promotes movement toward the counseling goal. This means that the validity of a specific technique in a specific situation will depend on (a) the characteristics of the client, (b) the characteristics of the counselor, and (c) the goal toward which they are mutually striving.

In order to impose some sort of meaningful organization on the wide variety of counseling techniques, these techniques have been arranged along a dimension of degree of counselor influence or verbalization. This is similar to the organization presented by Robinson (1950) and seems as useful as any.

Listening Techniques

Much of the counselor's behavior, especially in the early stages of counseling, is concerned with helping the client to describe himself and his problem as well as developing an atmosphere which the client can use constructively. This is congruent with the first phase of counseling, establishing a counseling purpose, described at the beginning of this chapter.

The counselor in this stage attempts, therefore, to be an active listener, injecting comments and questions only to the extent necessary to start the client talking and to keep him going. The counselor's primary concern is to communicate to the client that he is paying attention to him and that he is interested in him. The verbal involvement necessary to do this may be minimal, depending on the anxiety level and verbal ability of the client. To begin with, the counselor will probably need to make a general statement or ask a general question to get the client started. Examples might be, "What brings you in?" or "What can I do for you?" Any such comment which indicates to the client that the counselor expects him to describe his reason for coming should be sufficient.

With many clients the counselor then needs only to indicate his attention and interest, perhaps by an "Uh-huh" or "Yes, I see," from time to time, interspersed when necessary with general questions or comments to keep the client moving. Nonverbal behaviors, such as an attentive posture and an occasional nod of the head at appropriate times, can also be important in communicating interest and attention.

Reflection and Clarification Techniques

Many counselors, especially those of a nondirective orientation, believe that reflection and clarification are the heart of counseling, and some even feel that counselors should go no further. Although we will go into more directive techniques in this discussion, it is with the belief that reflection and clarification are basic to counseling, and that the beginning counselor should be most concerned with mastering these skills. The listening techniques described above are not difficult, inasmuch as they are often used in non-counseling interactions, while the more leading techniques to be described later are most useful when combined with the counselor's experience. Any counselor, however, can be of some help to most clients even if he goes no further than reflection and clarification, while the counselor who has not mastered these skills is severely limited.

Reflection and clarification techniques are statements by the counselor which attempt to feed back to the client the essence of the client's own expressions. This means that the counselor is concerned with perceiving and responding to both the thoughts and feelings of the client. The counselor has two purposes in doing this, which interact with one another: (a) He wants to show the client that he is listening and trying to understand him, and he is giving the client an opportunity to correct him if he misunderstands. (b) He is trying to help the client clarify the essence of what he is expressing in a rather confused way.

Some writers stress that the focus of reflection and clarification should be on the underlying feeling rather than the content, but this seems an extreme view. The typical client is struggling with both intellectual and emotional aspects of his problem, and he needs help in recognizing and clarifying both. In most cases they cannot be separated, and the counselor will need to respond to both.

Robinson (1950) suggests that reflection and clarification techniques may be subdivided into three categories: restatement, clarification, and summary clarification. Although these are useful classifications for purposes of discussion, in practice it is often difficult to assign a specific counselor response to one or another category. The essential difference between restatement and clarification is that in restatement the counselor is simply rephrasing what the client has just said, perhaps picking out what seems to be the most important aspect for emphasis. Clarification, on the other hand, includes an estimate on the part of the counselor, in which he adds an idea of his own which seems to be implied by the client's expression, with summary clarification being a broader statement covering a series of client expressions. A clarification response might be made, for example, to an emotional expression of the client, such as crying. The counselor would attempt to reflect the feeling which the client seems to be expressing through crying, although the counselor has to exercise some judgment in assessing the nature of the feeling and thus runs the risk of being wrong. Restatement, by being limited to an idea which the client has expressed directly, is less risky, but at times would be completely inappropriate. For example, the counselor would probably not respond to a weeping client by crying himself, and it would be almost equally inane for him to say, "You seem to be crying."

Reflection and clarification techniques seem deceptively simple, but in reality they are among the most difficult for counselors to learn. Of special importance are the timing and accuracy of the reflections. The counselor must learn to perceive the essence of the client's expressions and to reflect it in the most helpful way. Robinson (1950) stresses that the counselor must learn to deal with the "core" of what the client is saying, to see through the verbal facade and perceive the underlying meaning. He must then reflect it in a way helpful to the client, avoiding stock phrases which can easily become stilted and stereotyped, and using language which will communicate effectively in a nonthreatening manner.

The counselor must also make frequent judgments as to which feelings to reflect and when to reflect them. Often the client will express several ideas and feelings in one sentence, and the counselor must decide on which to focus at this time. He may, in fact, choose not to reflect any, but instead simply encourage the client to talk further in hopes that the client himself will pursue the idea which seems most important to him. The counselor must also decide at what point it is appropriate to attempt to clarify certain ideas raised by the client, in terms of the client's readiness to deal constructively with them. Clients are often not aware of the possible implications of their thoughts and feelings, and part of the counselor's job is to suggest such implications. This will be helpful to the client, however, only if he is able to use it constructively.

Thus the counselor must decide, when an idea is raised, whether the client is ready to have it clarified and to face the implications of the clarification. Even a seemingly nondirective clarification statement may push the client beyond the point he can now handle, which may in turn force him to increase his defenses and guard his verbalizations more carefully.

Leading Techniques

The concept of "leading" implies that the counselor is playing a more active role in the counseling process, interjecting some of his own ideas and taking some responsibility for the direction in which he and the client are moving. Not all counselors believe in the value of leading techniques, but most consider them an essential part of their counseling repertoire.

The extent to which a given counselor will use leading techniques depends on his concept of his role in the counseling relationship. Nondirective counselors try to avoid leading the client, on the assumption that this puts the counselor in the role of an authority figure and thus tends to undermine the kind of relationship they are trying to develop. They believe that the client must take the responsibility for the direction in which the counseling moves and that he must be the one to initiate any new developments in the counseling. Counselors of other persuasions, however, argue that they have some responsibility for taking part in the choice of direction for counseling, and some would go so far as to feel that they are letting the client down if they do not make use of their greater counseling experience to increase the efficiency of the client's progress toward his counseling goal.

Before we examine the techniques of leading, two aspects need further clarification. First of all, the term "leading" does not imply that the counselor is forcefully moving off in some direction, dragging the client behind him. The client has already determined his counseling goal and the counselor is simply trying to help him reach it, so that any leading done by the counselor is to facilitate movement in a direction already initiated by the client. Robinson (1950) uses the term "counseling ladder" to describe the concept of leading, meaning that the client moves upward toward his goal rung by rung, and the counselor's job is to help him get from one rung to the next. The client must progress one rung at a time and cannot be expected to jump from the bottom rung to one near the top. Thus any attempt by the counselor to lead him abruptly would in most cases be futile.

The concept of leading may also be likened to a forward pass in football, in which the passer throws the ball ahead of the receiver, so that both the ball and receiver arrive at the same spot at the same time. If the ball is underthrown or overthrown they don't make contact, and the pass is incomplete. The same applies to counseling: the counselor who underleads or overleads his client will frequently find himself out of contact with him, and loss of contact is a good indication of a poor lead.

In a sense, then, the counselor and client are moving together through unknown territory toward their goal, with first one and then the other leading the way, depending on who has the clearest perception of the path at the moment. Presumably neither the counselor nor the client will always lead. The important thing is that they not lose touch with one another, regardless of who is leading at a given time.

A second point that must be made concerning leading is that all counseling techniques—including those thought to be "nondirective"— have leading components. There is considerable evidence, for example, that supposedly neutral responses, such as "uhmm" or even a nod of the head, can influence the content of the client's verbalization, and presumably of his thinking, depending on when and in what manner they are interjected. The primary question, therefore, is not *whether* the counselor should lead his client, but *when* and *how* it can best be done.

The most common leading technique is a general question, such as, "What jobs have you considered entering?" or "Tell me something about your family." The purpose is to encourage the client to explore an area which the counselor believes may be related to his problem. It does not necessarily imply that the counselor assumes it to be of great importance or significance, but simply suggests an area which might prove relevant. Once he has responded to the question or suggestion by discussing the topic briefly, the client should feel free to move elsewhere or to explore it in greater depth, depending on his perception of its relevance at that time.

An analogy may be helpful at this point. It is as though the counselor and the client are exploring a house, looking for ideas which will help the client reach his counseling goal. The counselor, by virtue of his experience and perspective, sees rooms in the house which the client has not yet noticed. The counselor then, in effect, opens a door to a room with a question or comment, suggesting that the client might want to look around in it. The client does so, and either decides there is nothing of value for him there and moves on, or considers it promising enough to examine in greater detail. The "leading" thus shifts back and forth, in this instance beginning with the counselor and being transferred to the client.

Ultimately, of course, the client benefits from the counselor's suggestions only to the extent that they open a meaningful area. Since the counselor is not omniscient, it is inevitable that some of his leads will prove fruitless, or that the client will reject them. This should have no detrimental effect on the counseling relationship, provided that the leads are presented in such a way that the client feels free to accept or reject them. If the counselor tries too hard to stress the importance of an area, such as, for example, by saying "I think it's very important that you consider this aspect carefully," or by resisting when the client rejects a suggestion, the counseling relationship may be damaged. In most cases, therefore, the counselor should accept the client's rejection of a lead and move on to something else. Even if the counselor believes strongly that he was on the right track, the timing may have been wrong. Given time, the client may himself return to the idea which the counselor originally raised, or the counselor may be able to refer to it again in a different context.

The counselor should also keep in mind that clients very often do not accomplish everything that the counselor believes they should or could accomplish with counseling. The student, for example, who brings to counseling a question concerning curriculum choice may indicate that he is also having problems in getting along with the opposite sex. The counselor's attempts to lead him to explore this further may, however, be rejected, leaving the counselor feeling frustrated. The counselor must nevertheless accept the client's decision not to use counseling to deal with the social relationship problem; having given the client the opportunity to do so, the counselor should concentrate on the problem which the client wants to work on. The result may be less complete than the counselor would like, but it is not his life that is involved. In short, you can lead a client to water, but you can't make him think.

Interpretation

Interpretation of the client's behavior, thoughts, or feelings is the most controversial of counseling techniques. Some counselors, especially those of a nondirective orientation, recoil at the thought of interpretation, rejecting it on the grounds that the client benefits only from those ideas which he himself conceives and develops. Other counselors hold a strongly opposing opinion, believing that interpretation is the ultimate counseling skill, and that artful and insightful interpretations are the mark of the highly proficient counselor.

In order to come to a conclusion concerning the role of interpretation in counseling, we must first clarify the concept. Interpretation refers to an attempt on the part of the counselor to aid the client in progressing toward his counseling goal by helping the client put his thoughts and feelings into a more coherent and organized structure. As Levy (1963) describes it, interpretation is necessary because the client's current way of looking at himself and his problems is not helpful to him. A fresh approach, or a new perception, is needed. According to Levy, psychological interpretation consists of "a redefining or restructuring of the situation through the presentation of an alternate description of some behavioral datum. . . . Interpretation occurs whenever a new or different frame of reference, or language, is brought to bear on some problem or event [p. 5]," with the purpose of making the problem or event more amenable to manipulation. In this sense, then, interpretation can be a means by which the counselor helps the client gain control over problems and feelings which heretofore he has been unable to cope with adequately.

Most writers agree that interpretation cannot be forced: the counselor's suggestions are helpful to the client only if he is free to accept or reject them and to the extent that they fit the client's thinking at that point (see, for example, Robinson, 1950; Schonbar, 1965; Wolberg, 1967).

This still leaves a large question unanswered: on what basis does the counselor make an interpretation? How is he able to explain things which are unclear and confusing to the client?

The answer depends on one's conception of the nature of an interpretation. Most persons would assume, at first glance, that an interpretation represents some reasonable approximation of the "truth," and that the truer the interpretation turns out to be the more helpful it will be for the client. This is in turn based on the assumption that the client is searching for an explanation of his behavior, and therefore the closer the interpretation is to reality, the more meaning it will have for him. Thus if the counselor says, "You have trouble reacting to authority figures because you were afraid of your father as a child," the client will accept or reject this interpretation, and subsequently find it useful or not useful, depending on whether it is the true explanation of his difficulty.

This concept of interpretation, propounded explicitly or implicitly by many writers (for example, Schonbar, 1965; Wolberg, 1967), puts a great burden on the wisdom of the counselor. His job becomes one of "figuring out the client," much as if he were a detective and the client were a suspected criminal. At the proper time the counselor puts the pieces together and announces the solution which, if his timing is correct, the client will hug to his bosom as his source of strength. Small wonder that counselors who want to avoid playing an authoritarian and omniscient role may reject interpretation as an appropriate technique.

There is, however, an alternate concept of interpretation, as presented by Hobbs (1962) and Levy (1963), which allows the counselor to make interpretations without playing detective or assuming omniscience. This is possible when one rejects the notion that the counseling process is a search for truth and that interpretation must therefore be concerned with truth. Instead of self-understanding, the goal of counseling can be conceived as self-control. The client is trying to learn how to cope more effectively with some aspect of his environment. He is confused and overwhelmed by thoughts and feelings which he cannot control, in the sense that he is unable to behave as he wants to behave in a given situation. Self-understanding is thus only a means to an end. In order to be a self-confident, self-directing person, he must be able to put his thoughts and feelings into some kind of perspective which will enable him to exercise some degree of control over them. If he is having trouble, for example, in reacting to persons in authority, his major goal is to gain control of his behavior in such situations. Self-understanding may help, but the important thing is that he become able to behave more effectively when the situation arises.

Interpretation can therefore be viewed as a means by which the counselor helps the client to gain control over his thoughts and feelings by suggesting a way of looking at them which puts them into a perspective which the client is capable of handling. Thus the client who cannot deal effectively with authority figures is groping for some way to control his behavior in such situations. An explanation that his problem stems from a poor relationship with his father may be helpful, if by thinking through this relationship and putting it into a perspective commensurate with his current status as an adult he acquires a way of thinking which he can apply to anxiety-producing situations involving contemporary authority figures. If this serves to reduce his anxiety in such situations, he should then become able to handle them more effectively.[1]

[1] Levy (1963) has developed a theoretical model, based on dissonance theory, to explain the process of interpretation. He proposes that the therapist's interpreta-

This approach to interpretation means that "truth" is no longer of primary concern. As Levy says, "The interpretation of an event is not a search for the true meaning of the event. Every event is subject to a vast range of interpretations [p. 10]." The purpose of interpretation is to impose a structure on an event or a series of events which brings it within the client's control. To be sure, the interpretation must have some element of truth to it, or the client will probably not find it helpful. "Truth" in this sense, however, means that it must be consistent with the client's perception of the problem and of himself; in other words, it must "make sense" to him.

This concept of interpretation has several advantages for the counselor. It allows him to incorporate interpretation as part of the counseling process, rather than as the solution to a mystery. It does not violate any of the principles of counseling that have been presented thus far but instead allows the counselor to play an important and useful role without detracting from the integrity and responsibility of the client.

We have not yet considered the basis on which the counselor makes an interpretation, within this framework. How does he decide which of many possible explanations will be most helpful to a specific client? To some extent, of course, this depends on the nature of the client, but an additional important factor is the counselor's own frame of reference or theoretical structure, as described in the previous chapter. Within this framework, he looks for meaning and order in the thoughts and feelings of the client, and as he finds it he passes it on to the client, who in turn is able to apply it to gain better control of these thoughts and feelings. This view of interpretation is consistent with that presented by Hobbs (1962), who says:

> The occurrence of an insight merely means that the client is catching on to the therapist's personal system for interpreting the world of behavior. The therapist does not have to be right; he mainly has to be convincing [p. 742].

Interpretation in educational and vocational counseling can be seen to operate in a similar manner. In interpreting the results of an interest or ability test, for example, the counselor attempts to put the test data into a framework which will be meaningful to the client, while the client in turn is groping for the "meaning" which the test results have for him. The counselor presents an interpretive framework in which he believes; if he is successful, the client accepts the framework and uses it accordingly. It is evident that different counselors often obtain different meanings from the same test data, primarily because they view it within different frameworks. Their clients can be expected to learn to view it in a similar manner.

---

tion arouses dissonance within the client which he must reduce, either by rejecting the interpretation—and perhaps the therapist—or by modifying his thinking, and perhaps ultimately his behavior, so as to take this view into account.

Instruction

Dynamically-oriented counseling approaches tend to make considerable use of interpretation, encouraging the client to formulate an explanatory structure for his thoughts and feelings from which he develops more appropriate coping behaviors. Learning-oriented approaches, however, deal directly with the behavior itself and are little concerned with analyzing its causes. The counselor who uses a behavior modification approach will therefore supply certain instructions to the client in order to produce specific changes in the client's behavior.

These instructions are designed to clarify the nature of the behavior to be changed and to test out certain procedures which may effect the desired change. An early instruction might simply be for the client to keep a record of the number of times, and under what circumstances, the behavior occurs. When the frequency and context of the maladaptive behavior has been established, the counselor may then recommend certain techniques, such as a system by which the desired behavior is rewarded, or techniques of relaxation or anxiety reduction.

The effort here is still a cooperative one, with the counselor offering some suggestions which may be helpful, but with the suggestions aimed at the behavior itself rather than at the underlying dynamics. As the client learns to use the techniques being taught him by the counselor, he not only experiences the desired behavior change but also becomes able to apply the principles behind the techniques for himself.

Counselors who do not accept the principles of the learning-oriented approaches would probably strongly reject instruction as a technique, but it is a basic element of the behavior modification approaches.

Structuring

Structuring occurs when the counselor makes a statement to the client describing his view of the nature of the counseling relationship and the way in which he hopes the counseling will proceed. Its major purpose is to orient the client to his counseling experience in order that he may make effective use of it and, if necessary, to correct any misconceptions he may have when he first enters counseling.

Structuring may be accomplished in many ways, including both direct and indirect methods. Most counselors employ a combination of both, assuming that a formal statement concerning the nature of counseling is only the first step and that the client learns what counseling is all about through the experience itself. It is the structuring statement *per se* that we are concerned with at this point. This statement is not, in itself, a counseling technique, but it is a means of setting the stage so that the client can use counseling profitably.

Some counselors, following Rogers, avoid making structuring statements, believing that this puts the counselor in an authoritative role, which he is trying to avoid, and that the client can learn about counseling in more subtle ways. Others, however, find that a structuring statement is helpful with some clients and believe that it is an appropriate way to respond to a client's expressed or implied need for structure.

Not only may a structuring statement by the counselor help the client to use counseling more effectively and perhaps correct some of his misconceptions about counseling, but it may also help him to feel more secure in the counseling relationship. Some clients feel anxious and insecure in strange, ambiguous situations, and counseling may be no exception. A brief statement by the counselor describing the nature of counseling and of the counseling process may serve to reduce the client's anxiety and thereby increase his positive attitude toward the counselor.

A structuring statement is not always necessary, since some clients show no need for one. Like any counseling technique, the structuring statement should be the counselor's response to the client's need, expressed directly or indirectly. A client who needs structure will probably indicate this need in some manner, perhaps by asking openly for a description of counseling, or perhaps in more subtle ways, such as by requests for advice, asking the counselor to take the responsibility for deciding on a discussion topic, or testing the limits of the counseling situation. Each of these behaviors may be an indication of a need for structure, to which the counselor may choose to respond. If the client is quite insecure, frequent structuring may be necessary, and decreased need for structure may be one sign of counseling progress and improvement. If a structuring approach is not sufficient to alleviate the client's anxiety, the counselor may find it helpful to discuss with the client his need for structure, attempting to relate the client's need to other situations outside of counseling.

Silence

The most common error made by beginning counselors is that they talk too much. If successful counseling is to take place the client must be actively involved, and he is more likely to be involved when he is talking than when he is not. The counselor should, of course, be involved too, but less verbally. He should make a contribution when he thinks it would help keep the client moving or when he has information or an idea to contribute which may be useful to the client. But for the most part the client progresses toward his goal by learning about himself and his world and by integrating this learning into a coherent framework. To do this, he must have the opportunity to think as well as talk.

Thus, counseling is generally not a smooth flow of verbalizations back and forth between two persons, as is a social conversation. Silences are common in counseling, and the counselor should be able to handle them effectively and make constructive use of them.

Silences may become a problem in counseling if they are interpreted as undesirable. This is a normal tendency, since in the usual social conversation silence is to be avoided. Most persons become embarrassed when a silence arises and feel a responsibility to fill the gap with some kind of talk, even if it is meaningless or trivial. This is not only unnecessary in counseling, but it may actually serve to obstruct counseling progress. The counselor must therefore be able to handle silences comfortably. He should anticipate that they will arise and allow them to be resolved naturally, either by himself or by the client, when either he or the client has something worthwhile to say. By reacting calmly, the counselor shows the client that silence is expected and acceptable.

A major problem in handling silence is that it is often difficult for the counselor to determine its meaning or cause. This is because a silence may be initiated by either party, due to a failure to respond when the other person expects a response. If, for example, the client makes a statement or asks a question to which a response from the counselor would be expected, and the counselor does not respond, this initiates a silence over which the counselor has control. He is indicating to the client that he expects him to say more about this, to explore it further, and it may be difficult for the client to avoid succumbing to the pressure. In this sense, silence initiated by the counselor can be a powerful directive technique, since it may force the client, who is less adept at handling the situation, to say more than he had originally intended. Whether this is desirable will depend on the stage of counseling and the nature of the relationship between the counselor and client. It is probably unwise to use this technique much during the early stages, since it runs the risk that the client may become overly anxious and perhaps hostile toward the counselor. Later, when the relationship has been more firmly established, it may be quite useful.

At other times, a silence may be initiated by the client, by failing to respond to the counselor's question or statement. This need not necessarily be an open refusal to respond; it may instead be a brief response which avoids the main implication of the counselor's remark. In this case, the counselor may have trouble determining why the client does not respond further and how he should handle the silence. Wolberg (1967) believes that client-initiated silence is usually an indication of resistance and should be dealt with accordingly. Tyler (1961), on the other hand, points out that, at least in the early stages, a client's silences may be the result of a misconception of the nature of counseling. He may expect that counseling will be a series of questions and answers, and he is simply waiting for the next question. In this situation, a structuring statement by the counselor may be helpful.

Silence does not necessarily indicate a halt in the counseling. It may, instead, be a period during which the client is thinking about himself or experiencing a feeling of which he was not formerly aware. The counselor who insists that the client talk most of the time may not be giving him an opportunity to introspect. The counselor too will probably need to remain silent at times while he collects his thoughts.

Ideally, silence should fit naturally into the counseling. The client should feel that he need not talk if he does not want to, that he is free to use the counseling situation to think, as well as to express his thoughts, and that he will be accepted even if he is quiet. The latter point deserves further emphasis. Some people are "naturally" quiet. The emphasis in counseling on expressing oneself may be difficult for them to adapt to. If the counselor insists that they talk more, as do most of their acquaintances and teachers, they may feel rejected, as though they are less important or worthwhile because they have trouble expressing themselves. As noted earlier, the attitude that must first be communicated to the client is one of acceptance. The counselor who insists that his clients verbalize a great deal is not indicating an acceptance of the quiet, nonverbal client.

Résumé

We have considered a number of counseling techniques. None of these is intrinsically good or bad, wise or foolish. Each will be of value at certain times, with certain clients. As was stressed earlier, the major consideration is not *what* technique to use at a given time, but *why*. The outcome is much more important than the process.

This means that the counselor should have a repertoire of techniques from which he can draw. He should not feel so committed to the validity of one technique that he ignores all others. To do so would be like trying to drive a car with only one gear. Although one of the gears may be most useful most of the time, there are times when the others are indispensable. The person who doesn't know how to shift from one to another will make poor progress and will be restricted in the directions in which he can move.

DYNAMICS OF THE COUNSELING RELATIONSHIP

The verbal interaction represented by the techniques described in the previous section takes place within the context of the client-counselor relationship. It can thus be argued that the relationship itself is the key to progress in counseling, and that the nature of this relationship will overshadow the specific techniques that the counselor chooses to use.

There is abundant evidence to support this contention, although research which has attempted to establish associations between counselor-client relationships and counseling outcomes has generally allowed the two variables to contaminate one another. Thus it is not surprising to find that when the client feels he has been helped by counseling he believes the relationship with his counselor to have been an effective one, and vice-versa (Gardner, 1964). Despite this limitation, however, Gardner is impressed with the consistency with which research of various kinds shows the importance of the relationship in influencing the outcomes of counseling.

Many writers have made the relationship the focus of their counseling approach, stressing above all else the importance of the counselor establishing an effective relationship with the client. Foremost among these has been Carl Rogers, who emphasized the importance of the relationship in his first major book, *Counseling and Psychotherapy* (1942), and has continued to propound this point of view in his more recent writings (see Rogers, 1962).

Not all authorities, however, agree on the importance of the relationship in counseling. Some argue that the relationship is more appropriately of concern in psychotherapy, which has long stressed the use of the therapist-patient relationship as a therapeutic tool. Most of those who have written on the nature of the relationship, such as Gardner (1964), have been primarily concerned with its importance in psychotherapy rather than in counseling.

This is not a problem so long as counseling and psychotherapy are considered to be essentially synonymous, but it becomes an issue if an attempt is made to differentiate between them, as we have done here. If the counselor-client relationship is to be considered as an important element of the counseling process, it must be shown that this relationship plays a major role in promoting the goals of counseling rather than those of psychotherapy.

This becomes possible if the concept of the "working relationship," as described by Robinson (1950), is substituted for "therapeutic relationship." We have repeatedly stressed in these pages that the goals of counseling are achieved by a cooperative effort of the client and counselor. This effort must take place in the context of a relationship between them; any two persons working together toward a common goal must of necessity develop some sort of working relationship. The nature of this relationship will thus have an important bearing on the efficiency and effectiveness of the counseling process.

Gardner (1964), in his research survey, points out that the ideal therapeutic relationship, as described by numerous writers and supported by research evidence, is probably a variant of helping relationships in general. Thus many of the characteristics typically stressed as important in therapeutic relationships—warmth, acceptance, permissiveness, respect for the client, interest, and so on—are undoubtedly applicable to the counseling relationship as well. Those qualities and behaviors of the counselor which help the client to feel relaxed and secure and which encourage him to express himself freely and frankly will promote the client's effective use of the counseling experience.

The counselor's major task in establishing an effective working relationship with a client may be likened to a tennis match. The client's tendency, at the beginning, will generally be to assume this to be like a singles game, with him and the counselor on opposite sides of the net, batting the ball back and forth. Thus he expects to ask and answer questions, to tell the counselor what he (the counselor) wants to know and to get a prescription in return. The counselor, however, wants to be on the client's side of the net, playing doubles with him against an imaginary opponent (perhaps the cause of the client's problem). The development of a working relationship means that the counselor moves around the net to the client's side. With some clients this occurs with little difficulty, as the client readily accepts the counselor's definition of the relationship, and even welcomes it. Others, however, may be resistant, perhaps due to a general difficulty in handling personal relationships of any sort. As the counselor attempts to help the client overcome this difficulty and accept a relationship, the relationship itself may assume therapeutic aspects, and the client may be able to generalize from this experience to others outside the counseling office.

Limitations of the Counseling Relationship

Although the client may learn things about himself within the counseling relationship which he can generalize to other relationships, it must be recognized that the counseling relationship is not a typical one. Contrary to most interpersonal relationships, it is established for a specific purpose, and it terminates when that purpose is achieved. In this sense it is typical of most professional relationships, as contrasted with social relationships, but with the additional complication that the goals of counseling can best be attained when a certain degree of "rapport" exists between the client and the counselor. Because counseling deals with the private thoughts and feelings of the client, their relationship often becomes something more than a typical professional relationship. One might say that the counselor and client enter a "no-man's land" in that their relationship is not comparable to any other.

Another important limitation of the counseling relationship is that it is *controlled* by the counselor. Here again, this is typical of professional relationships in that the professional person is almost always in control, defining the limits of the relationship and telling the patient or client what he is expected to do. One of the general tenets of counseling, however, is that the counselor should not be authoritarian. The client should have some responsibility for setting the counseling goals and for determining how they are to be attained. The counselor and client should develop a cooperative working relationship, rather than viewing one another from different levels.

On the surface, this would seem to imply that within the counseling relationship the professional person (the counselor) does not impose direct controls. In fact, however, this is not the case, as Haley (1963) has described. It is necessary that the counselor exert some degree of control over the counseling situation, partly to ensure that the relationship will be used effectively by the client, and partly to help the client feel secure. The client needs to feel that, despite his own confusions and anxieties, the counselor is confident that something can be accomplished. In order to feel and communicate this confidence, the counselor must be operating in a situation in which he feels reasonably secure and which he can control.

Thus counseling resembles most professional relationships in that the professional person assumes control, but it differs from others because the controls which the counselor imposes are more subtle. It is important that the counselor's control of the counseling relationship be within the framework of helping the client to take more responsibility for himself and for the direction of the counseling. Many of the controls, therefore, are in the form of limitations on the relationship, rather than by direction itself. For example, most counseling interviews are by appointment and for a limited period of time; expressions of affection are limited; and the focus is on the needs of the client rather than those of the counselor.

The counselor also maintains a subtle control of the counseling relationship through his permissive and accepting attitude. In more typical interpersonal relationships, control is established when one of the members imposes his will on the other. This in turn can only become evident when there is a recognized difference of opinion or desire. The counselor, by refusing to be drawn into a contest of wills, cannot be controlled. By accepting the client's statements and behaviors, no matter how hostile or outrageous they may seem, he in effect "allows" the client to express them. In this way, the client is simply doing and saying what is permitted by the counselor.[2]

Such controls are necessary if the client is to use the counseling experience effectively. Presumably the counselor, by virtue of his training and experience, has a clearer idea than does the client of the nature of an effective counseling relationship. It is contrary to accepted counseling

---

[2] The extreme form of control is expressed in the story of the mental patient who informed his therapist, "I am God," to which the therapist replied, "All right, I'll let you be God."

philosophy to attempt to *impose* the counselor's concept of counseling directly on the client, and it is doubtful if it would have any great effect anyway. But the counselor can and does define the counseling relationship by more subtle means, and thus establishes for the client a situation in which he can achieve his counseling goal.[3]

The Concept of Transference

Transference is a concept originally developed by Freud and his followers to account for the strong and often embarrassing emotional reactions which patients tend to develop toward their therapists. In its strictest sense, transference means that the client places the therapist in the role of a person with whom he (the client) has a strong unresolved emotional relationship, such as a parent. The therapist thus becomes the object of the feelings toward that person which the client is unable to express openly to him. These are most likely to be "unacceptable" feelings, such as anger and hate, plus positive feelings of a sexual nature that are taboo. The therapist, by remaining objective and calm in the face of these emotional outbursts, is able to help the client acknowledge his feelings and deal with them in a more mature way. A great deal of the analytically oriented psychotherapy literature is concerned with how the therapist can promote the development of a transference relationship and subsequently how it can best be resolved.

As with many psychoanalytic concepts, the concept of transference has been "borrowed" by therapists who do not themselves adhere to analytic theory. In the process it has been distorted, so that much of the current writings about the role of transference in psychotherapy does not refer to transference in its original analytic meaning. Many writers now use the term "transference" to refer to the feelings that the client develops toward the counselor, which may include the counselor's role in the client's eyes as an authority figure, the client's feelings of dependency on the counselor, and affectional feelings which the client may have toward the counselor (Brammer and Shostrom, 1968). In any case, there is considerable agreement that the transference aspects of the relationship enable the therapist to help the client uncover emotional facets of his problem which might not otherwise

---

[3] Although it is seldom explicitly acknowledged by counseling supervisors, one of the skills which neophyte counselors learn is how to *control* the counseling relationship. It seems likely, therefore, that counselor training may prove attractive to individuals who lack security in normal interpersonal relationships. In the counseling program they are able to learn skills which enhance their feeling of security within a limited relationship. This is not to imply that this is a poor motive. Coupled with a genuine desire to help people, it may provide an important incentive for the beginning counselor. It is simply to suggest that persons who become counselors are not necessarily those who are highly skilled in controlling interpersonal relationships in general.

be evident (see, for instance, the discussions of transference by Patterson, 1959, and by Brammer and Shostrom, 1968).

Therapists who stress the importance of the transference relationship believe that it provides an avenue by which the client can learn appropriate emotional responses which can in turn help him to develop more adequate and satisfying relationships in his everyday life. In this sense, the client's emotional experiences in his relationship with the therapist are "transferred" to his relationships with others. The therapist-client relationship becomes a microcosm of the client's relationships with people in general and a testing ground for the development of improved relationships. Viewed in this light, the therapeutic relationship becomes a powerful therapeutic tool.

Not all psychotherapists, however, accept the concept of transference. It is strongly rejected by the nondirective school on the ground that the therapist, by stressing his genuineness as a person, does not allow himself to be distorted and to be misperceived as another person (Rogers, 1951; Patterson, 1959; Arbuckle, 1961a). This seems to be essentially a rejection of the analytic concept of transference rather than a repudiation of the importance of the therapist-client relationship. Nondirective therapists would certainly agree that one of the major goals of their approach is to enable the client to become fully himself and to express his feelings, and that the therapist's job is to provide a relationship within which this self-expression can take place. As the client learns to relate more securely to the therapist, he should be able to generalize this ability to his experience with people in the outside world.

The emotional aspects of the therapist-client relationship operate on a two-way street, and the analysts created the term "countertransference" to denote the emotional attachment which the therapist may develop toward a client. Therapists are only human, and their feelings sometimes become involved. This must of course be kept within strict limits, otherwise the client's progress would be impeded. On the other hand, the nondirective therapists argue that if the therapist is to be a genuine person within the relationship his feelings cannot be repressed and that his ability to be himself may have a therapeutic effect on the client, who is trying to learn how to become more real. In any case, both the client and the therapist are expected to limit their expression of feelings to those appropriate to a professional relationship, and presumably the therapist would be expected to have better control of this than would the client.

It may be evident to the reader by this time that the transference aspects of the relationship which we have discussed have been placed within a therapeutic rather than a counseling context. This has been deliberate. The emotional aspects of the relationship play a much more important role in psychotherapy than in counseling, and in fact may represent a distinction between the two processes in addition to those described in an earlier chapter. Although it is reasonable to speak of the "counseling relationship" as an important element in the counseling process, the emotional aspects of the relationship are not prominent. Instead, the working relationship, as described earlier, is the central focus of counseling. It has emotional overtones, to be sure, but these are not central to the counseling process nor are they usually highly developed. In psychotherapy, the therapist deliberately utilizes the emotional aspects of the relationship (through transference) to help the client perceive and understand his feelings toward other people. In counseling, the counselor and client form a working relationship to help the client solve a problem or arrive at a decision.

As with any distinction between counseling and psychotherapy, it is obvious that this one is not clear-cut. A relationship that begins as a counseling (working) relationship may eventually acquire important emotional overtones. If these overtones become the focus of the relationship, however, it is likely that the process has become psychotherapy rather than counseling. One reason why counselors are not encouraged to drift casually into a therapeutic relationship with their clients is because they may not have the training and experience to handle the transference elements of the relationship. This can create unnecessary difficulties both for the client and the counselor. The transference relationship is a complex one and should not be entered into lightly by inexperienced counselors.

We can conclude, therefore, that a transference relationship is not necessary to the counseling process and may in fact interfere with counseling, turning it into something else. The counselor should concentrate on developing an effective working relationship with his clients. If he finds a transference relationship developing instead, he should examine the situation carefully to determine whether it is becoming something other than counseling and, if so, whether he should continue the relationship under those circumstances.

5

Variables Which Affect
the Counseling Process

No two clients share exactly the same counseling experience, and in some instances their experiences may differ greatly. In addition to individual differences in counseling purpose, there are three general sources of variance which affect the counseling process in important ways. These are differences among clients, differences among counselors, and characteristics of the setting in which the counseling takes place.

CLIENT VARIABLES

Age

Counseling, as it has been defined here, is most effective with persons who can set a counseling goal, can express their thoughts and feelings in a systematic way, and can assume a significant degree of responsibility for their own behavior. This view calls into question the appropriateness of counseling with *children,* who generally do not meet these criteria.[1] Counseling services are, however, being extended to children (see the description of elementary school counseling in Chapter 11), which suggests that a framework can be devised within which children can make some use of counseling.

[1] Psychotherapy may, however, be quite appropriate with children. Discussions of psychotherapy with children may be found in several sources, including the volume edited by Haworth (1964).

Since a child is not expected to be entirely responsible for himself, a more mature person, usually a parent, is expected to help him in a rather direct way. The definition of a counseling need for a child therefore usually involves the child's parents, with the child perhaps participating in the decision. The counselor who works with children is well advised not to begin counseling with a child without gaining the approval of his parents and to attempt to involve them in the counseling as much as possible, because of their great influence on the child's life and development.

Counseling with children generally takes one of two forms. With children who exhibit rather specific behavior problems, behavior modification techniques have proved quite successful (Bijou, 1966; Gelfand and Hartmann, 1968), generally more so than techniques which require verbalizations of feelings and self-insight. Some counselors, however, work with children in a developmental sense, not focusing on specific problems but instead on helping the child develop self-awareness and self-identity. Such efforts may set the stage for more direct use of counseling during the later stages of growing up.

Sometime during adolescence the individual gains sufficient maturity and independence to profit more directly from counseling, but at what point is uncertain. This varies from one person to another, and the professional counselor who is working with adolescents will have to make individual assessments as to their amenability to counseling.

Counseling with *adolescents* generally involves consideration of present and future plans. In school settings, this is usually related to curriculum planning and vocational choice; in other settings, the plans may have a different orientation. Adolescents may also use counseling to help them deal more effectively with other kinds of problems such as family conflict, peer group pressure, or sexual confusion.

The counselor who works with adolescents must be aware of certain of their characteristics which may affect his approach (Nichols and Rutledge, 1965). Although the adolescent is gaining maturity and independence, he is by definition not yet fully emancipated from his family. His parents still have legal and social responsibility for him and thus cannot be ignored in the counseling. If possible, the parents should be informed of the counseling—preferably by the adolescent himself—and should agree to it. In some instances, the counselor may find it helpful to include both the adolescent and his parents in the counseling. However, it must be emphasized that counseling assumes that the client—the adolescent, in this case—has some degree of maturity and personal independence, so that any direct involvement of the parents should be by prior agreement between the adolescent and the counselor and for the purpose of furthering the adolescent's counseling goal. Therefore it is generally unwise for the counselor to discuss an adolescent's counseling with his parents without the client present. If the counselor develops a relationship with the parents apart from the client, the counseling goals of independence, maturity, and self-development are likely to be undermined. In counseling with adolescents it is often desirable to include the parents at certain points, but this can be better accomplished with a joint interview involving both the client and his parents than by the counselor seeing the parents alone.

Counseling as we know it has been developed primarily from work with older adolescents and young adults, and these continue to be the groups toward which counseling is largely aimed. There seems to be a tacit assumption that counseling resources should be focused on this age group, undoubtedly based in part on the recognition that decisions and adjustments made during this period can have a profound impact on the remainder of the person's life. The scarcity of counseling services for persons beyond this age range seems to imply that such services are not needed, which is highly unrealistic. It has been well established that as persons move through adulthood they frequently encounter difficulties which counseling might help them handle more constructively. The man who is dissatisfied with his job, the woman who finds being a housewife unstimulating, the couple who hit snags in their marriage—all are potential candidates for counseling.

With the exception of the concern of sociologists and social workers for marriage counseling, counselors have been slow to make themselves available to *adults*. It has been convenient to develop counseling services within high schools and colleges, where they have flourished, but this is not enough. Counseling services must continue to be extended to the adult population, with the recognition that persons of all ages may be able to profit from them. Unfortunately, there is no single institution, such as the public school or university, which could logically be expected to assume this responsibility for adults. Counseling services now available to adults are offered by a variety of agencies and institutions, such as schools, churches, family service agencies, and businesses. Generally they are aimed at a rather specific group and their efforts are not well integrated. The result is that there is no logical source of help for many adults in need of counseling, and many for whom help is available are unaware of its existence.

Counselors accustomed to working with young people may have to make some adjustments in their approach when counseling with adults (Thoroman, 1968). In many cases, the number of options open to the adult is considerably more restricted; he has already closed off some alternatives by his past decisions, and this must be accepted. This is not to imply that the counselor of adults must be pessimistic, but simply that he must be realistic. The adult will also usually come to a counselor with a rather specific problem and will be satisfied if a satisfactory solution can be found. Counseling with adults is therefore likely to be of a shorter duration than counseling with young persons, since the adult's way of life is generally more firmly set.

An age group which is much in need of counseling help, and at the same time one of the most neglected, is the *aged*. The person in his later years faces many changes in his life with which he may be unable to cope adequately: retirement from his job, loss of loved ones, restricted social interactions, physical infirmities, and so on. Society is slowly moving to deal constructively with the physical needs of the aged, but it has been even slower to recognize and to meet the psychological needs of this group.

One reason for the slow development of counseling services for the aged is that older persons are less willing to discuss their problems with others and to engage in self-exploration (Kowal and others, 1964). To some extent this is undoubtedly due to a greater rigidity on their part coupled with a fear of losing the defenses which they have built up over the years. A complicating factor, however, is that counselors tend to be young persons, who may have difficulty in empathizing with the problems of later life and who may not inspire confidence in older clients.

Kastenbaum (1963) has suggested that therapists have traditionally avoided working with the aged for several reasons. Among these are the lower status of old people in our society, plus the feeling that they probably will not live long enough to make the effort worthwhile. Most counselors presumably get more satisfaction out of helping a young person, since they can feel that they may have had an important influence on the remainder of the person's life. Older persons, of course, have needs as serious and important as those of youth, but counselors have chosen to overlook them. Perhaps, as Kastenbaum has suggested, acknowledging the problems of old age is too threatening for the young counselor. In this case we may expect that as the current generation of counselors grows older they may develop an increased interest in the counseling needs of the aged.

Counseling facilities for the aged are available through a variety of resources, but they have not been systematically developed as have facilities for adolescents and young adults. Older persons are often helped by social agencies, and a few churches have also established counseling facilities for them (see, for instance, the program described by Brown, 1964). There remains, however, a great need for the development of wide-spread counseling services for the aged.[2]

Sex

The sex of the client assumes particular importance in vocational and educational counseling. Counselors who work primarily with young people tend to assume that their clients are concerned with making educational and vocational plans consistent with their development as individuals. This

---

[2] The reader is also referred to a review of the literature concerning psychotherapy with geriatric patients by Rechtschaffen (1959).

assumption generally holds true for boys, but often not for girls. There is considerable evidence that girls of high school and college age are concerned primarily with getting married and raising children (Empey, 1958) and that their vocational plans typically are focused on the immediate future prior to marriage and children, rather than being put in the perspective of their entire life (Siegel and Curtis, 1963).

This difference occurs because of the different sex-role expectations for males and females in our society. Girls are raised to believe that marriage and children is the culmination of a woman's life, and only after they have experienced this role do many women find that it is not enough. When their children are of school age, many women return to school or to work, and it is at this stage that women could profit from counseling services. Prior to marriage, however, girls are usually reluctant to plan very far in advance. This is in some respects only realistic, in view of the uncertainties which influence the vocational activities of a woman: whom she will marry, where they will live, how her husband will feel about a working wife, and so on.

There are, of course, exceptions—girls who have decided on a career and who want help in making plans accordingly. These girls can be counseled more like boys of their own age, although the probability of marriage in the future may make their plans a little less certain than those of boys. In any case, the counselor should not assume that a female client will put educational and vocational planning in the same perspective as will a boy, and he should likewise not assume that she will automatically choose to follow the traditional female pattern.[3]

Counselors are also handicapped in working with girls by the inadequacy of many of the tools frequently used in educational and vocational counseling. Most test data, for instance, are based on boys and are often misapplied to girls (Tyler, 1962). Occupational information for women is likewise limited to those fields in which women traditionally predominate. As a result, the counselor who looks for tests and information appropriate for his female clients will quickly become frustrated. Resources suitable for use in counseling with girls are badly needed.

The sex of the client may also influence the counseling process in more subtle ways. It is likely, for example, that the counseling relationship will vary depending on the sex of the client as well as that of the counselor, although there is little evidence to specify the nature of this variation. Certain transference aspects, likely to emerge in counseling with more deep-seated emotional problems, will almost certainly be affected by the sex of the participants. There is also some evidence that continuation in counseling is related to different personality variables among females than among males.

[3] For more extended discussions of the counseling needs of girls, see Zapoleon (1961) and Lewis (1968).

The influence on the counseling process of sex differences among coun-selees would be less important if counselors would remember to focus on the individual. Many counselors, however, fall into a rut and begin to make assumptions from their experience which may not apply to all clients. Thus they expect girls to make the same kinds of plans as do boys, overlooking the obvious differences in the career development of males and females in our society. In addition, counselors are likely to be as constricted as most laymen by attitudes concerning the "appropriate" role for women in our society, which may make it difficult for them to provide a girl with a coun-seling experience which she can use for self-development as an individual.[4]

Social Class

It is becoming increasingly evident that the social status of the client has an important effect on the kind of help he receives and on its ultimate effectiveness. Much of the evidence for this conclusion comes from studies of psychiatric patients,[5] including the monumental work of Hollingshead and Redlich (1958), who established that the verbal methods of psycho-therapy are utilized most frequently with persons from the middle and upper classes, while the lower classes more often receive organic treatment.[6] Although there has been little comparable study within counseling settings, it is generally agreed that counselors are more effective with clients with a middle-class background than with those from the lower classes.

Several factors combine to account for this discrepancy. One is that both the goals and methods of counseling have traditionally reflected a middle-class culture and middle-class values (Hunt, 1960; McMahon, 1964; Schneiderman, 1965). A premium is put on verbal expression and on introspection of motives and feelings, and it is assumed that the client can gain some degree of control over his environment. These criteria are gen-erally met by upper- and middle-class clients, but they may not be realistic for those from the lower class. This has led several writers, including Hunt (1960), to conclude that it is inevitable that counseling will have more value for middle-class persons.

[4] This problem is, obviously, more acute for male counselors than for females. Most counselors, however, are male, which makes it worthy of attention. In addition female counselors, by virtue of their professional status, are atypical females in our society, and thus they may have as much difficulty in empathizing with needs of many of their female clients as will their male counterparts.

[5] For an extensive critical discussion of the literature on the relationship be-tween social class and mental illness, see Petras and Curtis (1968).

[6] A ten-year follow-up of the group originally studied by Hollingshead and Red-lich found that persons from the lower social class levels were more likely to be institutionalized for treatment and therefore have more difficulty in readjusting to the community after their release than those from the middle and upper classes, who were treated within the community itself (Myers and Bean, 1968).

A related difficulty is the expectations which persons of different social classes have of a professional person in a "helping" role. Again, most of the evidence comes from psychiatric studies, but the results seem applicable to counseling. It is generally agreed that lower-class people expect the therapist to play an active role, similar to that of a physician (Patterson, 1959; Overall and Aronson, 1963; McMahon, 1964). Not surprisingly, those persons whose expectations are not met are likely to discontinue therapy (Overall and Aronson, 1963), which leads McMahon (1964) to suggest that the therapist working with lower-class persons must attempt to meet their expectations, at least in the initial stages of therapy. This seems to be reflected in the greater tendency of therapists to provide supportive therapy instead of insight therapy for persons with lower-class backgrounds (Patterson, 1959). Although there is some disagreement as to the validity of a supportive approach, in view of the characteristics of lower-class patients it seems reasonable.

How can this information be applied to counseling? It may, first of all, help us to understand why persons of the middle and upper classes may find more potential profit in a counseling approach to their difficulties than will persons with lower-class backgrounds. The lower-class individual may have difficulty in accepting some of the assumptions concerning the nature of personal problems which are necessary if counseling is to be helpful. The counselor, however, must recognize that there are broad individual differences in this respect which cut across class lines.

Social class differences also become important as the counselor and client attempt to communicate with one another. Most counselors come from the middle class, which enables them to perceive, empathize, and communicate most effectively with middle-class clients. The counselor's own experiences and values are more likely to become barriers when he is facing a client from the lower class, possibly resulting in inadequate counseling. Thus the failure of persons from the lower class to derive as much benefit from counseling as do those of the middle class, and their reluctance to seek counseling when they are in difficulty, may be as much the fault of counselors as of the inability of lower-class persons to accept the process as potentially useful.

Counselors must recognize, too, that the lower-class client may be handicapped not only by failure to use his own resources effectively, but also by severe limitations of his environment. Schneiderman (1965) has suggested that many lower-class characteristics which are barriers to the client's effective functioning in society in general may be a realistic way of adapting to a poor environmental situation. Thus the counselor must be aware of the client's environment and work within this framework, at least at the beginning. As Schneiderman (1965) has said:

> To start where the client is means, in the case of the impoverished, to start
> with the impoverished nature of goods, services and opportunities which

exist in his reality. In this reality, middle-class attitudes may be non-functional [p. 104].

The gap between the middle-class orientation of counseling and the needs of the lower-class client leads one to question whether counseling, in its traditional form, can be effectively utilized by persons of the lower class. In many cases it undoubtedly can be effective. However, as several writers (for instance, Gordon, 1964; McMahon, 1964) have suggested, counselors who work with lower-class clients, especially with adolescents, may have to take more responsibility for promoting environmental change as well as utilizing the more traditional counseling framework with their clients. The latter alone will often not be enough.

Race

The combination of counselors and clients of different races has been studied only meagerly thus far. Rosen and Frank (1962) have reported that black patients of white therapists tend to be race-conscious, with detrimental effects on the therapeutic relationship, while Banks, Berenson, and Carkhuff (1967) found that black clients preferred black rather than white counselors. The conclusions of both studies can be only tentative, due to the small numbers of subjects in each, but they suggest that race probably has an important influence on the counseling relationship. In view of the current concern with the problems of racial minorities in this country, Island (1969) is probably right in predicting: "Studies of counseling with ethnic and cultural minorities will undoubtedly increase dramatically during the next few years [p. 243]."

Personality Characteristics

Although it is generally assumed that certain kinds of persons are better candidates for counseling than others, there is little systematic evidence to enable counselors to make a differentiation with a high degree of confidence. As Truax and Carkhuff (1967) have pointed out, most of the research in this area has failed to distinguish between clients who improved *because* of the counseling or psychotherapy they received and those who would have improved anyway. More will be said about this problem in Chapter 10.

On the basis of his analysis of the psychotherapy literature, Frank (1961) has suggested a number of characteristics of patients who respond well to psychotherapy, bearing in mind the limitation noted above. These include perseverance and dependability (impulsive persons are more likely to drop out early), capacity for self-understanding, suggestibility, previous participation in group activities (isolates are poor candidates), and emotional responsiveness. Frank also says that patients whose difficulties are related to severe environmental stress have a better prognosis than those who are having trouble dealing with a normal degree of stress, since the former probably have a greater degree of adaptability. In addition, Truax and Carkhuff (1967) report research which indicates that a high level of "felt" disturbance, as measured by self-report instruments, plus a low level of "overt" disturbance, as indicated by behavior problems annoying to others, is most predictive of a positive outcome.

More specifically in the counseling realm, Heilbrun has developed a Counseling Readiness Scale, adapted from Gough's Adjective Check List and derived from the responses of clients at a university counseling service, using the criterion of early termination (Heilbrun and Sullivan, 1962; Heilbrun, 1964). He has also related performance on this scale to personality characteristics, as measured by the California Psychological Inventory (Heilbrun, 1962), and to dependency in problem-solving tasks (Heilbrun, 1968), both with university students. Among males, Heilbrun found that high "counseling readiness" was related to low self-acceptance and high dependency, while among females it was related to lack of concern with maintaining social appearances and low dependency. Among both sexes, counseling readiness was inversely related to the ability to think in psychological terms and the willingness to take responsibility. The latter suggests that persons who can think in psychological terms and can take responsibility for their problems are less likely to seek out counseling when in difficulty. This supports Heilbrun's (1961) earlier finding that males who continue in counseling tend to have "feminine" personality characteristics, while females who remain tend to be more "masculine."

The question of readiness for counseling can easily be oversimplified, since much probably depends on the specific counselor and the situation as well as on the characteristics of the client. As Truax and Carkhuff (1967) have noted:

> It may very well be that the diagnostic type of patient with the best prognosis varies from therapeutic setting to therapeutic setting, depending to some degree upon the biases and expectations of the counselors or therapists themselves [p. 183].

Although this statement is based primarily on research with psychiatric patients, and Heilbrun's research suggests some communality among personality characteristics which are related to counseling readiness in several settings, it seems likely that the expectations of the counselor do play an important role in influencing the readiness of a given client.

Motivation

Counseling cannot take place with a client who has no counseling need. This is a generalization with which nearly all counselors, regardless of their theoretical orientation, would probably agree. The person who enters the counselor's office with no reason of his own for being there is not at the moment a client. He may become one eventually, but his motivation must first be aroused.

Most clients are, of course, motivated for counseling, otherwise they would be spending their time elsewhere. The counselor can legitimately assume that when a person asks to see him professionally it is because he has a reason, and that this reason will in most instances involve a counseling need. This need may not be immediately clear either to the counselor or the client, which is why the first phase of counseling is the establishment of a counseling goal, but the client is nonetheless motivated to do something and the counselor's job is to help him channel this motivation in a constructive direction.

There are, however, instances in which the counselor sees a person who is not motivated for counseling. Such might be the case, for example, with a high school or college student referred to a counselor because of a disciplinary infraction. Although it should be clear that the counselor's role is not that of disciplinarian, the person responsible for handling the problem (the principal or dean) may believe that this student needs a counselor's help in overcoming the difficulties which led to the misbehavior in the first place. The referral source cannot be faulted for this kind of thinking, and the counselor must do what he can under the circumstances.

Another example is the spouse of a person who comes for marriage counseling. As we will discuss in greater detail later, marriage counseling moves more smoothly if both parties are involved. Thus the counselor will probably make some attempt to get the marital partner involved in the counseling too, although this person may at first be reluctant.

These examples illustrate that the counselor will occasionally find himself talking to a person who is not at the moment motivated for counseling, but who is there primarily at the insistence of someone else. What should be the counselor's role under these circumstances?

One approach would be to terminate the interview immediately on the grounds that nothing can be accomplished until the client decides for himself that he is interested in counseling. This seems unwise, for two reasons: (a) Client motivation is a continuum, not a dichotomy, which means that this person may have some latent counseling motivation that may be aroused if he is given the chance to consider the situation thoroughly.

(b) The hopes of the referral source must also be considered. Although the counselor cannot perform miracles, both he and the referral source should be able to agree that every effort was made to help the person referred. The counselor may, however, have to educate his referral sources as to what they can reasonably expect him to accomplish with reluctant clients.

The problem of dealing with the reluctant client has been discussed by several writers (for example, Dean, 1958; Snoxell, 1960), and their conclusion seems to be that clients who come to see a counselor under pressure are not good counseling prospects, regardless of the counselor's skills. Tyler (1961) cites several studies which indicate that such clients are likely to terminate early and to be judged to have made little progress. This suggests that the counselor should not exert undue effort to persuade reluctant clients to try counseling, nor should he expect to perform miracles with such persons. The chances are great that most clients who come involuntarily are not good prospects for counseling, at least not at that time.

On the positive side, however, the counselor should talk with a reluctant client and should attempt to get across at least two points. First, he should accept the client's negativism and encourage him to discuss the reasons behind it (Beier, 1952; Wolberg, 1967). If the client is willing to do this, a first step has been taken, and an understanding of the causes of the resistance may reveal some latent counseling motivation. Wolberg (1954), for example, describes a client who was highly resistant to psychotherapy because of a previous negative experience with a therapist. The current therapist, by accepting the negativism and discussing it with her, was able to help her recognize that underneath her hostility lay a strong need for help, and a therapeutic relationship was subsequently established.

Above all, the counselor should try to lay groundwork such that if the individual later recognizes a need for counseling, he will not be hesitant to return. Thus it is important that the counselor communicate to the client that the decision to begin counseling is entirely his; the counselor must then accept the client's decision. The counselor should discuss with the client the reason for the referral, to the extent that the client is willing to talk about it, and he can describe the counseling process if the client wants. But to be consistent with the philosophy and goals of counseling, the decision to continue must ultimately be the client's.

This also holds true with clients who have sought counseling voluntarily, but whose counseling goal is not that which the counselor thinks would be most meaningful. An example might be a student who wants help in learning to study better. It may become evident to both the counselor and the client that other difficulties, such as family conflicts, are contributing significantly to his academic problems and might be dealt with through counseling. The decision to do so, however, is up to the client. The counselor may raise the possibility, but the client should be free to accept or reject it.

Thus, in this example, the client may decide to continue to concentrate on the study problems and not use counseling to deal further with his family difficulties. The counselor must respect this decision if any counseling is to continue.

To return to the involuntary client, it is obvious that as many clients as possible should come to the counselor of their own free will, which means that the counselor should do what he can to promote self-referrals and to minimize forced referrals. Robinson (1950) suggests that counselors who work within institutions, such as a school setting, can promote self-referrals through several techniques. These include developing good relations within the school, and stimulating interest in counseling-related questions through the use of occupational information and psychological testing. Perhaps the best way, however, to build a clientele is through successful counseling. No one can proselyte quite as effectively as a "saved soul." The counselor will often find that persons who have completed counseling and are pleased with the outcome are his most effective boosters.

Motivation is not an all-or-none characteristic. Some clients enter counseling with enough motivation to get them started, but their interest may wane as counseling progresses. This may occur because the anxiety which initially propelled them into counseling has been reduced and the goal which they set no longer seems important enough to be worth the effort. When this happens, the client may fail to return for further interviews as expected, and in most cases the counselor should allow him to terminate. In some instances, the client may continue to come for counseling but resist working on his problem. He may come because the counseling relationship represents a kind of security to him, or he may simply be reluctant to take the initiative to terminate out of fear of hurting the counselor's feelings. The counselor should be sensitive to the current motivational state of the client and should discuss with him any perceived decline in motivation.

COUNSELOR VARIABLES

Age

Clients will have somewhat different perceptions and expectations of a counselor depending on his age. Some clients may have less confidence in a young counselor, especially if he is younger than they. On the other hand, an older counselor may be perceived in a parental role by a young client which may in turn interfere with the development of an optimum working relationship.

On the basis of such speculation, the beginning counselor may be tempted to try to fake his age, especially if he is youthful in appearance.

This is inadvisable, partly because there is little factual evidence to support a belief that counselors of certain ages are more effective than others and also because it is most important that the counselor present himself honestly and not try to be something he is not. Certainly he should dress and behave in a manner appropriate to his age and role, but he should not make a direct effort to age himself. The counselor should not attempt to be all things to all people.

Experience

Experience as a counselor is, of course, highly correlated with age, but whereas age has its greatest impact in terms of the client's perceptions and expectations, experience influences more strongly the behavior and effectiveness of the counselor. There is general agreement that experience has a positive influence on counseling, and that most counselors improve with experience. This is especially true among counselors who work in settings in which they have frequent contact with other counselors and who continue to grow professionally, such as by attending conferences, reading professional books and journals, and conducting research. Experience itself is not automatically profitable; a person can continue to make the same mistakes repeatedly and learn nothing from them.

Several studies (for instance, Fiedler, 1950a, 1950b; Strupp, 1955) have suggested that the greatest difference between experienced and inexperienced counselors and therapists is in flexibility. Inexperienced counselors tend to be rigidly attached to a theoretical orientation and set of techniques and are reluctant to venture beyond the bounds of their training, whereas with experience they gain confidence and dare to try new ideas and approaches. Experienced counselors tend to behave more like one another than do those who are beginning, since the experienced persons are less bound by a single theory and are more free to gear their approach to the varying needs and personalities of their clients.

Sex

As with age, the sex of the counselor affects the counseling relationship, primarily in terms of the client's reactions. In general, male counselors are preferred over female counselors by incoming clients when given their choice, although female clients prefer female counselors for the discussion of more emotionally loaded problems (Koile and Bird, 1956; Fuller, 1963, 1964). In these studies, however, the clients' opinions were sought prior to the counseling itself; there is no evidence that clients are more likely to reject female than male counselors once they have been assigned to them.

As noted in the discussion of the influence of the client's sex on counseling, the sex of the counselor may be important with certain clients, depending on the ease or difficulty with which they can communicate with males and females. Thus, for example, a female counselor may be more effective than a male in working with a male client whose difficulties involve his relationship with his father.

The range of variability among counselors is great, and the sex of the counselor is not a major component. Nevertheless, it can be argued that a counseling agency should employ both male and female counselors, just as it should employ counselors who vary in other respects too. In any case, the female counselor should anticipate that some clients will initially come to her with less confidence than they would approach a male counselor, and she may therefore have to work a little harder to establish her competence in their eyes.

Personality Characteristics

There is no ideal counselor personality. Research concerning the characteristics of counselors tells us only that many different kinds of persons can become effective counselors. Partly this is because no one person has the ideal combination of strengths. A specific counselor may be able to compensate for a lower level of skill in one area by strength in another, and thus he may be as effective as the next person but for different reasons. Even if it were possible to design a hypothetically ideal counselor, no human being could be expected to fit the model perfectly.

The complex nature of the counseling relationship presents an additional complication. No matter how skillful a counselor may be, he will not be equally effective with all clients. He may, in fact, be ineffective with some with whom another counselor could do much better. This is because clients enter counseling with preconceived personal likes and dislikes, and they quickly develop a reaction to the counselor as a person. No counselor can expect to be all things to all clients and still be a genuine, honest person, which seems to be a prime requisite. This suggests that a counseling agency which employs several counselors should avoid hiring new counselors who are carbon copies of those already on the staff.

Several studies have attempted to determine the ideal degree of counselor-client similarity in relation to counseling outcomes, but the results have been inconclusive. Tuma and Gustad (1957) found that the same counselors had different effects on different clients, as would be expected, but that close counselor-client similarity in personality characteristics produced the greatest degree of client learning. Mendelsohn and Geller (1965), on the other hand, found a curvilinear relationship between client attitudes toward counseling and client-counselor personality similarity. The difference may be a reflection of criterion differences, but it does indicate the complexity of the problem.

Despite the variation among successful counselors, it may be profitable to consider briefly some of the traits which have been suggested by several writers as desirable (see Weitz, 1957; Snyder, 1961; Tyler, 1961). It must be kept in mind, however, that the evidence is not conclusive and that a specific person may show a deficiency in one trait and still become a good counselor. Perhaps we can conclude only that this represents a desirable constellation of personality characteristics and that a person who lacks several is unlikely to be successful in counseling. (More will be said about this in a later chapter concerning the selection of counselors.)

Interest in Helping People. It seems axiomatic that to be successful a counselor must have a genuine interest in helping others. Grater, Kell, and Morse (1961) have suggested that a "social service need" is probably necessary not only for success but also for satisfaction with the job of counseling, and several studies (for example, Stefflre, King, and Leafgren, 1962; Mills, Chestnut, and Hartzell, 1966; Demos and Zuwaylif, 1966) have consistently found that counselors like people and want to help them. This attitude is presumably communicated to the client, who thereby feels comfortable in the counselor's presence and feels free to talk about himself.

Perceptual Sensitivity. Much emphasis has been placed on the counselor's ability to perceive the thoughts and feelings of the client, despite the confused manner in which they may be presented. He should be sensitive to the clues which the client presents and be able to help the client to clarify his thoughts and feelings.

Personal Adjustment. There is some disagreement as to the extent to which counselors should themselves be free of adjustment problems. Some writers believe that the counselor should serve as a model of effective adjustment for his clients and that he can be of help only to the extent that he can successfully cope with the kinds of problems which are giving his clients trouble. Others, however, argue that this requirement is unrealistic and perhaps also unwise. Although it is generally agreed that counselors should be reasonably well-adjusted themselves, it may not be necessary to expect them to be free of adjustment problems. Snyder (1961) suggests that they should be "normally adjusted" but not necessarily "perfectly adjusted," if indeed this were possible.

The most reasonable conclusion seems to be that the counselor should be able to deal with his problems in a constructive manner and that he should not attempt to help clients deal with problems with which he himself is having trouble. The latter statement is open to question, since it can be argued that the counselor's problems need have nothing to do with those of the client. A marriage counselor, for example, could conceivably be able to counsel effectively with a client who is having marital problems, even though the counselor's marriage were breaking up at the same time. Ideally the counselor should be able to separate these two situations and not let his own difficulties intrude on his counseling. In practice, however, this may be asking for superhuman strength from the counselor and may therefore be an unrealistic expectation. Counselors would therefore be well advised, when possible, to refer elsewhere clients whose difficulties are quite similar to their own.

It should also be recognized that the counselor's adjustment and personality may vary somewhat between the counseling situation and the outside world. Weitz (1957), for example, suggests that personal security is an important requisite of the successful counselor. Security, however, is essentially a function of one's feeling of ability to cope with a given situation and may therefore vary from one situation to another for a given person. A counselor may, by virtue of his experience and training, feel secure in his counseling role but feel insecure in certain areas outside of counseling. By the same token, another person who is secure in most situations might be insecure as a counselor. Thus the important consideration is how the counselor presents himself in the counseling situation, not what he is like in all facets of his life.

Genuineness. Most counselors would agree with Rogers (1958a) that the counselor should be a real person to his clients. This means that he must be able to provide a genuine relationship which they can use to achieve their counseling goals. To some extent this is related to the counselor's authenticity in other settings, in that reality and honesty cannot be turned on and off like a faucet. This seems to relate to the point made above, concerning the counselor's personal security: if the counselor feels secure in the counseling situation, he is more free to be himself. The same, of course, applies to the client and is what the counselor is trying to promote. The client has little chance of experiencing his own reality in the presence of a person who refuses to be real himself.

THE PHYSICAL SETTING

The new client's first impressions of counseling are obtained not only from the appearance and manner of the counselor but also from the setting in which counseling takes place. The nature of this setting reflects in many subtle ways the concept of counseling either of the counselor himself or of the agency which employs him. For this reason it should be unnecessary here to spell out in detail the most desirable arrangement of offices, furniture, and so on.[7] The counselor should make this determination for himself, by considering how the various aspects of the setting contribute to the kind of counseling climate he is hoping to establish.

In selecting his office, the counselor's primary concern should be with privacy. No office, no matter how tastefully furnished, can lend itself to counseling purposes if conversations can be easily overheard and distractions are frequent. Once a private office has been located, the counselor should try to furnish it in such a way as to produce a relaxed atmosphere. Any office will, of course, reflect the personality of its occupant, and there is no need for the counselor to make his office any less personal than that of any other professional person.

To minimize distractions, it is desirable that a counselor or a counseling agency have a receptionist to answer the telephone and make appointments as well as to do the routine clerical work. Since the receptionist will provide most new clients with their first impression of the counseling agency, it is important that she have a "counseling attitude" toward persons who enter the office, meaning simply that she be pleasant and friendly. Since many persons who come to see a counselor are under some stress at the time, it is also important that she be able to handle emergencies calmly.

An aspect of the physical setting that communicates the counselor's attitudes in a subtle but important way is the arrangement of furniture. Most counselors work from behind a desk, often because their office space is limited and it is impossible to have several chairs in the office. The arrangement of the client's chair in relation to that of the counselor is significant. If the desk is between them, this communicates a somewhat different relationship than if the desk is to one side so that there are no barriers between the counselor and client. Several possible furniture arrangements are depicted in Figure 5.1. The writer knows of no evidence to show that one arrangement is inherently superior to another, but it seems indisputable that the arrangement which the counselor selects will reflect his own personality and his expectations as to the nature of the counseling relationship. (Compare, for example, arrangements A and C in Figure 5.1.) Some counselors give the client a choice, having several chairs in various positions and allowing the client to indicate his preference. His choice presumably says something about his expectations of counseling.

In offices large enough to permit further permutations of furniture, it may be possible to establish a counseling area removed entirely from the

---

[7] Some writers take considerable pains to dictate office arrangements to the neophyte counselor or psychotherapist. Wolberg (1967), for example, makes very specific suggestions, even to the point of advising that the therapist should not keep a pet in his office as it may frighten insecure clients.

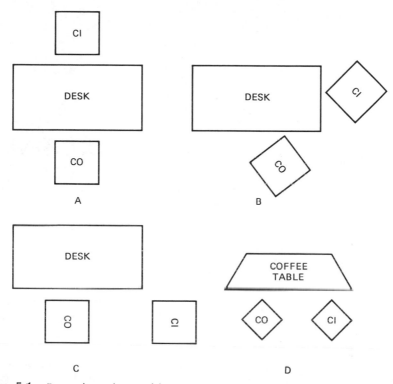

Figure 5.1 *Examples of possible arrangements of furniture in counseling offices.*

desk (for example, arrangement D in Figure 5.1), perhaps equipped with more comfortable chairs. Presumably this would promote an even more relaxed and intimate atmosphere.

The only advice that can be offered as to the optimal arrangement of furniture is that the beginning counselor should try various arrangements; eventually he will come to prefer the one in which he feels most comfortable and which seems to him to communicate best the kind of counseling relationship which he hopes to establish with his clients.

6

Group Counseling

To most people, counseling implies a private interaction between two persons, and this is in fact by far the common situation. In recent years, however, a growing interest has developed in the counseling of persons in groups, rather than individually. Although *group counseling* [1] is probably discussed more than it is actually practiced, and it is doubtful that it will ever become highly popular, exploring it in some detail should add to our understanding of the counseling process.

The origins of group counseling are obscure and can probably be traced to several influences. Group dynamics, the study of the interactions among persons in groups, has been of interest to sociologists and social psychologists for many years, and as knowledge concerning group inter-actions grew it was inevitable that practical applications would eventually be attempted. The popularity of group psychotherapy, resulting from its extensive use in veterans' hospitals during and after World War II, drama-tized the potential of the group process for changing individual behavior. Inevitably, counselors began to apply group processes to their work, with enough success to warrant the continued study of counseling in group set-tings.

Some of the interest in group counseling probably came from a hope that it would prove to be more efficient than individual counseling, thereby enabling the hard-pressed counselor to see more clients. In some cases this

[1] Other terms, such as "multiple counseling," are sometimes used, but group counseling seems to be the most popular term and will therefore be used here.

has proved to be a valid outcome, but even if it is not always more efficient, group counseling can add an important dimension to the counseling process. This aspect will be discussed further in a later section.

RELATIONSHIP TO OTHER GROUP APPROACHES

To clarify the nature of group counseling, it is necessary to differentiate it from other group approaches also aimed at behavior change. To a large extent the distinctions to be made here parallel those made in the first chapter between counseling and other forms of interpersonal interaction. Thus group counseling can be most simply defined as counseling persons in groups rather than individually, with the definition of counseling itself remaining the same.

As noted above, much of the impetus for group counseling came from the success with *group therapy,* but group counseling differs from group therapy in the same ways that individual counseling differs from individual psychotherapy. Persons who prefer to blur the distinction between individual counseling and psychotherapy will also deny a meaningful distinction between group counseling and group therapy, but this writer prefers to maintain a distinction along the lines discussed in Chapter 1, that is, in terms of objectives and techniques.[2]

This distinction is, however, admittedly more difficult to maintain clearly when groups rather than individuals are being considered, simply because the various individuals within a group will not have identical goals. Thus it is conceivable that within a given group, some persons could be working toward therapy-type goals—that is, a rather fundamental change in personality—whereas others could be working toward counseling goals, or a more effective utilization of their present resources. Such confusion is especially apparent in groups designed to help persons learn more about themselves and to become more sensitive to others, such as the Sensitivity Training groups (T-groups)[3] sponsored by the National Training Laboratory, the "Self-Actualization" groups described by Brammer and Shostrom (1968), and "encounter groups" (Rogers, 1967). Also in a gray zone are groups such as Alcoholics Anonymous, designed primarily to prevent an alcoholic relapse on the part of its members, and Recovery Incorporated, composed of groups of persons once hospitalized as mental patients. Many

[2] Readers interested in a summary of group therapy approaches may consult Rosenbaum (1965) or Coffey (1966).

[3] Campbell and Dunnette (1968) have published a critical review of research concerning the effectiveness of T-groups in the development of managerial personnel. See also the comment by Dunnette (1969).

of these groups are designed to fulfill needs which could not be met efficiently, if at all, by either individual counseling or psychotherapy.

The present discussion of group counseling will, however, be limited to groups with traditional counseling goals, rather than the self-actualization or maintenance types of groups noted above.

Since most of the explorations with group counseling have taken place in educational settings, it is sometimes confused with *group guidance*. Here again, the distinction made earlier between guidance and counseling remains appropriate; group counseling may be one aspect of group guidance, but they are not synonymous.

Group guidance refers essentially to any phase of guidance done with groups rather than with individual students (Bennett, 1963), usually with an emphasis on the presentation of guidance-related information. Originally group guidance was combined with regular classroom activities and therefore resembled teaching rather strongly (Koile, 1955; Warters, 1960), but it is becoming increasingly accepted that effective group guidance is best handled outside of the regular classroom and by specially trained persons rather than by classroom teachers (Goldman, 1962). In this respect, group guidance programs are slowly catching up with the prevailing philosophy of guidance in general.

GROUP COUNSELING IN OPERATION

Objectives of Group Counseling

The operation of group counseling makes sense only in light of its objectives, and not all writers agree as to what these objectives should be. Although most writers begin by stating that the objectives of group counseling are not those of individual counseling, their subsequent lists of objectives scarcely suggest a meaningful distinction.

Writers on the subject also disagree as to the variability of objectives within the group. Warters (1960), for example, states that the goals of group counseling are the goals of the various individuals within the group, rather than the goal of the group as a whole. While it is probably true that the individuals within a group cannot be expected to set identical goals nor to agree on a single goal for the group, this writer is inclined to agree with Wright (1959) that group counseling is more effective when the members of the group share a reasonably common problem. Each may define the problem according to his individual needs and may arrive at a unique solution, but the concern of the group members should have essentially a single focus.

When the objectives of individual counseling are set aside, group counseling seems to have two major purposes, only one of which is really psychologically defensible. The less desirable purpose is efficiency and economy. Some counselors believe that group counseling will enable them to "process" more clients, and in some cases this is probably true. But most proponents of group counseling tend to play down this aspect and argue instead for its value on more meaningful bases.

The most acceptable objective of group counseling, then, lies in the positive use which can be made of the group situation to help the individual members reach their counseling goals. The counseling group represents, in a sense, a half-way situation between the individual counseling relationship and the real world. In Warters's (1960) terms, it is a "protected group." If operated properly, group counseling should provide the individual members with an opportunity to interact with others who are striving to reach similar counseling goals and to give to and accept help from them, as well as from the counselor. Although only one member of the group is a professional counselor, all members act as "counselors" for each other, and by so doing experience personal growth in the ability to interact meaningfully with other people as well as progressing toward the solution of their individual problems. By means of the interaction within the group, the individual members gain insight into themselves and have the opportunity to try out new behaviors in a relatively protected setting. Group counseling thus removes some of the artificiality of the individual counselor-client relationship.

Uses of Group Counseling

The following list of examples of the ways in which group counseling might be, and has been, utilized may help to clarify its nature. This list is representative but is not intended to cover the entire range of possible uses.

Problem Sharing and Developmental Understanding. Perhaps the most fundamental use of group counseling, especially with elementary and high school students, is to encourage the members to share their feelings and concerns with one another so that each may recognize that he is not alone. The group member should, by this process, gain a better picture of himself as a developing human being and be better able to place himself in a developmental perspective. Adolescents in particular tend to view themselves as unique and peculiar, and group exchange of personal concerns, under the guidance of a counselor, may relieve individual anxiety as well as provide suggestions for constructive approaches to certain problems.[4]

[4] See Cohn and Sniffen (1962) and Cohn and others (1963) for examples of group counseling used primarily for this purpose.

Readiness for Counseling. Some counselors have found that group counseling is a helpful starting point for persons who seem to be in need of counseling but who are not yet enthusiastic about undertaking it. Group counseling for this purpose would probably focus on the nature of counseling and the benefits which might be gained from it. Not all members of such a group will subsequently enter individual counseling, but enough might do so to make it worthwhile, and even those who do not continue may have gotten something of value from the group experience.

Vocational Development. Since counseling in general deals frequently with questions of vocational concern, it is to be expected that group counseling will also often be concerned with vocationally related questions. Group counseling, however, is more likely to emphasize general principles of vocational development rather than the vocational choice of a specific individual. Group counseling might, for example, be appropriate at stages at which the group members must make vocationally relevant decisions, such as choosing courses in high school, or deciding what to do following graduation. Warters (1960) speaks of the latter as an "exit group" and notes that group counseling can be helpful with persons who will soon be moving from one situation into another. Problems such as lack of interests, or difficulty in the curriculum of one's choice, may also be appropriately handled through group counseling.[5]

Assimilation of Information. Both test interpretation and the discussion of occupational information may be done effectively in groups. In some cases this may be a special case of the vocational development use, but in others it may be the primary purpose of the group's existence. The latter is especially true when the tests have been administered to a group of students for reasons other than an expressed need on their part, and yet the counselor believes that the students may benefit from knowledge of their results. Not only may test interpretation of this sort be done more economically in groups rather than individually, but the questions raised by some group members may stimulate others to consider possible implications that they might have missed had they reviewed them alone with a counselor. If the student was coerced into taking a test in the first place, a group interpretation may be a more powerful device to stimulate his use of the results than would individual counseling.

Adjustment to School. Since most group counseling takes place in school settings, it is hardly surprising that some counselors have tried to

[5] See Volsky and Hewer (1960) for an example of group counseling at the University of Minnesota which deals primarily with questions pertaining to vocational development.

use it as a means of helping students who are having academic difficulties or are behavior problems (see, for example, Cohn and Sniffen, 1962). Although the results have not been dramatic, the group approach seems promising enough to warrant further study.

Remediation. Linked closely with school adjustment problems is the use of group counseling for academic remediation. Thus a group counseling approach, combined perhaps with a teaching situation, may be helpful to students with problems in study methods or in specific subjects. Often a purely didactic approach will not be successful, since motivation and attitude play a major role in students' deficiencies, and the inclusion of group counseling may help to deal more directly with the underlying cause of the difficulty.

Techniques of Group Counseling

Since the goals of group counseling are essentially the same as those of individual counseling, the techniques employed by the counselor are basically the same in both situations. As with individual counseling, the counselor himself must determine which techniques seem to achieve most effectively those goals which he believes are desirable. No manual of group counseling can therefore be written, and the effective counselor is one who is goal-oriented rather than technique-oriented.

The above description implies that any person skilled in individual counseling can conduct a group counseling session with little difficulty. In actuality this is seldom the case, since the group situation is considerably more complex. The counselor must be concerned not only with his interactions with each member of the group, but also with their interactions with one another. He relies more on techniques which help encourage the group to interact freely and will probably interject less of his own ideas if the group is making good progress itself. Although the effective group counselor is probably a person who has first learned the skills of individual counseling well, he has in addition mastered the complexities of group dynamics. Successful group counseling requires a period of training and experience, as does learning to become a skilled individual counselor.

The group situation does provide an opportunity to make use of certain techniques, in addition to those of individual counseling, which may prove helpful. Among these are case discussions and role-playing. A case discussion generally concentrates on the needs and concerns of one member of the group, with the other members contributing to the solution of that person's problem or the making of a decision. Role-playing, in which the group members assume certain roles to help clarify a problem situation, may range further afield and provide a way of bringing "significant others" into the group. Role-playing can be an effective device in helping a person to learn more appropriate ways to handle situations or relationships which give him trouble, and a group setting is more suitable than individual counseling for such an attempt.

Composition of the Group

Several issues with regard to the composition of a group for counseling purposes remain to be resolved. Most writers on this topic speculate freely, drawing heavily from the literature on group therapy, which does not necessarily apply to group counseling.

Homogeneity versus Heterogeneity. Should a group be composed of persons who are relatively similar, or should an attempt be made to obtain as much diversity as possible? This is a controversial issue among group therapists, but most group counselors (for instance, Bennett, 1964; Cohn and others, 1963) prefer grouping on the basis of a common problem. Cohn and his co-workers (1963), for example, suggest that groups may be organized to deal with problems of underachievement, behavior problems in school, vocational choice, and so on. Although there is little research evidence to demonstrate the superiority of either approach, it seems logical that a group would be of greater value to the individuals involved if the group members shared the general concern on which the group was focused.

Bennett (1964) also recommends that the maturity of the group members should be relatively similar, especially if a topic such as vocational development is to be a major concern of the group.

Size of the Group. Group counselors have also speculated, with some disagreement, as to the optimum size of a group. Warters (1960), for example, says that a group may vary from six to fifteen members, while Glanz and Hayes (1967) recommend a range of between five and ten persons. Again, there is little research evidence to support any specific number as being optimum, although a study by Castore (1962) is suggestive. He investigated the breadth of interaction within therapy groups as a function of the size of the group and found that the verbal interrelationships—the number of different members with whom an individual group member interacted—decreased significantly when the group reached nine members and decreased again when it reached seventeen. Apparently the interactions within groups of between nine and seventeen members are fairly similar.

In reviewing the literature on the influence of size on group psychotherapy, Goldstein, Heller, and Sechrest (1966) conclude, "Size assumes meaning for group psychotherapy only as it influences and interacts with other patient, therapist, and group characteristics which, in turn, appear to influence therapeutic outcome [p. 343]." Perhaps, therefore, the issue of size is in itself superficial and can only be settled when more is learned about the nature of group interaction.

In the meantime, however, a few general guidelines with regard to group size seem reasonable. Certainly the group must be small enough so that meaningful interaction can take place among the group members. At some point—probably around twenty—the group becomes so large that the activity becomes more like teaching than counseling. On the other hand, the group must be large enough to provide sufficient variety in group members to stimulate group interaction and profitable consideration of the problem. Furthermore a group which is too small may suffer from the domination of one individual. At what point this becomes likely is uncertain, but five or six members would seem the minimum.

Open versus Closed Groups. A controversy also exists in group therapy as to whether therapy groups should be open or closed. A closed group is one in which the members may not leave until the group as a whole decides to disband, and to which no new members may be added. In an open group, by contrast, members may withdraw whenever they desire and new members may be added at the group's discretion.

In group counseling, closed groups would seem more feasible. Since the group is presumably created to deal with a problem area common to the group members, all members should feel an obligation to remain in the group until its purpose has been fulfilled. By the same token, allowing new members to enter is likely to disrupt the rapport among the group members and thereby prolong their activities.

The Role of the Counselor

Basically the role of the counselor in a group situation is the same as in individual counseling: to provide a relationship in which the client can feel free to express his thoughts and feelings and to aid in the development of more satisfying behaviors on the part of the client. Because of the complexity of the group situation, however, the counselor may have to modify his normal role in order that these goals can be reached. It is for this reason that the group counselor should have a sound understanding of group dynamics as well as a repertoire of skills of individual counseling.

Group counseling requires, for example, that the counselor establish a meaningful relationship with each group member, which may require greater flexibility than does individual counseling (Cohn and others, 1963). The counselor who concentrates on only a few members of the group and pays little attention to the others not only does the remainder of the group a disservice but also probably negates the effectiveness of the group as such.

He is simply carrying on individual counseling with spectators. It is the counselor's responsibility to get the group working together as a unit, and to avoid allowing the group to rely on him for direction (Warters, 1960). Questions to the counselor, for example, can be redirected to the group, as an indication of their responsibility for helping one another.

In one sense, then, the group counselor may not need to involve himself a great deal in the interactions within the group, especially as the group develops greater cohesiveness. On the other hand, in the early stages the counselor may need to play a more directive role in structuring and in setting limits for the group. The more vulnerable group members, for example, may need to be protected against the onslaughts of those who are more aggressive, at least until the group itself can assume this responsibility. Unfortunately, little is known as to the optimum amount of involvement for the group counselor. Goldstein, Heller, and Sechrest (1966) have summarized the research regarding the amount of involvement by group therapists and find the evidence inconclusive. No better evidence is available to guide the group counselor. As with many other aspects of counseling, the group counselor must first determine his concept of effective group interaction and then develop a role and techniques which seem best to achieve this sort of interaction.

Because of the complexity of the group situation, a single counselor may be unable to handle a group with optimum effectiveness. Some group psychotherapists have developed a "co-therapist" approach to meet this problem, in which two therapists work together with the same group, each playing a somewhat different role. Often the two therapists are male and female, or represent some other sort of obvious distinction. Glanz and Hayes (1967) have suggested that a similar approach might work well in group counseling, but thus far it seems to have been neglected. Given the complexity of the group situation, a co-counselor approach would seem worthy of study.

THE USEFULNESS OF GROUP COUNSELING

Given the difficulty and complexity of group counseling, one may reasonably ask whether it is really worth the trouble. The answer seems to be that it is, at least in certain circumstances, for a number of reasons.

Strengths

The group situation helps the members gain *a better perspective on themselves and their problems* by demonstrating that others have similar difficulties and by allowing them to share their concerns with one another. Facing one's problems frankly is often a major first step in arriving at a solution, and the group setting may encourage some clients to do this more readily than would individual counseling.

The group also enables its members to engage in *reality testing* in a relatively safe setting. One limitation of individual counseling is that it is an artificial situation, in that the counselor seldom reacts to the client as would the typical person. While this presumably makes the client feel more secure and thereby more willing to expose himself as a person, it does not give him a realistic means of trying out new behaviors. The group setting, being a closer approximation of real life, provides a sort of "half-way house" for clients who are trying to develop new ways of coping with their environment.

The uncertain client may also gain needed *support from the group* for ideas which he is afraid to advance or behaviors which he is reluctant to adopt. The feeling that others think he can succeed may enhance his confidence in himself. Glanz and Hayes (1967), for example, have described the value of group support in the counseling of underachievers.

The pressure of the group may also be *an impetus* to the client who might otherwise fail to do something constructive about his difficulties. Some clients who progress quite slowly in individual counseling might move more rapidly if they felt the pressure of the group to do so. Obviously this could be a two-edged weapon, since the group might push a member too hard, and it would be the counselor's responsibility to determine whether the individual did in fact seem ready to move in the direction in which the group was urging him.

A group setting may be more helpful than individual counseling to *clients who tend to be nonverbal or who tend to withdraw quickly when threatened*. Both types of clients may have difficulty in individual counseling because their failure to verbalize retards or even prevents their progress. In a group setting, however, something is going on even if they are not actively participating in it, and they may learn something from the discussions of the other members. Furthermore, the group will probably not allow a member to withdraw completely and may be more successful than would the counselor in drawing out the reluctant client.

Group counseling may be a helpful *prelude to individual counseling,* by giving a reluctant client a taste of counseling with a lesser degree of threat than in an individual setting, and by helping the counselor to identify those members who are in need of individual help.

Last and probably least, group counseling may be *more economical* of the counselor's time and effort, at least in certain kinds of situations, as the group members move together toward a common goal. As noted earlier, economy alone is a poor rationale for group counseling and it may not always be true anyway, but when economy of the counselor's resources is achieved, in addition to the advantages already described, it is a worthwhile bonus.

Drawbacks

Group counseling is not without its drawbacks. An understanding of the potential pitfalls of group counseling should enable the counselor to make a wiser decision as to when to use it and the safeguards to employ.

Perhaps the greatest difficulty in group counseling is the *demands it makes on the counselor's skills and energies,* coupled with his *lesser degree of control* of the situation. A group setting is no place for an inexperienced or insecure counselor. As noted earlier, successful group counseling requires training, and the individual counselor should not assume that he will automatically be effective in a group. Group counseling is best approached cautiously.

Successful group counseling assumes that the group is working together as a unit and that rapport has been established among the members. The presence in the group of a single *disruptive individual* can therefore destroy the effectiveness of the group. For this reason, it is important that the group members be selected carefully, to try to screen out any persons who might cause trouble for the group. Such screening cannot, of course, be entirely accurate, and it is the counselor's responsibility to make sure that the group is not disrupted unduly by any of its members. This may require individual counseling with the person causing difficulty, and perhaps a decision that he should no longer continue as a member of the group (Ohlsen, 1967).

A more subtle problem arises when *a member of the group is progressing at a much slower rate* than the other members, thereby retarding the progress of the group. Here again, individual counseling may be helpful and may allow the member to continue in the group.

Confidentiality may also be a source of concern in a group, since the individual members are bound only by their trust and respect for one another rather than by the ethics of the professional counselor. In a test interpretation session, for example, some members of the group may be reluctant to reveal their test scores to the others, yet all such information should be shared if effective group counseling is to take place.

The logical answer to this problem is that rapport within the group should be developed first, so that the group members trust each other and want to share not only information but personal thoughts and feelings. The extent to which this may be accomplished, however, will vary, depending on the maturity of the members as well as the setting which they are in. There may be less concern with confidentiality, for example, if the group members have little interaction with one another outside of the counseling itself. Most group therapy situations are composed of persons who have no other relationship with one another, and this may also be desirable in group counseling. This is hardly possible, however, in a closed setting, such as a school, which may mean that group counseling is likely to be less successful in such a situation, although there is no firm evidence to support this contention. The counselor who attempts group counseling with high school students should at least be aware of the potential risks involved if confidentiality is breached.

Finally, it must be recognized that *not all clients can be helped* through group counseling. Some presenting problems are simply inappropriate for a group, and some clients cannot operate effectively in a group situation. Group counseling may be helpful for some persons under some circumstances, but it is far from being a replacement for individual counseling.

Age Levels

Group counseling has been undertaken primarily with high school and college students, since these are the groups for which individual counseling has been most prominent. As counseling in general, however, has been extended both up and down the age range, group counseling has likewise become more prevalent at other age levels.

Much of the group work with children, labeled "group counseling," is actually concerned primarily with preparation for vocational choice (Bennett, 1963; Patterson, 1962). Typically these group sessions are part of the activities of an elementary classroom, and can be considered as "counseling" only by a very broad definition of the term. A more explicit approach to group counseling with elementary children has been described by Ohlsen (1967), who appears to be one of the few persons to have studied group counseling at this level. He suggests that group counseling may be helpful for children who are shy and withdrawn, who want to make friends, or who are underachievers.

Ohlsen (1967) points out, however, that group counseling with children seems to require some modifications in the typical techniques. Children, for example, generally need more structure by the counselor as well as more active participation on his part to keep the group moving in a constructive direction. The size of the group should also be smaller than with adolescents (Mayer and Baker, 1967), and Ohlsen suggests that it may be desirable to separate boys and girls into separate groups, although he admits to some indecision as to this latter point. He notes that role-playing is an especially effective technique in group counseling with children, and that the use of play materials can be quite helpful.

Group counseling is, of course, of demonstrated value for high school and college students, for a wide variety of problem situations. As noted earlier, the concern with confidentiality may pose a problem especially for high school students, who are less mature and may have frequent contacts with one another outside of the group. But the value of group approaches with late adolescents and young adults seems firmly established.

Beyond the college years, little has been written about group counseling as such. Group counseling approaches are frequently used in marriage counseling, sometimes extended to the inclusion of the entire family, children and all. Other group approaches, such as sensitivity groups, have also become popular, but these can hardly be classified as counseling *per se,* although some of their members may achieve counseling-type goals. The possibilities of group counseling seem yet to be explored with other adults, especially among the aged.

Group counseling, then, seems to be potentially appropriate for all age levels for which individual counseling is used, but to date its proponents have concentrated almost entirely on the high school and college population.

Interrelations of Group and Individual Counseling

Discussions of group counseling often give the impression that group and individual counseling are in some way opposed to one another, in that a client must choose between them. In actuality, they are complementary rather than opposing facets of the same general process and can effectively supplement rather than duplicate each other.

Individual and group counseling can coexist well together, often for the same individual. Some clients may progress more rapidly with a combination of group and individual counseling, which Glanz and Hayes (1967) refer to as "parallel counseling." As noted earlier, group counseling may also serve as an effective prelude to individual counseling for the person who wants to get a conception of what counseling is all about before plunging in.

A counseling agency or office, then, need not choose between individual and group counseling. It should instead strive to provide the most effective possible services for its clients, which should include both individual and group approaches. Little is known as to the optimum combination of these approaches, but it seems reasonable to conclude that both should be available to all clients.

Effectiveness of Group Counseling

Most attempts to evaluate the effectiveness of group counseling have concluded that it achieves the same criteria of effectiveness as does individual counseling (see, for example, the literature summaries by Wright, 1959; by Shaw and Wursten, 1965; and by LeMay, 1967). Given the problems involved in the evaluation of individual counseling, to be described in a later chapter, this is hardly an impressive documentation, but it must suffice for the present.

More specifically, group counseling has been demonstrated to be as effective as individual counseling in test interpretation (Wright, 1963) and in model-reinforcement counseling (Krumboltz and Thoreson, 1964). The latter study noted that males seemed to benefit more from group than from individual counseling, within the framework of the approach and criteria employed, whereas females gained about the same amount from both. This suggests that investigators might more profitably study the specific processes by which group counseling effects behavior change rather than concerning themselves further with global assessments of its effectiveness.

Present State of the Art

The major drawback to group counseling at this point is that its development has been essentially pragmatic rather than systematic. As Anderson (1969) has noted, "There is still no body of theoretically related knowledge on which the practice of group counseling can be solidly grounded [p. 209]." He goes on to point out that "research is needed which will help to predict how a given client will respond under a given set of conditions and with a particular combination of other group members, including the leader [p. 212]." Until the nature of the group interaction is better understood, counselors are essentially "flying blind" in their efforts to conduct counseling in group settings. The fact that many counselors nonetheless are convinced of its value suggests that group counseling may be an important trend of the future.

7

Some Issues in Counseling: Diagnosis, Information, and Records

The diversity in counseling approaches is most evident in the varying attitudes of counselors toward certain activities related to counseling. Each of these activities may be viewed as essential by some counselors and unimportant by others, while a third group may feel strongly that it should be excluded from counseling altogether.

These disagreements arise partly out of the nature of the counseling experience. Much as counselors may recognize the importance of relying on scientifically produced knowledge to guide them in their practice of counseling, they nonetheless confront questions of technique and procedure for which science does not provide clear-cut answers. As knowledge about counseling increases, these issues may resolve themselves. In the meantime, the practicing counselor must deal with them in the best way he can, relying primarily on his philosophy of counseling as a guide.

The purpose of this chapter is to describe a few of the most common issues about which counselors disagree and to suggest some resolutions. Not all counselors would agree with the writer's views on these issues, and it must be remembered that what works well for one counselor may not be appropriate for another. Ultimately, each counselor must resolve these problems in a way consistent with his own concept of counseling.

DIAGNOSIS

Diagnosis in Medicine

The concept of diagnosis is basic to a medical model of treatment. Medicine has developed a standard procedure in which diagnosis plays a major role: the patient describes his symptoms, the physician makes an examination, then *diagnoses* the patient's ailment which in turn leads him to prescribe a treatment which has been judged appropriate for that particular illness. The diagnosis is a label attached to the patient's symptoms which results in a certain treatment being applied. If the diagnosis is correct the patient should improve, assuming he suffers no unusual reaction to the treatment. If the diagnosis is incorrect, the patient presumably should not improve and may likely get worse, although many patients undoubtedly recover despite an inaccurate diagnosis. In any case, however, diagnosis is considered as one of the fundamental skills of the physician, and the proficient diagnostician is highly esteemed by his colleagues.

As the profession of psychiatry evolved as a medical specialty concerned with the treatment of emotional disorders, it was natural that these practitioners would attempt to apply the traditional medical therapeutic procedures to their patients. In some instances this worked quite well, especially for the organic psychoses, but the sequence of examination-diagnosis-treatment proved less successful with persons whose difficulties did not have a somatic basis. Because of their commitment to the medical model, however, psychiatrists have been reluctant to abandon the traditional system. Instead they have worked to sharpen their diagnostic system on the apparent assumption that its inadequacies are due to a lack of refinement in the labels rather than to a basic fallacy in the system itself. The result has been the development of a highly intricate system of categories of mental disorder, the Standard Psychiatric Nomenclature, presented in the *Diagnostic and Statistical Manual of Mental Disorders* (American Psychiatric Association, 1952).

The *Manual* divides mental illness into five general categories—organic psychoses, functional psychoses, neuroses, personality disorders, and mental defects—and further subdivides each of these into a variety of specific ailments. This system of classification has been criticized on various grounds, questions most often being raised concerning the validity and reliability of the categories. The reliability of the more specific categories is between thirty and forty percent agreement (Beck, 1962), which is not impressive if diagnosis is primarily for the purpose of determining treatment. This would imply that more than half the time a mentally ill patient is being treated for the wrong illness. Agreement concerning the broader categories is of course much higher and probably serves to limit the range of treatment error. Most psychiatrists would agree that the *Manual* could be improved, and a revision is currently in progress (Brill, 1965), but the majority of psychiatrists appear to be committed to maintaining the current system in some form.

This is not the place to debate the validity of the Standard Psychiatric Nomenclature, since counselors should have little reason to make use of it anyway. More important, for our purposes, is the value of diagnosis in the medical form for clients with emotional problems. The general attitude of most counselors and psychotherapists outside the profession of psychiatry—and some psychiatrists, too, for that matter—is that the medical concept of diagnosis has not proved useful for emotional problems and should be abandoned except in instances in which an organic cause can definitely be established. One of the major limitations of medically oriented diagnosis when applied to emotional problems is that the label assigned to the patient is not very helpful in determining the most appropriate treatment. There is no close correspondence between diagnosis and treatment of emotional problems (or "mental illness") as there is in the case of physical disorders. Most physical illnesses can be traced to rather specific physical causes which can be dealt with by a specific treatment which attacks the cause. Most psychological difficulties, on the other hand, do not have specific causes; they are part of the life pattern of the individual and must be dealt with as such. In the case of a physical illness, a physician can do something *to the patient* which should further the patient's recovery. A client with a psychological problem, however, must do something *for himself*. Another person may help him do this, but the client himself must take action if change is to take place.

Harrower (1965a) has suggested that diagnosis ". . . is relevant only insofar as the therapeutic fate of the patient depends on it [p. 381]." If it can be established that what happens to a client within counseling is dependent on a diagnosis, then a diagnostic step might be justified. At the present time, however, diagnosis is seldom crucial. Most counselors and psychotherapists have found that they are able to be of help to persons with problems without first having to attach a label to their difficulties, and some feel strongly that such labeling only inserts a barrier to the relationship between the counselor and his client. Surgeons have a habit of referring to a particular case as "the appendix" or "the gall bladder," and the danger exists that counselors who become too label-oriented may begin to perceive a client as " the college choice problem" or "the lack of interests problem" rather than as a person whose current difficulty happens to involve a question as to which college to enter or an inability to commit himself to a single interest area.

Diagnosis in Counseling

Despite the arguments raised against the desirability of including a diagnostic step in counseling, there have been occasional attempts to develop diagnostic systems appropriate to adjustment problems rather than to emotional disorders. The creators of these systems do not seem to have expected that they would be used in the medical sense: that is, as a definite step in the counseling process which would determine the nature of counseling with a specific client. Instead their purpose has been to locate meaningful categories of client problems which would be helpful in research concerning the nature of counseling, and which might ultimately lead to a better understanding of the situations in which certain counseling tools and techniques would be most appropriate.

An early attempt of this sort was made by Williamson and Darley (1937), who suggested that the problems of college students could be arranged into five categories: personality problems, educational problems, vocational problems, financial problems, and health problems. These categories are obviously only descriptive, and their major value would be to suggest which person or agency might provide the most appropriate help for the individual. (In most schools, for example, financial and health problems would not be handled by a counselor, but problems in the first three categories probably would be.)

Dissatisfied with the superficial nature of Williamson and Darley's categories, Bordin (1946) devised a system which focused on the psychological basis of the problem rather than on its symptoms. He suggested that student problems could be attributed to one of four basic sources of difficulty: dependence, lack of information, self-conflict, and choice anxiety. He also included a fifth category which he called "no problem." Pepinsky (1948) subsequently changed the latter to "lack of assurance," added an additional category called "lack of skill," and subdivided the "self-conflict" category into cultural, interpersonal, and intrapersonal self-conflict. Pepinsky's research showed that counselors could assign clients to these categories with a fair degree of reliability, the "lack of assurance" category being the best separated from the others, but the degree of agreement was not remarkable and research on this system seems to have reached a dead end.

More recently, Callis (1965) has proposed a two-way classification combining categories from the Williamson and Darley system—vocational, educational, and emotional—with modifications of those developed by Bordin and Pepinsky—lack of information about or understanding of self, lack of information about or understanding of environment, motivational conflict within self, conflict with significant others, and lack of skill. Callis reports that half of the cases seen at the University of Missouri Counseling Service fell into the category of vocational problems caused by lack of information about self, and he suggests that this system might be used to study differences among counseling agencies or differences within an agency at various times.

Robinson (1963) has also proposed a two-way diagnostic system which includes five areas—personal adjustment, relating to others, knowledge, maturity, and skills—and two levels, remedial and developing strengths. He suggests that this classification could be related to counseling techniques to determine which approaches produce the greatest degree of client learning within each category.

Diagnostic categories are not currently in vogue in counseling, and it is doubtful if there will be an upsurge of interest in the near future. Not since the work of Bordin and Pepinsky has a classification system stimulated a substantial number of counselors, and there is little danger that a "Standard Counseling Nomenclature" will be developed. Bordin (1968) himself has confessed to having lost some of his original enthusiasm for diagnostic categories, and few counselors seem to feel that their skills are being hampered by the lack of a diagnostic system to guide them.

We should not, however, be too quick to discard the idea of diagnosis altogether. During the early stages of counseling in particular, the counselor must make various decisions concerning the client and the counseling process, and these decisions seem to involve a kind of diagnostic activity. For example, the counselor must decide whether counseling is the most appropriate way to meet the client's needs. Should the counselor commit himself to counseling with this person, or should he refer him elsewhere, perhaps to a source of information or perhaps to a psychotherapist? If the counselor decides to begin counseling with this person, he must then make some initial decisions as to how to proceed. Should he ask questions, or remain silent until the client feels like talking? Should he accept or reject the client's dependency overtures? These and many other questions may arise, and the counselor must meet them as best he can.

The common thread running through these examples is that the counselor is attempting to develop an *understanding* of his client so that he can be as helpful to him as possible. In a sense this can be called diagnostic activity, but not in the medical form. In counseling, understanding develops during the course of the counseling and is not a separate step prior to the treatment itself, as in medicine. Nor is the counselor concerned with labeling the client; his goal is to understand the client as a person, not to pigeonhole him as a problem.

The most valid conception of diagnosis in counseling is that the counselor gradually gains understanding of the client as the counseling progresses, and that the counselor's behavior in counseling is determined to some extent by his degree of understanding at that moment. Tyler (1961) has proposed that the counselor develops a "working image" of the client, a view substantiated by research (for example, McArthur, 1954) which indicates that the counselor seems to build a model of the client from the information available to him, a model which presumably becomes more accurate as the counseling progresses.

The Counselor as Evaluator

From time to time the counselor may be asked to advise persons who must make decisions concerning certain individuals. Examples might include a college admissions committee which must decide whether to admit a borderline student, or a social security officer who must decide whether an applicant for social security benefits is sufficiently disabled to be unable to work. In making such an evaluation the counselor must, in effect, make a prediction about the individual's subsequent behavior under various circumstances. He does so by gathering relevant information concerning the person and drawing a conclusion; in a sense, this is also a form of diagnostic activity.

A word should be said at this point concerning the counselor's role as an evaluator. At first glance it would seem that evaluation and counseling cannot coexist. Earlier we described counseling as a non-threatening, non-evaluative relationship, and it may seem strange that we now suggest that a counselor may at times engage in evaluation for others. Evaluation, however, is a legitimate activity for the counselor *as long as he does not attempt to evaluate persons with whom he has or has had a counseling relationship.* There are many situations in which a counselor, by virtue of his training and experience, may be the person best qualified to make a recommendation concerning a decision to be made about someone. The counselor should avoid having to make the decision himself, but he can legitimately advise whoever must make the decision. He should, however, refuse to advise on a decision concerning a person with whom he is counseling or has counseled in the past. To outsiders, the counselor's refusal to do this may seem peculiar, since to them the counselor knows more about this person than anyone else does. But evaluation is contrary to the basic principles of counseling, and the counselor should not try to mix the two. If decisions are to be made about his clients, they should be evaluated by someone else.

This principle also implies that a person coming to a counselor should know whether he is there for counseling or evaluation. If evaluation is the purpose, then certain rules apply which would not be applicable in counseling. No counselor would last long who attempted to use counseling as a guise by which to make evaluations of his clients, and ethical counselors would be leading the drive to get rid of him.

THE ROLE OF INFORMATION IN COUNSELING

To deal effectively with a problem, a client must have relevant information. In many cases, a client's difficulty may be in part due to a lack of necessary information. The student who is having trouble locating an occupation to enter may not know enough about the fields which he is considering to make an intelligent choice. A husband and wife who are worried about their sexual relationship may lack information concerning sexual physiology which could alleviate their anxiety. A "senior citizen" concerned about what to do following retirement might benefit from information about hobbies and retirement communities.

In the cases just cited, lack of information plays an important role in the problem which has brought the person to a counselor. This is not to say that lack of information is the sole difficulty, but it does suggest that until these clients obtain some relevant information they will be severely handicapped in dealing constructively with their problems.

It seems unquestionable, therefore, that the obtaining of relevant information by the client can often make an important contribution to the goals of counseling. Few counselors would dispute this, but they would disagree as to how this need for information fits into the counseling process itself. Specifically, counselors do not have a uniform position concerning the extent to which information should be a part of counseling, when information should be introduced (if at all), and the counselor's role in helping the client locate relevant information. We shall consider each of these issues separately.

Should Information Be Part of Counseling?

Some counselors believe that lack of information is an appropriate counseling problem and that the counselor should be responsible for helping the client locate relevant information. Others, especially those of a non-directive orientation, reject information-seeking as a part of counseling on the grounds that such concerns are superficial and tend to get the counseling relationship off the track. They fear that to focus on the cognitive difficulties of the client is to risk ignoring the more important emotional elements. They believe that once the client has come to grips with himself as a person, he can then make use of information which is available to him. They have nothing against the obtaining of information, but they do not believe it should be included in counseling.

Some compromise between these views seems necessary. The problems which a client brings to counseling may be complicated by the client's ignorance, and in such cases it would be to the client's benefit to obtain some relevant information. However, the search for information is not, in itself, counseling. Many persons other than a counselor might have directed the client to an appropriate source of information. If this is all that is necessary, then the counselor may have served a useful purpose, but not in a counseling role.

Information becomes a tool of counseling when it is *integrated* into the counseling process. This means (a) that the need for information grew out of the client's basic counseling goal but is not the entire goal; and (b) that the information, once obtained, is discussed by the client and counselor within the context of the client's major counseling goal. The counselor does not impose information on the client, and the client remains responsible for deciding that certain information might be useful. The client is also responsible for obtaining the information, with help from the counselor. Once obtained, this information is assimilated into the counseling so that it becomes a part of the cognitive world of the client, to be used as he thinks appropriate. If these conditions are met, the basic principles of counseling are maintained and information becomes a tool of counseling rather than an end in itself.

When Should Information Be Introduced?

Information is useful to the extent that the client is ready for it. Information introduced too early will, at best, be ignored and may actually shift the counseling in an inappropriate direction. On the other hand, if the client's need for information is not met by the counselor the client may feel rejected and may in turn reject the counseling. The question of timing is therefore critical.

Most counselors agree that information should be introduced when the client is "ready," but they disagree on the meaning of readiness in this context. One group, represented by Baer and Roeber (1964) among others, believes that information may be introduced early in counseling, especially if the client is quite interested in it. To them, information can serve as a stimulant to the client's thinking, and may also in the long run result in further self-exploration on the part of the client:

> The single, overriding purpose of the use of information in counseling [is] to introduce counselees to indirect experiences with occupations and schools as a means of stimulating self-study through projections into work and educational roles [p. 431].

Opposed to this view are counselors who believe that information should be introduced in the later stages of counseling, after the client has spent some time considering himself as a person. This viewpoint, expressed by Brayfield (1948) and by Kirk and Michels (1964), is based on the assumption that the client cannot use information meaningfully until he has gained a clear picture of himself as a person, and that to introduce information before this has occurred may encourage him to focus on superficial aspects of his problem.

It may not be necessary to adopt one of these views and exclude the other. If we accept the principle stated earlier that the use of information in counseling should arise out of the client's need, it seems likely that information can serve different purposes at different stages of counseling. In the early stages, information might well stimulate self-exploration, providing that the client recognizes that information obtained at this stage cannot yet provide direct answers to his questions. If he intends to use it this way, then counseling *per se* is not taking place and perhaps was actually not necessary. The true counseling use of information would come later and would in most cases require self-exploration first.

It seems evident that the timing of information in counseling depends largely on the counselor's concept of the nature of counseling. To some counselors, counseling is primarily information-giving of one sort or another, either information about the client or about the world, and the early introduction of information would therefore not be inappropriate. The concept of counseling presented in this book, however, is quite different and suggests that information must be related to the client's needs in a way which is personally meaningful and useful to him.

The Counselor's Role in the Dissemination of Information

The counselor has some important responsibilities relative to the dissemination of information in counseling, but there are some limitations on his role that should first be considered.

The counselor is not a storehouse of information. Some writers imply that the counselor should have a vast range of information at his disposal to interject during the interview when necessary to help the client. This is probably not possible, and certainly not necessary. The counselor cannot be expected to be up-to-date in all areas in which his clients may need information, and the counselor who tries to assume this role will sooner or later fall on his face. His clients are in danger of being both misinformed and miscounseled.

Most psychologists agree that people learn more when they seek information themselves than when it is handed to them. The client who actively engages in a search for information will probably gain more from it and feel more responsible for using it than will the client who receives it directly from the counselor. The counselor's job is to guide the client in his search for information so that the client uses his time efficiently and obtains information which is worthwhile.

The counselor should not assume the role of expert. In some cases, especially when occupational information is needed, the counselor, by virtue of his background and training, could legitimately qualify as an "expert" source of information. An example might be a client who is interested in the teaching profession being counseled by a counselor who is a former teacher. In such a situation the counselor should resist the temptation to insert himself as an expert, even though he may be well qualified to do so, for two reasons: (a) Despite his best intentions to be objective, the counselor may unconsciously color his information with his own attitudes and experiences. Published information is usually a distillation of the opinions of many persons and is not as likely to be biased. (b) Even more important, the client cannot be expected to shift relationships with the counselor. As noted earlier, the counseling relationship is unique, and any behavior on the part of the counselor which distorts the relationship can destroy this unique quality. This is especially critical if the client is attempting to make a decision and needs to have the counselor as a neutral person to talk to. In the example given above, the client may now find it difficult to discuss the pros and cons of teaching with the counselor, and even more difficult to tell the counselor that he is considering rejecting teaching as an alternative.

To some counselors, this point seems trivial. If the client needs some information, and the counselor can supply it for him, why make him go to the trouble of searching it out himself? The answer depends on one's concept of counseling. To this writer, the potential danger to the counseling relationship of the counselor shifting roles far outweighs any slight inconvenience to the client.

So much for what the counselor should *not* do in the dissemination of information. What are his responsibilities, consistent with a counseling point of view?

The counselor should be able to guide his clients to appropriate sources of information. "Guidance" in this case means that the counselor suggests sources of potentially useful information when the client indicates a need for information. He does not *direct* the client to a specific source, but he suggests as many alternatives as seem reasonable and the client makes the final decision as to which one or ones he will use. It is evident, then, that the range of alternatives from which the client can obtain information is limited by the available sources of good information and by the counselor's awareness of these sources. The client, too, may have some ideas as to possible sources of information, some of which may be unknown to the counselor. Thus the location of sources of information is a cooperative process, as is all of counseling.

The counselor cannot be expected to be familiar with sources of information in all possible areas. He can, however, be expected to be familiar with information which is most likely to be needed by his clientele. Thus if he works primarily with high school seniors he should know, among other things, where they can find information about colleges and about jobs. If he is a marriage counselor, he should know where his clients can get information about sex or about legal aspects of marriage. To repeat, he need not have all of this information at his fingertips, but he should know the valid sources.

Because most counselors traditionally work with young people, and because their problems frequently involve vocational choice, a great deal of concern has been directed to the collection and dissemination of occupational information. Any counselor who plans to work in a high school or college setting, or in an agency in which vocational counseling with adults is common, should be quite familiar with the various sources of occupational information. There are a number of general textbooks (for example, Baer and Roeber, 1964) which describe the field of occupational information and list the various kinds of published information available. The counselor should know something about the kinds of questions which various forms of information are designed to answer, and he should be able to direct his clients to the most useful sources.

If the counselor is in a setting in which a sizeable number of clients need information in a certain area, such as occupations, it may be expedient for the counselor to assemble this information and make it available to them. The client must still take the responsibility for reading the material, but unless the counselor collects it in one place it may not be available for persons who need it.

In setting up such a "library," the counselor should attempt to include material which is "accurate, unbiased, complete, and timely" (Kirk and Michels, 1964). These requirements apply not only to occupational information, but to information in any area.

The counselor need not, however, limit his suggestions for occupational information to published materials. In many cases, the client may be referred to local persons who are employed in a field about which he wants to learn more. There are some obvious risks in this procedure: the "expert" may not be a typical person in his field, or he may not have the information which the client needs. On the other hand, there is something to be said for providing a more realistic perception of the field than the client can obtain from printed material. Probably the best procedure is a combination of both approaches, when practical. The client can obtain objective data from published material, but he may become more involved in the field itself by becoming acquainted with persons actually engaged in it.

The counselor should help the client to interpret the information in light of his needs. Earlier we stressed that information becomes a legitimate part of the counseling process only when it is sought as a response to a need expressed in counseling, and when the obtained information is discussed in a counseling context. This means that it is the counselor's responsibility to help the client make meaningful use of the information he has located in light of his personal needs and goals.

Counselors may use various techniques to help the client assimilate and use information. Some encourage the client to bring the material to the counseling interview so that the counselor and client can read it together and discuss it. More commonly, the client returns to the counselor after having located certain information and they discuss it in relation to the question that originally prompted the search. The major point is that the counseling use of information requires that there be a follow-up discussion of some sort. The counselor's failure to encourage such a discussion may leave the client dangling with an incomplete counseling experience.

THE ROLE OF BACKGROUND INFORMATION AND RECORDS

Background Information

In most agencies, a person who wants to talk with a counselor for the first time will find that his route to the counselor's office is barred by paper. Before he can see a counselor, he must declare himself in writing, usually on a standard form. The amount of information required may vary from a few items to several pages of detailed information concerning his past and present life, but seldom will a new client see a counselor without having first completed at least a routine questionnaire. In a high school setting, the information may already be contained in the student's cumulative folder to which the counselor has access, which serves the same purpose as the personal data sheet elsewhere.

The great emphasis which is placed on information collected from and about the client prior to the first counseling interview suggests that this information plays a crucial role in the initial phase of counseling. Many counselors are reluctant to talk with a client about whom they have no previous information. In their minds, they cannot actually begin counseling with a person until they first know something about him, and preferably they want this information before their first face-to-face contact with him.

How important in fact is background information in counseling? Is it worth the time and trouble required of the new client to fill out the forms expected by the agency, at the risk that he will become frustrated or annoyed and withdraw from counseling before he begins? The answer is unknown. Although many counselors believe strongly in the importance of background information and others are opposed to it with equal vigor, there is little evidence to support either view. We can, therefore, only speculate as to the value of background information for the counselor.

"Background information" refers to anything that the counselor learns about the client before the counseling actually begins. This may include information provided by the client himself, usually in response to a standard questionnaire; information supplied orally or in writing by someone who knows the client, such as a referral source; and information collected in the client's cumulative folder, as is typical in most school systems. Most counselors look at whatever information is available, and the general view seems to be "the more the better."

With the practice of obtaining background information concerning new clients so prevalent, it may be foolhardy to question its value, and yet close inspection of the procedure makes one wonder whether the emperor is in fact wearing any clothes. Not only may the collection of information not be worth the trouble, but the information itself may have a negative effect on the counseling process. Following are some of the potential *disadvantages* of obtaining background information about the client.

Information obtained from cumulative records is likely to be incomplete, inaccurate, and out-of-date. Seldom does a cumulative record provide a complete picture of the student; the best that the counselor can hope for is bits and pieces of information which he can put together to form a reasonably coherent picture. The problem, however, is that the counselor does not know how accurate this picture actually is. It may in fact be quite inaccurate, and he may waste valuable time readjusting the picture of the client which he has developed on the basis of the inadequate information available.

Counselors, because of their role, must assume that people can and do change, and yet they often use background information as though the individual were static. Change is, of course, developmental, and information about the client obtained several years ago may be relevant to the kind of person he is now, but the information itself may no longer describe him accurately. The counselor should be concerned primarily with the client as he *is,* not as he *was.*

Information may encourage the counselor to begin counseling with the wrong set. Few counselors, when presented with background information concerning a new client, can resist the temptation to use it to make some predictions about the client; they try to get to know him even before they have met him. It is probably natural that counselors, when faced with an ambiguous situation such as meeting a client for the first time, will look for ways to reduce the ambiguity. Some authorities, in fact, encourage the use of background information in this way. The counselor is encouraged to pursue the information with his mind on questions such as, "Why is this person coming to see me?" "What are some of the major influences in his life?" "What kind of person is he?" And he has not yet even seen the client for the first time.

Why the rush? Why not simply wait for the counseling to begin, and learn this from the client himself? Some authorities argue that the formation of early hypotheses saves time, but it is just as likely that time will be wasted while they are being corrected. Counselors are not omniscient, but the attempts of some to use background information as though it were a fortune-teller's crystal ball suggest that they have delusions in that direction.

Information about the client is more meaningful when obtained in a counseling context. Here again, the time-saving argument is raised by those who favor background information. In their view, routine information can be obtained by a precounseling questionnaire, thus saving the counselor's time in extracting the information during the counseling interview.

This view may have some merit if the counselor sees his role during the early stages of counseling as primarily that of obtaining factual information. As we have earlier described the counseling process this would not be the case, although a certain amount of factual information would, of course, be discussed during counseling. The focus, however, should be on the client as a person and his reasons for coming to counseling, rather than on the client as a statistical object.

The concept of "routine information" may also be questioned. In a counseling context, little information is "routine," and much may depend on how the information is brought out during counseling. A client, for example, might have responded in a routine fashion to questions concerning his mother and father on a precounseling questionnaire, but in response to the counselor's suggestion that he describe his parents, he might spend twenty minutes talking about his mother and thirty seconds about his father. In the latter case his relationships with his parents are presented much more meaningfully. In other words, by *not* having collected routine information prior to counseling, the counselor is in a better position to suggest an area for discussion during the counseling itself, and thereby learn more than the client could or would have revealed on a questionnaire.

Proponents of background information may want to argue at this point that responses to a precounseling questionnaire may suggest areas for the counselor to pursue during counseling, and that without this information the area might not have been explored. This, of course, is possible, but two points can be made in rebuttal: (a) The skillful counselor will probably touch on most potentially relevant areas during his discussion with the client; in any case, he will very likely touch on those which would be included on the typical information form. (b) No questionnaire can be complete enough to uncover every relevant point. The agency which tried to design such an instrument would have to require its clients to spend long hours completing it and would probably soon be out of business.

The completion of a questionnaire may have a negative impact on the client. The client who wants to see a counselor may well resent being required to fill out a form as an initiation rite. The client who has taken the trouble to make an appointment with a counselor is probably motivated at that time, but his motivation may not be sufficient to carry him through the rigors of the questionnaire. Perhaps, then, the completion of the questionnaire is a way of weeding out those persons who have insufficient motivation to benefit from counseling, but with no evidence to support this view it is dangerous to operate on this assumption.

More importantly, perhaps, the questionnaire is presented to the client as the first step in the counseling process and therefore provides him with an initial set toward counseling. In his mind, counseling becomes a question-and-answer process, and it is little wonder that many clients, when they finally do get to see a counselor, expect him to continue in the same vein.

Clients who have misgivings about counseling may use the questionnaire to resist becoming involved in counseling. In response to the counselor's question, "How have your grades been in school?" the client may reply, "I answered that on the questionnaire," or "It's in my record." The counselor can, of course, structure this appropriately for the client, but the client is certainly entitled to wonder why he was asked to take time to give this information on the questionnaire in the first place.

Can a defense be made of background information in counseling? Yes, although some of the legitimate uses have little to do with the counseling process *per se*. A counseling office or agency, for example, may need to maintain records of its clients, and collecting routine information as the clients enter may be the most efficient way to get it. This kind of information may be especially important for research purposes. Anyone who has tried to utilize background information in a research study has probably experienced the frustrations of incomplete data.

Background information may also provide a developmental picture of the client, which may be especially useful to a school counselor. Information for this purpose, however, might best be obtained *after* at least one interview with the client, when the counselor has begun to develop a picture of the client and needs information to fill in gaps. The counselor formulates certain questions about the client, on the basis of his contacts with him, and then searches for information which will help him answer those questions. Not only does this approach enable the counselor to take a fresh look at the client when he first meets him, but a directed search for certain kinds of information is probably more helpful to the counseling than an undifferentiated mass of information presented before the counseling begins.

Perhaps the strongest reason for dependence on background information is that it provides a structure for the beginning counselor and makes him feel more secure. Presumably as a counselor becomes more experienced and more confident, he should have less need for background information to help him get started with a new client.

Records of Counseling Interviews

Perhaps one reason for the popularity of background information among counselors is that it is provided by someone else. Written records of counseling interviews, however, are another story. The only person who can make a professional record of the counseling interview is the counselor himself. Therefore, whether a record is kept depends on whether the counselor is willing to take the time and trouble to do it.

Records of counseling interviews may take two forms: (a) descriptions of individual interviews, and (b) a summary of a series of counseling interviews with a single client. Which form a counselor will choose is a matter of individual preference, within the limits of policy set by his agency; many counselors and agencies prefer a combination of both. Notes of individual interviews obviously require more of the counselor's time, but they provide a more detailed description of the counseling and can reveal changes over time which may not be evident in a summary.

Keeping notes of counseling interviews does take time which might well be spent in other activities. Is it worth the trouble? The answer depends partly on the extent of the notes themselves. Notes which take five minutes to write are certainly more economical than notes which require fifteen or twenty minutes of the counselor's time, and the former may be nearly as useful. But why bother at all?

Perhaps the major value of notes is that they help keep the counselor up-to-date concerning his progress with a given client. Earlier we stressed that to be effective the client and counselor must be working together, moving toward a common goal. The counselor who has a number of clients, seeing each only once a week, may find it difficult to keep track of where things stand with each of them without notes. It is quite helpful to the counselor to be able to look over a set of notes from a week-old interview just prior to seeing the client again, to refresh his memory as to where they left off and where they planned to go the next time. Some counselors may be able to recall this without notes, but trusting entirely to memory is risky. The counselor who begins a counseling interview disoriented with regard to the client is in danger of losing the client's confidence.

Notes from a series of counseling interviews may also be useful in providing the counselor with a picture of the client's growth during counselling. At times, client progress may be difficult to see unless the counselor can view it from the perspective provided by his notes. The counselor may also find that a rereading of notes made of earlier interviews suggests ideas as to where to go with a particular client at a later stage in the counseling.

Notes can also be an important source of information concerning clients who have terminated counseling. A client may return later for further counseling, and a thorough set of notes may help the counselor become re-oriented to him quickly, or perhaps may be useful to a new counselor if his former counselor is no longer available. Similarly, questions are sometimes raised concerning clients who have been seen by an agency at some time in the past, and a set of records concerning that client may be useful to whoever must respond to the questions.

Finally, comprehensive records are often of value for research purposes. Much valuable data concerning counseling have been obtained through the study of counselors' notes. A typical limitation, however, is that counselors differ greatly in their note-taking style, so that it is often difficult for a researcher to extract comparable data from the notes of several different counselors. This might argue for the use of a standard format for notes within an agency, but most counselors would probably resist being tied down by a stereotyped form.

Like background information, notes are an accepted part of counseling, and yet, also like background information, some serious doubts can be raised as to their value. Several of these objections are mirror images of some of the points just made concerning the importance of keeping notes. One has to do with confidentiality. Anything written down may fall into the wrong hands, and the counselor's notes may be utilized for purposes for which they were not originally intended. Counseling agencies are frequently asked questions concerning past clients, and the counselor's notes are a tempting source of information. Counselors are, of course, bound by ethics of confidentiality (which will be discussed further in a later chapter), but they may have little control over how their notes are used once they are made a part of the client's counseling record. For this reason, some counselors believe that it is best to keep no notes at all, or at least to destroy the notes when the client terminates counseling.

The last suggestion seems a little drastic and would interfere seriously with counseling research. A better plan might be to utilize two sets of notes: (a) those of individual interviews, which contain more detailed information as well as the counselor's own observations, which the counselor keeps privately; and (b) a summary of the counseling with a client, to be filed either in the records of the counseling agency or, in a school system, in the student's cumulative folder. This summary would present only a minimum of information, enough to inform the reader that the person has been counseled and perhaps a little as to the nature of the outcome. The exact content of the summary statement would depend partly on to whom the records would be available, but in any case it should be brief and objective.

Most counselors take record-keeping so much for granted that they overlook the possibility that the client may be apprehensive about it. A client who is aware that the counselor keeps notes of the interviews—and the counselor should not try to hide this—may be inhibited as to what he discusses. The counselor should be alert to any such concern on the part of the client and deal with it directly when it arises. In most cases, the client will probably be most apprehensive as to who might see the notes, and the counselor should be as honest as possible in responding.

One way in which the counselor may reassure the client is to let the client read his notes. Whether this is desirable would depend both on the nature of the specific counselor-client relationship as well as the content of the notes themselves. Some counselors write their notes in a highly personal style, including their own reactions and impressions which they might not be ready to communicate to the client. In some instances, however, the counselor's willingness to show the client his notes from past interviews may be an important way of impressing the client with the counselor's honesty and openness. The client who is refused this request may well wonder whether openness and honesty are one-way streets in counseling.

Some counselors, primarily those of a nondirective orientation, oppose note-taking altogether on the grounds that it has too much of a diagnostic flavor. They argue that the counselor's rereading of the notes from a previous session may actually be detrimental to counseling, in that it focuses attention on the client as he was during the last interview rather than on how he is now. They fear that a rereading of notes from the previous interview might cause the counselor to become so intent on following a point raised then that he would thwart the client's desire to work on something new which has arisen in the meantime. The experienced counselor, however, avoids this pitfall by giving the client the lead at the beginning of the interview. It is likely that the client will resume where he left off at the last session, and the counselor who has forgotten what happened then may immediately be lost.

Notes do take time to prepare, and to be worth the time they should be as useful as possible. One principle to follow in preparing notes is that descriptions of specific behaviors are worth much more than are vague impressions, which may be totally inaccurate. The counselor's impressions and hypotheses may be included in his notes, but they should be written in such a way as to make it obvious that they are not facts. Some counselors do this by putting their impressions or inferences in a separate section of their notes, others by interspersing them with the relevant factual material but setting off the impressions by parentheses. In any case, anyone reading the notes should be able to separate the material which is descriptive of the counseling interview itself from the counselor's subjective impressions. This is important even if the counselor himself is the only person who will see the notes, since after a lapse of time the difference between facts and impressions may no longer be clear without some guidelines.

Notes are of greatest value when made shortly after the interview, the sooner the better. If the counselor does not have enough time to write a full set of notes immediately, he should jot down some key words which he can elaborate later. The counselor who trusts entirely to his memory to carry him through several sessions before writing notes will probably find that they have become hopelessly jumbled in his mind.

What specifically should notes include? They should not attempt to be a verbatim transcript of everything that went on in the interview, even if the counselor could hope to remember it all. Instead, the notes should provide a synopsis of the interview, highlighting the major events, with enough specific information to give them form. They should also include the counselor's impressions, hunches, and feelings, but as noted earlier these should be separated from the events themselves. The exact content of a set of notes will depend on the individual counselor; the principal criterion of a good set of notes is that they should be *useful* to the persons who are most likely to use them.

The beginning counselor will probably find it difficult to remember what goes on during the counseling interview and feel lost when he begins to write his notes. This is partly because he is concentrating so hard on what he is going to say that he has little energy left over for remembering what the client said. As he becomes more relaxed in counseling, his memory should improve. The experienced counselor also has the advantage of knowing more about the pattern of a counseling interview. He is able to recall much of what goes on in an interview by applying a structure derived from his experience in counseling. Nevertheless, few counselors are able to recall a counseling interview with perfect accuracy, although no one has yet demonstrated that this is necessary.

At this point someone will want to suggest the use of a tape recorder as a means of maintaining an accurate record of a counseling interview. Although tape recording of interviews may be useful for several purposes, keeping records of counseling interviews is not one of them. For one thing, it would be prohibitively expensive, both in terms of storage space as well as the cost of tapes themselves, to attempt to maintain recordings of all interviews. An equally limiting factor is that tape recordings are an extremely inefficient way to refresh one's memory concerning a previous counseling session. No counselor can afford to spend time equal to that of the interview itself in reviewing the interview, not to mention the boredom that would soon set in.

Tape recording of interviews does have some worthwhile uses however. One is their use in the supervision of beginning counselors. Counselors-in-training find it quite instructive to listen to their counseling performances, as well as having them criticized by experienced counselors. Even the experienced counselor can benefit by listening to himself from time to time, especially with a client with whom he is having trouble. The purpose here, however, is improvement as a counselor, not the keeping of a record of the counseling interview.

Tape recordings are also valuable tools in counseling research. Most studies of the counseling process are based on analysis of transcripts of counseling interviews, and often of recordings themselves.

A recent development in the recording of counseling interviews is the use of closed-circuit television and the taping of televised sessions. Equipment is now available which can televise counseling interviews with a minimum of distraction to the counselor and client, and the behavior which can be observed in this manner is much more varied than can be provided by the typical tape recording, which is limited to verbal behavior. As the cost of television equipment for this purpose comes within range of more agencies, and as counselors become familiar with its use, television is becoming a valuable tool in the training of counselors as well as in counseling research.

Although counselors are concerned with supervision and with the importance of keeping records, they are also concerned that this process not interfere with the counseling itself. It is for this reason that most counselors prefer to write their notes after the completion of an interview rather than during the interview itself. This procedure may sacrifice something in accuracy, but it is less disturbing to the client-counselor rapport.

There are several risks in taking notes during the interview. One is that the writing of notes distracts the counselor from what the client is saying. It is psychologically difficult to attend to more than one stimulus at a time; the counselor cannot listen well and write simultaneously. Since it seems of basic importance to the development of rapport as well as to the progress of the counseling that the counselor pay close attention to the client, anything which might interfere with this should be avoided. A related disadvantage of note-taking during the interview is that it may tend to make the client overly conscious of the importance which the counselor attaches to a particular statement. The client may well ask himself, "Why did he write that down?" or "Why didn't he make a note of that?" What the counselor was writing may actually have had little to do with what the client was saying

at the time, but this is not clear to the client. Despite the added time required, note-taking seems best left until after the interview.

Tape recording must, of course, be done during the counseling itself.
Although there is no consistent evidence to suggest that the recording of an
interview is at all harmful (Tyler, 1961), a recorder may tend to make both
the counselor and client self-conscious. One possibility is to record unob-
trusively and not tell the client that it is being done, but this suggestion must
be rejected on the grounds that nothing should be done behind the client's
back. Not only is this unethical, but it also runs the risk that the client
might eventually learn of the recording, with potentially disastrous effects
on the counseling relationship.

Whether a tape recording interferes with the counseling will depend on
at least two factors: the counselor's own attitude toward it, and how ob-
trusive it is. If the counselor introduces it in a matter-of-fact way, the client
will probably accept it as a natural part of the counseling situation. If, on
the other hand, it obviously makes the counselor nervous, the client will
be justified in being apprehensive about it. It is also desirable to minimize
the physical distraction which may be caused by the mechanical operation
of the tape recorder. Some counseling agencies are designed so that the
recording is made in a central location, with only the microphone in the
office itself. It is still necessary, of course, to call the client's attention to
the recording at the beginning of the interview and to ask his permission
that it be made, but beyond that the counseling should be able to proceed
in an entirely normal manner.

PART III

Contributions of Psychology to Counseling

8

The Role of Tests
in Counseling: Basic Principles

Psychologists have long been interested in the study of individual differences and in the measurement of meaningful dimensions along which individuals vary. The construction of instruments for the measurement of psychological traits has therefore been of major concern to psychologists and has comprised much of their activity, especially in the early decades of this century.

This activity had an important influence on the development of counseling. As psychologists devised instruments to measure various kinds of abilities and personality characteristics, counselors began to use these instruments to help their clients make vocational and educational decisions. Much of the early vocational counseling relied heavily on the assessment of the client's characteristics, by means of psychological tests, and the matching of these characteristics with appropriate jobs, a method still known as the "trait-and-factor" approach. Although modern counselors tend to rely less heavily on tests than did their predecessors, most still believe that an understanding of psychological tests should be an important part of the counselor's repertoire and that they can be quite useful in appropriate situations.

THE TEST AS A COUNSELING TOOL

A test is a sample of behavior which provides information not readily available in other ways. By presenting a comparison of the client's performance with that of persons in some relevant group, a test may help the client move toward his counseling goal. In a counseling context, therefore, a test is a tool, with the strengths and weaknesses inherent in any tool.

The discussion of tests in this chapter and the next is limited to their use *in a counseling context*. Counselors sometimes make use of tests in ways which are not directly related to the needs of the client. This may include the use of test results to help the counselor make an early decision concerning the client, such as whether to refer him elsewhere; to provide information to aid in an evaluation; or to provide comparable research data for a large number of clients. Testing in these instances is initiated by the counselor rather than by the client. The results may, however, become part of counseling at a later time if the client decides that such information is now related to his counseling goal.

Tests may be useful tools in some counseling situations and of little value in others, depending on a number of variables. These include the orientation of the counselor and the client, the available data concerning test results in relation to the client's problem, the availability of the tests themselves, and the time and effort required for taking the tests.

Counselor Orientation

Whether testing will be included in the counseling process depends most strongly on the orientation of the counselor. Some counselors rely heavily on tests, while others avoid them. Some feel that counseling is incomplete without testing and routinely expect their clients to take tests, while others believe that testing focuses attention on superficial elements of the counseling process.

To some extent, these differences have a reasonable basis. Whether a counselor makes frequent use of tests will depend somewhat on his own background and his familiarity with tests. Most counselors whose background is in psychology or education have learned enough about psychological tests to feel comfortable in their use. Others may have had little experience with tests and therefore find them of little value.

Even within education and psychology, however, there are wide differences in counselor attitudes toward the use of tests. These differences are largely based on one's philosophy of counseling. Some counselors feel that the information gained from tests is central to the counseling process by virtue of its objectivity, while others, especially those of a nondirective orientation, reject the rather directive role that they see implied in the administration and interpretation of tests and prefer to focus instead on the dynamics of the individual client.

It is difficult to separate the attitude of a counselor toward tests from the setting in which he works. As we will see shortly, tests are much more useful in certain kinds of counseling situations than in others. Counselors who frequently encounter "test-appropriate" situations are more likely to emphasize the value of tests than are those whose work is in other areas. But which comes first? It is likely that counselors who are inclined to be test-oriented anyway tend to gravitate to counseling settings in which tests are usually appropriate. But even within such a setting there may be marked variation in the extent to which the counselors rely on tests.

It seems unwise for a counselor to take a strong position either for or against the use of tests in counseling. There is ample evidence that test information can be useful in certain situations and of little value in others. As with any counseling tool, the decision to use or not to use it should be based on its potential value for a given client rather than on a blind doctrine.

Client Orientation

The value of tests for a given client will also depend on that client's attitude toward tests. Our society is strongly test-oriented, and the typical client enters counseling having had some previous experience with tests and with either a positive or negative attitude toward their use. Most often, the new client expects tests to be the focus of the counseling, and he may in fact state that he has come "to take some tests." Before tests can be useful, however, he and the counselor must agree as to the purpose for which they will be used.

In the areas of vocational and educational counseling, most clients expect to take tests. If the counselor decides that tests might be useful, it is unlikely that the client will reject the suggestion. But there are exceptions. Some clients are suspicious or afraid of tests, perhaps due to an unpleasant experience with tests earlier in their lives or a fear of failing. Such a client is unlikely to benefit from taking a test, and the counselor's attempt to force testing on him will probably only succeed in driving him away from counseling. A client who has little faith in tests will probably gain little from them, and there seems no point in requiring that testing be a part of the counseling procedure for all clients.

Available Data

Test results are useful in counseling to the extent that there is a known relationship between the data provided by the test and a question which the client is trying to answer. For example, a high school student who is trying to decide whether to go to college or take a job after graduation may find information from an intelligence test useful *to the extent that performance on that test is known to be related to performance in college*. In some areas, relationships of this sort have been well established, but in others such relationships are slight or nonexistent and there would be little purpose in using tests at our present state of knowledge. Thus a counselor working in the area of educational or vocational counseling would probably be able to make frequent use of tests, while a counselor dealing primarily with marital problems would find few tests that would be helpful.

As new tests are developed and old ones are improved, the area in which testing can be useful in counseling expands. Therefore it seems desirable for a beginning counselor to have some knowledge of general principles of the use of tests in counseling, even though he may be planning to work primarily in an area in which tests are of little value at the present time.

Other Considerations

Also to be considered in the decision to include testing as a part of counseling are the availability of specific tests and the time and effort required to take them. Most counselors work on a limited budget and must therefore restrict their supply of tests to those they use frequently. This means that tests may not be given to a specific client, not because a test is not deemed useful, but because the useful test is not available. This situation will probably arise infrequently, if only because most counselors are familiar with only a limited range of tests and tend to rely primarily on these.

The potential value of information to be obtained from a test must be weighed against the time and effort required of the client to take that test. This decision is ultimately the responsibility of the client, although the counselor should be able to give him some idea as to what he might expect to gain from a specific test so that he can decide whether it is worth the effort.

JUDGING THE VALUE OF A TEST

Information obtained from a test is of value to a client to the extent that the meaning of the test has been established, the client's score is accurate, and the form in which the data are presented is relevant to the client. In technical terms, this refers respectively to the test's validity, its reliability, and its norms. These concepts are basic to psychological measurement, and it is assumed that the reader has had some earlier contact with them. If not, basic measurement textbooks, such as those by Anastasi (1968), Brown (1970), and Cronbach (1960), are recommended as sources of background information. The discussion of these concepts presented here will concentrate on their importance in the counseling use of tests and will stress those aspects which are of special concern in counseling.

In determining the potential value of a specific test, the counselor need not rely solely on his own opinion. Any published test should be accompanied by a test manual, which can be expected to provide information concerning the technical aspects of the test as recommended in the 1966 version of the *Standards for Educational and Psychological Tests and Manuals* [1] (French and Michael, 1966), prepared jointly by the American Psychological Association, the American Educational Research Association, and the National Council on Measurement in Education. A manual which follows these guidelines should provide the counselor with a wealth of information about a specific test. Specimen sets of tests are often available from test publishers, so that the counselor can make some preliminary investigation of the potential value of the test for himself. An additional source of information is the *Mental Measurements Yearbook,* published at intervals of a few years by Oscar Buros, which contains critical reviews of tests by experts in educational and psychological measurement. These sources should provide the basic information needed to assess the value of a specific test.

In most cases, the counselor will rely on published tests, but in some instances he may want to make use of one which has not been formally published. This may be a test which has been designed for use in a specific setting, such as a school or an industry, or it may be in the early stages of development. In any case, however, the basic principles of measurement still apply, and the counselor should evaluate unpublished tests by the same criteria that he applies to those produced by test publishers.

Validity

To be useful in counseling, a test score must bear a *meaningful relationship* to the client's problem. If, for example, the client believes that an ability test may help him decide which of several careers to pursue, there must be evidence that differential performance on that test is in fact reflected in differential performance in the jobs under consideration or in training programs required to enter the field.

Perhaps the most frequent single error in the use of tests in counseling is the tendency to overgeneralize from a test score, by assuming that a test provides information which in fact it does not. Clients cannot be blamed for such overgeneralizations, but counselors can. It is the counselor's responsibility to *know* what a given test measures, to know what questions it can

---

[1] Available for $1.00 from the American Psychological Association, 1200 Sixteenth St., N.W., Washington, D.C.

and cannot answer, and to guide the client in interpreting the test scores within these limits.

This means that it is wrong to speak of *the* validity of a test, as though a test is or is not valid in an absolute sense. A test has numerous validities, depending on the nature of the client and the kind of question he is trying to answer. A case in point is the American College Testing Program, a widely-used series of achievement tests which are designed to predict the potential college performance of high school seniors. Data provided by the ACT office (Hoyt and Munday, 1968), presented in Table 8.1, show a wide range of validity coefficients for this test. This means that a high school student who is considering several different colleges will find his ACT score to be more helpful in predicting his performance at some than at others. This situation is typical of any test, but in most cases the specific validity coefficients for various predictions are not stated explicitly and may perhaps

Table 8.1. *Distribution of T-Index R's, 1965–67 Standard Research Service Participants, American College Testing Program.*[a]

Interval Midpoint	Frequency
.71	2
.68	3
.65	12
.62	21
.59	32
.56	37
.53	44
.50	54
.47	59
.44	53
.41	25
.38	38
.35	21
.32	12
.29	8
Below	16
Median	.479
No. of Colleges	437
No. of Students	272,995

[a] Source: Hoyt and Munday, 1968, p. 206. By permission of the American College Testing Program.

not even be known. A test may therefore be quite valid for one purpose and invalid for another, even though the two may logically not be very different.

The most recent version of the *Standards for Educational and Psychological Tests and Manuals* (French and Michael, 1966) deals at length with the concept of validity and suggests that there are basically three kinds: content, criterion-related,[2] and construct.

Content validity refers to the extent to which a test is representative of the universe of behaviors which are of concern. Content validity is of greatest importance in achievement tests, which are used to determine a client's degree of knowledge in a given area. A client who has been out of school for awhile and who is considering entering college might want to have some idea of his current level of knowledge in a certain academic area. An achievement test would be the most appropriate way to determine this, provided that the content of the test were relevant to the kind of question that was being asked. (For example, an English test which stressed grammar might be of little value to the client who needed to determine his level of knowledge in English literature.)

Construct validity is the most difficult to define and is probably of least importance in counseling. In construct validity, the author of the test begins with a theoretical concept in mind and attempts to devise a test which will measure this concept. A test of "ego-strength" would be an example. Construct validity is important for tests used for research purposes and in theory construction, but it can be dangerous as the sole basis for test validity in counseling. Even if the test is a valid measure of the construct, which is difficult to determine, the relevance of the construct to the counseling problem may be obscure. There is a great risk that both the client and counselor will tend to assume relationships between the construct and the problem at hand for which there is little evidence. In the absence of more definite evidence, the counselor and client may be forced to rely on construct validity, but they should be very much aware of the assumptions on which it is based and the limitations which it imposes.

For most counseling purposes, *criterion-related validity* is of greatest importance. Clients use tests to help gain a clearer picture of themselves in relation to some future status: performance in college, satisfaction on a job, happiness in marriage, and many others. Therefore a test will prove useful to the extent that the relationship between one's present performance and the desired outcome is known. The basic question is: how well does performance on this test predict the outcome in which the client is interested?

---

[2] Criterion-related validity is a combination of two kinds of validity—concurrent and predictive—that were formerly presented separately.

The most valid test is therefore the one which will predict most accurately *for a given client in a given situation.*

Since the validity of a test may vary considerably from one client and situation to another, it is the counselor's responsibility to know as much as possible about all validities of the tests that he would consider using. This may at first glance seem to be an impossible job, but the counselor's task is reduced in scope by several factors.

One is that in most counseling settings the range of clients and their problems is restricted. Therefore the counselor should concentrate on becoming familiar with the validities of various tests in relation to the kinds of questions his clients are likely to raise. The counselor cannot anticipate all possible questions, and at times he may be unsure as to how valid a test will be for a certain purpose, but most of the time he should be able to suggest tests for a client with a reasonable degree of confidence in their validity in that situation.

A second limitation is that the number of potentially good tests is not large. A glance at the *Mental Measurements Yearbooks* can be frightening to the beginning counselor, since they include an overwhelming number of tests. But a reading of the reviews shows clearly that only a minority of these tests have been studied sufficiently to be of value in counseling. It is not surprising, therefore, to find that most counselors tend to rely on a relatively small number of tests which they believe are generally most valid for the needs of their clients.

Because of the time required to accumulate validity data concerning a test, some authorities suggest that old tests are the best. This advice may be true up to a point but it should not be taken too literally. Test construction is becoming more sophisticated, and counselors should be alert to the development of new tests which will be potentially more useful to their clients than those currently popular. Validity data can be accumulated only if a test is used, and to rely exclusively on old tests would make it quite difficult for a new test to gain a foothold.

Old tests may also become less valid with time, as the criterion groups on which the validities were originally based are no longer representative. A certain college, for example, may have up-graded its entrance requirements, so that the students with whom the client would be competing are considerably more capable than those with whom the test validities were originally determined. For this reason, the *Standards for Educational and Psychological Tests and Manuals* (French and Michael, 1966) recommends that a test which has not been revised for fifteen years should be withdrawn from the market. Revision is, of course, primarily the responsibility of the test publisher, but publishers would be more motivated to revise their tests if counselors refused to use those which have become senile.

Reliability

To be useful in counseling, a client's test score must be accurate and reasonably stable. Both of these characteristics are aspects of reliability, but evidence of one does not guarantee the other.

If a test is *accurate,* this means that the score closely represents the person's true level of performance at the time he took it. It is unlikely that a test will be perfectly accurate, due to random fluctuations in the individual and in the test itself, but unless the test measures with a reasonable degree of accuracy the results will be meaningless. A common example of an inaccurate instrument is an elastic tape measure, which produces different results each time it is used to measure the same thing. The accuracy of a test is usually determined by comparing performance of a large number of persons on comparable parts of the tests, such as the odd- and even-numbered items.

Stability of performance is another aspect of reliability, and a more complicated one. If predictions are to be made from a client's test score, it must be assumed that the test measures a characteristic which is reasonably stable over time. This is obviously more true of some characteristics than of others. Abilities, for example, are unlikely to change drastically, while some interests may appear and others disappear with the passage of time. In a sense, therefore, unreliability over time may be caused by the characteristic being measured as well as by the test. It is the counselor's responsibility to know something about the consistency of various characteristics and to know which tests are capable of measuring the consistent elements. Reliability in the form of consistency is usually measured by retesting the same group with the same test at two different times.

In addition to variation in the characteristic being measured, as well as inaccuracies in the test itself, there are other factors which may lower the reliability of tests used in counseling. One is the conditions under which the test is given. Administration by a poorly trained person, or in conditions not conducive to optimum performance, can lower the reliability of a test in a given instance. Directions should be carefully explained, timing should be accurate, and distractions should be minimized if the client's score is to represent a reasonably true picture of the characteristic in question.

The reliability of a test also depends on the client's attitude toward it. Most tests assume that the person will try to do his best or present himself as honestly as possible, whichever is required, but it is evident that in many cases this does not happen. Much has been made of the problem of *faking* of psychological tests, and it is generally accepted that all interest and personality measures can be faked, some more easily than others. In that case, how can the counselor be sure that a test result does not represent a client's cleverness in faking rather than a true picture of himself?

The answer, of course, is that this cannot be known with certainty. With some tests it is possible to spot evidence which suggests faking, but the best safeguard in counseling is to introduce the test in such a way as to minimize the client's desire to fake it. Presumably the client should recognize that it is to his advantage to represent himself as accurately as possible on the tests, since the information is to be used by him to deal with the problem which brought him to counseling. In this respect the counselor has a great advantage over persons who must make use of the results of tests taken against the will of the subject, such as for personnel selection or in school testing programs. One should be suspicious of test results obtained under forced circumstances and should avoid using them for counseling purposes.

A more difficult type of faking to handle is that in which the client may have faked his responses without deliberately meaning to. An example might be a college student who has committed himself to becoming a doctor but who is having difficulty with pre-med courses. Although his true interests may not be in medicine, he may feel compelled to "fake" medical interests for fear of the potential damage to his self-concept otherwise. In this case, the client himself may suspect that he was not being entirely honest, yet he was not deliberately trying to fake, either.

This problem is difficult to resolve, partly because no one can be sure what a "true" interest is. Interests are the product of a variety of forces, and it is risky to attempt to tell a person that, by claiming to have certain interests, "he's only fooling himself." A better approach would be to help the client who is unsure of the reliability of his scores on an interest inventory to think carefully about himself and his interests, rather than either accepting or rejecting the test results out of hand. As we shall see later in our consideration of the test interpretation process, a test is of much greater value when it stimulates self-exploration than when it ends it.

Since no test is perfectly reliable, the client's exact score is not very important. What is important is the range of scores it represents. The reliability of the test determines the breadth of this range, and the narrower the range the more specific the interpretation can be. The major difficulty with tests of low reliability is that the information they provide must be considered highly tentative, but in some areas such information may be the best that can be obtained and therefore better than nothing.

Norms

An individual's score on a test means little in isolation. It takes on meaning when compared with the scores of a relevant group, usually called "norms." In counseling, this group should approximate as closely as possible the present or future status of the client in terms of the questions he is asking about himself.

Since both validity and norms are concerned with the meaning of the test score to the client, it is not surprising that these concepts are easily confused. Both are necessary in a test, but the establishment of one does not guarantee the other. For example, a test of "academic aptitude" may provide norms based on entering college freshmen, against which a high school student's score can be compared. From this comparison, the student and the counselor could determine that he performed, perhaps, at an above-average level on the test as compared with the norm group. They therefore know something about his score, but they do not yet know whether this test is in fact related to college performance. Evidence is needed to show that persons who perform differently on this test do in fact also perform differently in college. If this can be established, then the normative data become more meaningful.

This suggests that, to be useful in counseling, norms should meet two criteria: (a) they should present a distribution of scores based on a group relevant to the person who is taking the test, and (b) they should be based on evidence which shows a relationship between that group's performance on the test and their performance on some external criterion. Perhaps the most serious violators of these requirements are the personality inventories, which often provide normative data on a wide variety of groups, but with little or no indication as to the relationships between scores on the inventory and performance in real-life situations.

It is quite important that the counselor know the norm group with which the client is being compared, lest conclusions be reached which are inappropriate. For example, the oldest norm group presented in the manual of the *Differential Aptitudes Tests* is twelfth-grade students. A counselor who attempts to use the DAT with college freshmen will find that his clients will probably score spuriously high on several of the scales, since they are a select group. Unless the client recognizes that the group to which he is being compared is high school students rather than college students, he may be tempted to seize on a high score as indicative of probable success in that area in college, not realizing that he will be competing with many others who have scored at the same level or better.

The more closely the norm group approximates the client's own status, the more meaningful will be the interpretation. A high school senior trying to choose a college will gain something from an academic aptitude test which compares him with college freshmen around the country, but he will learn more from comparisons with students at the specific schools which he is considering attending. It is the counselor's responsibility to seek out normative data likely to be relevant for his clients; if none are available he should collect them himself. In counseling, *local norms* are often quite useful in providing data specific to a particular setting that cannot be obtained from published test norms, which must be based on a broad sample and would be legitimately criticized if they were limited to a single setting.

Published normative information is sometimes made more specific by organizing it into broad groups. The most common groupings are by age, grade, and sex. Such groupings are of value to the extent that there are consistent differences between one group and another so that a client can make more accurate predictions on the basis of the grouping.

This criterion is met better by age and grade norms than by sex norms. The performance requirements of being a certain age or in a certain grade are distinct, at least within the limitations of school-related areas. This is not true, however, for sex differences. Although it is evident that men and women tend to gravitate toward different occupations, the distinction is by no means complete, and in some fields the sex ratio is nearly even. In academic situations the differences are even less noticeable; there are few curricula in which one sex or the other strongly predominates or in which an individual would be at a definite disadvantage by virtue of being male or female. This means that the criterion groups to which the test is designed to predict are themselves composed of both males and females. Presenting normative data in terms of one sex or the other therefore lowers the validity of the prediction.[3]

Suppose, for example, that a high school girl obtains a high "mechanical" score on an interest inventory, according to the norms for females. How is she to use this information in making a decision about her future? The most that can be said is that she is an atypical girl; whether she will get along well in a mechanical field is another question. Since most girls do not enter mechanical fields, the fact that her mechanical interests are higher than those of most girls is not very relevant. More important is how her interests compare with those of boys, many of whom do enter mechanical fields. This necessitates a comparison with boys' norms, which in this case is probably more meaningful than a comparison with girls' norms, but even then the comparison is not as accurate as would be desired. It seems unnecessary in this case, and potentially misleading, to provide separate sex norms in the first place.

The two major disadvantages of separate sex norms are that (a) they provide information which is potentially misleading, and (b) they tend to imply that men and women ought to lead separate lives. Perhaps one of the barriers standing in the way of true equality of opportunity for women in our society is our continued tendency to think of men and women as completely different kinds of persons.

According to the *Standards for Educational and Psychological Tests and Manuals* (French and Michael, 1966), there are two acceptable ways in which normative data may be presented: by percentiles and by standard scores. *Percentiles* are the most familiar and easiest for clients to understand,

[3] For a more thorough discussion of this point, see Bauernfeind (1956).

but they are also more likely to be misinterpreted. A percentile score indicates the percentage of persons in the norm group who obtained a score
below that particular raw score. Thus a percentile score of fifty would mean
that half of the norm group fell below that score (and half were above it);
a percentile score above ninety would put the person in the upper ten
percent, and so on.

The major limitation of percentiles is that equal percentile distances do
not represent equal raw-score distances. This occurs because most psychological characteristics fall into a normal distribution, with a large proportion
of the population near the center and fewer persons at each point as the
distance from the center increases (see Figure 8.1). Since percentiles are
based on the proportion of people lying between any two given scores, it
is evident that equidistant percentiles will represent a much smaller range
of raw scores near the center of the distribution than will the same percentile distance toward the extremes. Thus, in Figure 8.1, the percentile
distance between the 45th and 55th percentiles covers a much smaller range
of raw scores than does the same distance of ten points between the 85th
and 95th percentiles.

An important result of this inequality of percentile distances at different
places on the distribution is that the reliability of the difference between
two percentile scores will be much greater at the extremes of the distribution than near the middle. For this reason, it is advisable to interpret exact
percentiles only near the extremes, and to describe a score anywhere near

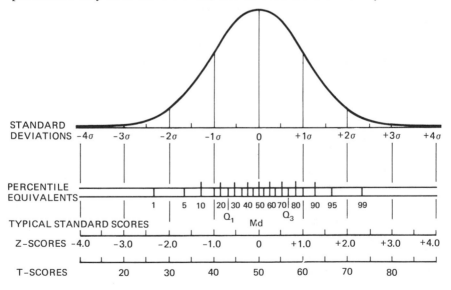

Figure 8.1 *Distribution of percentiles and standard scores. Source: Seashore, 1955, p. 8.*

the center of the distribution as "average." The latter will usually be more relevant to the client's questions, anyway. Exactly where interpretive lines can be drawn will depend on both the reliability of the test itself and the spread of scores within the distribution. The counselor must understand the nature of percentiles thoroughly so as to guide the client in interpreting a percentile score properly. Visual aids, such as a normal percentile chart, may help make this clear to the client.

The *standard score,* based on standard deviation units rather than on units of people, avoids most of the statistical pitfalls inherent in percentiles, since equidistant standard score units do correspond to equidistant raw score units (see Figure 8.1). Standard scores are especially useful when comparisons are to be made of the client's performance on several different tests. If percentiles are used for such comparisons, they must be shown on a scale which adjusts for the unequal intervals, and even this may be misleading if different norm groups with different distributions are included. Standard scores, being based on an equal-interval scale, are preferable.

The major drawback to the use of standard scores in test interpretation Is that the concept is difficult for most clients to grasp. For those clients who are judged capable of understanding them, the presentation of test results in terms of standard scores is desirable; but for others, presentation in percentiles, despite their limitations, is probably best.

TYPES OF TESTS USEFUL IN COUNSELING

Dimensions for Describing Tests

The wide variety of psychological tests which may be used in counseling requires some form of organization for purposes of discussion. They are grouped here according to several dimensions which seem relevant to their use for counseling purposes.

Group versus Individual. Most tests used in counseling are group tests, meaning that they are designed to be given to a group of persons at the same time. Usually they are pencil-and-paper tests, although there are a few performance measures that can be given to several persons at once. An advantage of group tests is that they do not require a high degree of training to administer, although some training is necessary. Often when group tests are used for counseling purposes they are administered to clients individually, as the need arises.

Maximum versus Typical Performance. The purpose of a test of ability or achievement is to determine how well the person can perform in that area. It is assumed that he is trying to do the best he can when he takes the test; therefore such a test is one of *maximum* performance. Interest and personality measures, by contrast, are designed to present a *typical* picture of the individual. The individual's purpose in taking the latter tests should be to present himself as accurately as possible, not to try to present the best possible picture.

This distinction is quite important for the counseling use of tests, since many clients tend to approach all test situations with a "maximum performance" set. It is important that the client understand that he is to respond to an interest or personality inventory in terms of how he really feels rather than how he thinks he "ought" to feel.

Objective versus Subjective.   Counselors generally prefer to rely on tests in which the administration and scoring are objective, meaning that no subjective judgment is required in determining how the test should be given and how a specific response should be scored. The most commonly used subjective tests are the projective personality inventories. These are popular among clinical psychologists for diagnostic purposes, but they have proved to be of little value in counseling.

The major drawback of nonobjective measures is that direct relationships with external criteria are difficult to establish. We have repeatedly emphasized that a test is of value in counseling to the extent that its relationship to some external criterion is known. Such relationships are not evident with subjective tests, primarily because the scores obtained from them are not reliable enough to permit validation. Counselors are well advised to stick to objective tests for which validity evidence has been established.

Speed versus Power.   Some tests set time limits, while others allow the testee as much time as he needs to complete them. Speed tests are common among ability tests, although in some cases the time limit is quite generous and all but the slowest persons will finish. Other ability tests, however, have narrow time limits, and speed of response then becomes a major factor in the individual's score.

Tests with restrictive time limits are often criticized on the grounds that they produce invalid results for persons who for one reason or another work slowly at a task. Whether they are in fact invalid depends on the nature of the criterion they are designed to predict. If speed is an important variable in performance on the criterion, then a speed test will probably predict it better than will a power test. For example, most academic aptitude tests have generous time limits and therefore are primarily power tests. It is evident, when performance on these tests is compared with performance on comparable untimed tests, that some people are penalized on the timed tests due to slow working habits. The criterion, however—in this case, academic performance—also puts some emphasis on speed. The slow student will have difficulty keeping up, both in his schoolwork and on classroom tests, and his grades are therefore likely to suffer. Such a student might benefit by carrying a reduced load, in which case the criterion is altered and the speed factor becomes less important.

Time limits have also been found to be unduly restrictive for older persons, who do relatively better on power tests. Here again, speed may also play a part in performance on the criterion to be predicted, but if it is known that an individual's performance is likely to be slow, the criterion situation may be adjusted accordingly.

If a speed test is to be considered for use in counseling, the counselor should know to what extent speed of performance is important in the criterion to be predicted, and also whether the criterion can be adjusted if it can be established that slow response is causing a significant underestimation of the person's true ability.

Normative versus Ipsative. Most tests are designed to be *normative,* meaning that a single score or a series of scores are reported by comparing them with the performance of some norm group. In an *ipsative* test, on the other hand, the testee's status in one area is compared with his status in another, so that he is being compared with himself rather than with a norm group. This format is found in certain interest and personality inventories, which present scores in various interest areas or personality traits obtained by asking the testee to make choices among them. Thus a high score on one scale and a low score on another means that the testee selected items scored on the first scale more frequently than items scored on the second, under circumstances in which he had to choose one or the other.

The value of an ipsative type of inventory is that it provides a picture of the relationship among various interests or personality traits *within the same individual.* Thus the person who says, "I like everything," and who might well respond favorably to everything on a list of interests, is forced to discriminate degrees of attraction among various interests. A pattern of interests emerges where one was not previously evident.

The disadvantage of the ipsative approach is that the meaning of high and low scores is difficult to interpret. One person may have a number of strong interests, for example, but on an ipsative inventory those which are not quite so strong may appear low. Another person, who may have generally weak interests, may seem to have several strong ones on the profile because these happen to be less weak than the others. In other words, the results of an ipsative instrument are easily misinterpreted, since the nature of the test tends to exaggerate a pattern and does not indicate the overall degree of strength or weakness.

Some ipsative tests attempt to overcome this problem by including normative data. Thus the profile not only shows the relative pattern of scores within the individual, but it also compares the strength of his scores in each area with a norm group. This helps to clarify the meaning of the scores, but it does not solve the problem, since certain areas may still be unrealistically high or low.

It is important that the counselor understand the nature of ipsative inventories and be prepared to help the client interpret the meaning of scores obtained on them.

Areas of Measurement

Tests used in counseling can be conveniently grouped into four areas: ability, achievement, interests, and personality characteristics. This leaves a few tests not covered, but most would be included in one of these categories. Because of the large number, it is impractical to discuss specific tests in each of these areas. It is assumed that the reader has some background knowledge of specific tests and has access to sources such as the *Mental Measurements Yearbooks, Tests in Print,* and *Appraising Vocational Fitness* (Super and Crites, 1962). Our purpose here is to describe how tests in these areas may be useful in counseling and to point out some of the potential pitfalls in their use.

Ability or Aptitude Tests

Role of Ability in Counseling.   Knowledge of one's abilities should play an important role in the formulation of his life plans. The person who is considering various forms of education or training, or who is trying to decide among several career fields, should be concerned with making a choice which is reasonably consistent with his abilities. Many unwise choices have been made because abilities were not carefully considered, and only through failure and frustration did the individual learn that his choice was inappropriate for him.

The best indication of a person's ability is his experience up to the present. This in fact is the meaning of *ability* in its narrow sense: that which an individual can do at the present time. The client who is unsure of his abilities should therefore be encouraged first to examine his performance in various areas as indications of strengths and weaknesses which can then be related to his current question.

Often, however, such an exploration will not clarify the situation much, which may be why the person has sought counseling. Perhaps he feels that his past performance may not be predictive of his future performance in similar areas (for example, the college freshman to whom grades came easily in high school but who is now confronted with more difficult competion); or perhaps he has had no previous experience which is related to his current question (for example, the young man who is considering taking a sales job but who has had no previous sales experience). In these cases, the questions being asked can be stated more specifically: what are the odds that the client will be able to learn the skills required for success in the field under consideration? Thus, in the examples presented above, the clients are probably asking, "Can I perform well in college?" or "Can I learn to become a successful salesman?" In psychological terminology, we are now talking about aptitude (future performance) rather than ability; the distinction has some important psychological implications, but in the typical counseling situation it is probably not worth worrying about.[4]

Ability is usually considered to have a cognitive basis, meaning that the individual *could* profit to a certain extent from a learning experience in that area, assuming a sufficient level of motivation. It is therefore quite important to establish whether the client is asking, *"Can I be successful in this area?"* or *"Will I be successful?"* The first question focuses primarily on his aptitude for learning in that area, while the second incorporates motivation and interest. This distinction eludes many clients, just as it eludes many parents, teachers, and even counselors who urge a student in a certain direction on the basis of his "test scores" or performance in school, with little consideration as to whether he is really interested in that field.

It is important, therefore, to help the client determine whether he truly needs to know more about his abilities, or whether consideration of interests and personality characteristics may be more relevant. Some clients, upon reflection, decide that they know a good bit already about their abilities as such, and that their uncertainties are due primarily to confusion about noncognitive aspects of themselves.

The predictive value of an ability measure also depends on the criterion of outcome. Earlier, in the discussion of test validity, it was noted that a single "academic ability" test may predict performance at one college quite well but be unhelpful in predicting performance at another school. This means that a question such as, "Will I be able to graduate from college?" will be rather difficult to answer on the basis of an ability test since the results may suggest a high probability of success at College A but not at College B. Therefore a more meaningful question is, "What are my chances of graduating from College A?" If evidence is available which relates performance on an ability test to performance at College A, the question may be answered with a fairly high degree of certainty.

The same problem exists for questions of vocational success. As

---

[4] For more detailed discussions of the nuances in differences among terms such as ability, aptitude, capacity, talent, etc., see Seashore (1956), English and English (1958, pp. 1–2), and Super and Crites (1962, pp. 70–73).

Ghiselli (1966) has noted, criteria of occupational success vary greatly, and ability tests have generally not proven to be highly predictive of success in a given occupation. Part of the trouble, Ghiselli suggests, is a failure to differentiate between training and proficiency criteria. The former criteria— the likelihood of reaching a minimal level of performance as a result of training—are predicted more accurately than are measures of on-the-job performance, in which a variety of factors seem to conspire to determine an individual's success.

Not only do outcome criteria vary objectively, but clients also vary in their implicit definitions of "success." One prospective college freshman may be satisfied to learn that at College A he has a reasonably good chance of making a "C" average and graduating. Another student may reject this as an acceptable outcome, and prefer a college in which his chances of making the Dean's List are high. The same holds true for on-the-job performance criteria: one person may be satisfied with a field in which his income will not be great, while another wants to find something in which he can earn a lot of money.

It should be evident by now that the relationship between a score on an ability test and a criterion of outcome in some field is quite complex and will vary from one client to another. The counselor's job is not only to help the client locate a test which will provide a measure of his ability relevant to the questions he is asking, but first to encourage him to clarify the question being asked and then to help him integrate the results into his thinking about himself as a person.

Value of Ability Tests. What can we conclude, then, about the value of ability measurement in counseling? Although ability tests can provide worthwhile information for a client, the results are often not as clearcut and useful as clients would like to believe. The typical client tends to attribute an almost magical quality to tests of ability, assuming that they can reveal to him the one area in which he has a high probability of success. Unfortunately, as we have seen, the abilities required to perform well in a given area are not that specific. For most jobs for which some degree of formal education or training is required, general intelligence is the most important consideration. In a few areas, special abilities become important—for example, mechanical comprehension or perceptual speed and accuracy—but even here there are few jobs which correspond closely to the abilities measured by tests of special abilities. For the most part, ability tests are used in counseling to help resolve the client's doubts as to whether he will profit from a certain kind of learning experience: college, trade school, on-the-job training, or others. Since general intelligence tests are primarily measures of learning ability, they are more likely to be helpful than are tests of more limited scope, although tests designed to predict learning ability in a restricted setting, such as tests of academic aptitude, are often more useful for predictions of performance in that setting.

Lest this discussion seem overly pessimistic, we should point out that ability measures can do two things fairly well.

They can suggest occupational areas for consideration, although they cannot predict success in specific occupations within these areas. On the basis of an extensive survey of the predictive power of aptitude tests for personnel selection purposes, Ghiselli (1966) has concluded that there are three ability dimensions—intellectual and perceptual, motor, and spatial and mechanical—and that these dimensions form the basis for job clusters.

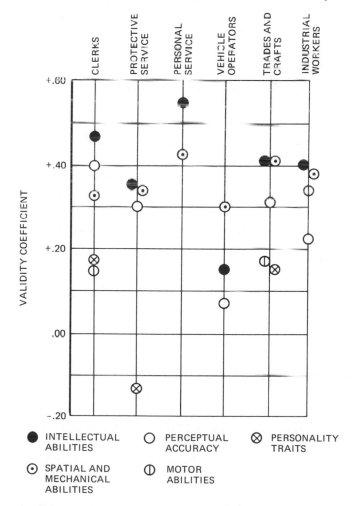

Figure 8.2 *Validity coefficients of tests for training criteria. Source: Ghiselli, 1966, p. 62.*

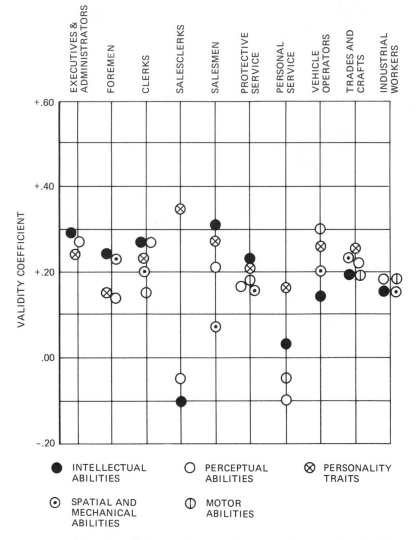

Figure 8.3 *Validity coefficients of tests for proficiency criteria. Source: Ghiselli, 1966, p. 63.*

Figures 8.2 and 8.3 summarize the relationship between various kinds of tests and performance in various kinds of jobs. It is evident from these figures that training criteria are predicted better by ability tests than by personality measures, that the distinction is less clear for proficiency criteria, and that intellectual abilities are generally more predictive than are special abilities. Ability measures can thus be helpful in narrowing the client's range of choices, but they will probably not provide him with a final answer.

Low scores on an ability test are more informative than are high scores. It is reasonable to assume that a minimal level of ability is necessary for a person to be able to learn how to perform a certain skill. If his ability in that area is quite low, his chances of success are therefore poor. The belief that high motivation can compensate for low ability is seldom borne out. Above the minimum level, however, personality characteristics such as interest and motivation become quite important. A person with high intelligence, for example, could probably perform well in almost any field which interested him enough. Therefore, once his ability is shown to be high, it will be more profitable in counseling to concentrate on his interests and personality characteristics as indicators of fields which he might choose to enter.

Achievement Tests

Achievement tests represent a special case of ability tests, aimed specif ically at assessing the testee's present level of knowledge or performance in a given area. Such tests may be useful for a person who is considering entering a certain training program or taking certain courses in school. He may want to know at what level he should begin, or whether he has the background necessary to meet the demands of the new situation.

Some tests may be used as either tests of ability or achievement, depending on whether the testee's major purpose is to assess his present level of performance or to predict performance in a future learning situation. Usually, though, ability tests have a broader range of items, whereas achievement tests are restricted to items from a more limited content area.

Measurement of Interests

Role of Interests in Counseling. As noted earlier, the question of what a client *can* do often turns out to be more accurately a question of what he *wants* to do. It seems indisputable that an individual's feelings of personal satisfaction and well-being throughout his life, as well as the full development and use of his potentials, depend greatly on his being engaged in activities consistent with his interests. It follows, then, that a client concerned with planning his future should be encouraged to examine his interests, both as a means of gaining greater understanding of himself as a person as well as helping him narrow his choices to those consistent with his interests. Small wonder that somewhere along the line in most counseling cases in which plans for the future are discussed, the client's interests are a focus of the discussion.

It seems unnecessary to develop an elaborate definition of "interest" for the present discussion. We can assume, with Strong (1955), that an interest has an emotional element, that it relates to some object or activity —and for counseling purposes the activity aspect is of prime importance— and that it implies some fairly persistent degree of attention on the "interest." An interest, then, is a selective feeling, which causes the individual to seek out and engage in certain activities at the expense of others.

In recent years, much research has been concerned with the origin and development of interests.[5] From this work, some general comments relevant to the role of interests in counseling can be made.

1. Interests are a product of the individual's experiences, which in turn are dependent on his opportunities. Any assessment of a client's interests, especially if he is young, must recognize that his experiences are limited and many potential areas of interest may therefore be unknown to him. It would be foolhardy, therefore, for a client to base his decision on only those interests of which he is certain at present. A better approach is for the client and counselor to attempt to make some generalizations out of the client's likes and dislikes, based on his experiences up to that point, from which they can extrapolate as to the probability of the client liking or disliking certain potential new experiences.

2. Interests are highly related to the individual's personal needs. The reasons why one person develops one sort of interest, and another person the opposite, are unclear, but it seems evident that the personal needs and motives of the individual must play a major role. Thus a consideration of a client's interests is really, in a broad sense, a consideration of his personality. This view of interests recognizes their dynamic quality and may help the client to understand himself better as he examines his interests and how they grew.

By the same token, two persons may share the same interest, but for very different reasons. One individual may, for example, be interested in musical activities because of self-satisfaction derived from performing a beautiful piece of music well; another may enjoy the praise of others for his performance; and still a third may find in music an opportunity for socialization with persons with similar interests. Actually, of course, the motivations of any individual are complex, and a person with musical interests probably combines all three of these motives in some proportion. But this complexity suggests that dealing with interests as surface phenomena may cause the client and counselor to miss their most important implications.

3. Interests are related to role expectations. The assumption of appropriate interests is one important feature of the learning of a suitable role. This is especially evident in the case of sex-role development, in which interests are a central feature of the traditional distinctions. Boys and girls,

[5] See, for example, the reports by Tyler (1960, 1962), Darley and Hagenah (1955), Super and Crites (1962), and Roe and Seligman (1964).

in other words, tend to develop certain sex-appropriate interests simply because they *are* boys or girls. This comes about, not because of any known sex-linked genetic influence, but simply because society exerts certain pressures on children to conform to the traditional sex-role pattern. Very small boys, for example, are frequently interested in playing with dolls, but they are usually strongly discouraged from such activity and the more appropriate "masculine" interests soon take its place.

A related influence is the child's desire to identify with the parent of the same sex, which not only results in the adoption of sex-appropriate interests but also in the development of more specific interests which are characteristic of the parent's vocational or avocational activities. To what extent the child completely adopts the parent's interests will vary depending on many factors, including the closeness of the parent-child relationship. Persons who have had a poor relationship with the parent of the same sex may have greater difficulty in "finding themselves"; their interests may, in other words, develop more slowly.

4. A fairly persistent pattern of interests begins to emerge in middle adolescence, although the rate of crystallization varies considerably from one person to another. Before adolescence, interests tend to be transitory and often conflicting, although the antecedents of adult interests are often evident in retrospect. Eventually, however, patterns begin to form and to persist, so that it becomes possible to make some predictions as to the individual's interests at some time in the future. We shall return to this point in a moment.

5. Perhaps the most surprising finding is that the development of interests is not highly related to abilities. Correlations between interests and abilities are seldom higher than .30 (Strong, 1955) and in some cases are actually negative. Although it is likely that abilities have something to do with the development of certain interests initially, the sustaining of the interest seems to depend much more on its relation to the personal needs of the individual than to its congruence with his abilities. We must bear in mind, too, that despite the continued search for "ability factors," most learning situations depend primarily on general intelligence rather than on a specific ability.

Interests are of special importance in vocational counseling because of the abundant evidence that persons in various jobs and in various academic curricula can be differentiated reasonably well on the basis of interests (see Darley and Hagenah, 1955; Berdie, 1960; Super and Crites, 1962). Therefore a client's interests may be compared with those of persons in various occupations and in various curricula, to determine which kinds of persons he is most like or unlike. This in turn should provide the client with useful information to help him come to a decision concerning his plans for the future.

Stability of Interests.   The prediction of a client's future interests in terms of his present interests is warranted only if it can be assumed that the client's interest pattern is reasonably stable. If interest patterns are unstable and liable to shift unpredictably, they do not provide an adequate basis on which to form a decision concerning the future. If, on the other hand, interest patterns are reasonably consistent, such predictions can be made with some degree of confidence.

The question of stability of interests is central to the role of interests in counseling and has been the subject of a considerable amount of research. The results indicate that, by the age of twenty, most people have established a fairly stable interest pattern (Darley and Hagenah, 1955; Strong, 1955),[6] and most authorities agree that some tentative decisions can be made by high school students on the basis of their interest pattern at that time. The immature client may, of course, not yet have established a sufficiently stable interest pattern to warrant predictions based on his current interests. The counselor should be alert to evidence that this is the case and should call it to the client's attention.

The question of stability and prediction has another facet: if the client is to base his vocational decision on the degree of similarity of his interests to those of persons currently employed in certain occupations, this implies that the characteristics of persons in those fields are not expected to shift much for some time in the future. Is this assumption warranted? What little evidence is available tells us that it is, at least within limits (Campbell, 1966b, 1966c). It seems that the kinds of persons who enter an occupation do not change radically over time, so that a young person may expect that if it seems likely that he would fit into a certain field as he is now, he can predict with a fair degree of confidence that unless he or the occupation changes a great deal, he will fit in when he is older too.

Assessment Methods.   It should be obvious to the reader that all of this is leading up to a discussion of interest measurement, but let us pause first to remind ourselves that there are other, more direct, ways of ascertaining a client's interests. The typical client, for example, can describe his interests fairly well. The chances are good that he has already considered this area as a source of potential help in dealing with his problem, so it will come as no surprise when the counselor suggests that they explore it. If the client seems unsure as to how to begin, a few questions from the counselor (for example, "What do you think of the courses you've had in

---

[6] It should be noted that almost all of the data on which these statements are based have been obtained from men. Little is known as to the stability of interest patterns among women, although it is suspected that, in view of the discontinuity of most women's vocational lives, their interests may be less stable.

school?" or "What do you like to do in your spare time?") should be sufficient to get him started. And many high school and college students can predict their future vocational choices quite well on the basis of their present interests (Holland and Lutz, 1967).

In that case, why bother with interest tests in counseling? With some clients they are unnecessary, and the counselor who automatically pulls out an interest test for every client who has a vocational-choice problem is probably making unnecessary work for himself and some of his clients. Interest measures do come in handy, however, in several instances. Many clients need help in organizing their interests, putting them into a form which they can apply constructively to their problem. An interest inventory can provide this kind of information rather easily, and perhaps suggest relationships among his interests of which the client had not been aware.

An interest inventory can also provide information as to relationships between certain interest patterns and various predictive criteria, such as satisfaction, success, or persistence in certain job areas. These kinds of relationships are much more difficult to determine from a verbal discussion of interests, which would suffer from the lack of quantitative data.

Finally, there is some evidence, though not conclusive, that expressed and measured interests are far from identical. Darley and Hagenah (1955) believe that the discrepancy is large enough in many cases that basing counseling on the client's expressed interests is quite risky. In a situation in which the client's interests will play an important part in his decision or in the resolution of his difficulty, the counselor should probably suggest that an interest inventory might be helpful. Few clients will disagree, and those who do would probably not have allowed it to help them much anyway.

One further point needs to be emphasized concerning the role of interest measurement in counseling: it should be firmly understood, by both the client and the counselor, that, despite its potential value, an interest test simply *reflects* the client's interests; it does not *create* interests for him. The client who says, "I don't know what I'm interested in," may find this uncertainty confirmed by an interest inventory and be little better off than before. Whether he will be greatly disappointed by the failure of the test to discover some interests for him will depend on how the counselor has introduced the role of interest measurement in relation to the client's problem.

Major Approaches to Interest Measurement. Although there are a number of interest inventories on the market, two have so greatly overshadowed the others that they deserve extensive consideration. These two inventories—the Strong Vocational Interest Blank and the Kuder Preference Record—not only represent different approaches in the construction of interest measures, but they have each been the subject of a large amount of research, so that their value is more clearly evident than is true for their competitors.

The most respected interest inventory is the *Strong Vocational Interest Blank* (SVIB), originally published in 1927, revised in 1938, and revised again in 1966.[7] Most authorities would agree with the statement by Super and Crites (1962) that the SVIB is ". . . without question one of the most thoroughly studied and understood psychological instruments in existence [p. 418]." It has been the subject of hundreds of research studies, which provide a wealth of information for the counselor as to relationships between scores and pattterns of scores on the SVIB and various educational and vocational outcomes. The major value of the SVIB, then, is that a great deal is known about the meaning of scores obtained on it, and this information can be quite valuable in counseling.

The Strong Vocational Interest Blank comes in two forms, one for men and one for women. Each form consists of a set of 400 items—lists of activities, occupations, people, and so on—to which the subject is asked to respond in terms of whether he would like or dislike engaging in that activity or occupation. The SVIB has been administered to persons in a wide variety of occupational fields, and their responses compared with those of "men-in-general" or "women-in-general," so that it is possible to determine those items on which a specific occupational group responds differently from men- or women-in-general. The responses of an individual testee, then, can be compared with those of various occupational groups, and the extent to which his responses are similar to those of persons in a certain occupation can be indicated.

There is considerable evidence that performance on the SVIB is related to entrance into and persistence in an occupation (Strong, 1955; Darley and Hagenah, 1955; Berdie, 1960; Campbell, 1966d). It therefore does provide information useful in counseling. Persistence in an occupation implies at least a minimal degree of success or satisfaction in that occupation and, until more adequate criteria of success and satisfaction are devised, persistence is a reasonably good indication that the individual is employed in an occupation which is suitable for him.

The SVIB does have some limitations of which counselors should be aware. The fields it includes are primarily professional and managerial occupations, so that it is of greater value for college students and high school seniors who plan to attend college than for those who will enter the skilled trades. Because of the complicated scoring procedure, by which an in-

[7] The 1938 version, and research based on it, is described in detail in Strong's volume, *The Vocational Interests of Men and Women* (1943); the 1966 revision is described by Campbell (1966a); and the history of its development is described by Campbell (1968).

dividual's responses must be compared with those of a wide variety of criterion groups, it is almost impossible to score by hand. A number of commercial centers around the country will score the blanks by computer for a small fee, but the cost involved and the time required to mail the material back and forth may discourage some counselors from using it. Finally, the validity of the women's form is questionable. As noted earlier, there is some doubt as to whether separate forms of an interest inventory should be used for men and women in the first place. Strong continually insisted that they should, but the supporting evidence is not impressive and some counselors find it more useful to use the men's form with both sexes, or at least with girls who have strong career motivations. In defense of the SVIB, however, it should be said that no interest inventory has solved the problem of how to measure the interests of women in a way which can be meaningfully applied in counseling.

Despite its limitations, the Strong Vocational Interest Blank has two great advantages which make it the single most useful interest measure available: (a) it has been the subject of continuing research, so that a great deal is known about it; [8] and (b) it has been recently revised, so that it is up-to-date in the content of the items, the scoring procedure, and the criterion groups. Research with the SVIB is continuing to be prolific, and its value will undoubtedly continue to grow.

The only serious rival to the pre-eminence of the SVIB is the *Kuder Preference Record—Vocational* (KPR) which is worth considering here not only because of its widespread use but also because it was designed in a manner quite different from the SVIB.

The KPR was originally developed in the 1930s and the version currently in use was published in 1948, so that as compared with the current revision of the SVIB it is less contemporary. During the last decade or two, Kuder has concentrated his efforts on the development of a different kind of interest inventory, which will be described shortly.

The Kuder Preference Record describes an individual's interest patterns by comparing the strength of his interests in a number of relatively "pure" areas. The form currently in use includes ten areas: outdoor, mechanical, scientific, literary, musical, social service, computational, clerical, persuasive, and artistic. There is some evidence that these areas are relatively independent.[9] The format is in obvious contrast with the SVIB, in that relationships between interest patterns based on these areas, and per-

---

[8] A 1964 publication by the University of Minnesota's Center for Interest Measurement Research in honor of E. K. Strong listed 487 research studies using the men's form of the SVIB and 64 studies with the women's form.

[9] It is interesting to note that a factor analysis of the items on the men's form of the Strong Vocational Interest Blank (Cranny, 1967) located a series of factors which correspond closely to the Kuder scales.

formance and satisfaction in vocational areas, must be inferred; although Kuder provides a list of suggested occupations related to various interest combinations, the evidence for these relationships is tenuous.

The other distinguishing feature of the Kuder Preference Record is the forced-choice response mode. The testee is presented with a group of three activities, from which he must select the one he would like most to perform and the one he would like least. In some groups, it is probable that he would like to do all three, while in others he might not like any of them, but in all cases he must select one as most preferred and one as least preferred. This procedure is in contrast to that of the SVIB, in which the subject makes an independent response to each item.

The KPR has been used extensively at the high school level, less so with college students. There are several reasons for its popularity, some of which are legitimate and some not. One of its major advantages is that it is easily comprehended by most high school students. The items are simpler than those of the SVIB and more appropriate for younger persons. In addition, the concept of interest areas may be more appropriate in some respects for high school students than is Strong's approach of dealing with specific occupations. For the uncommitted high school student, a discussion of interest areas may be less threatening than a discussion of specific jobs.

One of the major attractions of the KPR is also a major drawback: it is easily administered and scored, so that it can be given to large groups of students and the profiles can be interpreted to the group as a whole. Unfortunately, despite (or perhaps because of) its apparent simplicity, the results are easily misinterpreted. No interest measure is of much value in a counseling sense if it is not administered and interpreted within the context of a counseling relationship. The simplicity of the KPR has tempted many high school counselors to use it in large groups, with little or no attempt to help the students relate the results to their personal needs. The result has often been confusion and annoyance on the part of the student, who felt his time was wasted and he got nothing useful from the experience. Most college counselors can attest to the fact that any previous "counseling" experience which their clients have had in high school has usually involved the administration of the KPR, and that the client's reaction was often negative. This is not an indictment of the KPR itself, but rather of its misuse by high school counselors.

Even when used individually, however, the KPR presents some difficulties in interpretation. The interpretation of the SVIB is relatively straightforward, the major limitation being to remind the client that the scores indicate degree of similarity to persons in an occupation rather than strength of interest in that occupation. The interpretation of the KPR, however, is more complicated because of its ipsative nature: the client has been forced to make discriminations among interest triads which may not represent a true picture of his own interests. As Bauernfeind (1962) has suggested, ipsative measures are often confusing when used in counseling because they tell nothing of an individual's actual degree of interest in a single area. In essence, an ipsative inventory indicates *relative* rather than *absolute* strengths of interest. Thus a person who is not interested in much of anything may demonstrate a high interest in, say, scientific activities because that interest is a little less low than the others, whereas a person who is interested in many areas may show a low scientific interest when actually his scientific interest is reasonably high.

This problem applies to any ipsative instrument, and it is true of the KPR because it happens to be ipsative. A related difficulty, more specific to the KPR, is the fact that the different interest areas on the KPR include varying numbers of items, which in turn means that the pairings among items for forced-choice purposes is unequal (Katz, 1962).

The upshot is that, despite its deceptively simple nature, the meaning of a KPR score or pattern of scores is difficult to interpret. This is not to say that the KPR should not be used in counseling. At the high school level, it may continue for some time to be the best inventory available. But counselors should recognize that its ipsative nature makes the interpretation of an individual's score or pattern debatable, while the relationships between various interest patterns and vocational outcomes have not yet been clearly established.

The SVIB and KPR are not, of course, the only interest inventories available, but they are by far the most widely used. Of the others, two newer inventories are worthy of consideration inasmuch as they represent potentially useful extensions of the SVIB and KPR.

The *Minnesota Vocational Interest Inventory* (MVII) (Clark, 1961; Clark and Campbell, 1965) was developed to meet the need for a Strong-type measure which included skilled trades occupations. In format much like the SVIB, the MVII compares the individual's scores with those of men in various skilled trades, such as bakers, carpenters, electricians, painters, and plumbers. Although it has not yet been the subject of extensive research, it shows promise of filling a major gap.

In recent years, Kuder has shifted his approach to interest measurement to one more closely resembling that of Strong. His most recent instrument, the *Occupational Interest Survey* (OIS) (Kuder, 1966), while still utilizing the familiar Kuder-style forced-choice triads, presents the individual's scores in terms of his degree of similarity to the responses of persons in various occupations. Although the method by which Kuder calculates degree of similarity is not the same as that of Strong, the manner in which the results are presented is more like Strong's than is the Preference Record.

Like the SVIB, the OIS provides comparisons primarily with persons in professional occupations. A major difference from the SVIB is that each occupational scale can be scored separately by hand, making it relatively easier to use if only a few comparisons are desired. The OIS is also open-ended, meaning that new occupational scales may be added as they become available. Its major disadvantage, relative to the SVIB, is that it does not yet have a large body of data available to aid in interpretation.

The Question of "Faking." Before leaving the topic of interest measurement, we should comment on a question which often worries counselors: can interest inventories be faked? The answer, very simply, is "Yes." The evidence is overwhelming that a reasonably intelligent person can deliberately distort his responses to an interest inventory to make it come out nearly any way he chooses (Darley and Hagenah, 1955). Most items on an interest inventory are obviously tapping one sort of interest rather than another; there is little attempt made in designing an interest inventory to disguise the purpose of an item, if indeed this were possible. Presumably a Kuder-style inventory could be faked more easily than the SVIB, since it would be rather difficult in some cases to guess the relationship between a certain response and a score on a specific occupational scale, but the evidence is clear that the SVIB can be faked too (Darley and Hagenah, 1955), so this seems not to be a significant difference.

For counseling purposes, a more important question is the extent to which it is likely that a client *will* fake his responses on an interest inventory. The answer probably depends a great deal on the client's attitude toward the test. If it has been introduced in such a way that he believes the results will be of value to him, he should then recognize that it is to his benefit to be as honest as possible in his responses. This is not to say that a client may not fake his responses despite the counselor's best efforts to prevent this, although it is often difficult to determine how much faking is deliberate and how much is unconscious. In the discussion of the results, the counselor should encourage the client to consider the truthfulness of his responses. But if the counselor has made a genuine effort to help the client approach the testing with the right attitude, he need not worry much about the likelihood that the client's responses will be faked.

Measurement of Personality Characteristics

Role of Personality Measures in Counseling. The role of personality measurement in counseling is more elusive than the areas previously discussed. Some counselors rely heavily on personality measures, while others reject them as being of little value.

Much of this confusion comes from differences in counselors' views as to the role of personality measures in counseling. In some roles they are of greater value than others, and the purpose should be carefully considered before a personality measure is introduced. There are three primary roles, any or all of which might be applicable in a given counseling situation:

1. *To help the client make a prediction about himself in some future situation.* This is the purpose for which ability and interest measures are most successful: they provide information which can help the client to judge the extent to which he will be able to profit from a certain learning experience or will gain satisfaction from a certain kind of activity. Although we have noted that the relationship between test scores and future performance is far from perfect, the information provided by a valid ability or interest test adds something of value to the client's knowledge about himself.

Unfortunately, personality measures do not provide information of this sort for counseling purposes. Most personality measures are not empirically validated; they rely instead on "construct validity," which is useful in some respects, but not for prediction (Vernon, 1964). For this reason, there is little evidence that personality measures can predict performance in school or on a job with any significant degree of accuracy (Super and Crites, 1962; Guion and Gottier, 1965), which means that for predictive purposes the use of a personality measure adds little or nothing to information obtainable by ability and interest tests. In specific settings, personality measures may add something useful to other information, but for the kinds of questions concerning the future with which most clients are dealing, personality scores are more likely to be misleading than helpful.

Does this mean that personality measures are of no value in counseling? The answer is "No," provided that they are used in ways consistent with what is known about them. Two other purposes, to be discussed below, represent more legitimate uses of personality measures in counseling.

2. *To help the counselor make decisions about the client.* As noted in an earlier discussion of diagnostic activity in counseling, a counselor may sometimes be called upon to answer questions about a client. In some cases the counselor may be asked by someone else for an evaluation, while in others the counselor may need to answer questions such as whether he should attempt to work with a certain client and, if so, what approach would be most helpful. In situations such as these, personality measures may supply useful diagnostic information, especially when the decision must be made before the counselor can get to know the client well. While personality measures used for this purpose have substantial limitations, they nevertheless may provide a useful supplement to information which the counselor can collect in other ways.

Perhaps even more than in the case of ability and interest measures, it is important that personality data used for assesment purposes be current. Personality characteristics are less stable than are interests and abilities, especially among young people, and data obtained several months ago may no longer describe the person at all accurately. Parker (1961), for example, found that students who came to a college counseling center for personal counseling showed a pattern of scores on the Minnesota Multiphasic Personality Inventory different from that which they had displayed when tested during freshman orientation. Part of this change is undoubtedly a reflection of differences in the situations within which the test was administered, but the results demonstrate that earlier personality data may present a grossly inaccurate picture of the person as he is at the present time.

3. To help the client better understand himself as a person. Perhaps the single most common, and defensible, use of personality measures in counseling is to promote the client's self-exploration. Some clients have difficulty in thinking about themselves in meaningful terms, and the constructs represented by personality scales may help them organize their thinking. In this sense, personality measures are used primarily as a stimulus, and they are useful to the extent that they promote critical and constructive thinking by the client. The counselor will find that some measures usually fulfill this function better than others. The client and counselor, in considering the client's responses to a personality measure, may gain insights into the client's behavior that were not evident before.

Assessment Methods. Personality measures come in two forms: self-report techniques (generally in the form of inventories), and projective tests. Of these, only the inventories have been found to be useful in counseling. Projective tests are clinical instruments primarily useful in the diagnosis of emotional disorders, and even their value for that purpose is hotly debated. For counseling purposes they are of little value, since relationships between their scores and other criteria have not been demonstrated and their reliability is poor (Patterson, 1957; Super and Crites, 1962). Few counselors have sufficient training to use projective techniques correctly, and there is little reason why they should spend their time obtaining such training.

There are a variety of personality inventories available which may be of value to the counselor, depending on the nature of the client and on the purpose for which they are to be used. For diagnostic purposes, the Minnesota Multiphasic Personality Inventory (MMPI) is probably the most useful for college students and adults, because it has been the subject of a great deal of research, but the type of questions asked and the labels of the scales are such that it is a difficult instrument for clients to use for self-exploration. Among those inventories which may satisfy the latter purpose reasonably well are the Guilford-Zimmerman Temperament Survey, the Edwards Personal Preference Schedule, the California Psychological Inventory, the Minnesota Counseling Inventory, and the Allport-Vernon-Lindzey Study of Values.[10] All of these inventories utilize items which are relatively non-threatening and report the scores on scales which deal with "normal" traits or needs and which the client can consider constructively. The counselor's preference will be determined by the extent to which the constructs on which the various inventories are based fit his own view of human personality, plus the applicability of the various instruments to the kinds of clients with whom he typically works.

[10] For further information concerning these and other potentially useful personality inventories, see the discussions by Super and Crites (1962), Berdie and others (1963), Vernon (1964), and Hathaway (1965), as well as the reviews in the *Mental Measurements Yearbooks* edited by Buros.

9

The Role of Tests
in Counseling:
Selection and Interpretation

After exploring the client's problem and determining the questions to be answered, the counselor and client may decide that test information may help the client to arrive at these answers. Whether the counselor or the client first suggests the introduction of tests is not important, provided that they both agree that test information is potentially of value for this client in this situation.

THE SELECTION OF TESTS

The decision to include testing may be made rather easily, but the choice of specific tests is usually a more complex process. Of major concern are the roles of the counselor and client. Should the assignment of tests be the responsibility of the counselor, or should the client take an active part in this decision? And, if the latter, what role should the client play?

One of the potential drawbacks to the use of tests in counseling is that it is easy for the counselor to lapse into an authoritative, omniscient role when tests are introduced. Psychological tests are, of course, technical in nature, and few clients enter counseling with substantial knowledge about them. Without some guidance from the counselor, the naive client would be likely to misuse and misinterpret the results of his tests, and the counseling would thereby do him a great disservice.

With this in mind, some counselors feel it necessary to assume a great deal of the responsibility for the assignment and interpretation of tests, assuming that the client knows little about tests and therefore cannot play a meaningful role in this phase of counseling. It is because of this attitude that some nondirective counselors avoid the use of tests altogether, believing that to include tests would force them into a relationship incompatible with that which they are trying to establish.

In the previous chapter we presented evidence that test information can be of value to clients, provided that it is used judiciously. Is it possible, therefore, to introduce tests into counseling in such a way that the client can benefit from the information to be obtained from them, yet without violating the basic principles of counseling? If the counselor suddenly assumes an authoritative role, the client is likely to become hopelessly confused as to the nature of counseling and subsequently look to the counselor to supply answers to his questions. Likewise, the client who has taken no responsibility for the tests he is assigned may not feel responsible for making constructive use of the results. The more that the client has been actively involved in the decision to take certain tests, the greater the likelihood that he will believe the results are worth using.

One way in which these goals can be accomplished is to encourage the client to make decisions within the limitations of his knowledge and experience. One decision that is more appropriately the client's than the counselor's is the kind of information the client wants to obtain from tests. For example, a client who is undecided as to a vocation might want information about his abilities, his interests, his personal characteristics, or other relevant areas. He might want information in all of these areas, but more likely only in some. He may feel that others are unrelated to his questions, or that his information in those areas is already sufficient. The counselor can help him formulate meaningful questions, but the nature of the questions must be left to the client.

Once the questions are posed, however, there is still a decision to be made as to the tests which will provide the most relevant and useful information. For example, the client may have decided he wants information about his academic ability, but there are a wide variety of tests he might take which could supply him with such data. It is at this point that the counselor should step in and determine the best test to use. Unless the client has had some experience with tests, he cannot be expected to make this decision alone. The counselor who asks the client, "Would you rather take the School and College Ability Test or the Ohio State Psychological Examination?" is putting the client in an impossible, and potentially embarrassing, situation. To attempt to explain the tests in sufficient detail so that the client can then make an intelligent choice among them seems highly inefficient. It is much simpler for the counselor to suggest that a certain test seems most likely to provide the client with the kind of information he is looking for. The client, having already asked for this information, can feel that he has played an important role in arriving at this final decision.

It should be evident that the technique of including the client in the test selection process will work well for some counselors and not for others, depending on their personal concept of counseling and of their role as a counselor. As Goldman (1961) has pointed out, it is important that the counselor use a method of test assignment with which he is comfortable. The counselor who includes the client in the process of selecting tests must truly believe that the client has something worthwhile to contribute; otherwise, the client will probably feel he is being manipulated, without understanding why. Likewise, the inclusion of the client encourages him to ask questions about various tests which the counselor may find difficult to answer. A more authoritarian approach will probably eliminate such trying moments, but at the risk of encouraging the client to become a passive taker of tests and recipient of information.

THE INTERPRETATION OF TEST RESULTS

The crucial phase in testing comes when the client attempts to learn something from his test results that will help him in resolving the difficulty which brought him to counseling. It is the counselor's responsibility to discuss the test results with the client in such a way that the client gains the maximum value from them.

To do this, the counselor should follow two basic principles: (a) test results should be related as closely as possible to the questions which the client originally hoped to answer; and (b) the results should be presented in a form which is as meaningful as possible for this particular client.

In a sense, the interpretation of test results is a translation process. The counselor, by virtue of his training and experience, can "read" the results in the form in which they are originally presented. Most clients cannot, without help, and the counselor must provide this help. It is for this reason that persons who are experts in psychological testing may do a poor job of interpreting test results to a naive client; effective test interpretation requires thorough knowledge of basic principles of psychological measurement, *plus* the counseling skills necessary to communicate this information to a client.

Communication is often enhanced by the use of concrete devices which express the information in a form more meaningful to the client. Devices such as expectancy tables and normative profiles (described more fully by Goldman, 1961) are often useful. They present the client with probability statements concerning future performance in areas related to the tested skill, or they graphically compare him with a relevant norm group in some relevant characteristic. The counselor may also create other devices which enable him to present test information to his clients in the most meaningful way possible.

In the interpretation of test results, the counselor must take into consideration characteristics of the client, such as age, intelligence, and background in determining the most meaningful form of presentation. Above all, the counselor should not limit himself to a single method of presentation; a method which is very effective with one client may be totally inappropriate for another.

Test interpretation need not be limited to "mechanical" devices such as expectancy tables. The counselor may also want to add his own "intuitive" impressions based on his experience, depending on the kind of questions the client is trying to answer. There is considerable evidence that specific predictions (for example, "What are my chances of graduating from college?") are more accurately made from statistical data, and that the counselor's impressions are likely not to be as valid (Mechl, 1954). On the other hand, there are some kinds of questions for which statistical data are inadequate (for instance, "What are my strengths and weaknesses as a person?"), and in these cases the counselor's impressions may add an important dimension to the interpretation process.

Techniques of Test Interpretation

There are many techniques by which test information can be presented. Some counselors simply explain the results in a rather didactic manner, while others try to include the client more actively, to the extent of holding back certain results until the client has expressed a specific interest in them or has raised a question to which they are relevant. Some counselors present the results of each test individually; others present results in the same area as a unit; while still others attempt to organize the results into a total pattern for presentation.

Despite these variations, however, there is little evidence to suggest that any one approach is more effective than another. Research on this question (Rogers, 1954; Gustad and Tuma, 1957) has failed to locate a superior technique; as with any counseling technique, effectiveness depends on the individual counselor. Presumably a counselor will be most effective using a technique with which he feels comfortable and that is consistent with the general approach to counseling which he is trying to present.

With this in mind, we can suggest some principles of test interpretation consistent with the view of counseling presented earlier,[1] with the under-

---

[1] For more detailed considerations of the interpretation of test results in counseling, see Goldman (1961) and Berdie and others (1963), as well as the casebook by Womer and Frick (1965).

standing that the basis for these suggestions is more philosophical than scientific.

The client's reactions to the test-taking process should be explored first. Most clients return to the counselor, after having taken tests, with reactions to the testing itself. Since these reactions may influence their acceptance of the test results, it is important that they be recognized and discussed. The opportunity provided the client to ventilate his feelings about the tests may produce a more objective and accepting attitude on his part toward the test results. Failure to take time to allow the client to express his reactions to the tests may negate much of the value of the testing.

Test interpretation is most effective if it is a cooperative process. The client should be actively involved, not a passive recipient of information. This principle is not always easily implemented, since the counselor must often "read" the information to the client, but the counselor should encourage the client to participate as much as possible.

One approach to involve the client actively is to allow him to see and react to the test results directly whenever possible, with the counselor's assistance. This is most feasible when the test results are presented in some form which the client can be expected to understand with a brief explanation from the counselor. For example, most college students can interpret a profile from the Strong Vocational Interest Blank after a brief explanation. For the counselor to interpret a profile to the client without showing it to him bears some resemblance to examining a crystal ball. The client who is encouraged to inspect the profile himself will probably get more out of it as well as believing that the counselor is being open and honest with him.

Some counselors object to showing the client a test profile on the grounds that he may misinterpret it. This risk depends somewhat on the age and intelligence of the client, but the risk is probably not as great as the potential damage of hiding it from him.

The client should, of course, be asked to describe his interpretation of the profile. If his impressions are at variance with those of the counselor, the discrepancy can be pointed out and discussed. Likewise, any errors in interpretation due to misunderstanding of the test itself can be corrected.

An additional value of allowing the client to react to the profile is that it provides some insight into the client as a person. In some cases, the client reacts first to an aspect that the counselor would have thought less important or might have ignored altogether. Whether it is really a significant point may be doubtful, but the fact that the client focused first on it may be of considerable importance.

The interpretation of ability test data may be facilitated by the use of an *expectancy table* which relates the client's test scores and other information to a relevant criterion by indicating the probability that a person with a given score will reach a certain level of performance on the criterion.[2] Examples of expectancy tables with college grades as the criterion are presented in Tables 9.1 and 9.2. The first shows the relationship of scores on a popular scholastic aptitude test to first-term grade-point-average at a midwestern university. The figures represent the percentage of students with a given test score who attain a certain grade average, as calculated on a 4.00 basis. Table 9.2 is based on the same group but combines two predictors: aptitude test scores and high school rank. The numbers within the cells represent the chances in 100 of attaining at least a 3.0, at least a 2.0, and below a 2.0 grade average, respectively. A blank cell indicates too few cases for a stable estimate, and a star (*) indicates less than one chance in 100.

The use of expectancy tables should help the client to participate in the extraction of information relevant to decisions he must make. The counselor must, of course, explain the nature of the table to him, but most clients should be able to participate in the discussion of the results using this device.

The general point to be made here is that the working relationship already established between the counselor and client should be extended to the interpretation of test results, with both parties as actively involved as possible and both making whatever contributions are appropriate for them.

The client should be encouraged to express his reactions to the test

Table 9.1. *Expectancy Table for Predicting First Quarter College Grades from a College Aptitude Test.*[a]

Test Raw Score	Grade-Point Average		
	≥ 3.0	≥ 2.0	< 2.0
32–	93	99+	1
30–31	58	97	3
28–29	34	89	11
26–27	19	75	25
24–25	14	63	37
22–23	5	52	48
20–21	4	49	51
18–19	2	44	56
16–17	3	36	64

[a] Source: Brown, 1970, p. 188.

[2] For a more detailed discussion of the use of expectancy tables, see Seashore (1949).

Table 9.2. Expectancy Table for Predicting First-Quarter College Grades from a College Aptitude Test and High School Rank.[a]

Test Raw Score	High School Rank (in tenths)						
	First	Second	Third	Fourth	Fifth	Sixth	Seventh–Tenth
30–	82–98–2	26–93–7	—	—	—	—	—
28–29	52–94–6	21–89–11	16–92–8	30–80–20	7–47–53	—	—
26–57	37–93–7	18–81–19	9–65–35	5–66–34	17–52–48	*–36–64	8–16–84
24–25	35–93–7	19–70–30	4–61–39	13–49–51	3–37–63	*–40–60	6–25–75
22–23	17–95–5	7–63–37	4–61–39	3–41–59	3–40–60	*–32–68	*–45–55
20–21	22–78–22	4–67–33	5–50–50	3–43–57	5–52–48	*–36–64	*–45–55
18–19	—	—	*–31–69	*–38–62	6–45–55	8–41–69	*–33–67
–17	—	—	—	—	*–20–80	—	4–26–74

[a] Source: Brown, 1970, p. 189.

results. These results are very personal to the cilent, and he should not be expected or encouraged to treat them as cold, objective facts. More important than the results themselves may be his feelings about them, and about himself. For example, the high school student who plans to become a doctor but who scores only within the average range on a test of academic ability may have some trouble integrating this information into his self-concept. It is the counselor's responsibility to encourage him to consider the meaning of this information to him and to help him handle his reaction in a constructive manner.

The client should be encouraged to relate the test information to the questions originally raised. The relationships may be obvious to the counselor, but not necessarily to the client. The client may need to be reminded that the tests were taken for a purpose, and he may need help in relating the test results to that purpose. Likewise, results from different tests should be interrelated and not treated as discrete facts. The client's performance on an interest inventory may or may not be consistent with his performance on an ability test; the client should be encouraged to consider relationships among the test results as well as how the picture painted by them relates to his original questions.

The test results should be presented in such a way as to make their limitations clear to the client. This does not mean that the counselor should undersell the tests, but he should not imply that they are more accurate than he knows to be true. For this reason, specific scores are seldom presented, especially in ability tests, since a specific score implies an accuracy that the test probably does not possess. The results should be presented as a range, in accordance with the known reliability of the test, and predictive information should be presented as probabilities rather than certainties. Clients often expect test information to be specific and are disappointed when it is not. The counselor must therefore guard against the client's tendency to read too much into the results by expressing them in terms which suggest their limitations.

The manner and vocabulary in which the results are presented may have an important bearing on the client's acceptance of the results. It is the counselor's responsibility to present the results as honestly and objectively as possible, without expressing value judgments and without prejudging the client's reaction. On ability tests, for example, high scores should not be presented as "good" and low scores as "poor." Whether a score is good or poor is a relative matter, to be determined by the individual client. The client should, of course, be encouraged to express his reactions to the results; if he feels he did poorly on a test, this should be discussed. But the counselor should not anticipate the client's feelings nor should he indicate by his choice of words how he expects the client to react.

This point is especially important when the counselor must interpret a low score to a client, especially in an ability area. The counselor may be hesitant to present the information, perhaps out of concern that the client's feelings will be hurt, and he may therefore become apologetic in tone. This kind of presentation does the client a disservice by implying that there is something wrong with his performance. If the client asked for the information originally, then he deserves to have it, and without prejudice from the counselor. If he is unhappy with the results, this reaction can then be discussed.

The counselor will also do well to avoid terminology which may be threatening to the client. The use of the term "academic ability," for example, is often preferable to "intelligence," not only because it is a more accurate description of most tests of this sort but also because "intelligence" has strong emotional connotations for some people. Likewise in the interpretation of personality inventories it is desirable to avoid terms that the client may misunderstand. In interpreting the MMPI, for example, it is well not to tell the client that he has a high score on the "schizophrenic" scale.[3] The meaning of a high score on this scale can be communicated in a manner which is less threatening and just as accurate.

Confusion regarding terminology can be avoided if the test performance is related to specific outcome criteria rather than described in terms of a possibly ambiguous label. This approach enables the client to put the information in a relevant perspective, rather than becoming overly involved in trying to decipher the meaning of the label.

INTERPRETING TEST INFORMATION OBTAINED ROUTINELY

Most schools routinely administer test batteries to their students, partly to obtain information of use to the school but also to provide the student or his parents with information that may be useful in helping them make plans for his future. Testing under these circumstances is not part of a counseling process, but inasmuch as the results may be useful in the student's planning, they require some interpretation to him or his parents.

One of the major complaints often made about school testing programs is the lack of feedback to the student. Except for unusual circumstances, it would seem that anyone who is asked to submit to testing deserves to know the results, especially if he may be able to make constructive use of

---

[3] With instruments such as the MMPI, in which the scale labels may be threatening to many clients, it may not be desirable to allow the client to view the profile as suggested earlier since he may want to know what each letter code signifies. Such instruments may therefore be of less value in counseling because they do not lend themselves to cooperative interpretation.

them. The difficulty in interpretation of the results is, obviously, that the administration of the tests was determined by a decision of the school rather than by a specific need of the student. Nevertheless, most students seem to recognize the value of tests and accept the results, if some feedback is offered (Rothney, 1952).

To be meaningful to the student or his parents, test results should be interpreted individually if possible, integrated with a discussion of the student's current concerns to which they may be related. This provides some students with an opportunity to raise questions and problems which they might not take the initiative to bring to the counselor otherwise. Thus a routine testing may be an overture to counseling rather than an outgrowth of it. Most students in this situation, however, are primarily concerned with learning something about themselves which may be useful, and the discussion will therefore usually be focused primarily on the test results themselves.

To the extent possible in this situation, the counselor should attempt to follow the principles described earlier. He should certainly try to get some idea as to whether the student has any questions which the tests might answer, and he should allow sufficient opportunity for the student to express his reactions to the results. Perhaps an extended discussion may be precipitated, although this is not nearly as likely as when the tests are the product of a counseling need.

SOCIAL IMPLICATIONS OF TESTING

The use of tests has been for so long a standard feature of our schools and colleges that we tend to assume they will always be with us, yet there are signs on the horizon that all is not well with the testing movement and that the public is coming increasingly to distrust and reject tests. As this distrust continues, counselors may find more resistance to the use of tests and may have to reassess their own thinking about the role of tests in counseling.

Part of the problem has been brought on by psychologists and counselors themselves. As testing gained in popularity, many counselors were too quick to respond to the public's demand for more and more testing. They increased their use of tests which were not always appropriate or well constructed, implying that more could be learned from them than was actually the case. Gradually the public has begun to wake up to this practice and has become increasingly skeptical of tests, even of those which are of real value. Unable to distinguish between the wheat and the chaff, the public has swung away from wholehearted acceptance of all tests toward complete rejection.

Complicating this tendency toward skepticism is the trend over the past generation toward more and more frequent testing within the schools, but with a minimum amount of feedback to the students and their parents. The public has become understandably hostile toward a practice which often seems to be a waste of time and perhaps even subversive. The failure of school guidance counselors to make a strong effort to explain their testing programs to their communities and to insure feedback to those directly involved has produced some of the current suspicion of tests and of data collection in all forms.

A more recent, but equally serious, threat to the testing movement is the increasing recognition that the role of tests in selection processes can have a stultifying effect on society by encouraging the continuation of the social status quo. Colleges, for example, have long collected data to describe the kinds of students who do well in their curricula and subsequently select students on this basis, thus insuring that the same standards of performance will be maintained. Counselors, knowing of such practices, have therefore been able to use test data to help clients make decisions as to the choice of a college, based on the client's probabilities of success at various schools.

There is growing concern, however, that such practices, by perpetuating the status quo, tend to discriminate against persons who do not meet the normal entrance requirements but who should be considered for admission anyway. This problem is most evident in the case of members of minority groups, who because of disadvantaged backgrounds do not perform well on the types of tests usually used as bases for selection, yet who are deemed deserving of an opportunity in an elite academic environment.

There is no easy answer to this dilemma. Certainly there is ample evidence that persons from disadvantaged backgrounds are handicapped in performance on tests of academic ability, although they are likewise handicapped in performance in the academic settings which these tests are designed to predict. In a sense, therefore, the tests themselves are not invalid: their prediction is accurate, so long as the criterion situation remains relatively stable. To ignore the person's test performance and admit him anyway is only to insure that he will probably fail, since the handicaps of his background continue to plague him. Only an alteration of the criterion situation—in this case, the academic setting—can increase the probability that the disadvantaged student will be successful and the test prediction will thereby be invalidated.[4] Such alterations can, of course, be effected through the use of special tutoring and remedial courses, and many colleges and universities are taking steps to do this. The same principle holds for job

[4] There is even considerable debate as to the extent to which special educational help, or "compensatory education," can reverse the impact of the earlier environment, especially at the college level. For examples of various positions in this debate see Jensen's paper in the Winter, 1969, issue of the *Harvard Educational Review* and the comments in the Spring issue of the same journal.

training situations as well, although pressures for modifications at this level have as yet been less severe.

The fault, it must be emphasized, lies in the restrictive nature of the criterion, not in the test itself. The counseling use of tests should emphasize their predictive value in terms of performance in some future criterion situation rather than a fixed judgment about the person himself. This means that the counselor must be sensitive to changes in the criterion situation which may change the prediction he would formerly have made for a given client. He may learn, for example, that a certain college has established a program to provide special help for disadvantaged students, an item of information which might provide an important supplement to the test data for certain clients.

It is the counselor's responsibility to insure that his clients obtain the most valid possible information about themselves and their environment in relation to the kinds of decisions they need to make. Knowing both the risks and potential rewards of a given situation, the client himself must make the decision as to the path on which to direct his life. The counselor must recognize that people and institutions do change, and that test data do not guarantee a static situation. He must use tests wisely and tentatively, to help the client develop as complete a picture as possible of the alternatives available to him. Above all, the counselor must respect the rights and needs of the individual and encourage him to make his decisions as free as possible from cultural stereotypes and in terms of himself as an individual.

10

The Evaluation
of Counseling

This is a scientific age, and counseling is therefore expected to provide scientific proof of its validity. A theory is a beginning, but it is not enough; the counselor has an obligation to provide evidence that the time he spends with his clients is well spent and that counseling does in fact help people. The public deserves assurance that counselors are sufficiently effective to warrant its support, and counselors should be concerned with improving their techniques through objective study. Counseling without a research base has feet of clay, which can easily crumble under the onslaught of disbelievers.

Most counselors acknowledge the importance of research, yet much of the dogma of counseling has little basis in scientific evidence. Why the gap? As compared with research in the physical and natural sciences, the study of human behavior is clumsy and messy, and counseling research is one of the most difficult areas of all. Yet to say that adequate research on counseling is difficult is not to say that it is impossible, nor does it warrant the abandonment of research attempts. It does mean, however, that persons conducting research in counseling must be especially aware of the methodological pitfalls they are likely to encounter.

A review of the journals reveals that counseling has not suffered from lack of research studies, but much of the research suffers from being either trivial or unsophisticated, or both. With a few outstanding exceptions, counseling has lacked sophisticated researchers who have systematically advanced our knowledge about counseling. The next generation of counselors must be better prepared to conduct relevant research and must be willing to invest the time and effort required to do it well. The longer that counselors continue to operate primarily on the basis of faith rather than evidence, the greater the risk that they will lose favor with the public as well as losing respect for themselves.

There will be no attempt made here either to provide a primer of research methods for counselors or a compendium of counseling research studies. Instead, two areas will be stressed: (a) methodological problems of special concern in counseling research, and (b) trends in counseling research, as exemplified in representative studies. For a thorough background in research methodology, the reader is referred to books on behavioral research, such as that by Kerlinger (1965), and to the discussion of experimental design in counseling research by Edwards and Cronbach (1952); the *Journal of Counseling Psychology* and the *Personnel and Guidance Journal* are the best sources of current research studies of counseling.

METHODOLOGICAL PROBLEMS IN COUNSELING RESEARCH

The Choice of a Criterion

Any attempt to study the counseling process must begin with a decision as to the expected outcome of counseling. It is against this *criterion* that the counseling process in general, or specific aspects of it, can be studied. If a satisfactory criterion cannot be specified, the research is meaningless. Much of the research in counseling is virtually worthless because the criteria employed were either ill-defined or of little relevance for most counselors. Therefore the determination of a suitable criterion is the first step in developing a worthwhile research study in counseling.

At first glance the criterion problem seems trivial. Counselors presumably know what they are trying to accomplish: improved adjustment, a sensible vocational choice, or a realistic self-concept are common goals. Not all counselors would accept all of these as criteria, but they represent broad areas of general agreement as to typical worthwhile outcomes.

A problem, however, arises when one attempts to specify the client behaviors which are indicative of these outcomes. In a research study, the criterion must be more clear and specific than a phrase such as "improved adjustment." In Astin's (1964) terms, it is the *criterion performance* rather than the *conceptual criterion* that must be studied directly. And it quickly becomes evident that there are few clear and simple criteria of "improved adjustment" available for study. One might use self-ratings, ratings by persons who know the client well, or changes on personality inventories, but pitfalls are evident in each of these. None clearly represents "improved adjustment" in a form acceptable to all counselors, which in turn means that whatever criterion is chosen for a particular study will cause many persons to reject the value of the study itself.[1]

With the variety of imperfect criteria from which to choose, it is necessary to consider how the most appropriate may be selected. The primary consideration is, of course, to choose the criterion performance which most closely fits the question under study. In other words, to be of value a criterion must be *relevant* to the problem which has been posed for study. Change in performance on a personality inventory would not, for example, be a relevant criterion for a study in which a realistic vocational choice was the desired counseling outcome.

A second attribute of a good criterion is that it be *measurable*. In one sense, of course, all concepts are measurable but, like Orwell's animals, some are more measurable than others. The more easily and accurately a criterion can be measured, the more valuable will be the results of the research in which it is employed.

Let it be said loud and clear that this is not a plea for an agreement on a single criterion: no one criterion is best, since relevance will vary depending on the question asked. If, however, the attributes of relevance and measurability are carefully considered in the selection of a criterion for a research study, the results of that study will be of much greater value than if this step had been passed over casually.

With this caution in mind, we can examine some of the criteria commonly used in counseling research, to consider which are more desirable and under what conditions they might be employed.

Internal versus External Criteria.   Criteria for counseling research can be categorized as to whether the data are obtained from within or outside of the counseling setting. *Internal criteria* may include the content of client verbalizations, or other indications of client improvement as reflected in client behavior during counseling. One example of the use of internal criteria is the research in the late 1940s by Robinson and his students at Ohio State University (summarized by Robinson, 1950), which concen-

---

[1] Astin (1964) has suggested that the status of a profession is related to the clarity of criteria by which its value can be judged. He cites as an example that surgery enjoys a higher status than psychiatry within medicine, because the surgeon can more clearly demonstrate the value of what he does. This may explain why clinical psychology has higher status than counseling psychology: the role of the clinical psychologist in the improvement of a schizophrenic is more obvious than is the role of a counseling psychologist in helping a student arrive at a satisfactory vocational choice.

trated on the development and utilization of criteria [2] such as "statements of insights and plans," "feeling reactions," "working relationship," and "division of responsibility." Thus a client would be judged to be improving if he made more frequent statements of insights and plans, expressed more positive feelings, indicated a favorable working relationship with the counselor, and assumed more responsibility for the direction of the counseling.

Other internal criteria, less dependent on client verbalization, may also be useful. These include the total number of counseling sessions, which assumes that clients who are benefiting from counseling are likely to continue longer; and physiological measures, such as GSR reactions, as involuntary indicators of decreased anxiety and tension. The former is highly suspect, since length of counseling duration probably depends substantially on the philosophy of the counselor and the time available to him as well as the attitude of the client (see the discussion by Frank, 1961, pp. 14–15). Physiological measures have seldom been used in counseling research, primarily because of the mechanical problems involved, and their value has not been thoroughly assessed. It may be argued, however, that the emotional cues which they tap are more relevant to behavior changes expected during psychotherapy than during counseling (see Dittes, 1957, for an example).

External criteria include evidence concerning client change which is not directly observable within the counseling situation itself. This would include client reports of behavior change or of his own attitude toward counseling, observations of the client by others, objective indicators such as grades or job success, and client statements to others about his counseling experiences. More will be said about some of these criteria in the following section.

Internal criteria have the advantage of being directly observable by the counselor or by other skilled professionals (from recorded transcripts of the counseling interview) under relatively controlled conditions. Their major drawback, however, is their questionable relevance to the client's counseling goal. Presumably all clients seek counseling because they want to change their behavior in their everyday lives, not just within the counseling setting itself. To the extent that behavior change within counseling can be shown to reflect change outside of counseling, internal criteria are certainly relevant. But such correspondence is not often demonstrated to a sufficient extent to impress other counselors. Most counselors would probably agree that, while internal criteria provide a more systematic and controlled manner of increasing our knowledge about the counseling process, concern must also be paid to evidence of client change obtained from the real world.

[2] Robinson actually used the term "immediate" rather than "internal" criteria, but the latter has been substituted here to avoid needless confusion with Thorndike's continuum of "immediate-intermediate-ultimate" criteria.

Objective versus Subjective Criteria. *Objective criteria* are those which do not rely on the judgment of someone connected with the counseling itself and are usually easily quantifiable. Popular objective criteria include grades in school, job tenure, job ratings by supervisors, number of dates, duration of a marriage, and so forth. Criteria such as these are appealing because they can be collected easily and are not subject to biases by the client or the counselor. Some, such as grades in courses or ratings by a job supervisor, do, of course, require subjective judgments by someone, but in most cases this person is not connected with the counseling and is probably not, in fact, aware that counseling has taken place. If he is aware of this, and if there is a possibility that he has some interest in either supporting or refuting the value of the counseling, then the use of such a judgment would become a subjective rather than an objective criterion of the counseling outcome.

The major drawback of the objective criteria described above is that to many counselors they seem superficial. While the object of counseling may, in some cases, be clearly the improvement of the client's grades or improved performance on a job, more often the goals of counseling are broader than this. Some counselors would reject objective criteria entirely as being too narrow and superficial while others would accept them under certain circumstances, but few counselors would agree that such criteria represent the general goals of counseling for most clients. Criteria with greater depth are needed for meaningful study of counseling.

This means that, while it may be perfectly appropriate to estimate the success of counseling with a given client on the basis of improved grades or increased frequency of dating, if these were the counseling goals of that client, it would seldom be appropriate to use such criteria as general indications of the value of counseling. Yet grades in school are probably the most frequently used criterion in counseling research, since most counseling is done within academic settings where such data are easily obtained. The relevance of such a criterion as a general indication of the value of counseling must, however, be subject to serious question and the validity of grades as a general criterion of counseling effectiveness is yet to be demonstrated (see, for example, the study reported by Hill and Grienecks, 1966).

The superficiality of objective criteria for the general evaluation of counseling effectiveness has led to an increased use of *subjective criteria*. These come in a variety of forms, but essentially they rely on the judgment of either the counselor or the client to determine that something worthwhile has been accomplished through counseling. To many counselors they represent a more meaningful dimension than do the objective criteria, yet they are severely limited by their subjective nature: satisfaction can be produced by a variety of influences, some of which may be only distantly related to the counseling goal. Proponents of subjective criteria have been hard-pressed to devise measures which are reliable enough to serve as adequate dependent variables and to demonstrate that these measures are closely related to client behavior outside of counseling.

Perhaps the most commonly used, and most controversial, subjective criterion is the client report of satisfaction with counseling. As has often been pointed out, for a counselor to ask a client as he leaves counseling whether he benefited from it is like a host asking a guest whether he enjoyed the party: the social expectations are obvious, and few persons are so callous as to take up another's time and then insult him with a negative reaction. Beginning counselors soon learn that an easy way to obtain rewards for the time spent with a client is to ask him, as he leaves, whether the counseling has helped him. Only after obtaining the same pleasant but stereotyped response from several clients may the counselor begin to question the value of such an inquiry.

Estimates of client satisfaction can, of course, be obtained in a manner less likely to produce distortion: for instance, a survey by an agency rather than by an individual counselor, with questions designed to elicit more specific evidence of the value of counseling for the client. As persons are pinned down by more specific questions, involuntary distortion becomes more difficult. Devices such as the Counselor Evaluation Inquiry (Linden and others, 1965) have been developed to measure client satisfaction more accurately, but many limitations in this process remain.

To use client satisfaction as a criterion implies that clients are capable of viewing themselves and their counseling experience accurately in terms of their personal needs, an assumption which is probably often unwarranted. Some clients may express satisfaction with no discernible change in behavior as a result of the counseling, while others may be dissatisfied because the counselor did not behave as they had hoped, despite other evidence that they gained something from counseling.

Another form of client judgment is the report of one's degree of personal adjustment or self-concept. Loevinger and Ossorio (1959) have pointed out that clients who remain in counseling for a time are probably more introspective than those who drop out early and that this difference is probably reflected in their self-reports. They also suggest that increased correspondence between actual and ideal self-concept, a frequent criterion of improved personal adjustment, may simply reflect a combination of naiveté plus some grasp of the purpose of counseling. In any case, self-reports do not correlate well with other evidence of improvement and are therefore of dubious value.

Asking the counselor to estimate client benefit from counseling is likewise a questionable criterion. To be sure, the counselor, being professionally trained, should be more aware than the client of the pitfalls of such estimates and might therefore be expected to rate improvement more accurately, although counselors suffer from the human frailties which contribute to invalid ratings under any circumstances. But even if it can be demonstrated that the counselor's ratings are more reliable than those of the client, the counselor is limited by a much more restricted range of evidence than the client has at his disposal. Counselor ratings may be useful in conjunction with ratings from other sources, but alone they are of dubious value as a criterion of counseling outcome.

Selecting the Best Criterion.   The picture painted here of the current status of criteria of counseling outcome is rather dark, but by no means hopeless. It is intended to emphasize that research in counseling must begin first with concern for the selection of a valid and reliable criterion. When this step is skipped, the study itself is of little value.

Basically the selection of a criterion for a given research study must depend on the question to be answered by the study, as well as the theoretical structure within which the investigator is working. To this extent, then, there can be no single ultimate criterion of counseling effectiveness. But within the limitations of theory, there is considerable room for improvement in the construction of the criterion measure. Much of the difficulty with the criteria typically used in counseling research is the lack of adequate measures rather than inappropriateness of the criterion itself. Counselors must concern themselves with devising better criterion measures before galloping off to conduct counseling research with inadequate criteria.

One promising approach to the improvement of counseling criteria involves the combining of criteria into multiple measures. This approach is based on the recognition that a single criterion is unlikely to be completely appropriate or adequate for a given study, whereas a combination of criteria may be more useful. The question remains, however, as to how these criteria should be combined. Perhaps techniques such as factor analysis will enable investigators to determine those criterion components which contribute independently to the total variance in client behavior and thereby to select those criteria which will most adequately represent the behaviors relevant to the study.

The Difficulty of Measuring Change.   Most criteria of counseling outcome involve the measurement of some sort of change in the client by comparing pre- and postcounseling scores on a relevant measuring instrument. This procedure, however, presents several difficulties which are often overlooked in the investigator's haste to compare the scores he has obtained.[3]

[3] The discussion here is derived largely from the writings of Bereiter (1962a, 1962b). The reader is referred to these, especially to the latter, for a more detailed discussion of the problem.

One problem is that the instruments, such as personality inventories, typically used in such studies are designed to measure stable characteristics and are therefore not sensitive to the kinds of changes which counseling is likely to produce. By the same token, however, an instrument which readily reflected change would be suspected of being unreliable, so that the meaning of a change in score would be difficult to interpret. In any case, however, attempting to measure client change on a variety of characteristics is more difficult than it first appears.

Even if an appropriate instrument could be found, however, and the statistical difficulties could be overcome, it must be recognized that change in human behavior normally does take place over time, and that it should therefore not be surprising to find that a client has changed during the course of counseling. Since the precounseling measure is generally obtained just prior to the beginning of counseling, it cannot be said that no evidence of change was present before. It is quite possible, in fact, that the motivation which causes a client to seek counseling may also stimulate the beginning of a behavior change, which may continue through counseling and be erroneously attributed to the counseling itself. If this were the case, then to match a group of "controls" with the clients as they began counseling might be misleading, since the clients may already be moving in an upward direction while the controls are probably a more stable group (see Figure 10.1). More will be said about the problem of controls shortly.

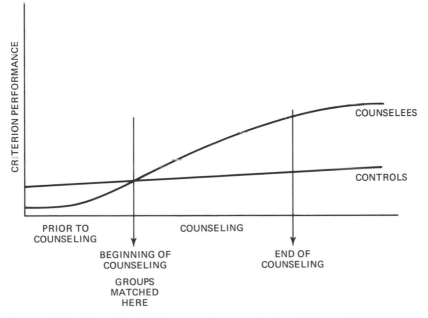

Figure 10.1 *Hypothetical changes in counseled and "control" groups.*

Perhaps the most reasonable way to deal with the problem of change as a counseling criterion is to specify more exactly the behaviors which a particular counseling approach is expected to influence, rather than simply to accept any change in the client as indicative of successful counseling.

Control of Extraneous Variance

It is undeniable that many persons behave differently after counseling than they did before: they make more rational decisions, they get along better with other people, or in some manner handle their problems more effectively. It is tempting to use this sort of evidence to prove the effectiveness of counseling, and thereby fall into the trap of *post hoc* reasoning: the fallacy that simply because two events occur together in time, the first must necessarily be the cause of the second. In this case, the occurrence of counseling prior to or during a behavior change on the part of the client demonstrates only some kind of association between the events. It does not prove that counseling *caused* the behavior change, since many other things have been happening to the client at the same time as the counseling which may have also contributed to the outcome.

This means that, in order to demonstrate that counseling produced the behavior change in question, it is necessary to demonstrate that the behavior change is the direct result of counseling. In technical terms, it is necessary to account for all other possible sources of variance and to demonstrate that the change in client behavior is associated with variance attributable only to counseling.

Most counseling research is *ex post facto,* which means that the investigator has no control over the selection of subjects for counseling nor over other variables which may contribute to variance in the criterion. Only by controlling all possible sources of extraneous variance, as is done in experimental research, is it possible to conclude that variation in the dependent variable (client behavior change) is directly related to variation in the independent variable (counseling). Control of this sort is seldom possible in counseling research, since selection of persons for counseling is not determined by the investigator: clients select themselves. Therefore to compare persons who have and have not undergone counseling is to compare two groups which are different in a very important variable—motivation for counseling—and quite likely therefore different in other ways as well. The fact that one group demonstrates certain behavior changes during the course of counseling may simply reflect differences in the two groups which existed prior to the counseling rather than to the influence of counseling itself, or perhaps an interaction effect.

This suggests that somehow a comparison must be made between two groups, both of whom are similar except for the variable of counseling and with the variable of motivation held constant. This might be accomplished in two ways: by selecting both groups from persons who have no immediate interest in counseling, or from persons who have sought counseling. Either approach should result in two groups which are alike in motivation as well as, presumably, other variables of possible relevance.

The first approach—selecting persons who have no immediate interest in counseling—has rarely been used in counseling research, primarily because it is difficult to approximate a true counseling situation without a motivated client. Since counseling is goal-directed, a counseling situation involving a client with no counseling goal is hardly an appropriate test of the effectiveness of counseling.

An evaluation of the effectiveness of counseling must be based, therefore, on persons who are motivated to seek counseling. A control group could then be established by providing counseling for some of those who seek it and denying counseling to others for a period of time, perhaps by putting them on a "waiting list," and subsequently comparing the two groups on a relevant criterion. If the counseling has been effective, then presumably the counseled group should show significant gains on the criterion as compared with the non-counseled (control) group.

At first glance this design is appealing, since it introduces a legitimate control group, but closer inspection reveals several flaws. One obvious limitation is an ethical one: is it fair to deny counseling to persons who need it, in the interests of research? Although the professional organizations have agreed that to deny counseling temporarily in the interests of scientific inquiry is not unethical, in practice it may work to the detriment of the image of the agency conducting the study. Thus most counselors, while perhaps agreeing in principle with the design described above, would prefer that such research be conducted elsewhere.

There are, however, more subtle handicaps in this design which make it less effective than it may appear. A control group selected in this manner is actually not a true control group, since these persons do not maintain themselves in suspended animation for the duration of the study. Presumably they have sought counseling because of some personal need or discomfort, which continues to bother them while they wait for help. It should come as no surprise to find that many seek out other sources of help— friends, ministers, other counselors—rather than waiting patiently until called by the agency (Frank, 1959; Bergin, 1963; LeMay, 1968). Whether such sources are better than nothing is debatable; it can be argued that more harm than good may be caused. It is also possible that a rejection by the counseling agency, even though only temporary, acts as a negative influence, causing the rejected group to become worse off than before. In any case, however, the "waiting list" group no longer fits the definition of a true control group: a group which represents the status of the experimental (counseled) group if the experimental treatment (counseling) had not been instituted.

In medical research this problem is avoided by providing the control group with a *placebo,* something indistinguishable from the treatment being tested, but which actually has no known medicinal value (such as a sugar pill instead of a wonder drug). In this way the control group continues to correspond to the experimental group, since both are receiving treatment which appears to be identical. The same principle could be applied to counseling research, except that no one has yet devised an adequate placebo for counseling. To maintain the control group as a true control, the members should be subjected to some activity which appears to be counseling, but which in fact is not. To devise such an activity would insure an instant reputation for its inventor.[4]

A major cause of the dilemma just described is that the variable, "counseling," is too complex and varied to be controlled adequately. Since it seems to be impossible to provide a no-counseling control group, it may be necessary to restructure the problem and to specify more clearly those aspects of counseling which are considered crucial parts of the process. It may then be possible to devise an experimental design in which only a single crucial element is varied, and the effects of the presence or absence of this independent variable can then be compared. An example of such a study, concerned with psychotherapy rather than counseling, is the research reported by Imber and his co-workers (1957), in which the variable of number and length of therapist-patient contacts was manipulated. Differences between the two groups suggested that this variable actually does have a bearing on the outcome of psychotherapy.

Similar studies may be the key to meaningful research on counseling outcomes. It will require, however, a more careful consideration of the nature of the counseling process than many counselors can be bothered to make, and it will not tell us whether "counseling," in general, is better than no counseling. The latter question may not, however, be amenable to scientific study under present social conditions, and partial answers based on ex post facto research may be the best that can be obtained.

The Role of Belief and Attitude

As knowledge about the influence of one's beliefs and attitudes on his perceptions has increased, there has developed what might be called the "social psychology of the experiment." It is becoming increasingly evident that an experiment involving human beings is a considerably more com-

---

[4] For a more extensive discussion of the placebo effect see Patterson (1959), Frank and others (1963), and Shapiro (1964).

plicated situation than its pencil-and-paper design suggests. And nowhere are these complications more obvious than in counseling research.

The Hawthorne Effect. One of the earliest instances in which the attitudes of the experimental subjects were found to influence the results was the Hawthorne studies. The "Hawthorne effect," in which subjects perform in accordance with the perceived desires of the experimenter simply because they are singled out as a special group, has subsequently been recognized in a variety of situations, including counseling. The Hawthorne effect is to be expected, for example, when a group of high school students is given extensive counseling and another group is not. In short order the experimental group will find that it is being given special treatment and will probably respond accordingly.

The Hawthorne effect cannot be entirely eliminated, but it can be reduced by minimizing the likelihood that the experimental group knows that it is being treated in a special manner and by obscuring the expected outcome from the subjects. Studies concerned with the global effects of counseling as opposed to no counseling are more subject to contamination from the Hawthorne effect than are studies of the relevance of specific aspects of counseling, since in the latter case the research hypotheses are much less obvious to the subjects.

Sensitization by Pre-measurement. If a group of subjects is given some sort of measurement device (a personality inventory or an attitude scale), then subjected to some special treatment (counseling), and subsequently given the same instrument again, many will recognize that some change is expected, and the direction of the change will probably not be difficult to determine. Since instruments of this sort are frequently used as criteria of counseling effectiveness, the possibility of pre-treatment sensitization must be considered. To reduce the likelihood of its occurrence, a variety of pre- and post-tests may be administered in order to obscure the true criterion, or control groups may be included so that a pre-experimental measure is not necessary. The latter approach, however, runs afoul of the complications in the selection of control groups discussed earlier.

Experimenter Bias. A more recently recognized source of difficulty in psychological experiments is the effects of the experimenter on the generation of data from the experiment. It is becoming increasingly evident, through the work of Rosenthal and others (see Rosenthal, 1966; Kintz and others, 1965), that psychological experiments are not as "objective" as was once assumed. Subjects are extremely sensitive to the desires of the experimenter and, since experiments are usually conducted by a person with a bias toward one outcome rather than another, it is not surprising that the subjects obtain subtle cues which guide their performance.[5] Thus for a dedicated counselor to demonstrate, under experimental conditions, that counseling is superior to no counseling, or for a counselor who espouses a new technique to demonstrate the comparative effectiveness of that technique, must be greeted with suspicion. The subjects may have simply picked up clues as to the desired performance on the criterion measure, probably without realizing it. The experimenters in such cases are not being deliberately dishonest; they are simply not aware of the power of their hopes in influencing the results of their research.

The influence of the experimenter on his results can be reduced by designing the study so as to minimize his opportunity to communicate performance expectations to the subjects, or perhaps even better by having the experiment conducted by a disinterested party. The disadvantage of the latter method, however, is that negative results will be discounted by true believers on the grounds that the person conducting the study did not use the experimental method properly. In a sense, however, such arguments only prove the importance of guarding against contamination by experimenter bias.

Sampling

Finally, a word should be said about the limited samples on which most counseling investigations are based. Most research in counseling utilizes the most easily available subjects, namely the clients of the agency with which the investigator is affiliated. At best, the results of such studies can be applied only to similar agencies, but in many cases even this much generalization is not warranted. One might assume offhand that a study conducted within a college counseling service would be relevant to other college counseling services, if not necessarily to employment services, but this conclusion is risky. Colleges and their student bodies differ widely, and data obtained from students at one school may have little relevance to students at a different sort of school. Even when similar schools are compared the results may be misleading, since the counseling agencies at the two schools may draw from different parts of the student population.

The greatest drawback in the sampling of subjects for counseling research is not, however, the restricted nature of a given study, but instead lies in the failure of most investigators adequately to describe their samples. Many seem to assume that simply to mention that the subjects came from a certain student body is sufficient, whereas such information may be more misleading than helpful. Persons reporting research in counseling have an

---

[5] Hansel (1966) has suggested a similar explanation for much of the evidence advanced to support theories of extrasensory perception.

obligation to describe their subjects as fully as possible so that the readers may determine to what extent their findings are applicable in another setting.

IS COUNSELING EFFECTIVE?

In view of the many difficulties inherent in the evaluation of counseling effectiveness, it is hardly surprising that counseling rests on a shaky scientific basis. The counseling literature is replete with studies attempting to demonstrate that counseling helps people, but when taken as a whole the evidence is not impressive. Most of the research can be discarded because of inattention to methodological pitfalls described earlier, and that which remains has provided ambiguous results.

In this area as in many others, more concern has been directed to psychotherapy than to counseling, and discussions as to the effectiveness of psychotherapy have often been heated. The lack of conclusive support for the effectiveness of psychotherapy has produced some sharp exchanges in the literature, with the most outspoken criticisms having been provided by Eysenck (1952), Levitt (1957), and Astin (1961). These writers have said, in effect, to psychotherapists, "Go away and don't come back until you can demonstrate that you have something worthwhile to offer." Not surprisingly, the reaction to such criticism has been equally strong, and the resulting debates have generally shed more heat than light on the question.

Once telling point made by the defenders of psychotherapy is that the interpretation of negative results is more complicated than previously appreciated and that it may be misleading to lump several counselors and several clients together into a single study. There is increasing evidence that some clients improve with therapy while others lose ground, probably due to differences among both counselors and clients. When these clients are combined, their changes cancel one another out, so that it appears that little gain has been made by the counseled group as a whole. This suggests that some clients do benefit from counseling but that their improvement is obscured when they are studied in combination with others who regress.

Evidence of Positive Effects

The critics of counseling seem to imply that counseling has been consistently shown to be ineffective, yet this is far from true. Several reasonably well-controlled studies have demonstrated that persons do benefit from counseling, although the differences between the counseled and the non-counseled are seldom large or dramatic. To review here all of the studies which support this contention would be both tedious and pointless. Two of the most extensive will serve as illustrations.

Rothney's Evaluation of a High-school Guidance Program. A series of studies has been reported by Rothney (1958), based on an experimental program of counseling and guidance established in four Wisconsin high schools. Students in these schools were randomly assigned to experimental and control groups. The experimental group was provided with extensive counseling and guidance services, and special attempts were made to involve them in these services as frequently as possible. The control group was not denied the services, but no special attempt was made to involve them. The experimental students did, in fact, avail themselves more often of the counseling. Rothney and his students conducted follow-up studies of both groups two and five years after graduation and found that the experimental students exceeded the control students on many relevant variables. Among other differences, the experimental students had better academic records, both in high school and after; they had made more realistic and more consistent vocational choices and were more likely to stick with their first choice; they had made more progress in their employment; they were more likely to have entered college and to have graduated; and they were more satisfied with their lives. None of these differences was large, yet the trend is obvious, and counseling must be considered to have been an important mediating variable.

Campbell's 25-year Follow-up of Students Counseled in College. One of the earliest attempts to evaluate the effectiveness of counseling was reported in 1940 by Williamson and Bordin.[6] Their subjects were 384 students who had voluntarily undergone counseling at the University of Minnesota Student Counseling Bureau early in their freshman year. These students were matched individually with students who had not sought counseling, and both groups were interviewed and rated as to adjustment approximately one year after the counseling had taken place. The counseled group had earned significantly better grades than the noncounseled in the interim and were also judged to be better adjusted.

As part of a larger study of university alumni, Campbell (1965a, 1965b) compared the same two groups 25 years later.[7] Although the differences between the two groups were slight, the counseled group reported higher income and were judged to have contributed more to society; on

---

[6] It is a commentary on the status of outcome research in counseling that few investigators have improved on Williamson and Bordin's research design in the intervening three decades.

[7] Campbell's thoroughness is evident in the fact that he was able to locate and test 761 of the original 768 subjects.

the other hand, there was little difference between the groups on measures of anxiety and self-confidence.

Campbell (1963) also reanalyzed Williamson and Bordin's data in an ingenious manner. He located the records of 62 students who had originally been in the control group but who had later voluntarily sought counseling while still in college. When compared with the other controls, in terms of the data collected during the original study, those who later became clients looked no different. After counseling, however, they resembled the original counseled group in terms of the criteria of the study. This suggests that changes did take place among these students and that these changes were associated with counseling.

Conclusions

These studies are representative of those which could be cited and from which the following conclusions can be drawn:

1. The effectiveness of counseling in general has not, and probably can never be, firmly proved. Stated in such a general and vague manner, this is probably not a researchable problem.

2. Motivated clients usually benefit from counseling, whatever criterion is employed. It is likely that their motivation plays an important role in this change, but then it is difficult to conceive of counseling with an unmotivated client anyway.

3. The effectiveness of counseling can be more easily demonstrated with the use of objective, but perhaps superficial, criteria. For example, counseling with college students clearly helps improve their grades and their probability of graduation (with the variable of motivation kept in mind as being of great importance). Many counselors do not find such goals to be very exciting or profound, but they do provide the best available evidence that counseling can do some good. As Campbell (1965a) has noted,

> Real differences appear, as a result of counseling, on variables that are important to the counselor and his client, i.e., grades and academic progress, but not on the sort of theoretical constructs that are important to these theorizing researchers. Perhaps we are not yet ready for such elaborate theoretical treatments; perhaps we have far more basic hard work to do before our data merit such extensive super-structures [p. 20].

4. No theoretical approach has proved superior to others. Variation in the behaviors of psychotherapists of different theoretical views has been demonstrated (Fey, 1958; Strupp, 1955), but few concomitant differences have been found among their clients (for example, Cartwright, 1966). Of the three major theoretical approaches—psychoanalytic, phenomenological,

and behavioral—the former has the poorest record of validation (Bergin, 1966; Paul, 1966, 1967), but inasmuch as psychoanalysts generally reject the scientific method anyway, these results seem to have had little impact on them. Such comparisons are not, however, very fruitful, since the gains produced by a given approach are generally specific to the method used and therefore probably not comparable to those produced by another approach (Fiske, Cartwright, and Kirtner, 1964).

To summarize, the effectiveness of counseling as a general process has not been firmly established in relation to all criteria, yet enough evidence has been uncovered to demonstrate that it is effective in helping clients achieve certain important goals. Moreover, the complexity of the counseling process is such that the lack of positive results in all cases cannot be construed to mean that counseling is ineffective in these instances. It simply means that in many areas the effectiveness of counseling remains to be scientifically demonstrated, although the indications of effectiveness are strong enough to warrant its continuation.

RESEARCH ON THE COUNSELING PROCESS

It is doubtful if the question of counseling effectiveness is really worth studying further, at least at our present stage of understanding. Enough evidence has been collected to show that counseling does do some persons some good. It is time, therefore, to abandon this question and move on to another, more sophisticated, one: what aspects of counseling produce what sorts of results? Or, to put it another way, if we assume that counseling is effective we must then explain *why* it is effective, in order to improve its value. At the present time, counseling comes in many shapes and sizes, all vying for attention as the most effective approach. It should be possible to resolve this confusion, at least to the extent of specifying the circumstances under which certain approaches are effective, and why.

This is obviously an argument in favor of research on the *process* rather than the *outcome* of counseling. Further demonstrations of effective outcome seem fruitless, if we do not understand why the outcome took place. It is time that counselors concentrated on this problem.

Process research provides an opportunity for the application of more sophisticated research techniques than are possible in studies of outcome. On the basis of a theoretical model, predictions can be made as to the effects of varying certain aspects of the counseling process, and the validity of these predictions can be observed in counseling. Some of the major theories of personality and of counseling have been discussed earlier, and Goldstein (1966) has described how other models, such as those derived from social psychology, may provide fruitful hypotheses for explaining client-counselor interaction (see also Goldstein, Heller, and Sechrest, 1966). Counselors must become more imaginative in their study of the counseling process, and familiarity with theoretical frameworks from other areas which deal with interpersonal interaction should be a helpful step.

It can be argued, however, that the natural counseling situation is too complicated for close experimental study, as well as not being subject to direct experimental manipulation. For this reason, counselors are turning more frequently to the *experimental analog* as a technique which approximates natural counseling, yet in which specific variables can be isolated and manipulated for closer study.[8]

Results of process research have been included in the discussion of the counseling process earlier in this book. Mention of the general approach is made here to point up the distinction between outcome and process research and to urge a greater concentration on the latter in the future. Further investigations of the effectiveness of counseling, except to demonstrate the value of specific programs under specific circumstances, would seem appropriate only for lemmings.

[8] For a more extensive discussion of the use of the experimental analog in counseling research, see Cowen (1961) and Zytowski (1966).

PART IV

The Professional Counselor

11

Professions
That Use
Counseling

The view of counseling presented in these pages has stressed that counseling is a process, not a profession. The process of counseling can occur in any relationship between two persons but, as explained in the first chapter, it is most efficient and effective when the relationship is a professional one. For this to occur, one of the parties in the relationship must be a professional person, and the other person must have sought him out specifically because of this professional identification.

Counseling is a basic tool of many professions, although it is more central to some than to others. The purpose of this chapter is to describe the professions which use counseling as a tool. Having considered counseling as a process in detail, we turn now to the question: who are the counselors?

In the first chapter it was noted that various concepts of counseling exist and that these can roughly be classified into two types: those based on an educational model and those based on a medical model. The emphasis here has been that counseling follows an educational model, in contrast with psychotherapy as based on a medical model. Nevertheless, professions which are primarily medical in orientation do make use of counseling tools, and these will be included in this discussion.

PROFESSIONS BASED IN EDUCATION

The modern history of counseling in America is generally considered to have begun with the work of Frank Parsons, a Boston educator, who in the first decade of this century established a vocational guidance service to help out-of-school youth find jobs consistent with their abilities and interests. His book, *Choosing a Vocation,* published posthumously in 1909, is considered a landmark in the development of vocational counseling.

Further impetus was provided by World War I, which stimulated the development of psychological measures of abilities, subsequently adapted for counseling use in the 1920s. The Depression of the 1930s further stimulated interest in the understanding of jobs, so that by the middle of the century the groundwork for modern counseling and guidance had been firmly established. (For more extensive discussions of the history of guidance in this country, see Norris, 1954; Borow, 1964; and Miller, 1964.)

School Counseling

Although vocational counseling began outside of the schools, the public schools soon assumed this responsibility as one of their legitimate functions. For many years, the schools engaged in counseling oriented primarily to helping graduates find jobs or select suitable further education. Gradually, however, as school counselors became more professionally sophisticated they grew dissatisfied with the restricted emphasis on vocational choice. They became aware that many student problems, although ostensibly concerned with educational or vocational confusion, in actuality reflected more deep-seated personal difficulties. At first, school counselors tended to avoid dealing with the latter kinds of problems and instead attempted to refer them elsewhere, but gradually, spurred by the writings of psychologists such as Carl Rogers, they began to extend their scope of responsibility, so that the range of their counseling became broader. The modern school counselor, therefore, would hardly consider vocational and educational counseling as his sole area of responsibility, although he probably spends most of his time helping students select courses, jobs, and colleges.

The belief that counseling is an important responsibility of the public schools is firmly established. As of 1960, only three-fourths of the high schools in this country employed counselors (Wrenn, 1962), but many of the remainder were small schools which would have probably been eager to hire a counselor if one were available. Certainly the need for counselors has exceeded the supply for many years, and there is yet no end to the gap in sight.

Partly because of the shortage of trained counselors as well as the desire to get more for their money, it has been the practice of some schools to employ "teacher-counselors," persons who work part-time as counselors and part-time as teachers. This combination, while perhaps necessary at one time as an expedient, has come under severe criticism as unprofessional and is disappearing. It is becoming increasingly expected that the school counselor be a professional in his own right, rather than simply a teacher who gets along well with students and is given some free time in which to talk with them about their problems.

The qualifications of school counselors have steadily risen, although their adequacy can still be questioned. Most states now certify counselors for work in the schools, and the certification requirements normally require education approaching or including a master's degree. The American Personnel and Guidance Association, the leading professional organization devoted to counseling, is becoming more involved in the upgrading of state certification requirements for counselors (Stoughton, 1965), and greater uniformity can be expected in the future.

Most state regulations include the requirement of teaching experience for certification as a school counselor. Whether teaching experience is necessary, or even desirable, is a controversial point. Some authorities (for example, Farwell, 1961; Hoyt, 1961, 1962) argue that it is necessary because the counselor must function as part of the teaching team and would not be accepted by teachers if he were not truly one of them. Others, such as Arbuckle (1961b), have suggested, however, that the roles of teacher and counselor have little in common and may, in fact, be incompatible. They point out that the teaching role requires direction and evaluation, both of which are inappropriate for counseling.

This writer has more sympathy for the latter position. In his experience, the teacher who becomes a counselor often has to unlearn certain attitudes and behaviors in order to be effective in his new role. In addition, the person whose background is limited to teaching may not be able effectively to counsel with the student who is not academically oriented. Certification standards often suggest that the counselor ought to have had experience in business or industry, but this is seldom enforced as rigidly as is the requirement of teaching experience. There is ample evidence that school counselors have consistently paid more attention to the bright, college-bound student and have had difficulty empathizing with the potential drop-out or otherwise academically retarded adolescent (Wrenn, 1962). In light of the current upheavals in our society, it is evident that counselors with a diversity of experiences and fresh ideas are badly needed.

It is important, of course, that the school counselor have a basic commitment to, and understanding of, the profession of education. But the belief that such a commitment and understanding can be gained only through teaching experience is a matter of opinion rather than of fact. As with many requirements within education, this dogma has persisted in the face of a sizeable body of evidence to the contrary.

Despite their historical antecedents, school counselors spend a relatively small amount of time in vocational counseling with students (Super, 1964). This probably reflects their lack of confidence in their knowledge of the world of work as well as their preference for working with the brighter students. Instead, most of their time is spent helping students to plan their high school programs and to plan for education beyond high school. School counselors are typically responsible for the school's guidance program, which includes not only counseling with individual students but also administering standardized tests, maintaining the students' cumulative folders, operating career days, and similar activities. In some schools the counselors are also responsible for student discipline, although the more enlightened schools recognize that this activity is incompatible with a counseling role.

The amount of time that counselors spend with individual students is minimal. They have responsibilities to too many students to allow any one student to take up a large share of their time. This situation is unfortunate, since it causes many students to miss an opportunity for constructive help with personal problems and development. Yet it must be recognized that the school counselor cannot, and should not, attempt psychotherapy. One of the unfortunate results of the blurring of the distinction between counseling and psychotherapy is that some counselors believe that psychotherapy with students is now their responsibility. This writer agrees with Moore (1961) that it is not, and it should not be. There are many competent psychotherapists outside of the school to whom referrals can be made. Most school counselors have neither the time nor the competence to undertake psychotherapy. They can render the greatest service to the greatest number of students by doing a good job of counseling.

The counseling-psychotherapy controversy has raised another issue which plagues school counseling: the conflict between directive and nondirective approaches. Many counselors, having defined their role primarily as that of facilitating personal growth, and having been indoctrinated in Rogers's client-centered approach, tend to counsel all students within a framework of reflection and apparent passivity. Not surprisingly, many students have reacted negatively to this approach, having expected the counselor to be of more active help to them. The result has been that the counselor often feels abused and misunderstood, when his attempts to provide a setting for the student's personal growth are rejected and as teachers and parents criticize him for not giving the students enough help.

Certainly a substantial amount of damage has been inflicted on students by counselors who were too intent on giving advice or urging a certain course of action to actually listen to the student and try to understand his point of view. And certainly the nondirective approach is safe, in that the counselor cannot be blamed for having influenced the student in a direction that later proved unwise. But for the counselor to attempt to be completely nondirective, ignoring relevant test data and other sources of information which may be useful to the student, seems equally irresponsible. The school counselor is expected to be an expert, in terms of knowledge of relevant information and the ability to ask helpful questions and to make relevant suggestions. This can be done without interfering with the client's responsibility for making his own decisions. The public has the right to be dissatisfied with the counselor who tries to cloak his lack of relevant knowledge behind the guise of nondirective techniques.

School Psychology

The distinction between the school counselor and school psychologist is unclear to many people, but the confusion is unnecessary. The school psychologist's role in most schools is clearly different from that of the counselor (Higgens, 1966). The psychologist acts as a consultant to teachers and administrators rather than being responsible directly for the students. He advises teachers in their work with individual pupils, especially with those who pose problems for the teacher, and he advises administrators regarding decisions to be made about certain pupils: for example, whether a pupil should be promoted despite a poor record, or whether he should be placed in a special class for slow learners. He may also counsel with parents to help them understand their child's problems in school and to advise them as to how they can help him.

School psychology has its historical antecedents in clinical psychology (to be discussed shortly). The school psychologist relies heavily on clinical tools, including measures of intellectual functioning and of personality traits. His first responsibility is diagnostic evaluation of pupils referred to him, on the basis of which he recommends a course of action. Because of the heavy workload in accomplishing this function, most school psychologists generally engage in a minimum of direct therapeutic work with individual pupils, referring instead to outside sources of help and acting as a liaison between the school and the outside agency.

The orientation of school psychologists is often divided, and the field thereby suffers from a kind of schizophrenia. Most school psychologists are certified by the state department of education, and certification usually requires a minimum of a master's degree obtained from an approved program. The locus of such programs varies, some being operated through psychology departments and others by departments of education or educational psychology. Many of the students in such programs have originally been teachers, and they are therefore torn between identification with education and psychology. Other psychologists often are not sure they are really psychologists, especially since they usually have only the master's degree, and teachers are dubious of their commitment to education. The result is a confused identity on the part of the school psychologist. This confusion is likely to increase as the profession of elementary school counseling becomes more widespread. Typically the school psychologists have worked primarily at the elementary level, leaving the high school to the school counselors. The encroachment of counselors into the territory of the school psychologist will require accommodation by both professions.

Bardon (1968) has suggested that the role of the school psychologist might well be considered analogous to that of the industrial psychologist, in that he is responsible for promoting optimum integration of the individual pupil with the educational setting. Such a view has the potential for freeing the school psychologist from a rather archaic diagnostic role and enabling him to make more meaningful use of his training as a psychologist and of his interest in the educational process.

Counseling Psychology

The counseling psychologist is ". . . a psychologist who uses varying combinations of exploratory experience, psychometric techniques, and psychotherapeutic interviewing to assist people to grow and to develop" (Pepinsky and others, 1956, p. 283). As compared with some of the other counseling professions, counseling psychology is of recent origin. It builds upon the vocational and educational concerns of school counseling, to which it applies the specialized knowledge and skills of the psychologist in helping normal persons with normal problems.

Counseling psychology has its roots in the psychometric tradition within psychology, which has stressed the isolating of ability and interest variables related to vocational success and satisfaction. To this have been added the therapeutic skills of the clinical psychologist, applied to help normal persons understand themselves more clearly in relation to their environment (Super, 1955). Only in the period since World War II has counseling psychology become clearly differentiated as a specialty area within psychology. The speed of its growth, however, has more than made up for its belated entry.

Counseling psychologists are concerned with service to those in need, but they also recognize a responsibility to operate as scientists, within the framework of basic psychology. They are concerned with increasing the understanding of the counseling process and of human development, and their training includes a strong emphasis on research. The result, however, is that the job responsibilities of counseling psychologists are not always clear. Many have strong service interests while others prefer to spend a substantial amount of their time engaged in research. Both roles are clearly appropriate, but the individual psychologist may have difficulty in arriving at an optimum combination.

Although the development of counseling psychology was given a major boost by the Veterans Administration following World War II, and a substantial number of counseling psychologists continue to work for the VA, the majority are employed in educational settings (Peterson and Featherstone, 1962; Yamamoto, 1963), primarily in colleges and universities rather than in the public schools. Perhaps this concentration is due, at least in part, to the scarcity of counseling psychologists in relation to the number of positions available to them. If so, we can expect them to appear in more diverse settings in the future.

About one-third of the counseling psychologists have substantial teaching responsibilities and about one-fourth are primarily administrators, which leaves less than half engaged primarily in service activities (Thompson and Super, 1964). They deal mainly with the typical adjustment problems of normal people and rely primarily on counseling and testing as their basic tools (Jordaan and others, 1968). Many, however, are also competent psychotherapists and engage in this activity at times, although few specialize in it.

The distinction between clinical and counseling psychology has never been entirely clear. Clinical psychology, having developed first and having been identified with the more prestigious medical profession, has enjoyed a higher status, which has prompted occasional attempts to merge the two fields. There appear, however, to be some important distinctions which warrant continued separation, albeit with close cooperation. The tools which each use most typically (for example, different kinds of psychological tests) are different enough to warrant separate, although overlapping, training programs, and the problems presented by their clients are also different enough to justify different practicum and internship experiences (Schofield, 1966). These differences are of degree, however, rather than of substance, and the job responsibilities of counseling and clinical psychologists working in the same setting are often not dramatically different.

The interests of counseling psychologists vary widely, which in part accounts for the confusion in relation to other fields. Some are primarily interested in vocational and educational problems and therefore have much in common with school counselors, while others are more attracted to personal problems and abnormal difficulties, a la the clinical psychologist. Some rely heavily on tests as tools in their work, while others are less interested in them. Some prefer to limit their service activities to one-to-one contacts with clients in their offices, while others take a more active responsibility in attempting to influence the environment of their clientele. At the present time, all of these roles are within the domain of the counseling psychologist, indicating that the label provides an umbrella which covers a wide range of activities. The major communality of all counseling psychologists is that they have an advanced degree in psychology and that their training program emphasized the acquisition of counseling skills and research tools for increasing our understanding of the adjustment problems of normal persons (Jordaan and others, 1968).

PROFESSIONS BASED IN MEDICINE

Abnormal behavior has always fascinated and disturbed society. The person who behaves irrationally seems frightening and dangerous, since one cannot cope with him by usual means. Attempts by society to explain and control such persons have often been as bizarre as the behavior itself.

For many centuries, persons who behaved irrationally were thought to be possessed of demons or of the devil and were often killed or imprisoned as a result. As man became more sophisticated, however, such explanations were no longer tenable. And since great strides were being made in understanding the nature of physical disorders, it was logical to ascribe the same sorts of causes to behavior disorders. Thus, during the nineteenth century, behavioral abnormalities became defined as "mental illness," and the treatment of these abnormalities became the province of the medical profession.

It is important to recognize that the medical model of treatment of behavior disorders rests on the assumption that the causes of such disorders are analogous to the causes of physical ailments, and that the same general treatment procedure is therefore applicable. This assumption is being increasingly questioned. As Szasz (1960, 1961) has pointed out, the concept of "mental illness" was developed partly as a way of making abnormal behavior socially acceptable and therefore treatable. He and many others have questioned whether a large share of behavior abnormalities are, in fact, illnesses. Some, of course, have clear organic causes and can therefore be treated medically. But the majority of emotional disorders have little, if any, known organic basis. To treat them as though they were truly illnesses may be fallacious. Yet the medical profession, which initially assumed responsibility for the care and treatment of persons with behavior abnormalities, has been reluctant to abandon the medical model of treatment. Instead, a large mental health industry has arisen, dominated by the medical profession, with satellite professions which operate within the general medical model.

Psychiatry

Psychiatrists are physicians who specialize in the treatment of behavior abnormalities. They are initially trained as medical doctors and become psychiatrists through further specialized experiences, in the same manner as a physician may specialize in pediatrics or surgery. Certification as a psychiatrist requires three years of residency in a psychiatric institution, plus two years of further practice (Wolberg, 1967).

The psychiatrist's specialized training is largely in the form of supervised, on-the-job experience, usually in a mental hospital. With the exception of a few training centers, the emphasis is on practical experience rather than on formal course work. Thus a psychiatrist, while being well grounded in the fundamentals of medicine, may know little basic psychology (Ausubel, 1956). He will have had considerable experience in dealing with the severely disturbed, but probably relatively little experience in working with persons with normal adjustment problems.

Some psychiatrists eventually become *psychoanalysts* by continuing their training in psychoanalytic training centers.[1] These persons generally engage in private practice, at least part-time, and emphasize techniques derived from the theories of Freud and his followers.

Psychiatrists vary greatly in their orientation and techniques. Some stick closely to their medical background and emphasize medically-oriented techniques, such as shock therapy (Pronko and others, 1960) and drug therapy (Battista, 1960; Sargant, 1965). Others rely more heavily on psychotherapy, and their clientele includes more patients who can make effective use of this approach.

The relationship between psychiatry and other professions has been stormy at times, the greatest conflict being with clinical psychology. Psychiatrists, because of the legal strength of their medical affiliation, have traditionally been accorded the top position among the mental health professions, and they have resisted attempts by other professions to challenge their supremacy. The psychiatrist is usually considered to be the leader of the psychiatric "team"—psychiatrist, clinical psychologist, and psychiatric social worker—in most clinics, although this rigid stratification is being increasingly challenged by the other professions. Conflict occurs mostly over the practice of psychotherapy, since it is generally conceded that persons without medical training should not be allowed to administer organic treatments, such as drugs.

Recent years have brought a rapid increase in publicly financed mental health facilities without a corresponding increase in the production of psychiatrists, resulting in a severe shortage. The length of training discourages many persons from entering the profession, as does the fact that psychiatry occupies a rather low status within the medical profession as a whole.[2] A contributing factor in this shortage is the desire of many psychiatrists to enter private practice rather than to work in a public agency or institution. As the state and federal governments, however, assume a larger role in the treatment of persons with behavioral disorders, the opportunities for psychiatrists in private practice may be gradually reduced.

---

[1] Some centers also train a few "laymen," such as clinical psychologists, as psychoanalysts, but most psychoanalysts have first been psychiatrists.

[2] It has been suggested that this status problem may augment the tendency of psychiatrists to be defensive toward threatened encroachments by non-medical professions.

Clinical Psychology

Many clinical psychologists would object strongly to being placed in such close conjunction with the medical profession. But because of the historical development of the field, as well as the medical orientation of some present clinicians, the field is placed here for purposes of discussion.

Clinical psychology traces its formal beginning to a psychological clinic founded by Witmer at the University of Pennsylvania in 1896. Witmer believed strongly that psychologists should put to use their knowledge of human behavior to help people with problems. His views initiated a controversy between applied and scientific psychology which persists to this day.

By the time psychologists entered the service arena, it had already been preempted by the medical profession. The role of the clinical psychologist therefore was defined as an adjunct to the psychiatrist. His special contribution was the assessment of psychological functioning by the use of psychological measurement devices, primarily individual intelligence tests and tests of personality characteristics, both objective and projective. As the Ph.D. degree became more common among clinical psychologists, they began to assume more responsibility for the research phase of the institution or agency in which they worked. For the most part, direct treatment remained the responsibility of the psychiatrist.

Prior to World War II the growth of clinical psychology was slow, and the employment of clinical psychologists outside of academic settings was limited mostly to child guidance clinics (Sundberg and Tyler, 1962). The war, however, produced a great need for the treatment of emotionally disturbed servicemen, a need which psychiatrists alone could not meet. Clinical psychologists were pressed into a treatment role and performed well enough to establish their competence in this area. On this basis, clinical psychologists were assigned a key role in the development of the Veterans Administration hospitals following the war, and the federal government provided stipends to support their training. The result was a sudden increase in the number of students entering clinical psychology, an upsurge in the size of the profession, and an upgrading and specification of training requirements (Santostefano and Kahn, 1966). A new force had emerged in the field of mental health.[3]

With this growth and professionalization, however, came a shift in role. The clinical psychologist, trained at the doctoral level and no longer content to operate within a limited role as defined by the psychiatric profession, moved more aggressively into psychotherapy and into private practice. Thus by 1960, Kelly (1961) could report that psychotherapy was the job

[3] For a more detailed discussion of the history of clinical psychology, see Reisman (1966).

activity most frequently cited by clinical psychologists he surveyed; psychological assessment had by then been relegated to second place.

The medical orientation of clinical psychologists, however, has by no means vanished. Kelly (1961) reported that, in 1960, approximately half of the clinical psychologists were employed in medical settings, with the next largest groups being in universities and private practice. This is consistent with the emphasis placed by clinical psychology on the medical model. Clinical psychologists, for the most part, work with behavioral abnormalities, although in settings such as colleges and universities they may also help normal persons with normal problems. They are more interested in personality reorganization than are counseling psychologists (Brigante, Haefner, and Woodson, 1962), and a substantial amount of their internship is in a mental hospital or mental health clinic. Their major tool is psychotherapy rather than counseling, although many clinicians are proficient in both.

To qualify as a clinical psychologist, a person must have a Ph.D. as well as appropriate internship experience (Hoch, Ross, and Winder, 1966). Some master's level persons function in clinical roles, generally in psychological assessment, under the supervision of a fully qualified clinical psychologist.

The ever greater involvement of clinical psychologists in psychotherapy, especially in combination with private practice, has aroused the antagonism of some psychiatrists, who view this as an infringement on the rights and responsibilities of the medical profession. Numerous attempts have been made, both on national and state levels, to reconcile the differences and to define the role of the clinical psychologist in a way acceptable to both professions. Progress has been made and issues have been clarified by such discussions (see, for example, the report by Kelly and Handler, 1960), but controversy still exists. The saddest part of the situation is that, considering the large number of persons in need of psychotherapy, both professions have more business than they can handle anyway. It is important that this issue be resolved as soon as possible so that the needs of the public can be more effectively met.

To imply that all psychiatrists are on one side of the controversy and all psychologists on the other would be misleading. Freud himself believed that competence in psychotherapy did not require a background in medicine, and many present-day psychiatrists concur. Wolberg (1967) has suggested that an interdisciplinary approach to the training of psychotherapists may be necessary, since at the present time much of the training of both professions is not directly relevant to psychotherapy. We will return to this issue in a later chapter.

Another current controversy, this time within the profession of clinical psychology itself, concerns relative emphasis on the research and service functions of the field. This dispute is also found within counseling psychology, although clinical psychologists have, over the years, made more substantial research contributions than have counseling psychologists.[4] Some clinical psychologists, especially those in academic settings, believe that the academic training of the psychologist obligates him to engage in research activities after obtaining his degree. Most of them will accept some service activity in addition, but their academic careers depend primarily on their scholarly productivity.

Clinical psychologists in service settings, on the other hand, tend to be heavily committed to service activities, often with little or no interest in research. To them, the doctorate is a union card which testifies to their high level of competence and, by entitling them to be called "Doctor," enables them to meet the psychiatrist on more-or-less equal ground. (Actually, the Ph.D. is a research degree whereas the M.D. is a professional degree, but both professions have been guilty of blurring this distinction.) As a result, the interests of the two groups of clinical psychologists are often at variance, and the continued conflict indicates that the profession of clinical psychology has not yet achieved a clear definition. It is this lack of agreement that makes it vulnerable to the onslaughts of other professions such as psychiatry.

Psychiatric Social Work

The traditional mental health team is a triumvirate: the psychiatrist, the clinical psychologist, and the psychiatric social worker. Originally, the role of the social worker was to gather data about incoming patients and to work with the patient's family to facilitate his progress in therapy. This role was a logical outgrowth of the social worker's training and experience in social agencies, and he adapted himself to the clinical and hospital setting accordingly.

Gradually, however, in the face of ever-increasing numbers of patients who needed psychotherapy, social workers began to assume this responsibility, under the supervision of psychiatrists. Out of this expansion a special branch of social work developed which came to be labeled *psychiatric social work,* and the social worker became a more direct part of the treatment phase of the clinic's operations.

To become a psychiatric social worker requires at least a master's

---

[4] One can only speculate on the reasons for this difference. In view of the greater prestige and financial support which clinical psychology has enjoyed, it is likely that the students entering clinical psychology are brighter on the average than those in counseling. It is also a fact that the doctorate is obtained at a younger age among clinicians than among counselors, which means that clinical psychologists have more of the creative years in which to be productive.

degree. The typical program covers two years, with one year spent in learning the basic skills and knowledge required for social work and the second in supervised internship in a clinic or hospital. The finished product is a person who is reasonably competent to conduct psychotherapy and who can fit smoothly into the typical team relationship.

Since the education of a psychiatric social worker requires less time than that of a psychiatrist or a clinical psychologist, and since the former is trained to work in a rather specific setting, it is not surprising that the supply of psychiatric social workers available to mental health clinics and similar agencies is greater than is the supply of psychiatrists and clinical psychologists. One result is that many clinics rely heavily on psychiatric social workers to conduct much of the actual treatment, other than that which is clearly medical. Psychiatric social workers are strongly service-oriented, and it has been speculated that the bulk of the psychotherapy in this country is probably being conducted by psychiatric social workers rather than by either psychiatrists or psychologists.

It may seem strange that the psychiatric profession has tolerated the increasing involvement of social workers in psychotherapy, in light of its constant friction with psychology over this issue. The explanation is that most psychiatric social workers view their role as supplementary to that of the psychiatrist rather than as independent of him. The social worker is trained to work in the clinic setting under the supervision of a psychiatrist, and few have the confidence or the aggressiveness to want to break away from this model. In most clinics, the arrangement is such that the social workers are presumably simply carrying out the instructions of the psychiatrist, who has first diagnosed the patient and prescribed the treatment. The amount of direct supervision which the psychiatrist provides will vary, depending in part on the skills and experience of the social worker. Nevertheless, in this arrangement the psychiatrist is clearly responsible for the patient, and he can be called to account for any inept therapy administered by a social worker under his supervision.

The clinical psychologist, on the other hand, trained at the doctoral level and identifying with a profession clearly distinct from psychiatry, is much more likely to expect to be treated as an independent and equal professional, in some cases to the extent of being permitted legally to engage in independent private practice, a status strongly opposed by the psychiatric profession. Few social workers would be so bold as to demand these prerogatives, and psychiatrists therefore see little threat from them as a group.

This is not to imply that psychiatric social workers necessarily engage in a strongly medically-oriented form of psychotherapy. Kaplan (1963) has argued that social work psychotherapy is different from psychiatric psychotherapy in stressing a psychosocial rather than a biosocial orientation. There are certainly many shades of orientation within both groups, but psychotherapy as conducted by social workers does add a worthwhile dimension to the treatment of persons with behavioral disorders.

OTHER PROFESSIONS THAT USE COUNSELING

In addition to those professions discussed up to now, there are others in which counseling skills may sometimes come into play although it is not their major role. Physicians and lawyers, for example, occasionally assume a temporary counseling relationship with a distraught or confused person, but their primary responsibility is for aid of another sort. If prolonged counseling or psychotherapy were needed, a referral would be made to a professional more directly skilled in that area.

Two other professions which are in a similar sort of position with regard to persons with problems are social workers and ministers. Because counseling situations may, however, arise more frequently for them than for physicians and lawyers, we will examine their counseling responsibilities in more detail.

Social Work

Earlier a distinction was drawn between the psychiatric social worker and the social case worker, primarily on the basis that the former is competent to conduct psychotherapy under supervision. Social workers in general are trained to give direct assistance to people with problems, primarily by administering welfare programs and aiding persons in trouble to arrange their lives more satisfactorily. Many social workers have only a bachelor's degree, and the turnover among them is great. They work primarily in social agencies, such as family service and adoption, and attempt to help people deal with specific problems that have brought them to the agency. Social workers tend to rely heavily on direct advice and on environmental manipulation rather than on counseling *per se,* a role which is usually appropriate to the type of clientele they serve and the problems which are brought to them.

The primary area in which social workers are apt to assume a counseling relationship is in handling family problems. From this activity a special area of counseling, called marriage counseling, has developed. It will be discussed in greater detail later.

Ministers

In a nationwide survey of where people with emotional problems are most apt to go first for help, the clergy led all professions by a wide margin

(Gurin, Veroff, and Feld, 1960).[5] The minister is thus the initial contact for many troubled persons, and in some instances they are unwilling to go elsewhere.

Ministers therefore have frequent opportunity to engage in counseling if they desire. It is generally agreed that the minister bears some responsibility for counseling with his parishioners, especially concerning problems with a religious involvement, but that he should not attempt to conduct psychotherapy (Pacella, 1966; Wolberg, 1967). It is also agreed that ministers who attempt to counsel should have sufficient training to do a competent job. There is an increasing emphasis on training in pastoral counseling in the education of ministers, and opportunities are available for more intensive training for those ministers who intend to specialize in counseling (Johnson, 1967; O'Sullivan, 1968). There is some concern, however, that the minister who invests a large amount of time in counseling may do so to the detriment of his other responsibilities (Pacella, 1966). For this reason, some authorities advise the minister to limit his counseling unless he is in a setting in which he can legitimately play a more specialized role.

Ministers who engage in counseling should, of course, recognize their professional limitations and be willing to refer to more skilled professionals when the need arises. There is some evidence that the better educated ministers are more likely to refer elsewhere, which means that some ministers may be attempting to conduct counseling for which they are not qualified (Bentz, 1962). It is important that the counseling competencies of ministers be upgraded as much as possible, not so that they will spend a large part of their time in counseling, but so that they can give the troubled person a favorable introduction to the counseling process and then make an appropriate referral.

HYBRID PROFESSIONS

The professions discussed thus far are established entities, although the identities of some are not entirely clear. As society changes, however, and new needs arise, new professions evolve to meet these needs. Such professions emerge first from existing professions and gradually solidify and differentiate into distinct entities. In the meantime, however, they draw from their roots in various traditional professions, so that they must be considered as hybrid professions. Two of this sort which will be discussed here are rehabilitation counseling and marriage counseling.

---

[5] Of the persons sampled, 42 percent said they would go first to a minister, 29 percent to a doctor, 18 percent to a psychiatrist or psychologist, and 13 percent to a social service agency.

Rehabilitation Counseling

Rehabilitation counseling is "an occupation concerned with assisting physically and emotionally disabled individuals to find satisfactory social and work roles in society" (Sussman and Haug, 1967b, p. 1). Like several others of the counseling professions, rehabilitation counseling developed first to provide help in vocational adjustment, in this case for disabled persons. Gradually, however, its scope has broadened to include counseling with disabled persons to facilitate their adjustment to themselves and to society.

Rehabilitation counselors deal not only with the effects of physical handicaps but also with mental and emotional disorders. Their potential clientele is therefore sizeable; DiMichael (1964) estimates that nearly three million adults and one-and-one-quarter million children would qualify for rehabilitation services in this country.

Although rehabilitation counseling was originally provided by private services, since World War II the field has been largely preempted by the Veterans Administration and by state departments of vocational rehabilitation, the latter assisted by the Vocational Rehabilitation Administration in the Department of Health, Education, and Welfare. Most of the rehabilitation counseling within the Veterans Administration is conducted by counseling psychologists and within the state agencies by rehabilitation counselors. The latter are less well trained, only forty percent having a master's degree (Sussman and Haug, 1967a).

The job of the rehabilitation counselor varies, depending partly on his training. In general, he works with persons with physical disabilities or emotional problems, helping them to adjust to society, with particular emphasis on vocational choice and adjustment. He attempts to encourage the client to focus on his assets rather than his limitations. Since he works with a group which is often shunned by society, in many cases he finds it necessary to make direct contacts with prospective employers, to help them accept and utilize handicapped persons. The role of the rehabilitation counselor in "environmental manipulation" may provide a model for future counselors responsible for other culturally anomalous groups.

Because of the relatively low level of training of rehabilitation counselors, as well as their scarcity, the amount of actual counseling which they conduct is often minimal (Peterson, 1964). This has led Patterson (1968) to recommend that the counseling function be separated from other aspects of rehabilitation work, to free those trained as counselors to spend more of their time in counseling. Although Patterson's concern is understandable, it would be unfortunate if rehabilitation counselors were encouraged to retreat behind the closed doors of their offices, as counselors in other areas have tended to do.

Part of the confusion concerning the role of the rehabilitation counselor has come about because several professions—including psychology, education, and social work—have contributed to the development of the field (Super, 1964). The divergent emphases of each of these professions has inevitably led to conflict, and the counselor trained in one orientation, such as psychology, may find it difficult to understand the concerns of one with a background in social work. Ultimately, however, one can hope that these various bloodlines will merge to produce a profession which combines the best traits of its parent professions to meet a major social need.

Certainly the knowledge and skills required of a rehabilitation counselor are broad. He should, of course, be well-grounded in counseling skills and in knowledge of the world of work, but in addition he should have sufficient medical background to understand the physical limitations of the client as well as his potentials (Lofquist, 1957; DiMichael, 1964). Few persons would come by such a background casually, and programs designed specifically to train rehabilitation counselors are becoming increasingly visible. Some counselors intensify their training and become specialists in working with clients with very specific disabilities, such as blindness, but in many agencies such narrow specialization is impractical.

Marriage Counseling

A major concern of modern society is the maintenance of family stability. The alarmingly high divorce rate is a sign that many couples marry with insufficient knowledge or consideration about the responsibility they are undertaking, while many others find themselves unable to adjust to the stresses and strains which are bound to arise when two persons attempt to merge their lives into one.

Out of this concern has developed marriage counseling, a counseling specialty which deals specifically with problems of marital adjustment. Begun within social agencies by members of the social work profession, it has gradually been infiltrated by professionals of varying backgrounds, so that present-day marriage counselors have their roots in several professions, some of which better equip their members to engage in marriage counseling than do others. Even within a single profession, however, there is unlikely to be any clear road by which one qualifies as a marriage counselor.

Marriage Counseling as a Profession.   Many persons who have wandered into marriage counseling as a specialty began with training in counseling to which they subsequently added an interest in problems of marriage and the family. Although their qualifications as counselors may be adequate, such persons may not have sufficient professional knowledge of family structure or of areas such as sexual physiology to prepare them to deal with marital problems. Others with a strong background in family dynamics may have little counseling training and view marriage counseling as an opportunity to impart advice to persons less well informed than they. Neither person, despite his good intentions, is truly qualified as a marriage counselor, but under present circumstances there is no clear way of specifying his deficiencies.

The lack of a clear definition of the qualifications of a marriage counselor has caused speculation as to whether marriage counseling should be considered a professional specialty. In some respects it already is: full-time marriage counselors tend to identify with a cohesive group, primarily represented by the American Association of Marriage Counselors and the National Council on Family Relations. Yet their backgrounds are diverse, encompassing psychiatry, psychology, and social work as well as law, medicine, and the ministry (Johnson, 1961). This situation has led Harper (1953) to recommend that special training programs for marriage counselors be developed and that marriage counseling be conducted on a full time basis. Many persons currently engaged in marriage counseling do not limit themselves to that activity, but instead combine it with individual counseling or psychotherapy. Harper believes that as long as this arrangement continues, marriage counseling cannot be established as a full-fledged professional specialty.

Whether marriage counseling should, in fact, be separated from other forms of counseling is debatable. Certainly it is foolish to believe that anyone trained in individual counseling can automatically counsel persons with marital problems; some specialized training and knowledge are clearly required. Yet to argue that marriage counselors should limit themselves to a specific problem area and a specific type of clientele seems to ignore some obvious similarities between counseling persons with marital problems and counseling persons with problems in other areas.

Clientele.   Persons come to a marriage counselor for help because they are having difficulty getting along together, or because one partner is unhappy and believes the marriage to be the cause of his distress. Among the areas of difficulty commonly presented are finances, sex, in-laws, religion, and job pressures. In some cases the problem is truly that specific and can be dealt with accordingly, but more often the presenting problem is only a symptom of a more basic difficulty. On the basis of their experience with a large number of marital problems, Hey and Mudd (1959) have suggested that the most frequently encountered problems are caused by loneliness, rejection (real or imagined), loss of perspective, a breakdown of communication, or a real-life trauma such as a death in the family or the loss of a job. All of these difficulties can have serious consequences, but their effects can also be amenable to the help of a counselor.

Sometimes a husband and wife seek marriage counseling together, but more often one partner—usually the wife—initiates it first. Although this is a beginning, most marriage counselors agree that much more can be accomplished if both the husband and wife are involved in the counseling (Saul and others, 1953). Since the focus in marriage counseling is on the relationship between the two, both must participate in the counseling if the relationship is to be substantially altered. Rarely is only one partner at fault, and change on the part of one will likely produce only frustration as no corresponding change comes from the other.

This is not to say that nothing can be accomplished if one member refuses to become involved in counseling. The motivated member may be helped to adjust more satisfactorily to the relationship as it exists, and may perhaps even learn how to exert more control over the relationship. But most marriage counselors will make every effort to encourage the resistant partner to enter counseling before agreeing to counsel with the one member alone.

The Role of the Marriage Counselor.   Marriage counseling deals primarily with a disordered relationship between two persons. The husband and wife must not, of course, be ignored as individuals, but their interaction is of chief concern to the marriage counselor. If it becomes evident that the root of the difficulty lies in adjustment problems of one or both of the parties, the emphasis shifts to them as individuals and the concern for the relationship is temporarily abandoned.

If either of the individuals appears to have deep-seated emotional problems which are contributing to the marital disruption, he will generally be advised to seek individual psychotherapy. Some marriage counselors undertake this responsibility themselves, but most prefer to refer the client elsewhere (Foster, 1956). If, at a later time, marriage counseling for the couple seems warranted it can be resumed. By the same token, the marriage counselor should feel free to refer to other professionals, such as a lawyer or physician, when their specialized knowledge may be of value to his clients.

Just as not all counselors would accept the distinction between counseling and psychotherapy proposed earlier in this book, not all marriage counselors would agree that emotionally disturbed persons should be treated individually first before marriage counseling can be successful. Some practitioners, in fact, speak of marriage *therapy* rather than marriage counseling (see, for example, Haley, 1963; Watson, 1963; Sager, 1966), by which they appear to mean a process which deals with rather seriously disturbed persons and highly neurotic relationships. Nevertheless, it is important to bear in mind that most marriage counseling deals with normal persons with normal problems of adjustment. Relatively few couples need the services of a marriage therapist.

The goal of marriage counseling is not, as many persons would suppose, the preservation of the marriage. As with any counseling, the client must be free to make his own decisions; it is the counselor's responsibility to help him think things through rationally and thoroughly, so that he can live with the decision he makes. Certainly, successful marriage counseling often results in a "saved" marriage, but divorce may be a reasonable solution for a husband and wife who are not able to adjust their differences despite the help of counseling.[6] Marriage counseling which ends in divorce does not therefore necessarily signify failure, although most marriage counselors would prefer to view their role as primarily that of preserving marriages rather than of terminating them.

Marriage Counseling Techniques. For the most part, the techniques of the marriage counselor are those basic to counseling of any type. The principles described in the early chapters of this book are followed, to achieve the same general purposes.

Because the marriage counselor usually has two clients rather than one, however, he may make use of some varied approaches which are seldom possible in individual counseling. These may include the involvement of more than one counselor, as well as joint interviews with both partners.

Despite the possible conflicts which may arise, most marriage counselors prefer to counsel with both parties of the marriage, usually at separate times. This means that the same marriage counselor conducts individual counseling interviews with both the husband and wife, perhaps occasionally seeing them together as well. This practice has been frequently debated, with both the advocates and critics presenting strong arguments.

The practice of one counselor working with both the husband and wife poses some obvious problems. He must be equally fair and objective with each partner, despite the temptation to weigh the evidence and to be more sympathetic to one side than the other. He may also easily be caught in the middle, since each partner may try to use him against the other. The adroit counselor will sidestep such attempts, and perhaps even use them constructively in the counseling, but the energy thus spent by the clients could be better utilized in working directly on their difficulties. The counselor may also find himself in the position of sharing a confidence with one party of which the other is unaware—for example, the husband's infidelity—which may cause him to be guarded in his relationship with the other party, to the detriment of the counseling itself.

---

[6] The acceptance of divorce as a possible solution to marital problems may be difficult, and perhaps impossible, for a counselor whose personal or religious values dictate otherwise. To be successful, such a counselor must separate his own values from those of his clients, or restrict himself to counseling only with persons who share his value system.

Most marriage counselors will argue that their client is the marriage, rather than either the husband or wife individually, and that they are better able to serve this client by counseling with both partners. To assign the clients to different counselors would, they believe, further disrupt a marriage which is already on shaky ground. Furthermore, these counselors believe that they can gain a better picture of the marriage by counseling with both clients: they can perceive distortions and inappropriate interactions which they can bring to the attention of the clients and thereby help them become more sensitive to their relationship.

Both views have merit and are to some extent a product of the varying backgrounds of different marriage counselors. Those trained in social work, accustomed to working with families and with groups, tend more naturally to prefer to see both partners, while those with a background in individual counseling, such as psychologists and psychiatrists, may feel more comfortable seeing only one member of the pair with another counselor responsible for the partner. In the latter case, however, it is important that the two counselors work closely together on the case; otherwise only individual counseling, not marriage counseling, is taking place.

The other issue of technique is whether it is better to see the two parties separately or together for counseling. The so-called "conjoint interview" has been much debated as a marriage counseling technique (see Karpf, 1951; Skidmore and Garrett, 1955; Smith and Anderson, 1963; and Leslie, 1964). These writers agree that it can be valuable if used sparingly, but they caution against using it to any great extent or without adequate preparation.

The joint interview is generally used when the clients have decided, in their individual sessions, that they need to discuss an area of difficulty together but that they seem unable to do so on their own. Often this is because the topic has strong emotional overtones for one or both persons, so that a typical discussion quickly degenerates into anger or tears. The presence of the counselor can provide a more secure, objective situation in which the husband and wife can discuss the issue without the usual stress. The counselor's role is to point out the basic areas of difficulty and to help the clients begin to deal with them constructively. A successful joint interview should enable the husband and wife to discuss the topic further outside of the counselor's office, based on the approach they learned during the counseling.

If a joint interview is undertaken too soon, or with insufficient preparation, it may accomplish little and may, in fact, make one or both parties dissatisfied with the entire counseling. It is desirable that the husband and wife each have become accustomed to individual counseling and have developed faith in the counselor before a joint interview is attempted.

The joint interview seems a logical step when one counselor is seeing both the husband and wife, but what if two counselors are involved? A joint interview can still be arranged, in which all four parties—the husband and wife, plus their respective counselors—are included. This sounds a little complicated, but it can work well if the counselors have agreed beforehand on the purpose and approach of the interview. To be even more complex, we might add a third counselor, who would deal with the marital relationship, leaving the other two counselors free to concentrate on the individual problems of their clients (see, for example, Fulcomer, Edelman, and Lewis, 1961). Anyone who wants to carry things this far had better have a large office in which to meet.

Premarital Counseling. Most marriage counselors do not limit their clientele to persons already married. Since they view one of their responsibilities as the prevention of marital disorder, as well as the alleviation of disorders which have already occurred, most marriage counselors welcome the opportunity to counsel with persons prior to marriage.

Premarital counseling may be initiated by a single person or by a couple planning on marriage, for a variety of reasons. The couple may anticipate an area of potential difficulty, such as differing religious views, which they hope to resolve prior to marriage. Or they may simply want an opportunity to discuss their views about family relationships with someone who can remain objective and who may suggest areas which they have overlooked. A single person, on the other hand, may be troubled by an inability to find a marital partner or perhaps by indecision among several marriage possibilities. In all cases, however, the emphasis is on the person or the couple in relation to a future marriage. This emphasis at least partially distinguishes premarital counseling from other forms of counseling, although the distinction is certainly often not clear-cut.[7]

Most ministers believe that one of their responsibilities is to interview couples at whose marriage they have been asked to officiate, in order to ascertain that the couple has considered the important issues in marriage and to provide an opportunity for discussion of any areas of potential difficulty. Some ministers are satisfied with one or two interviews with the couple, unless further sessions seem warranted, but others insist on an extensive series of "counseling" sessions. Whether counseling is actually taking place under such circumstances is debatable. In cases in which the couple has a strong religious commitment, such sessions may evolve into premarital counseling, but in many cases the couple simply goes through the prescribed ritual in a perfunctory manner because it is required. The minister who insists that the couple discuss personal areas with him may succeed only in alienating himself as a potential resource if difficulties later arise in the marriage (Furgeson, 1952).

---

[7] For a more extensive discussion of premarital counseling, see Rutledge (1966).

As with any form of counseling, the minister can only offer a service, he cannot impose it on anyone. The best guidelines for ministers interested in premarital counseling would seem to be (a) to acquire the training necessary to conduct counseling sessions with engaged couples, and (b) to be sensitive to the counseling motivation of the couple before embarking on an extensive series of interviews.

Family Counseling and Therapy.   Marriage counseling typically deals only with the husband and wife, but there is growing interest in viewing marital problems as involving the entire family, children as well as parents. This view seems most appropriate when the difficulties of one or more of the family members are creating considerable disruption within the family. Under such circumstances, some sort of family counseling or family therapy may be warranted.

It is beyond the scope of this book to consider family therapy in detail. The writers who have been most influential in the development of this approach, and whose work should be consulted for descriptions of goals and techniques, are Ackerman (1961a, 1961b, 1966; Ackerman and Behrens, 1967), Jackson (Jackson and Weaklund, 1961; Jackson and Yalom, 1965), and Satir (1967). Their orientations are more consistent with the principles of individual psychotherapy than of counseling, but they do present approaches to the treatment of disturbed individuals and families which are finding increasing acceptance.

SETTINGS FOR COUNSELING

Counseling takes place in many professional settings. The more common settings, to be described here, are the educational settings—elementary school, secondary school, and college—government settings, and community agencies. Counseling also takes place in other settings, but less frequently and less systematically.

One reason for a discussion of settings for counseling is that the setting tends to limit the counselor's clientele. A counselor who works in a college counseling service, for example, tends to see persons in late adolescence or early adulthood who are above average in intelligence. This restriction of clientele may cause the counselor to overlook the counseling needs of other groups and to lack understanding of the problems of counselors working in other settings. In order that the potential of counseling can be most effectively exploited, it is important for all counselors to bear in mind that there is no ideal counseling setting nor an ideal clientele. Each setting and each type of client presents its unique problems and challenges.

Counseling in the Public Schools

Most states require that counseling in the public schools be done only by persons certified as guidance counselors within the state. Therefore the counseling which is available in a school setting is limited to that within the competence and interest of the school *guidance counselor,* whose training and experience were described earlier. Some authorities have argued that the counseling services available within the schools should be broadened, at least by relaxing the requirements for certification, but few states have as yet responded to these suggestions. The rather rigid certification requirements in existence, while serving to maintain a minimum set of standards for guidance counselors, have the effect of preventing persons who might otherwise be highly qualified as counselors from offering their services to the schools.

The typical guidance counselor, as noted earlier, has a variety of responsibilities in addition to that of counseling with students. The basic guidance services for which he is responsible, as described by Thompson (1964), include the collation and dissemination of occupational information, personal data collection, counseling, placement, and follow-up and research. It is little wonder that time spent in actual counseling with students may be quite restricted and contacts with individual students may often appear brief and perfunctory.

The lack of time available in most school settings for extensive individual counseling may be one reason why guidance counselors do not enjoy a highly favorable public image (see, for example, Shertzer and Stone, 1963). The many responsibilities of the school counselor prevent him from establishing and maintaining the relationships with students necessary for effective counseling, with the result that the students are often frustrated and resentful after having undergone a superficial and incomplete counseling experience. It would seem to be one of the professional responsibilities of the school counselor to define his role so that he is able to provide the services which he believes are of greatest importance to his students.

Counseling in a school setting is also complicated by the multiple relationships which a counselor may have with the students. Although it is generally agreed that the teacher-counselor combination does not operate effectively, and such hybrids are being phased out by most schools, the guidance counselor may nonetheless find it more difficult than his counterpart in a college setting to limit his contacts with students to the confines of his office. He will be expected to work with student committees and activities and otherwise to develop contacts with students outside of his office. While such experiences may be useful in helping the counselor make initial contacts with students, they may tend to interfere with the development of an ideal counseling relationship. The counselor in a school setting will probably find it necessary to strike a balance between being aloof and overly involved with students.

Within recent years, guidance counseling has entered the elementary school (Faust, 1968; Van Hoose, 1968), generally following the model found in the secondary schools. As in the secondary schools, the elementary school counselor must meet requirements for state certification, which generally are quite similar to those required for certification at the secondary level.[8] Here again, it is quite difficult for persons without a traditional guidance background to work as counselors in an elementary setting.

The role of the counselor in the elementary school has been rather difficult to define, since it is not simply an elementary version of secondary school counseling. As noted in an earlier chapter, children differ from adolescents in several respects important to counseling, including less maturity and less sophisticated command of language (Peters, 1959; Aubrey, 1967). Moreover, the needs of children are different from those of adolescents, since they are not expected to make immediate plans for the future nor to take major responsibility for their decisions. As a result, elementary school counseling has emphasized the developmental needs of children and the promotion of social change (Gordon, 1966; Van Hoose, Peters, and Leonard, 1967; Van Hoose, 1968), with the counselor being encouraged to take more responsibility for direct assistance. It is assumed that the elementary school counselor works more closely with parents than at the secondary level and that more use is made of group and play techniques and less of individual interviews (Van Hoose, Peters, and Leonard, 1967; Van Hoose, 1968). The focus and future of elementary school counseling appear hazy at this point, but the profession seems to be here to stay.

Counseling in a College Setting [9]

It is generally accepted that the modern college has a responsibility to provide services to its students to enhance their educational experiences. These activities, commonly termed "student personnel services," grew originally out of a concern with the physical needs of students as expressed through residence halls and medical services which the college provided, but over the years there has developed a growing awareness of the impor-

[8] A 1967 study by Van Hoose and Vafakas (1968) reported that only 14 states had separate certification requirements for elementary school counselors; the remainder certified persons for the entire age range.

[9] Although this discussion deals primarily with counseling services in four-year colleges, the reader is also referred to the chapter on counseling in the junior college in the book by Thoroman (1968).

tance of attending to other developmental needs of the students as well. Among the student personnel services now provided by most colleges are admissions, an orientation program, advising for foreign students, development and supervision of extracurricular activities, financial aids, job placement, and of course counseling. Although in most institutions these services have developed more-or-less independently, in recent years there has been a trend toward coordinating them under a single administrator, generally at the level of a vice-president or executive dean.[10]

About two-thirds of all colleges have an organized counseling program (Albert, 1968), and many of the remainder have informal arrangements with qualified faculty members to conduct counseling with interested students. The function of the counseling agency within a college may, however, vary considerably from one school to another. Some college counseling services restrict their responsibilities almost exclusively to vocational and educational counseling, while others range more widely into personal counseling and psychotherapy (Warman, 1961). The scope depends partly on the interests and competence of the counselors employed by the agency as well as by the availability of other services. Some of the larger universities, for example, have both a counseling service and a psychological or psychiatric clinic, the latter staffed by psychiatrists and clinical psychologists dealing with the more disturbed individuals.[11] Yet even in this situation, some members of the counseling service may conduct psychotherapy at times, and the distinction between the functions of the agencies is far from clear. Other schools encompass a wide range of counseling and psychotherapy services within a single agency, which permits a more fluid coordination of services as well as more casual interchange among members of several different professions.

Many of the larger counseling agencies also assume responsibilities beyond that of counseling with students. Among these may be: (1) the administration of university-wide testing programs, such as orientation testing; (2) supervision of graduate students in counselor training programs within the university; (3) consultation with faculty members and with persons in other student personnel agencies regarding the problems of college students; (4) research concerning the characteristics of the student body and the extent to which the university is meeting the needs of its students. Ideally, the modern counseling service should provide all of these

[10] For more complete descriptions of the various student personnel services and their development, see Williamson (1961) and Siegel (1968b).

[11] The role of the university psychiatrist in a college setting has been stressed by Farnsworth (1957, 1966), who is in charge of psychiatric services at Harvard University. Many counselors, however, would probably not agree with the scope and authority which Farnsworth would assign to the psychiatrist at the expense of the counselor.

services, but in smaller colleges this may be impractical due to the limited size of the staff. Ivey and Oetting (1966) have stressed that the counseling function should be paramount, and that the other services should be included only as time and resources are available beyond that needed to do an adequate job of counseling with students.

The academic status of the college counselor has been the subject of some concern, especially in recent years. Originally it was assumed that the counselor's sole function was to provide services to students and staff and, as such, his academic credentials were of secondary importance. Over the years, however, as the educational background of counselors improved, they desired to become affiliated with academic departments so as to maintain and enhance their involvement with their academic discipline. As a result, many college counseling agencies now enable their professional staff to obtain an appointment in the appropriate academic department—usually in education, psychology, or sociology—so as to attract more highly qualified personnel and to become better integrated with the university as a whole (Koile, 1960). One result of this trend, however, is that a greater emphasis is being put on the Ph.D. as a requirement for an appointment in a college counseling service, since many departments are reluctant to grant academic rank to persons at the master's level. Since, however, counselors with the Ph.D. tend to have a stronger interest in research and less in service activities than do those at the master's level, the service activities of many counseling agencies are becoming less prominent. In addition, the necessity of hiring a Ph.D. instead of an M.A. or M.S. counselor puts much greater strain on the agency's budget. Proponents of this trend seem to have overlooked the lack of evidence that service activities, including counseling, are performed any better by persons with the Ph.D. than by those with only the master's degree. If the counseling service is to continue to fulfill its service responsibilities, it seems that room must be made for more persons at the master's level, without sacrificing the contributions which the Ph.D. can make in research, teaching, and other scholarly activities.

Counseling in Government Agencies

The bulk of vocational counseling with persons no longer in school takes place within state employment services. Most of the clients of these agencies represent the range of unskilled through skilled labor, with some technical jobs also included. The training and qualifications of employment service counselors vary widely from one state to another (Gellman, 1964), although many states are now making a concerted effort to encourage specialized training of their counselors. The counselor's role is primarily that of providing relevant information and then either placing the client on a job or making a referral to another agency. The sophisticated counselor will, of course, attempt to deal with the client as an individual, taking into account his interests and abilities in locating a suitable job for him, but if more extensive counseling is needed a referral is generally more appropriate.

Other government agencies which employ counselors include the Veterans Hospitals and Vocational Rehabilitation agencies which primarily employ rehabilitation counselors, as described earlier. The major responsibility of the counselor in these settings is to help the client adjust to a physical or emotional disability and to become reintegrated with the world at large.

Counseling in Community Agencies

Although vocational guidance began in voluntary community agencies, it has long since been taken over by the schools and the employment services, so that the voluntary community agency is no longer as prominent. Notable exceptions are found in a number of large metropolitan areas, such as the Jewish Vocational Service of Chicago (see Gellman, 1964), but such facilities have not proliferated in other areas. The major contribution of voluntary community guidance agencies is that they can meet the needs of out-of-school adults, for whom there is otherwise no convenient service. A drawback, however, is that such agencies are bound by no uniform standards for their counselors, as are schools and government agencies (Super, 1964), so that their quality is quite uneven.

Family service agencies, primarily sponsored by community funds, engage in a large amount of marriage and family counseling. Generally they are staffed by social workers, although persons from other disciplines may also be employed, and they concentrate on helping persons with rather immediate situational problems.

Mental health clinics also provide a certain amount of counseling, although their emphasis is on the treatment of emotional disorders, especially of a more severe nature. As noted earlier, the typical clinic team consists of psychiatrists, clinical psychologists, and psychiatric social workers, any of whom may engage in counseling as well as psychotherapy.

Conclusion

It is evident that, outside of the educational institutions, counseling facilities are few and far between. Those which are available to adults, such as within the employment service and family service agencies, tend to deal with rather narrow areas of concern. Our society has failed to meet the need for a broader type of counseling facility for adults similar to that available to high school and college students.

12

Professional Considerations in Counseling

Persons who engage in counseling as a professional activity have encountered problems common to most professional groups. Three of the most important of these will be discussed here: ethical problems in counseling, the legal status of counselors, and the selection and training of persons becoming professional counselors. Increased attention to these areas is a reflection of society's recognition of counselors and the responsibilities which accompany this recognition.

ETHICAL CONSIDERATIONS

A concern for ethical behavior invariably accompanies the development of a profession. As Wrenn (1952) has pointed out, a profession implies service to society, and as such it must be concerned with its relations with the members of that society. Moreover, because the relationship between the counselor and his clients is a highly personal one, the opportunity for abuse of this relationship is great. Few counselors would deliberately misuse this relationship, but the profession must protect itself and the public it serves against the possibility that such an abuse might occur.

At first glance, distinctions between ethical and unethical behavior seem obvious, since it is the flagrant cases of unethical activity which receive the greatest attention. But the situation is actually more complicated than a cursory view would suggest. One reason for this complexity is that the causes of unethical behavior are varied. Schwebel (1955) has suggested that unethical behavior may occur for any of three reasons: the counselor behaves out of ignorance, the counselor has been inadequately trained, or the counselor behaves out of self-interest. Only in the latter instance does Schwebel believe that the behavior can truly be called "unethical," since presumably the person who is ignorant or poorly trained is doing the best he can. It is necessary, however, that the public be protected from possible damage inflicted by persons in all three categories, since it is the effect rather than the cause of the behavior that is of greatest concern to society.

To determine that a given behavior is or is not unethical, a profession first needs some general principles to guide the practitioner in his everyday activity. The two major professional organizations with which counselors are affiliated—the American Psychological Association (1968) and the American Personnel and Guidance Association (1961)—have each published a code of ethics, to which it is expected that all members will conform. The codes provide a guideline for the beginning counselor, so that ignorance cannot be claimed as a legitimate defense of unethical behavior by a member of the organization, as well as providing a means by which to punish persons who violate any of the principles. Unless they are incorporated in state certification requirements these codes of ethics have no legal force, but they do enable an organization to suspend one of its members for a violation, thereby denying him the status of membership in that organization in his relations with the public.

Ethics codes do not, however, resolve many of the ethical dilemmas which counselors encounter. At best, they state a position on a given question which rules out extreme violations, so that the flagrant violator is obviously in error. Most ethical problems, however, lie in a gray area between behavior which is clearly ethical and behavior which is not. The resolution of these problems becomes a matter of personal judgment, and the ethics codes seldom provide a clear-cut answer. A person accused of violating an ethical principle seldom has done this deliberately; he believed he was acting in good faith and may find it hard to accept the opinion of his peers that his behavior was in error. Nevertheless, some people do not exercise good judgment, and a code of ethics, as interpreted by one's professional peers, seems to be the best way to control and educate these persons.

Although ethical problems may arise in a wide variety of areas, there are some in which counselors more often find themselves in a dilemma. The most common of these will be discussed here.

Conflicting Responsibilities

Depending on the kind of setting in which he works, the counselor may have a number of simultaneous responsibilities. His primary responsibility is *to his client* and, if the client is a child or otherwise not capable of assuming responsibility for himself, to those who are responsible for him. But other responsibilities may at times assert themselves, and the counselor should be aware that they exist.

If the counselor is employed by an agency or institution, he has a responsibility to meet whatever expectations his employer has set for him. At times these expectations may interfere with his responsibility to his clients, as for example when a school administrator expects his counselors to inform him of potentially disruptive students, and this conflict must somehow be resolved. If the counselor believes that the expectations of his employer may interfere with his responsibility to his client he should attempt to persuade the employer to modify the expectations; failing that, he should probably seek employment elsewhere. But the counselor cannot in good conscience ignore his employer's expectations, since they may have a valid basis. His primary responsibility is to his client, but this responsibilty does not necessarily override all other responsibilites.

Even if the counselor is self-employed, he has a responsibility *to society*. If he believes strongly that a client may be potentially destructive to others, he may find it necessary to take steps to prevent this behavior from occurring. Such an action could be construed as also being in the client's best interests, in the long run. In few instances do the client's needs and those of society come into direct conflict.

The counselor also has a responsibility *to his profession,* to represent that profession as well as possible. Little conflict should arise in this connection, since by fulfilling his other responsibilities in an ethical manner he should be presenting his profession in a favorable light. Problems sometimes arise when the counselor misconstrues his professional responsibility to include gaining status for his profession at the expense of others, such as by refusing to refer a client to a member of another profession for fear that this may make his own appear less competent. The counselor's responsibility for the welfare of his client dictates that such an attitude would be unethical.

Finally, the counselor has a responsibility *to himself* as a person. He is responsible for doing the best job of counseling that he can, but he is not responsible to his clients night and day. He and his family must sometimes come first, and the counselor who believes that his client's needs must always supersede his own, even outside of the counseling office, is likely to experience many frustrations.

The responsibilities described here are usually compatible and, in fact, reinforce one another. Occasionally, however, they may create a conflict situation for the counselor, which he must somehow resolve. Ethics codes are not very helpful at such a juncture. The counselor must ultimately rely on his own judgment, supplemented when possible by the opinions of colleagues with whom he discusses the situation.

Confidentiality

Probably no area of ethical concern is as much stressed as that of confidentiality of information imparted by the client within the counseling session. The ethics codes of all helping professions include a strong statement regarding confidentiality (see, for example, the statements by the American Personnel and Guidance Association, 1961; the American Psychiatric Association, 1961; and the American Psychological Association, 1968). The statement from the ethics code of the American Psychological Association (1968) is typical:

> Safeguarding information about an individual that has been obtained by the psychologist in the course of his teaching, practice, or investigation is a primary obligation of the psychologist. . . . Information received in confidence is revealed only after most careful deliberation and when there is clear and imminent danger to an individual or to society, and then only to appropriate professional workers or public authorities [p. 358].

The reason for the stress on confidentiality is evident. In addition to the obvious ethical considerations themselves, a counselor who talked freely about his clients would soon find himself with no clients to talk about. Only by keeping their confidences to himself can the counselor persuade his clients that he is to be trusted. Once this trust is violated, it may be impossible to regain.

The counselor cannot, however, assume that he has unlimited control over his ability to maintain confidentiality. In addition to the occasional legal complication, to be discussed in the following section, some institutions—such as high schools and colleges—expect their counselors to report to them any threats to the institution implicit in a student's admitted behavior. The counselor should try to reduce these limitations to those within which he can operate with reasonable comfort, but he need not necessarily assume that any restrictions imposed by his superiors make his job impossible. As Clark (1965) has described, it is possible to counsel effectively under conditions of limited confidentiality. To do so, however, both the counselor and the client must be clear as to the nature of these limits. It is the counselor's responsibility not to guarantee a degree of confidentiality to his clients which he is unable to carry out, and to head off discussions in areas in which the limits may be breached until the client fully understands the risks he is taking.

The statement of confidentiality presented earlier seems plain enough, but several questions may arise which it does not adequately cover:

1. Is it unethical to discuss a client with another professional person? Most counselors would agree that case conferences, in which they exchange ideas about their cases with other counselors, are quite helpful in their work, and all ethics codes permit the divulging of information for this purpose. It is assumed that discussions with other professionals are for the purpose of helping the counselor do a better job with his clients, and that neither party has any personal interest in the client being discussed. If, for some reason, the second counselor is interested in a specific client, then the discussion borders on the unethical.

2. How should the counselor handle requests for information or impressions from persons who have other relationships with the client, for example, a parent or a teacher? Except in unusual circumstances, the counselor should avoid providing any confidential information about the client without first asking the client's permission. A counselor may sometimes be tempted to violate this principle on the grounds that, by understanding the client better, the parent or teacher can handle him more effectively, but this is a risky assumption. The counselor cannot be certain that the information will be used wisely, and in the process he risks losing the client's trust in him.

It is generally preferable to acknowledge the value of the person's request and his obvious interest and concern about the client, and to suggest that the counselor and client discuss this interest and decide between them what their reaction should be. Perhaps a joint conference might be arranged, in which the counselor and client together can discuss the relevant information with the parent or teacher, or perhaps the client will want to do this alone. In any case, however, the counselor should table the request until the client can be consulted. If the person raising the question objects to the client knowing about the request in the first place, this is further evidence that the information may not be wisely used.

Although the counselor should, in most cases, refuse requests for information about his clients, he should bear in mind that there are many different ways of saying "No." It is important, both for himself as a counselor and for his client, to maintain the good will of the inquirer, so that a blunt refusal is seldom wise. A better approach is for the counselor to acknowledge the sincerity of the caller's concern and to explain as tactfully as possible why he cannot respond immediately. Often a parent or teacher requesting information is actually asking for reassurance that he is doing the right thing. The counselor who uses a code of ethics to berate persons who, in good faith, request information of him, is undoubtedly only increasing his client's problems.

3. How should the counselor respond to requests for information from prospective employers or the government? Here the dilemma is a little different than in the previous question, since the request usually comes some time after the counseling has been terminated. If the client is available for

consultation it would be best to discuss the request with him, but in many cases he will no longer be in the vicinity. Nevertheless, it is generally best to continue to hold that confidentiality is breached only with the expressed permission of the client. Most counseling agencies have a form which is sent to the inquiring party, by which the client can sign a release of information. The difficulty with such a form, however, is that the client's refusal to sign may place him in jeopardy with the inquirer, who may thereby assume he has something to hide. Most clients will sign the release and trust the counselor to use his best judgment. The counselor in turn should be cautious in the information he provides, even if he has the client's written approval for it.

The counselor in such a circumstance should remember that his information about the client only describes the client as he was when the counselor knew him, not as he is now. This is especially true of test data, which some people seem to believe describe a person for perpetuity. The counselor may perform a service both for the client and his prospective employer by advising that the employer seek a *current* evaluation rather than relying on information and impressions which may no longer be valid.

4. Who should have access to test data concerning the client? Test information obtained as part of the counseling process should be considered as confidential information imparted by the client and should be transmitted to others only with his permission. Some agencies treat test information rather loosely, apparently assuming that it is somehow less personal than material which the client provides verbally. In fact, however, if the client has taken the tests as part of the counseling process, the results are just as personal to him as other information he may have provided. Furthermore, the risk that the test information may be misused, or used against him, is just as great as if it had been provided verbally.

Test information obtained in a noncounseling context may be treated differently, or at least is not the direct responsibility of the counselor. A person may, for example, have been required to take certain tests as part of an employment selection procedure, or he may have routinely been administered certain standardized tests in school. Certainly any such tests should be supervised by a person trained in testing, and the results should be the responsibility of that person, but access to the results does not require the testee's permission. Presumably the tests were administered for a purpose, and anyone who the supervisor determines has a legitimate reason for needing the test information should have access to it. The public, however, is becoming more sensitive to the indiscriminate use of tests, and persons responsible for the collection and dissemination of test information must consider carefully to whom it should be exposed. If not, the time may not be far away when laws will be enacted which will severely restrict the administration of tests for any purpose.

5. Is it ethical to use tapes from counseling interviews for the training of counselors? This question is a tricky one and opinion is no longer entirely one-sided. It was once assumed that it was acceptable to use tapes in counseling classes in which graduate students were learning to become counselors, provided that the identities of the clients on the tapes were adequately disguised. There is a growing concern, however, with this practice, on the grounds that 100 percent disguise cannot be guaranteed and that the client might not approve even if it could be. It would seem that the tape of a counseling interview preserves a confidential relationship and, as such, should be used for another purpose only with the consent of both parties. Certainly few counselors would be willing to turn over a copy of the tape to the client, to use as he saw fit, but most counselors assume the right to do so themselves. It would seem more in keeping with the nature of the counseling relationship to specifically request the client's permission to use a tape of one or more of his sessions in a teaching situation. Most clients will probably give their permission; if one refuses to do so, it would have been a serious error to use the tape in the first place.

The underlying principle which seems evident in confidentiality is that information provided by the client within the counseling setting belongs to him until released by him for other use. It is permissible to reveal a client's confidences to others only when there is the likelihood of imminent danger, either to the client or to others. Such situations arise occasionally in psychotherapy, almost never in counseling. The counselor will find very few occasions in which there is a strong reason to reveal to another person something told to him in confidence by a client. If the counselor believes that such a situation has arisen, he should consult with his colleagues before taking the drastic step of breaking his client's confidence. Perhaps others can suggest alternate courses of action which he has not considered; at least they can help validate his opinion that it is necessary to break the client's confidence.

Competence and Representation

The ethical counselor restricts his services to those persons and problems which he believes he is qualified, by virtue of his training and experience, to handle, and he uses tools which he is trained to use competently. When a situation arises which he believes another counselor or psychotherapist could handle more successfully, he explains this to the client and makes a referral. He does not misrepresent his own qualifications, and he makes every effort to correct any false impressions which the client may derive concerning his qualifications and competence. When in doubt concerning the desirability of continuing with a client, the counselor should consult with his colleagues. It is also desirable for a counselor to maintain an informal relationship with a clinical psychologist or psychiatrist with whom he can discuss problem clients.

The issue of referral is sometimes not as simple as it may seem. Suppose, for example, that the client refuses to accept a referral. Should the counselor continue to counsel with him, even though he believes the client should actually be seeing someone else? The answer, in most cases, would be that the counselor would do better to terminate the relationship. If the client refuses to see the person whom the counselor recommends, the status of the relationship is in doubt anyway. Furthermore, the client should not be allowed to determine how the counseling is to proceed. Presumably the counselor used his best judgment in recommending a referral, and he should therefore back this judgment by refusing to continue counseling with the client. Perhaps the client is simply testing the counselor's resolve; once he becomes convinced that the counselor meant what he said, he may decide to accept the referral.

Another dilemma may arise if there is no appropriate person in the vicinity to whom the counselor can make a referral. Suppose that the counselor believes that a client needs psychiatric treatment, but there is no psychiatrist nearby. Should he continue to work with the client? Again, the best procedure is for the counselor not to attempt to undertake an activity which is outside of his competence. Perhaps counseling may be of help to the client, although not as much as psychotherapy, but for the counselor to attempt psychotherapy without adequate training could very likely cause more harm than good for the client. In most cases someone can be found to whom the client can be referred, although it may be less convenient for the client.

Ethics in Research

The ethical principles discussed heretofore have concerned themselves primarily with the counselor as practitioner. As research in counseling has increased, however, ethical dilemmas have also arisen in this area. This confusion reflects a more general awareness that scientific research which uses human beings as subjects—whether medical, psychological, or otherwise—presents some difficulties not encountered in research with laboratory animals.

The basic dilemma arises from a conflict between two highly valued rights: (a) the right of the individual to maintain his personal privacy and to control his own destiny, and (b) the right of the scientist to advance knowledge (Clark and others, 1967). In most research with human beings these rights are not at odds, but occasionally they may be.

Since behavioral science seeks to explore man's innermost personal life, it would seem that the potential subject has the right to decide whether he will allow himself to submit to such an exploration. It is generally agreed, therefore, that a person should not be studied without his consent and that this consent should be "informed"; that is, it should be based on sufficient knowledge and understanding of the nature of the study in which the person is being asked to participate. This principle is not accepted by all researchers, since it may at times interfere with the collection of data from a "random" sample, but most behavioral scientists agree that the subject should have the right to be informed as to the nature of the study to the extent that this is feasible or possible. This means, for example, that it is unethical for a counseling agency to require its clients to submit to a battery of tests for research purposes in order that they be accepted as clients. In few cases, however, will a person decline if the purpose of the testing is explained to him and he is given the option to refuse.

A more serious dilemma arises when it is not feasible to inform the person of the nature of the study, since to do so would invalidate it. Suppose, for example, that one wanted to compare the effects of a warm, pleasant counselor with one who would appear to be hostile and rejecting. It is conceivable that clients who were exposed to the latter counselor would find the experience unpleasant and should therefore presumably be given the opportunity to refuse to participate. But to inform them in advance that their counselor would only be acting and that it would be an artificial situation would probably eliminate any potential effects of the manipulation. In other words, in some research it is necessary for the client to be convinced that the situation is real in order that he will react in a normal manner, even though the experience may be unpleasant for him.

No statement of ethical principles has yet resolved this dilemma. The best any statement can do is to warn that such a study should be undertaken only if there is no other alternative and that the client should be "debriefed" —that is, be informed of the true nature of the study—after it is completed. These strictures do not, however, prevent the subject from suffering some anxious moments during the investigation itself, nor do they guarantee that the experience will have no long-term effects. The responsibility lies with the investigator to determine that the study is necessary and that no other approach is possible. Scientists, however, are not always sufficiently empathic with their subjects, and this procedure seems to run more risks than may be warranted.

At the very least, it would seem that an investigator should not undertake a study in which the subjects cannot give informed consent without first reviewing it with his colleagues and weighing their opinions in his judgment. The federal government now, in effect, requires such a procedure from persons applying for research grants: their design must be approved by an authorized group within their institution. Some scientists balk at this requirement, believing that it violates scientific freedom, but it seems necessary to impose some such restriction as a protection to the subjects.

A more fundamental issue, however, would seem to be whether some research questions simply cannot be answered. Interesting as the outcome might be—and there are few definitive studies in behavioral research anyway—the potential damage to an individual subject may be too great to warrant the risk. It may no longer be possible, in behavioral science at least, to accept the proposition that anything in the interest of science is legitimate. Perhaps the rights of the scientist ought not always to override other rights. And perhaps if scientists were denied certain techniques, they might be forced to use their creativity to devise others which would be more acceptable.

LEGAL CONSIDERATIONS

The legal implications of the counselor's activities are a frequent source of concern to the practitioner. In one sense, this concern can easily be overemphasized, since only rarely does the counselor actually encounter legal difficulties in his work. But the specter of the law is always hovering overhead, and the counselor should have some general knowledge of areas of potential difficulty so that he can sense when special steps ought to be taken.

The discussion here is not intended as a primer of law for counselors.[1] It touches on a few of the areas of greatest concern and suggests some guidelines to follow when problems arise, but it is by no means an authoritative dissertation. When a legal problem does arise, the counselor's best course of action is to consult a lawyer rather than to hope he can handle it himself. As lawyers themselves are fond of quoting, "The lawyer who defends himself has a fool for a client." This is even more true of the counselor who tries to act as his own attorney.

The Legal Recognition of Counselors

As a profession reaches maturity, it begins to seek legal recognition in the form of licensing or certification statutes.[2] The major intent of such legislation is to prevent the untrained or otherwise incompetent practitioner from cloaking his activities with a fraudulent professional title as well as

---

[1] The interested reader is referred to the volume of readings edited by Allen, Ferster, and Rubin (1968), a collection of articles, case transcripts, dialogues, and court opinions written primarily to help lawyers make better use of psychiatric and psychological testimony. Another useful collection is the volume edited by Ware (1964).

[2] Although both licensing and certification are used as the basis for legally controlling the practice of a profession in different states, there appears to be no meaningful distinction between the two relevant to the discussion here.

to set guidelines for the practice of those persons who meet the criteria for a license. The original issuance of a license is determined by requirements of training and experience, but the license may be revoked for violations generally drawn from the ethics code of the professional organization. Ethics and legal recognition thus go hand in hand, with an ethics code usually being a preliminary step for a profession which wishes eventually to obtain legal recognition.

In addition to protection of the public, legislation has a second benefit to the profession itself: it indicates to the public that the profession is recognized as performing a service of value to society, and that society should be protected against persons who are not members of the profession and are therefore deemed incompetent to perform this service. The status implications of such recognition are obvious.

Legal recognition of counselors is granted through state legislation regarding professions with which counselors are affiliated. Guidance counselors, for example, are certified in all states through state departments of education. This certification allows them to be employed by public educational institutions, but it does not protect them in any counseling they may do which is not under the aegis of such an employer. Psychologists are gradually gaining legal recognition across the country. As of August, 1969, 37 states had enacted legislation authorizing the licensing or certification of psychologists, and it seems inevitable that all states will eventually have some such arrangement. In order to minimize confusion among the various states, the American Psychological Association has issued guidelines for state legislation, to which the reader is referred (see American Psychological Association Committee on Legislation, 1967).

A counselor's legal position, then, depends largely on the legal status of the profession with which he is affiliated. Traditionally lawyers, physicians, and ministers have had the greatest legal protection in their counseling roles, but other professions have been demanding equal status and are gradually attaining it. But because legal recognition must come primarily through state legislation, it is possible to draw only general conclusions about the status of counselors across the country. Moreover, laws must be tested and interpreted by the courts, and it is only through litigation that the actual effect of a law can be determined. This is why lawyers tend to be very cautious in advising laymen as to the implications of a given law until the law has been tested through court cases. The discussion in these pages must be approached with these limitations in mind.

Privileged Communication

Privileged communication is defined by Geiser and Rheingold (1964) as:

. . . the legal right which exists either by statute or common law that protects the client from having his confidences revealed publicly from the witness stand during legal proceedings. It means that certain professionals cannot be legally compelled to testify to the content of the confidential relation they entered into with their client [p. 831].

The doctrine of privileged communication is derived from common law, in which it was limited to the husband-wife and lawyer-client relationships. Subsequently, however, other relationships, primarily those involving physicians and clergymen, have been recognized by statute as privileged (Ferster, 1962). Attempts have been made to extend privileged communication to other professional groups, but the courts have been resistant and progress has been slow (Volz, 1964).

The necessary conditions for the establishment of a privileged relationship are generally agreed to be those enunciated by Wigmore (described by Volz, 1964): (a) the communications must originate in a confidence that they will not be disclosed; (b) this element of confidentiality must be essential to the full and satisfactory maintenance of the relation between parties; (c) the relation must be one which in the opinion of the community ought to be sedulously fostered; and (d) the injury that would inure to the relation by the disclosure of the communications must be greater than the benefit thereby gained for the correct disposal of litigation. Many counselors would argue that the counselor-client relationship meets these conditions, but at this point these arguments have not been generally accepted by the courts.

It is often assumed that privileged communication is accorded to a profession, when in fact the privilege is actually assigned *to the client*. The concept of privileged communication exists to protect the individual, and it is therefore the *client's* disclosures that are privileged and the privilege is exercised at his option. As Geiser and Rheingold (1964) state: "The client's privilege imposes the legal obligation of secrecy upon the professional person in court, in those cases where the law recognizes a privilege [p. 831]." This means that the client may bar the professional person from testifying, even if he wishes to, or the client may waive his privilege, in which case the professional person can no longer legally withhold his testimony. The judgment as to whether the privilege should be exercised therefore lies with the client, not with the professional.

The counselor-client relationship is not generally recognized as privileged by most courts, although several of the counseling professions are attempting to gain such recognition. With regard to school counselors, for example, Volz (1964) says:

Since the doctrine of privileged communications does not extend to [school] counselors, . . . they can be compelled to reveal in court proceedings statements made to them by students, even in confidence, where such statements fall within one of the exceptions to the hearsay rule. However, there is no requirement that such statements be revealed to third persons outside of court, except to further the best interests of the school system or of the student [pp. 8–9].

As other professions, such as psychology, have gained legal recognition through state certification and licensing statutes, privileged communication has often been included, although most of these provisions have not yet been tested in the courts. Both Louisell (1957) and Geiser and Rheingold (1964) have objected to the tying of privileged communication to licensing on the grounds that the privilege is legally that of the client rather than of the professional person and therefore should not depend on whether the psychologist happens to be licensed. They contend that if it is in the best interests of society that communications between a psychologist and his client be privileged, then statutes should be enacted which spell out the privilege of the client who consults a professional counselor or psychotherapist, rather than emphasizing the specific profession. In any case, however, few of the recently enacted laws have been tested in the courts, and until such tests are conducted their strength is unknown.

What guidelines can be offered to the counselor whose relationship with a client is deemed not to be covered by a statute regarding privileged communication? Is he automatically required to testify against his client? Not necessarily. Geiser and Rheingold (1964) suggest two alternatives: the counselor may refuse to testify on ethical grounds and this argument might be accepted by the judge, or the court itself might create a privileged communication situation for this instance. In either case, the decision rests with the judge, and the counselor can only request, through an attorney, that an exception be made.

If a counselor keeps records of his interviews with his clients, as most do, these records may also be subject to scrutiny by others. Official records of a public agency or institution, such as a school, are generally considered to be "public" and therefore must be made available to anyone with a legitimate interest in them, whereas the counselor's notes and related material are considered his personal property and not open to others (Burt, 1964). It is therefore advisable for the counselor to keep a separate file of his counseling interviews rather than to include his notes in the client's "official" file (Burt, 1964; Rezny, 1964). These notes may, however, be subpoenaed anyway by a court, in the same manner that the counselor himself may be called to testify. Whatever statutes exist in the state regarding privileged communication for the counselor also apply to his notes. This suggests that, if the counselor believes that certain material in his notes might be detrimental to the client in a possible court action in the future, he should destroy the notes as soon as practical.

Expert Testimony

On occasion, the counselor may be requested to testify in court as to his professional opinion regarding a defendant. The defendant may have been a client, or he may have been referred to the counselor for a professional evaluation by an attorney, but in any case the counselor is asked to present his professional opinion rather than to testify as to any personal knowledge he has concerning the client. In this situation, the counselor is providing "expert testimony."

According to the Uniform Rules of Evidence, as quoted by Fox (1964):

> If the witness is testifying as an expert, testimony of the witness in the form of opinions or inferences is limited to such opinions as the judge finds are (a) based on facts or data perceived by or personally known or made known to the witness at the hearing and (b) within the scope of the special knowledge, skill, experience or training possessed by the witness [p. 113].

Fox goes on to explain:

> The expert witness generally has no personal familiarity with the facts he is asked to appraise. His opinions are drawn from his specialized knowledge on the subject of his testimony; and he testifies either on the basis of factual data given in a hypothetical question or on the basis of his observations in the court room during the interrogation of other witnesses [p. 114].

Controversy may arise when the qualifications of an "expert" are challenged, as is likely to occur when the expert's testimony conflicts with the arguments of the other side of the case. If such a challenge is issued, the court must rely partially on precedents which have been established as to the qualifications of a member of a given profession. Such precedents are of concern to the profession itself, since a refusal to accept a member of a given profession as an expert tends to cast doubt on the qualifications of all members of that profession.

For this reason, clinical psychologists have fought a hard battle to establish their qualifications as experts in the area of diagnosis of mental retardation and emotional disturbance, a field in which the medical profession has attained preeminence in the courts. Recent court cases (see, for example, Hoch and Darley, 1962) have laid the groundwork for the acceptance of the clinical psychologist as an expert witness in such cases, but the battle is by no means won.

Most counselors, however, would not claim expertise with regard to cases of emotional disturbance. Counselors are most likely to be asked to provide expert testimony in court cases involving educational or vocational questions. Wiener (1964) and Sinick (1964), for example, have described the role of the counselor as an expert witness in hearings involving questions about Social Security benefits, when the decision hinges on a determination of the physical or mental capabilities of the individual. The school counselor might play a similar role in proceedings involving the placement of a child in school. As long as the counselor restricts his testimony to areas in which his qualifications are secure, his testimony will probably not be severely challenged.

Liability for Negligence or Malpractice

The medical profession is plagued by suits for negligence or malpractice, and one might wonder whether counselors may also be subject to such harassment. On the basis of past experience there seems little need for concern, since both Schmidt (1962) and Krauskopf and Krauskopf (1965), in surveys of legal decisions concerning clinical and counseling psychologists, could find almost no cases of this sort. The lack of experience, however, simply means that the courts have seldom been called upon to rule on the liability of a counselor for negligence or malpractice, which leaves the issue open.

The case most frequently cited as an indication of the liability of the counselor involved the director of a college student personnel service in Wisconsin who counseled with a student who subsequently committed suicide (Butler, 1964). The girl's parents sued the counselor for damages on the grounds that he should have recognized her suicide potential and should have reported it to the parents. The court ruled in favor of the defendant on the grounds that the defendant, not being medically trained, could not be expected to diagnose mental illness, and that moreover it could not be concluded that had he done so the suicide would have been prevented. While the court's opinion of the limitations of psychologists may not be cheerfully accepted by the clinical branch of the profession, it appears that counselors would probably not be held liable for failure to make judgments which they are not assumed to be qualified to make.

There remains, however, a wide area in which lawsuits against counselors for negligence or malpractice are possible, if not probable. Although the evidence to date suggests that the counselor would be favored to win such a suit, unless he had been grossly derelict in his duty, the expense of fighting such a charge can in itself be a major problem. Krauskopf and Krauskopf (1965), in their review of the liability of counselors for court actions, suggest that counselors would be well advised to anticipate such difficulties and to protect themselves against the costs of a lawsuit, either through prior agreements with their employers or by personal insurance through their professional organizations.

Again it is necessary to stress that the material presented in this section is based primarily on opinion, and that in most cases there have been insufficient court tests to permit any firm statements as to the counselor's probable status if a legal question arises. The best advice remains: *When in doubt, consult a lawyer.*

SELECTION AND TRAINING OF COUNSELORS

Counselors vary in the quality of help they can provide. Those who are highly skilled generally produce more effective outcomes with their clients than do those who are less skilled. It is therefore the obligation of the professions concerned with counseling to do their utmost to produce the most highly skilled counselors possible. They will not always succeed, but they should know the procedures by which this goal can most likely be attained.

It is generally agreed that effective counselors are both born and made, meaning that a person with an aptitude for counseling, by virtue of being the kind of person he is, can be helped through a training program to use his personal skills effectively. Without the training program he might have been a reasonably effective counselor anyway, but with training he should do better. On the other hand, any training program is limited by the raw material with which it begins. This means that a training institution must concern itself both with the selection of persons with good "counseling potential" as well as with providing these persons with the program which can best enable them to develop this potential.

Selection of Potential Counselors

Selection Criteria. Compared with the high ideals to which counselor training programs subscribe, their selection procedures are typically mundane and unimaginative. As Hill (1961) has pointed out, the counseling professions have devoted little effort to research concerning the process or criteria by which prospective counselors are selected, with the result that ". . . supervisors in counseling and psychotherapy tend to select potential trainees on the same bases that they select patients or clients: intelligent, verbal, well-motivated, high socioeconomic status, high ego-strength, etc." (Truax and Carkhuff, 1967, p. 233). It is apparently persons with these characteristics that counselor educators most enjoy teaching.

One of the major reasons for the apparent lack of concern with selection criteria is that most training in counseling is incorporated in programs leading to a graduate degree. The typical criteria for the selection of students are therefore those which seem most likely to predict performance in the graduate program: undergraduate grades (the single most popular criterion), tests such as the Graduate Record Examination and the Miller Analogies, and letters of recommendation.[3] The prospective student, once past these hurdles, need only declare an interest in counseling to be accepted into the counseling program, at least on a tentative basis.

Most counseling programs do, however, provide opportunities for ongoing selection of their students, especially during the practicum. Thus a student who makes slow progress in acquiring counseling skills or who demonstrates characteristics that appear to mitigate against his success as a counselor may be "counseled" into another field. Although there appear to be no clear data as to the proportion of persons admitted to counseling programs who are dropped for such reasons, it is probably low. The student who is intelligent enough to master the course work and who maintains an interest in counseling will probably progress satisfactorily through the program. Whether this means he will necessarily perform effectively in a subsequent counseling job is, however, less certain. It is likely that counseling, as an occupation, follows the pattern noted by Ghiselli (1966) in many other occupations: performance in the training program is more easily predicted than is performance on the job.

It would seem, then, that the two most valid selection criteria for persons interested in a graduate program in counseling are intelligence and interest. The prospective counselor must have the ability to cope with the didactic material in his graduate courses, and he must have the motivation to sustain him through the program. This suggests that a prospective candidate may be initially screened out on the basis of inadequate intellectual ability, as reflected in test scores and undergraduate grades, or on the basis of inappropriate motivation. While it is improbable that a person who has little interest in counseling would apply for admission to a counselor training program, those responsible for the selection of students should be alert to those candidates whose motivation appears to be inappropriate: persons who want to become counselors for the "wrong" reasons, such as a desire to manipulate others or to direct their lives. Some candidates, too, enter a counselor training program with inadequate knowledge of the field, and subsequently become dissatisfied as they gain a clearer picture of the counselor's job. These persons will probably leave the program of their own accord, but they may welcome an opportunity to discuss their growing doubts with their instructors and supervisors.

Most authorities agree that the most effective selection process stresses self-selection. Presumably as a person progresses through a counselor train-

[3] A 1953 survey of counseling training programs by a subcommittee of the APA Division of Counseling Psychology reported that many of the respondents who required letters of recommendation actually had little faith in their validity (Gustad and others, 1954). They continue to be used, however, perhaps more as a ritual than because of any more recent evidence of their value.

ing program he should develop increased self-awareness, which may in turn cause him to recognize that counseling would be an inappropriate profession for him. Although self-selection should be welcomed, it should not be stressed too early. Some potentially competent counselors tend to be overly critical of themselves and may be quickly overwhelmed by the high standards which a counselor is expected to meet. The person who is sincerely motivated to become a counselor, but who doubts his potential, should be encouraged to continue in the program long enough to determine whether he can grow in skill and security in the role. Neither the decision to become a counselor nor the decision to withdraw from a counselor training program should be made impulsively.

Personality Characteristics. A great deal has been written concerning the personality characteristics desirable in fledgling counselors, most of which has been based on speculation rather than evidence. Such lists of desirable traits could be applied equally well to persons in any profession, and few practicing counselors would be so bold as to claim that they measure up completely in all areas. At best such lists serve as a goal toward which counselors can strive, but they risk discouraging those persons who are honest enough about themselves to recognize their shortcomings.

A more serious problem, however, is the lack of evidence to support the belief that any single constellation of personality characteristics can describe the ideal counselor. It is generally agreed that the range of personalities among effective counselors is wide, as is the range of personalities among persons who can become effective clients. Perhaps an optimum matching of counselor and client personalities would produce an optimum counseling relationship, but the evidence is too sparse yet to provide a basis for such combinations.

The effectiveness of a counselor also depends on the goals which he is attempting to achieve with his clients, which means that a counselor tends to define the characteristics of the ideal counselor in terms of his own model of counseling. On this basis it is possible to locate some personality differences between more and less effective counselors (see, for example, Truax and Carkhuff, 1967), but the biases on which such research is based must be borne in mind.[4]

It may be misleading to berate the lack of evidence as to personal qualities which delineate the effective counselor. This is a problem which plagues all professions, since a profession by its nature implies varied

---

[4] For example, both Arbuckle (1965) and Brammer and Shostrom (1968), two textbooks which stress therapeutic counseling, devote a considerable amount of space to discussions of the desirable personal characteristics of counselors. Their speculations make sense in light of their theoretical views about counseling, but counselors of differing theoretical persuasions could legitimately offer a different list.

job requirements. A wide variety of personalities may therefore perform well in a given profession for a wide variety of reasons; a person's strengths in certain areas may compensate for weaknesses in others. Jobs in which performance requirements are narrowly restricted are more amenable to a limited list of desirable personailty traits.

Furthermore, there is no sound theoretical basis for predicting the relationships between specific personality traits of counselors and their counseling skills. This gap has led Whiteley (1969) to conclude that it is "fruitless to continue this inquiry of particular traits. . . . The focus must be shifted from what the counselor *is* in terms of a static model to an evaluation of what the counselor actually *does* that is effective [p. 175]." Ultimately, research of this nature may lead to a more sophisticated picture of the personality characteristics of the effective counselor, but for the present there is little helpful evidence.

It would seem, therefore, that any attempt to include personality assessment in the selection of students for a counselor training program is both baseless and unnecessary. Certainly as the person progresses through the program continual evaluation should be made of his interactions with others, especially in counseling situations. He should be able to demonstrate that he is a person to whom others can talk freely and easily, who does not appear to be trying to satisfy neurotic needs for omnipotence or manipulation,[5] and who does not need to promote and maintain the dependency of others.

In Chapter 5, we discussed several characteristics which seem to be necessary for effective counseling: interest in helping people, perceptual sensitivity, personal adjustment, and genuineness. With the possible exception of the first, without which a person would be unlikely to enter a counseling program anyway, all can be developed in an effective counselor training program. It is therefore not necessary to screen applicants for these characteristics, but it is essential that continual evaluation be made of the student's growth in these areas during the program. The person who can demonstrate growth during a training program is a good bet to continue growing beyond it, while the person who shows little sign of change will probably not change substantially afterward either.

Training of Counselors

The core of the process by which counselors are produced is the training program. In light of the disparity of views among counselors concerning the nature and practice of counseling, it is hardly surprising to find disagreement as to the procedures by which counselors should be prepared. Most would agree that some combination of content and skill learning is neces-

---

[5] See Bugental (1964) for a useful discussion of the role of the counselor's personal needs, both positively and negatively.

sary, but the ratio of these two forms and the ultimate goals to be achieved are areas of controversy.

Goals of Counselor Training. Some counselors will have already balked at the heading of this section, "training," and will argue that "counselor education" is a more appropriate term. As Kinzer (1961) has noted, the counselor must be more than a technician, as implied in the term "training"; he should be a well-educated person who can interact freely with a wide variety of individuals, and who can adapt to new knowledge in his field. The person who simply performs certain skills with little understanding of their origin or intent is doomed to a life of mediocrity in his profession. Certainly few would dispute that the expert counselor must first be an educated person.

Yet is education, in a broad sense, a responsibility of a program of counselor preparation? If we assume that persons selected for such a program have already acquired a considerable amount of education, as signified by their earned academic degrees, then it is hardly necessary that general education be a major concern of the counseling program itself. And if a person has managed to achieve a college degree without having become educated, it is unlikely that the counseling program will have much effect in this direction.

This suggests, then, that the major responsibility of a program of counselor preparation is the *training* of counselors. To be sure, they must learn as much as possible about the nature of the counseling process, and in that sense are becoming further educated, but they must also learn to function effectively as counselors. As McGowan and Schmidt (1962) have pointed out:

> Counselors can be highly knowledgeable and conventional about theory and techniques of counseling and still be quite ineffective counselors themselves. . . . It is one thing to know what counseling is and what counselors should do but quite another to be able actually to do it [p. 32].

Confusion between the education and training of counselors probably stems in part from the fact that most programs of counselor preparation operate as part of programs leading to a graduate degree, usually in either education or psychology. Most of the requirements for this degree are academic in nature—courses, seminars, and research activity—much of it having little or no direct bearing on the learning of counseling skills. Because of this stress on academic requirements, many programs tend to slight the learning of counseling skills, a neglect which they justify on the grounds that they are producing "educated" counselors, with the implication that "training" is really rather unimportant. There is growing evidence, however, that counseling skills can be taught effectively to persons outside of the typical academic setting, and that a program which purports to prepare persons to become counselors has a responsibility to insure that its students have the broadest possible opportunity to learn how to counsel effectively.

Controversy also exists as to the most important goal of the counselor training program itself. Some writers, such as Arnold (1961), believe that the program should concentrate on the personal growth of the student, on the assumption that the counselor as a person is the major instrument of the counseling process. Others, however, including the present writer, would agree with Krumboltz (1967) that counselors should be trained to specify their goals in counseling and to learn techniques by which they can most effectively reach these goals. The distinction between these two viewpoints may not be great, but a relative emphasis on one or the other will probably be reflected in the procedures and expectations within a given training program.

Approaches to Counselor Training. This lack of agreement as to the major goals of a counselor training program is reflected in the differing approaches of various programs. Some programs emphasize a thorough grounding in the basic knowledge of the behavioral sciences before the student embarks on the learning of counseling skills *per se,* while others expose the student immediately to training in counseling and put relatively less emphasis on didactic knowledge about human behavior.

The advantage of the former approach is that it probably produces a person who better understands the basis for the techniques he is being taught and who will be able to adapt more readily to increased knowledge in the future, but there is little firm evidence as to the specific academic background which a counselor should have in order to become such a person. It is likely that the more academically demanding programs produce better counselors simply because a student must be more intelligent and more highly motivated to complete such a program than to complete one in which less is required of him intellectually. This kind of evidence obviously does not validate the effectiveness of the program itself, and there is little research of an objective nature which has attempted to do so. A suggestion as to what might be found in such studies comes from a study by Joslin (1965), who found no relationship between counselors' knowledge of counseling principles and their skill in counseling itself.

The necessity of extensive academic background as preparation for counseling has thus not been clearly demonstrated. On the other hand, most educators would probably contend that a well-educated person is ultimately better equipped to counsel with a wider range of clients and to adapt to innovations in the field, an argument which is hard to dispute. Some combination of education and training obviously must be set, but there is little basis at the present time to insure that a given program has achieved the optimum balance.

Content Learning. The nature of the didactic experience for counselors-in-training will depend largely on the professional field with which they plan to identify. To be sure, the neophyte counselor should be provided with a conceptual understanding of the skills which he is attempting to learn, so that a course in the nature of counseling seems a logical starting point, as well as course work to help him understand the tools he will use in counseling, such as psychological tests. Otherwise, however, the content and objectives of his courses will depend on the nature of the field. Thus a graduate student in counseling psychology will be expected to master the basic content of psychology, whereas a graduate student in education or a student in a professional social work program will concentrate on different content areas. It is apparent, therefore, that the didactic courses ✓ which are a major part of most counseling training programs are designed primarily to mold the student into an acceptable member of his profession rather than to enhance his counseling skills as such.

Practicum Training. The practicum experience—in which the student performs as a counselor, under supervision is the heart of the learning of counseling skills, and a great deal of consideration has therefore been given to the nature of the practicum. Here again, one's concept of the ideal practicum is a function of one's concept of the nature of counseling, and no single practicum experience can therefore suit everyone. We can only suggest here some principles regarding the practicum experience which seem consistent with the nature of counseling as we view it.

The student comes to the practicum with a background of knowledge about counseling theory and process, but with as yet little or no formal opportunity in which to apply his knowledge. To throw him immediately into a real-life counseling situation on a sink-or-swim basis would therefore seem unfair, both to him and to his clients. Most counselor training programs, therefore, provide some sort of "bridge" between the content material and the real-life experience, so as to prepare the student as fully as possible for his role as a counselor. This "pre-practicum" experience usually includes exposure to the counseling situation, as provided by audio and video tapes of professional counselors at work and by case books such as that by Evraiff (1963), as well as an artificial simulation of counseling, through role playing. Once the student has developed his counseling skills in this setting, he is ready to proceed to counsel with real clients in a true counseling situation.

Even at this point the student is obviously not yet a skilled counselor. The practicum experience requires, therefore, that the student be closely supervised by an experienced counselor. In this way, the student counselor is guided in his early steps as a counselor, and his clients are presumably protected from any gross errors in judgment on his part due to his lack of experience. The practicum should provide for close supervision; a practicum in which only token or minimal supervision is provided is cheating its students out of a major educational opportunity. As the student gains in experience the amount of supervision may be decreased, but even professional counselors find it helpful to keep in touch with their colleagues for guidance with problem clients.

The practicum should enable the student to enhance and master his repertoire of counseling skills, which suggests that it should provide him with both breadth and depth of experience.[6] The practicum student should not, therefore, be restricted to a single type of client (for example, college students only) nor should a single counseling technique be emphasized to the exclusion of all others. To achieve such breadth will probably require that the practicum student be involved in a variety of counseling settings and with several supervisors of differing theoretical persuasions. Only from such broad exposure to the range of counseling techniques can the neophyte counselor select those aspects which will form his own unique approach to counseling.

The core of the practicum experience is the relationship between the student and his supervisor. Some authorities believe that this relationship should approximate a counseling relationship, with the supervisor acting as a counselor to the student, while others view the supervisor's role as more similar to that of a teacher. Obviously, the nature of the relationship will depend on which of these roles the supervisor chooses to emphasize; he may, moreover, shift his role from one student to another, or from one time to another with the same student. Presumably the supervisor, whatever his role, is trying to provide the student with a relationship to promote his optimum development as a counselor, as the supervisor sees it.

Whatever the supervisor's role, it seems important that he be a practicing counselor, primarily because of the role model he provides for his students. The noncounseling supervisor may have difficulty establishing his credibility in the eyes of the students he supervises, and it is likely that the influence of the supervisor, like that of the counselor, depends in large part on the status invested in him by those whose behavior he is attempting to influence.

The supervisor who attempts to play a counseling role with his students may find himself in conflict if one of his supervisory responsibilities is to evaluate the student's ability as a counselor. A practicum without evaluation seems impossible, since it may be the first opportunity for those responsible for the training program to estimate the student's counseling potential. Yet the supervisor who wants to develop a close relationship with his students may find himself thwarted if he must eventually evaluate their progress as counselors. It is therefore probably desirable to invest the responsibilities of supervision and evaluation in two different persons, so that the super-

---

[6] For specific suggestions as to the design of a practicum, see Nachman and others (1960), Arbuckle (1963), Patterson (1964), and Truax and Carkhuff (1967).

visor is not called upon to evaluate anyone. The person responsible for the practicum should make the evaluation, on whatever bases he chooses. Information available to him would probably include video or audio tapes of the student's counseling sessions, as well as discussions with the student himself. The evaluator should point out areas of difficulty to the student and encourage the student to work on these with his supervisor. The evaluator should consider in his evaluation the progress which the student has made during the practicum, as evidence of whether he will be likely to continue to progress when he is no longer so closely supervised. The student who shows little sign of change during the course of a practicum is a good bet not to change much afterwards either, and would therefore probably not be a good counseling risk.

As noted earlier, the trainee should gain experience in a variety of counseling settings. Since most counselor training programs are operated within academic settings, the first practicum experience for the trainee is usually in an agency attached to the university, such as a student counseling service. This may serve as a fine starting point, but the trainee's experience should not stop there. To locate other settings, however, may require the program to go afield, such as into a hospital setting or a community agency. In so doing, those persons responsible for the training program may find themselves placing students in practicum settings over which they have no direct control. If the practicum is to provide the student with an appropriate educational experience, it is necessary that the training program exercise a certain amount of control of the practicum experience, even within an outside agency. Otherwise the student's time may be wasted, or his training may be in conflict with the principles stressed in the training program. It is therefore important that the persons responsible for the program reach an understanding with the agency in which a practicum is being proposed concerning the nature of the practicum experience and its supervision, and that they maintain close contact with the agency to determine that the student's needs are being adequately met.

Professional Accreditation. The primary responsibility for the quality of a counselor training program lies with the educational institution which sponsors the program. As the counseling professions have reached maturity, however, their professional organizations have made increasingly strong attempts to impose some sort of structure on these programs in the form of standards or guidelines. In their ultimate form, such guidelines become a basis for the *accreditation* of a given program, accreditation signifying that the program has achieved an acceptable level of quality in the eyes of the profession. The American Psychological Association, for example, has established accreditation procedures for counseling psychology programs (Super and others, 1952), and the American Association of Counselor Educators and Supervisors has developed Standards for the Preparation of Secondary School Counselors (Hill, 1968). The latter group is also developing similar standards for elementary school counselors (Ohlsen, 1968) and for college student personnel workers (Isaacson, 1968), although actual accreditation of the latter group may be far distant.

The establishment of professional accreditation programs has been the subject of considerable controversy. Stripling (1968) has presented a number of arguments in support of professional accreditation, primarily stressing that accreditation is a means of protecting society from poorly prepared counselors as well as assisting institutions in initiating and evaluating programs of counselor training. He believes that, in the future, accreditation will proliferate to include programs in employment service counseling, rehabilitation counseling, junior college counseling, and university counseling and student personnel work.

While the desirability of protecting society from the ill effects of counselors produced by shoddy training programs cannot be denied, accreditation by professional organizations carries with it risks as well as benefits. The major risk is that accreditation standards tend to become fixed and thereby may hamper the development of a field. Educational programs in any profession which are bound by certain criteria in order to retain accreditation may be hesitant to experiment or to embark on a novel approach. In view of the youth of counselor training, it could be disastrous to fix criteria of preparation too soon. An innovative, creative program may not meet the criteria and therefore not be allowed to prove its value, and the field thereby may become more and more rigid.

It is primarily for this reason that academic institutions resist accreditation of their programs by professional organizations. The university believes that it must be free to pursue truth in whatever direction it leads, and archaic standards of accreditation tend to impede rather than facilitate this mission. Proponents of accreditation (for example, Hill, 1968) argue that the criteria will be constantly reviewed and modified, but their efforts may not keep pace with their good intentions. At the present time, therefore, professional accreditation of counseling programs in academic settings is only advisory to the university and to the professional world. In the long run, the product of a given counselor training program must be judged primarily on the known quality of the program which produced him rather than on its accreditation status.

Professional accreditation is more defensible when it applies to counselor training programs which are not directly under the control of a college or university. If, as seems likely, such programs will expand in the future, the need for professional accreditation may become more evident.

Effectiveness of Training.   How effective are counselor training programs? This question has received surprisingly little study, and the results of the studies to date have not been impressive. Carkhuff (1968a), in summarizing the evidence, says flatly that "no traditional preparation programs have demonstrated their constructive consequences [p. 257]." While this statement seems to overstate the case a bit, it is true that one is hard-put to point to any clear evidence of the effectiveness of a given training program. While a training program undoubtedly does help some persons to function more effectively as counselors, it may have little effect on others (Munger, Myers, and Brown, 1963) and may, in fact, reduce the effectiveness of the poorest of the students (Carkhuff, 1968a). Such an outcome is hardly impressive.

A dramatic indication of the ineffectiveness of many programs comes from research by Carkhuff and his coworkers (summarized by Carkhuff, 1968a) which demonstrates that the highest level of functioning, by their measures, occurs at the *beginning* of the graduate program and that the students in general deteriorate as counselors thereafter. Carkhuff suggests that the typical training program, accompanied by the stress of academic demands, presents the student with a crisis situation which he is unable to resolve successfully. This suggests that it may be more effective to separate the learning of counseling skills from the didactic demands of a graduate program; perhaps the two kinds of learning experiences impede rather than complement one another.

It is worth noting, however, that the evidence cited above has been drawn almost entirely from training programs in psychotherapy rather than counseling. It is possible that the kinds of skills required for counseling may be more readily taught in an academic setting than those required for psychotherapy. Further research on this question is obviously needed.

Training of Lay Counselors. The lack of convincing proof that the traditional counselor training programs have an appreciable influence on their students has led to a reassessment of many long-held assumptions about the training of counselors. One of these is the assumption that counselor training must take place within a graduate or professional school. Within the past few years, several training programs have been established to train persons as counselors outside of the traditional academic setting. These programs concentrate on teaching basic skills of counseling to persons who are effective in interpersonal relationships. Some attempt is made to provide a conceptual basis for the training, but the academic content is much more limited than in the traditional program.

Programs to train "laymen" as counselors are still in the experimental stage and are quite varied in nature. Among those which have proved successful are a program at the University of Maryland to train housewives as psychotherapists (Magoon and Golann, 1966), a program at the Chester County Mental Health Center to train housewives as therapists for children and adolescents (Siegle, 1968), and a program established by Rioch and her associates at the National Institute for Mental Health (Rioch and others, 1963; Rioch, 1966), as well as programs to train "mental health technicians" in community colleges (Wellner and Simon, 1969). The evidence indicates that these programs, and others like them, produce counselors who perform as effectively as traditionally trained persons, at least within a limited setting (Carkhuff, 1968b), and in some cases even better (Poser, 1966).

Not surprisingly, this innovation has met with resistance within the counseling professions. Many counselors would probably agree with Patterson's (1965) contention that laymen may be trained to perform subprofessional functions as "counselor aides," but that they should neither be expected nor encouraged to replace professional counselors. On the other hand, the substantial shortage of qualified counselors suggests that all possible sources of counselors must be explored, and the evidence that lay counselors generally are as effective as those with more impressive credentials cannot be ignored.

This writer believes that lay counselors can serve a useful function in meeting the counseling needs of society. As the skills of the effective counselor become better understood through research, it should become increasingly easier to train laymen to perform these skills. Such persons will, however, be restricted by their limited formal background and understanding of the nature of the counseling process, as well as by a lack of professional identification. The latter point seems especially important: the lay counselor is essentially a technician rather than a professional. As a technician, he is less likely to be committed to maintaining a professional involvement in his field. He is not bound by the ethics of a profession, nor is he likely to continue to grow as a counselor through continued professional involvement. His effectiveness will therefore be restricted to a limited range of problems and clients, and it may decrease with time as new techniques are devised with which he does not become familiar.

This suggests that the lay counselor, as a technician, should work under the supervision of a professional counselor. Such an arrangement should prove beneficial to both groups, as well as to society in general. The lay counselor can provide effective help for persons with problems, thus bringing counseling services to many who would otherwise have to go without due to the shortage of professional counselors. The professional, on the other hand, should be challenged by his responsibility to the lay counselors whom he supervises to enhance his own skills and to maintain an involvement in his profession. At the present time many "professional" counselors are probably in fact little more than technicians anyway, and a graduate or professional program is an inefficient way to train technicians. With the judicious use of lay counselors, the skills and education acquired by counselors in the course of a professional training program can be put to more effective use.

References

Ackerman, N. W. *The Psychodynamics of Family Life*. New York: Basic Books, 1960.

Ackerman, N. W. Emergence of family psychotherapy on the present scene. In M. I. Stein (Ed.), *Contemporary Psychotherapies*. New York: Free Press, 1961. Pp. 228–244. (a)

Ackerman, N. W. Further comments on family psychotherapy. In M. I. Stein (Ed.), *Contemporary Psychotherapies*. New York: Free Press, 1961. Pp. 245–255. (b)

Ackerman, N. W. *Treating the Troubled Family*. New York: Basic Books, 1966.

Ackerman, N. W., and Marjorie Behrens. The uses of family psychotherapy. *American Journal of Orthopsychiatry*, 1967, **37,** 391–392.

Albert, G. Advanced psychological training for marriage counselors—necessity or luxury? *Marriage and Family Living*, 1963, **25,** 181–183.

Albert, G. A survey of college counseling facilities. *Personnel and Guidance Journal*, 1968, **46,** 540–543.

Allen, R. C., Elyce Ferster, and J. G. Rubin (Eds.). *Readings in Law and Psychiatry*. Baltimore: Johns Hopkins Press, 1968.

American Personnel and Guidance Association. Code of ethics. *Personnel and Guidance Journal*, 1961, **40,** 206–209.

American Psychiatric Association. *Mental Disorders: Diagnostic and Statistical Manual*. Washington: American Psychiatric Association, 1952.

American Psychiatric Association. Statement on confidentiality. *Mental Hygiene*, 1961, **45,** 478.

American Psychological Association. *Casebook on Ethical Standards of Psychologists*. Washington: American Psychological Association, 1967.

American Psychological Association. Ethical standards of psychologists. *American Psychologist*, 1968, **23,** 357–361.

American Psychological Association Committee on Legislation. A model for state legislation affecting the practice of psychology, 1967. *American Psychologist*, 1967, **22,** 1095–1103.

Anastasi, Anne. *Fields of Applied Psychology*. New York: McGraw-Hill, 1964.

Anastasi, Anne. *Psychological Testing*. 3rd edition. New York: Macmillan, 1968.

Anderson, A. R. Group counseling. *Review of Educational Research*, 1969, **39,** 209–226.

Arbuckle, D. S. The education of the school counselor. *Journal of Counseling Psychology*, 1958, **5,** 58–62.

Arbuckle, D. S. *Counseling: An Introduction*. Boston: Allyn & Bacon, 1961. (a)

Arbuckle, D. S. The conflicting functions of the school counselor. *Counselor Education and Supervision*, 1961, **1,** 54–59. (b)

Arbuckle, D. S. The learning of counseling: process not product. *Journal of Counseling Psychology*, 1963, **10,** 163–168.

Arbuckle, D. S. *Counseling: Philosophy, Theory, and Practice*. Boston: Allyn & Bacon, 1965.

Arbuckle, D. S. (Ed.). *Counseling and Psychotherapy: An Overview*. New York: McGraw-Hill, 1967.

Arnold, D. L. Counselor education as responsible self-development. *Counselor Education and Supervision*, 1961, **1,** 185–192.

Astin, A. W. The functional autonomy of psychotherapy. *American Psychologist*, 1961, **16,** 75–78.

Astin, A. W. Criterion-centered research. *Educational and Psychological Measurement*, 1964, **24,** 807–822.

Aubrey, R. F. The legitimacy of elementary school counseling: Some unresolved issues and conflicts. *Personnel and Guidance Journal*, 1967, **46,** 355–359.

Ausubel, D. P. Relationships between psychology and psychiatry: The hidden issues. *American Psychologist*, 1956, **11,** 99–104.

Bachrach, A. J. Some applications of operant conditioning to behavior therapy. In J. Wolpe, A. Salter, and L. J. Reyna (Eds.), *The Conditioning Therapies*. New York: Holt, Rinehart and Winston, 1965. Pp. 62–78.

Bachrach, A. J., and W. A. Quigley. Direct methods of treatment. In I. A. Berg and L. A. Pennington (Eds.), *An Introduction to Clinical Psychology*. 3rd edition. New York: Ronald Press, 1966. Pp. 482–560.

Baer, M. F., and E. C. Roeber. *Occupational Information: The Dynamics of Its Nature and Use*. 3rd edition. Chicago: Science Research Associates, 1964.

Bandura, A. Psychotherapy as a learning process. *Psychological Bulletin*, 1961, **58,** 143–159.

Bandura, A. Behavioral modification through modeling procedures. In L. Krasner and L P. Ullmann (Eds.), *Research in Behavior Modification*. New York: Holt, Rinehart and Winston, 1965. Pp. 310–340.

Bandura, A. Behavioral psychotherapy. *Scientific American*, March 1967, **216,** 78–86.

Banks, G., B. G. Berenson, and R. R. Carkhuff. The effects of counselor race and training upon the counseling process with Negro clients in initial interviews. *Journal of Clinical Psychology,* 1967, **23,** 70–72.

Bardon, J. I. School psychology and school psychologists: An approach to an old problem. *American Psychologist,* 1968, **23,** 187–194.

Barron, F. X. *Creativity and Psychological Health.* Princeton, N.J.: Van Nostrand, 1963.

Battista, O. A. *Mental Drugs: Chemistry's Challenge to Psychotherapy.* Philadelphia: Chilton, 1960.

Bauernfeind, R. H. Are sex norms necessary? *Journal of Counseling Psychology,* 1956, **3,** 57–63.

Bauernfeind, R. H. The matter of "ipsative scores." *Personnel and Guidance Journal,* 1962, **41,** 210–217.

Bauernfeind, R. H. What to look for in a review of an interest inventory. *Personnel and Guidance Journal,* 1964, **42,** 925–927.

Beck, A. T. Reliability of psychiatric diagnoses: I. A critique of systematic studies. *American Journal of Psychiatry,* 1962, **119,** 210–216.

Beier, E. G. Client-centered therapy and the involuntary client. *Journal of Consulting Psychology,* 1952, **16,** 332–337.

Beisser, A. The paradox of public belief and psychotherapy. *Psychotherapy: Theory, Research, and Practice,* 1965, **2,** 92–94.

Bell, J. E. Contrasting approaches in marital counseling. *Family Process,* 1967, **6,** 16–26.

Bennett, Margaret. *Guidance and Counseling in Groups.* 2nd edition. New York: McGraw-Hill, 1963.

Bennett, Margaret. Strategies of vocational guidance in groups. In H. Borow (Ed.), *Man in a World at Work.* Boston: Houghton Mifflin, 1964. Pp. 460–486.

Bentz, W. K. The relationship between educational background and the referral role of ministers. *Sociology and Social Research,* 1962, **51,** 199–208.

Berdie, R. F. Changes in self-ratings as a method of evaluating counseling. *Journal of Counseling Psychology,* 1954, **1,** 49–54.

Berdie, R. F. Validities of the Strong Vocational Interest Blank. In W. L. Layton (Ed.), *The Strong Vocational Interest Blank: Research and Uses.* Minneapolis: University of Minnesota Press, 1960. Pp. 18–61.

Berdie, R. F., W. L. Layton, E. O. Swanson, and Theda Hagenah. *Testing in Guidance and Counseling.* New York: McGraw-Hill, 1963.

Bereiter, C. Using tests to measure change. *Personnel and Guidance Journal,* 1962, **41,** 6–11. (a)

Bereiter, C. Some persisting dilemmas in the measurement of change. In C. Harris (Ed.), *Problems in Measuring Change.* Madison, Wisconsin: University of Wisconsin Press, 1962. Pp. 3–20. (b)

Berenson, B. G., and R. R. Carkhuff (Eds.). *Sources of Gain in Counseling and Psychotherapy: Readings and Commentary.* New York: Holt, Rinehart and Winston, 1967.

Berg, I. A. The use of human subjects in psychological research. *American Psychologist,* 1954, **9,** 108–111.

Berg, I. A., and L. A. Pennington (Eds.). *An Introduction to Clinical Psychology*. 3rd edition. New York: Ronald Press, 1966.

Bergin, A. E. The effects of psychotherapy: Negative results revisited. *Journal of Counseling Psychology,* 1963, **10,** 244–250.

Bergin, A. E. Some implications of psychotherapy research for therapeutic practice. *Journal of Abnormal Psychology,* 1966, **71,** 235–246.

Bernstein, A. The psychoanalytic technique. In B. B. Wolman (Ed.), *Handbook of Clinical Psychology*. New York: McGraw-Hill, 1965. Pp. 1168–1199.

Bijou, S. W. Implications of behavioral science for counseling and guidance. In J. D. Krumboltz (Ed.), *Revolution in Counseling: Implications of Behavioral Science*. Boston: Houghton Mifflin, 1966. Pp. 27–48.

Bixler, R. H. The irrelevancy of wishful thinking. *Counselor Education and Supervision,* 1964, **3,** 214–219.

Blaine, G. B. Divided loyalties: The college therapist's responsibility to the student, the university, and the parents. *American Journal of Orthopsychiatry,* 1964, **34,** 481–485.

Blaine, G. B., and C. C. McArthur. *Emotional Problems of the Student*. New York: Appleton-Century-Crofts, 1961.

Blocher, D., W. W. Tennyson, and R. Johnson. The dilemma of counselor identity. *Journal of Counseling Psychology,* 1963, **10,** 344–349.

Blos, P. Psychological counseling of college students. *American Journal of Orthopsychiatry,* 1946, **16,** 571–580.

Bordin, E. S. Diagnosis in counseling and psychotherapy. *Educational and Psychological Measurement,* 1946, **6,** 169–184.

Bordin, E. S. *Psychological Counseling*. 2nd edition. New York: Appleton-Century-Crofts, 1968.

Borow, H. Vocational developmental research: Some problems of logical and experimental form. *Personnel and Guidance Journal,* 1961, **40,** 21–25.

Borow, H. Milestones: A chronology of notable events in the history of vocational guidance. In H. Borow (Ed.), *Man in a World at Work*. Boston: Houghton Mifflin, 1964. Pp. 45–64. (a)

Borow, H. (Ed.). *Man in a World at Work*. Boston: Houghton Mifflin, 1964. (b)

Brammer, L. M., and E. L. Shostrom. *Therapeutic Psychology*. 2nd edition. Englewood Cliffs, N.J.: Prentice-Hall, 1968.

Braun, J. R. (Ed.). *Clinical Psychology in Transition: Selected Readings*. Rev. Ed. Cleveland: World Publishing Co., 1966.

Brayfield, A. H. Putting occupational information across. *Educational and Psychological Measurement,* 1948, **8,** 493–495.

Breger, L., and J. McGaugh. Critique and reformulation of "learning-theory" approaches to psychotherapy and neurosis. *Psychological Bulletin,* 1965, **63,** 338–358.

Brigante, T., D. Haefner, and W. Woodson. Clinical and counseling psychologists' perceptions of their specialties. *Journal of Counseling Psychology,* 1962, **9,** 225–231.

Brill, H. Psychiatric diagnosis, nomenclature, and classification. In B. B. Wolman (Ed.), *Handbook of Clinical Psychology*. New York: McGraw-Hill, 1965. Pp. 639–650.

Brown, F. G. *Principles of Educational and Psychological Testing.* Hinsdale, Ill.: The Dryden Press Inc., 1970.

Brown, J. P. *Counseling with Older Citizens.* Englewood Cliffs, N.J.: Prentice-Hall, 1964.

Bryan, J. H., and Mary Ann Test. Models and helping: Naturalistic studies in aiding behavior. *Journal of Personality and Social Psychology,* 1967, **6,** 400–407.

Buchheimer, A. The development of ideas about empathy. *Journal of Counseling Psychology,* 1963, **10,** 61–70.

Buchheimer, A., and Sara Balogh. *The Counseling Relationship, a Casebook.* Chicago: Science Research Associates, 1961.

Buchwald, A. Values and the use of tests. *Journal of Consulting Psychology,* 1965, **29,** 49–54.

Bugental, J. F. T. The person who is the psychotherapist. *Journal of Consulting Psychology,* 1964, **28,** 272–277.

Bugental, J. F. T. (Ed.). *Challenges of Humanistic Psychology.* New York: McGraw-Hill, 1967.

Burt, L. A. Inspection and release of records to parents. In Martha Ware (Ed.), *Law of Guidance and Counseling.* Cincinnati: W. H. Anderson, 1964. Pp. 37–49.

Butler, H. E. Duties and liabilities of counselors. In Martha Ware (Ed.), *Law of Guidance and Counseling.* Cincinnati: W. H. Anderson, 1964. Pp. 159–170.

Byrne, R. H. High school counseling—conditions for change. In Margaret Smith (Ed.), *Guidance-Personnel Work: Future Tense.* New York: Teachers College Press, 1966. Pp. 41–50.

Cahoon, D. D. Symptom substitution and the behavior therapies: A reappraisal. *Psychological Bulletin,* 1968, **69,** 149–156.

Callis, R. Diagnostic classification as a research tool. *Journal of Counseling Psychology,* 1965, **12,** 238–243.

Campbell, D. P. A counseling evaluation with a "better" control group. *Journal of Counseling Psychology,* 1963, **10,** 334–338.

Campbell, D. P. *The Results of Counseling: Twenty-five Years Later.* Philadelphia: Saunders, 1965. (a)

Campbell, D. P. Achievements of counseled and non-counseled students twenty-five years after counseling. *Journal of Counseling Psychology,* 1965, **12,** 287–293. (b)

Campbell, D. P. The 1966 revision of the Strong Vocational Interest Blank. *Personnel and Guidance Journal,* 1966, **44,** 744–749. (a)

Campbell, D. P. The stability of vocational interests within occupations over long time spans. *Personnel and Guidance Journal,* 1966, **44,** 1012–1019. (b)

Campbell, D. P. Stability of interests within an occupation over thirty years. *Journal of Applied Psychology,* 1966, **50,** 51–56. (c)

Campbell, D. P. Occupations ten years later of high school seniors with high scores on the SVIB Life Insurance Salesman Scale. *Journal of Applied Psychology,* 1966, **50,** 369–372. (d)

Campbell, D. P. The development of the SVIB: 1927–67. In P. McReynolds (Ed.), *Advances in Psychological Assessment.* Vol. 1. Palo Alto, California: Science and Behavior Books, 1968. Pp. 105–130.

Campbell, J., and M. D. Dunnette. Effectiveness of T-group experiences in managerial training and development. *Psychological Bulletin,* 1968, **79,** 73–104.

Carkhuff, R. R. A "non-traditional" assessment of graduate education in the helping professions. *Counselor Education and Supervision,* 1968, **7,** 252–261. (a)

Carkhuff, R. R. Differential functioning of lay and professional helpers. *Journal of Counseling Psychology,* 1968, **15,** 117–126. (b)

Carkhuff, R. R., D. Kratochvil, and T. Friel. Effects of professional training: Communication and discrimination of facilitative conditions. *Journal of Counseling Psychology,* 1968, **15,** 68–74.

Carkhuff, R. R., and C. B. Truax. Toward explaining success and failure in interpersonal learning experiences. *Personnel and Guidance Journal,* 1966, **44,** 723–728.

Cartwright, D. S. Methodology in counseling evaluation. *Journal of Counseling Psychology,* 1957, **4,** 263–267.

Cartwright, D. S., and Rosalind Cartwright. Faith and improvement in psychotherapy. *Journal of Counseling Psychology,* 1958, **5,** 174–177.

Cartwright, Rosalind. A comparison of the response to psychoanalytic and client-centered psychotherapy. In L. Gottschalk and A. Auerbach (Eds.), *Methods of Research in Psychotherapy.* New York: Appleton-Century-Crofts, 1966. Pp. 517–529.

Castore, G. F. Number of verbal interrelationships as a determinant of group size. *Journal of Abnormal and Social Psychology,* 1962, **64,** 456–457.

Cattell, R. B. What is "objective" in "objective personality tests"? *Journal of Counseling Psychology,* 1958, **5,** 285–289.

Center for Interest Measurement Research. *In Honor of Professor Edward K. Strong, Jr.* Minneapolis: Center for Interest Measurement Research, University of Minnesota, 1964.

Clark, C. M. Confidentiality and the school counselor. *Personnel and Guidance Journal,* 1965, **43,** 482–484.

Clark, K. E. *The Vocational Interests of Nonprofessional Men.* Minneapolis: University of Minnesota Press, 1961.

Clark, K. E., and D. P. Campbell. *Minnesota Vocational Interest Inventory: Manual.* New York: Psychological Corporation, 1965.

Clark, K. E., and others. Privacy and behavioral research: Preliminary summary of the report of the panel on privacy and behavioral research. *Science,* 1967, **155,** 535–538.

Clemes, S. R., and V. J. D'Andrea. Patients' anxiety as a function of expectation and degree of initial interview ambiguity. *Journal of Consulting Psychology,* 1965, **29,** 397–404.

Coffey, H. S. Group psychotherapy. In I. A. Berg and L. A. Pennington (Eds.), *An Introduction to Clinical Psychology.* 3rd edition. New York: Ronald Press, 1966. Pp. 624–651.

Cohn, B., C. F. Combs, E. J. Gibian, and A. M. Sniffen. Group counseling: An orientation. *Personnel and Guidance Journal,* 1963, **42,** 355–358.

Cohn, B., and A. M. Sniffen. A school report on group counseling. *Personnel and Guidance Journal,* 1962, **41,** 133–138.

Colby, K. M. Computer simulation of change in personal belief systems. *Behavioral Science,* 1967, **12,** 248–253.

College Entrance Examination Board. *Financing a College Education: A Guide for Counselors.* Princeton, N.J.: College Entrance Examination Board, 1966.

Combs, A. Counseling as a learning process. *Journal of Counseling Psychology,* 1954, **1,** 31–36.

Coogan, J. P. The program and the patient. *S K & F Psychiatric Reporter,* May–June 1967, No. 32, 3–6.

Cottle, W. C. Personal characteristics of counselors: I. *Personnel and Guidance Journal,* 1953, **31,** 445–450.

Cowen, E. L. The experimental analogue: An approach to research in psychotherapy. *Psychological Reports,* 1961, **8,** 9 10.

Cranny, C. J. Factor analytically derived scales for the Strong Vocational Interest Blank. Unpublished doctoral dissertation, Iowa State University, 1967.

Crites, J., and others. Symposium. New research in vocational development. *Personnel and Guidance Journal,* 1963, **41,** 766–782.

Cronbach, L. J. *Essentials of Psychological Testing.* 2nd edition. New York: Harper & Row, 1960.

Cross, H. J. The outcome of psychotherapy: A selected analysis of research findings. *Journal of Consulting Psychology,* 1964, **28,** 413–417.

Crowne, D., and M. Stephens. Self-acceptance and self-evaluation behavior: A critique of methodology. *Psychological Bulletin,* 1961, **58,** 104–121.

Darley, J. G. The theoretical basis of interests. In W. L. Layton (Ed.), *The Strong Vocational Interest Blank: Research and Uses.* Minneapolis: University of Minnesota Press, 1960. Pp. 118–145.

Darley, J. G., and Theda Hagenah. *Vocational Interest Measurement.* Minneapolis: University of Minnesota Press, 1955.

Dean, S. I. Treatment of the reluctant client. *American Psychologist,* 1958, **13,** 627–630.

Demos, G., and F. Zuwaylif. Characteristics of effective counselors. *Counselor Education and Supervision,* 1966, **5,** 163–165.

Deutsch, Cynthia. A personal counseling service in a liberal arts college. *Personnel and Guidance Journal,* 1958, **37,** 193–197.

DiMichael, S. G. Vocational rehabilitation: A major social force. In H. Borow (Ed.), *Man in a World at Work.* Boston: Houghton Mifflin, 1964. Pp. 534–556.

Dittes, J. E. Galvanic skin response as a measure of patient's reaction to therapist's permissiveness. *Journal of Abnormal and Social Psychology,* 1957, **55,** 295–303.

Dollard, J., and N. E. Miller. *Personality and Psychotherapy.* New York: McGraw-Hill, 1950.

Dreikurs, R. The Adlerian approach to therapy. In M. I. Stein (Ed.), *Contemporary Psychotherapies.* New York: Free Press, 1963. Pp. 80–93.

Dunnette, M. D. People feeling: Joy, more joy, and the "slough of despond." *Journal of Applied Behavioral Science,* 1969, **5,** 25–44.

Ebel, R. L. Must all tests be valid? *American Psychologist,* 1961, **16,** 640–647.

Eckerson, Louise. Realities confronting elementary school guidance. *Personnel and Guidance Journal,* 1967, **46,** 350–354.

Edwards, A. L., and L. J. Cronbach. Experimental design for research in psychotherapy. *Journal of Clinical Psychology,* 1952, **8,** 51–59.

Empey, L. T. Role expectations of young women regarding marriage and a career. *Marriage and Family Living,* 1958, **20,** 152–155.

English, H. B., and Ava C. English. *A Comprehensive Dictionary of Psychological and Psychoanalytical Terms.* New York: Longmans, Green, 1958.

Evraiff, W. *Helping Counselors Grow Professionally.* Englewood Cliffs, N.J.: Prentice-Hall, 1963.

Eysenck, H. J. The effects of psychotherapy: An evaluation. *Journal of Consulting Psychology,* 1952, **16,** 319–342.

Eysenck, H. J. Behavior therapy, spontaneous remission, and transference in neurotics. *American Journal of Psychiatry,* 1963, **119,** 867–871.

Eysenck, H. J. The nature of behavior therapy. In H. J. Eysenck (Ed.), *Experiments in Behavior Therapy.* New York: Macmillan, 1964. Pp. 1–20. (a)

Eysenck, H. J. (Ed.). *Experiments in Behavior Therapy.* New York: Macmillan, 1964. (b)

Eysenck, H. J., and S. Rachman. *The Causes and Cures of Neurosis.* San Diego, California: Robert Knapp, 1965.

Farnsworth, D. L. *Mental Health in College and University.* Cambridge, Massachusetts: Harvard University Press, 1957.

Farnsworth, D. L. *Psychiatry, Education, and the Young Adult.* Springfield, Illinois: Charles C Thomas, 1966.

Farwell, G. The role of the school counselor. *Counselor Education and Supervision,* 1961, **1,** 40–43.

Faust, V. *History of Elementary School Counseling.* Boston: Houghton Mifflin, 1968.

Feifel, H., and Janet Eells. Patients and therapists assess the same psychotherapy. *Journal of Consulting Psychology,* 1963, **27,** 310–318.

Feldman, M. P. Aversion therapy for sexual deviations: A critical review. *Psychological Bulletin,* 1966, **65,** 65–79.

Ferster, Elyce Z. Confidential and privileged communications. *Journal of the American Medical Association,* 1962, **182,** 656–662.

Ferster, Elyce Z. Statutory summary of physician-patient privileged communication laws. In R. C. Allen, Elyce Ferster, and J. G. Rubin (Eds.), *Readings in Law and Psychiatry.* Baltimore: Johns Hopkins Press, 1968. Pp. 161–165.

Fey, W. F. Doctrine and experience: Their influence upon the psychotherapist. *Journal of Consulting Psychology,* 1958, **22,** 403–409.

Fiedler, F. The concept of an ideal therapeutic relationship. *Journal of Consulting Psychology,* 1950, **14,** 239–245. (a)

Fiedler, F. A comparison of therapeutic relationships in psychoanalytic, non-directive, and Adlerian therapy. *Journal of Consulting Psychology,* 1950, **14,** 436–445. (b)

Fiske, D., D. Cartwright, and W. Kirtner. Are psychotherapeutic changes predictable? *Journal of Abnormal and Social Psychology,* 1964, **69,** 418–426.

Fitzgerald, P. W. The professional role of school counselors. In J. W. Loughary (Ed.), *Counseling, a Growing Profession.* Washington: American Personnel and Guidance Association, 1965. Pp. 31–41.

Ford, D. H., and H. B. Urban. *Systems of Psychotherapy.* New York: Wiley, 1963.

Foster, R. G. A point of view on marriage counseling. *Journal of Counseling Psychology,* 1956, **3,** 212–215.

Fox, J. Use of records in court and other legal proceedings. In Martha Ware (Ed.), *Law of Guidance and Counseling.* Cincinnati: W. H. Anderson, 1964. Pp. 87–128.

Frank, J. D. Problems of controls in psychotherapy as exemplified by the psychotherapy research project of the Phipps Psychiatric Clinic. In E. A. Rubinstein and M. R. Parloff (Eds.), *Research in Psychotherapy.* Washington: American Psychological Association, 1959. Pp. 10–26.

Frank, J. D. *Persuasion and Healing.* Baltimore: Johns Hopkins Press, 1961.

Frank, J. D., E. H. Nash, A. R. Stone, and S. D. Imber. Immediate and long-term symptomatic course of psychiatric outpatients. *American Journal of Psychiatry,* 1963, **120,** 429–439.

Franks, C. M. (Ed.). *Conditioning Techniques in Clinical Practice and Research.* New York: Springer, 1964.

Franks, C. M. Behavior therapy, psychology, and the psychiatrist. *American Journal of Orthopsychiatry,* 1965, **35,** 145–151.

French, J., and W. Michael. *Standards for Educational and Psychological Tests and Manuals.* Washington: American Psychological Association, 1966.

Froelich, C. P. Must counseling be individual? *Educational and Psychological Measurement,* 1958, **18,** 681–689.

Fulcomer, D. M., S. K. Edelman, and E. C. Lewis. Interdisciplinary marriage counseling in a university counseling service. *Marriage and Family Living,* 1961, **23,** 273–275.

Fuller, Frances. Influence of sex of counselor and of client on client expressions of feeling. *Journal of Counseling Psychology,* 1963, **10,** 34–40.

Fuller, Frances. Preferences for male and female counselors. *Personnel and Guidance Journal,* 1964, **42,** 463–467.

Furgeson, E. H. The aims of premarital counseling. *Journal of Pastoral Care,* 1952, **6,** 30–39.

Gardner, G. G. The psychotherapeutic relationship. *Psychological Bulletin,* 1964, **61,** 426–437.

Gazda, G. M., J. A. Duncan, and M. E. Meadows. Group counseling and group procedures: Report of a survey. *Counselor Education and Supervision,* 1967, **6,** 305–310.

Geer, J. H., and E. S. Katkin. Treatment of insomnia using a variant of systematic desensitization: A case report. *Journal of Abnormal Psychology,* 1966, **71,** 161–164.

Geiser, R., and P. Rheingold. Psychology and the legal process: Testimonial privileged communications. *American Psychologist,* 1964, **19,** 831–837.

Gelfand, D., and D. P. Hartmann. Behavior therapy with children: A review and evaluation of research methodology. *Psychological Bulletin,* 1968, **69,** 204–215.

Gellman, W. Government and community settings for vocational guidance. In H. Borow (Ed.), *Man in a World at Work.* Boston: Houghton Mifflin, 1964. Pp. 510–533.

Ghiselli, E. E. *The Validity of Occupational Aptitude Tests.* New York: Wiley, 1966.

Ginzberg, E., S. W. Ginsburg, S. Axelrad, and J. L. Herma. *Occupational Choice.* New York: Columbia University Press, 1951.

Glad, D. G. *Operational Values in Psychotherapy.* New York: Oxford University Press, 1959.

Glanz, E. C., and R. W. Hayes. *Groups in Guidance.* 2nd edition. Boston: Allyn & Bacon, 1967.

Goldiamond, I. Self-control procedures in personal behavior problems. *Psychological Reports,* 1965, **17,** 851–868.

Goldman, L. *Using Tests in Counseling.* New York: Appleton-Century-Crofts, 1961.

Goldman, L. Group guidance: Content and process. *Personnel and Guidance Journal,* 1962, **40,** 518–522.

Goldman, L. Information and counseling: A dilemma. *Personnel and Guidance Journal,* 1967, **46,** 42–46.

Goldstein, A. P. *Therapist-Patient Expectancies in Psychotherapy.* New York: Macmillan, 1962.

Goldstein, A. P. Psychotherapy research by extrapolation from social psychology. In A. P. Goldstein and S. J. Dean (Eds.), *The Investigation of Psychotherapy: Commentaries and Readings.* New York: Wiley, 1966. Pp. 36–42.

Goldstein, A. P., and S. J. Dean. *The Investigation of Psychotherapy: Commentaries and Readings.* New York: Wiley, 1966.

Goldstein, A. P., K. Heller, and L. B. Sechrest. *Psychotherapy and the Psychology of Behavior Change.* New York: Wiley, 1966.

Gometz, L., and C. A. Parker. Disciplinary counseling: A contradiction? *Personnel and Guidance Journal,* 1968, **46,** 437–443.

Gonyea, G. G. Appropriateness-of-vocational-choice as a criterion of counseling outcome. *Journal of Counseling Psychology,* 1962, **9,** 213–219.

Goodstein, L. D. Behavior theoretical views of counseling. In B. S. Stefflre (Ed.), *Theories of Counseling.* New York: McGraw-Hill, 1965. Pp. 140–192.

Goodstein, L. D., and A. E. Grigg. Client satisfaction, counselors, and the counseling process. *Personnel and Guidance Journal,* 1959, **38,** 19–24.

Gordon, E. W. Counseling socially disadvantaged children. In F. Riessman, J. Cohen, and A. Pearl (Eds.), *Mental Health of the Poor.* New York: Free Press, 1964. Pp. 275–282.

Gordon, I. J. Elementary school guidance: Prospectus. In Margaret Smith (Ed.), *Guidance-Personnel Work: Future Tense*. New York: Teachers College Press, Columbia University, 1966. Pp. 31–40.

Goslin, D. A. The social impact of testing. *Personnel and Guidance Journal*, 1967, **45**, 676–682.

Gottschalk, L., and A. Auerbach (Eds.). *Methods of Research in Psychotherapy*. New York: Appleton-Century-Crofts, 1966.

Grater, H. A., B. L. Kell, and Josephine Morse. The social service interest: Roadblock and road to creativity. *Journal of Counseling Psychology*, 1961, **8**, 9–12.

Grigg, A. E. Client response to counselors at different levels of experience. *Journal of Counseling Psychology*, 1961, **8**, 217–222.

Gross, E. Counselors under fire: Opportunity centers. *Personnel and Guidance Journal*, 1969, **47**, 404–409.

Grossberg, J. M. Behavior therapy. A review. *Psychological Bulletin*, 1964, **62**, 73–88.

Grummon, D. L. Client-centered theory. In B. Steffle (Ed.), *Theories of Counseling*. New York: McGraw-Hill, 1965. Pp. 30–90.

Guion, R. M., and R. F. Gottier. Validity of personality measures in personnel selection. *Personnel Psychology*, 1965, **18**, 135–164.

Gurin, G., J. Veroff, and Sheila Feld. *Americans View Their Mental Health*. New York: Basic Books, 1960.

Gustad, J. W. The definition of counseling. In R. F. Berdie (Ed.), *Roles and Relationships in Counseling*. Minnesota Studies in Student Personnel Work No. 3. Minneapolis: University of Minnesota Press, 1953. Pp. 3–19.

Gustad, J. W., J. D. Black, Dorothy Clendenen, E. S. Roeber, and D. E. Swanson. An analysis of practices in counselor trainee selection. *Journal of Counseling Psychology*, 1954, **1**, 174–179.

Gustad, J. W., and A. H. Tuma. The effects of different methods of test introduction and interpretation on client learning in counseling. *Journal of Counseling Psychology*, 1957, **4**, 313–317.

Haley, J. *Strategies of Psychotherapy*. New York: Grune & Stratton, 1963.

Hall, C. S. *A Primer of Freudian Psychology*. New York: World Publishing Company, 1954.

Hall, C. S., and G. Lindzey. *Theories of Personality*. New York: Wiley, 1957.

Hanfmann, Eugenia, R. M. Jones, E. Baker, and L. Kovar. *Psychological Counseling in a Small College*. Cambridge, Massachusetts: Schenkman, 1963.

Hansel, C. E. M. *ESP: A Scientific Evaluation*. New York: Scribner's, 1966.

Hansen, D. A. The indifferent intercourse of counseling and sociology. *Journal of Counseling Psychology*, 1963, **10**, 3–13.

Harper, R. A. Should marriage counseling become a full-fledged specialty? *Marriage and Family Living*, 1953, **15**, 338–340.

Harrower, Molly. Differential diagnosis. In B. B. Wolman (Ed.), *Handbook of Clinical Psychology*. New York: McGraw-Hill, 1965. Pp. 381–402. (a)

Harrower, Molly. Clinical psychologists at work. In B. B. Wolman (Ed.), *Handbook of Clinical Psychology*. New York: McGraw-Hill, 1965. Pp. 1443–1458. (b)

Hathaway, S. Personality inventories. In B. B. Wolman (Ed.), *Handbook of Clinical Psychology*. New York: McGraw-Hill, 1965. Pp. 451–476.

Haworth, Mary R. (Ed.). *Child Psychotherapy*. New York: Basic Books, 1964.

Heilbrun, A. B. Male and female personality correlates of early termination in counseling. *Journal of Counseling Psychology*, 1961, **8**, 31–36.

Heilbrun, A. B. Psychological factors related to counseling readiness and implications for counselor behavior. *Journal of Counseling Psychology*, 1962, **9**, 353–358.

Heilbrun, A. B. Further validation of a counseling readiness scale. *Journal of Counseling Psychology*, 1964, **11**, 290–292.

Heilbrun, A. B. Counseling readiness and the problem-solving behavior of clients. *Journal of Consulting and Clinical Psychology*, 1968, **32**, 396–399.

Heilbrun, A. B., and D. Sullivan. The prediction of counseling readiness. *Personnel and Guidance Journal*, 1962, **41**, 112–117.

Helm, C. Computer simulation techniques for research on guidance problems. *Personnel and Guidance Journal*, 1967, **46**, 47–52.

Hewer, Vivian. What do theories of vocational choice mean to the counselor? *Journal of Counseling Psychology*, 1963, **10**, 118–125.

Hewer, Vivian. Evaluation of a criterion: Realism of vocational choice. *Journal of Counseling Psychology*, 1966, **13**, 289–294.

Hey, R. H., and Emily Mudd. Recurring problems in marriage counseling. *Marriage and Family Living*, 1959, **21**, 127–129.

Higgens, R. E. The school psychologist versus the school counselor? *Journal of School Psychology*, 1966, **4**, 59–63.

Hill, A. H., and Laurabeth Grienecks. Criteria in the evaluation of educational and vocational counseling in college. *Journal of Counseling Psychology*, 1966, **13**, 198–201.

Hill, G. E. The selection of school counselors. *Personnel and Guidance Journal*, 1961, **39**, 355–360.

Hill, G. E. Standards for the preparation of secondary school counselors. *Counselor Education and Supervision*, 1968, **7**, 179–186.

Hill, G. E., and P. F. Munger (Eds.). Up-grading guidance practices through improved preparation of guidance workers. *Counselor Education and Supervision*, 1968, **7**, No. 3SP.

Hobbs, N. Sources of gain in psychotherapy. *American Psychologist*, 1962, **17**, 741–747.

Hobbs, N. Ethics in clinical psychology. In B. B. Wolman (Ed.), *Handbook of Clinical Psychology*. New York: McGraw-Hill, 1965. Pp. 1507–1514.

Hoch, E. L., and J. G. Darley. A case at law. *American Psychologist*, 1962, **17**, 623–654.

Hoch, E. L., A. O. Ross, and C. L. Winder (Eds.). *Professional Preparation of Clinical Psychologists*. Washington: American Psychological Association, 1966.

Hogan, R. A. Implosive therapy in the short term treatment of psychotics. *Psychotherapy: Theory, Research, and Practice*, 1966, **3**, 25–32.

Holland, J. L. A theory of vocational choice. *Journal of Counseling Psychology*, 1959, **6**, 35–45.

Holland, J. L. Major programs of research on vocational behavior. In H. Borow (Ed.), *Man in a World at Work*. Boston: Houghton Mifflin, 1964. Pp. 259–284.

Holland, J. L., and Sandra Lutz. Predicting a student's vocational choice. *ACT Research Reports*, 1967, No. 18.

Holland, J. L., and D. R. Whitney. Career development. *Review of Educational Research*, 1969, **39**, 227–237.

Hollingshead, A., and F. Redlich. *Social Class and Mental Illness*. New York: Wiley, 1958.

Holtzman, W. Some problems in defining ethical behavior. *American Psychologist*, 1960, **15**, 247–250.

Hoyt, D. P., and L. A. Munday. *Your College Freshmen*. Iowa City, Iowa: American College Testing Program, 1968.

Hoyt, K. B. What the school has a right to expect of its counselor. *Personnel and Guidance Journal*, 1961, **40**, 129–134.

Hoyt, K. B. Guidance: A constellation of services. *Personnel and Guidance Journal*, 1962, **40**, 690–697.

Hunt, R. G. Social class and mental illness: Some implications for clinical theory and practice. *American Journal of Psychiatry*, 1960, **116**, 1065–1069.

Imber, S. D., J. D. Frank, E. H. Nash, A. R. Stone, and L. H. Gliedman. Improvement and amount of therapeutic contact: An alternative to the use of no-treatment controls in psychotherapy. *Journal of Consulting Psychology*, 1957, **21**, 309–315.

Isaacson, L. E. Standards for the preparation of guidance and personnel workers—in colleges and universities. *Counselor Education and Supervision*, 1968, **7**, 187–192.

Island, D. D. Counseling students with special problems. *Review of Educational Research*, 1969, **39**, 239–250.

Ivey, A. E., and E. R. Oetting. The counselor in the small college. *Journal of Higher Education*, 1966, **37**, 396–402.

Jackson, D. D., and J. H. Weaklund. Conjoint family therapy: Some considerations on theory, technique, and results. *Psychiatry*, 1961, **24** (Suppl. No. 2), 30–45.

Jackson, D. D., and I. Yalom. Conjoint family therapy as an aid to intensive psychotherapy. In A. Burton (Ed.), *Modern Psychotherapeutic Practice*. Palo Alto, California: Science and Behavior Books, 1965. Pp. 80–98.

Jensen, B. T., G. Coles, and Beatrice Nestor. The criterion problem in guidance research. *Journal of Counseling Psychology*, 1955, **2**, 58–61.

Johnson, D. *Marriage Counseling: Theory and Practice*. Englewood Cliffs, N.J.: Prentice-Hall, 1961.

Johnson, P. E. *Person and Counselor*. Nashville: Abingdon Press, 1967.

Jordaan, J. P., R. A. Myers, W. L. Layton, and H. H. Morgan. *The Counseling Psychologist*. New York: Teachers College Press, Columbia University, 1968.

Joslin, L. C. Knowledge and counseling competence. *Personnel and Guidance Journal*, 1965, **43**, 790–795.

Kalish, H. I. Behavior therapy. In B. B. Wolman (Ed.), *Handbook of Clinical Psychology*. New York: McGraw-Hill, 1965. Pp. 1230–1253.

Kanfer, F. H. Implications of conditioning techniques for interview therapy. *Journal of Counseling Psychology*, 1966, **13**, 171–177.

Kaplan, A. H. Social work therapy and psychiatric psychotherapy: An attempt at differentiation. *Archives of General Psychiatry*, 1963, **9**, 497–503.

Karpf, M. J. Some guiding principles in marriage counseling. *Marriage and Family Living*, 1951, **13**, 49–52.

Kastenbaum, R. The reluctant therapist. *Geriatrics*, 1963, **18**, 296–301.

Katz, M. Interpreting Kuder Preference Record—Vocational scores: Ipsative or normative? Paper presented at the annual meeting of the American Psychological Association, 1962.

Katz, R. L. *Empathy*. New York: Free Press, 1963.

Kauffman, J. F. Student personnel services in higher education. *Educational Record*, 1964, **45**, 355–365.

Kelly, E. L. Clinical psychology—1960: A report of survey findings. *Newsletter, Division of Clinical Psychology, American Psychological Association*, 1961, **14** (Winter), 1–11.

Kelly, G. A., and J. S. Handler. Joint report on relations between psychology and psychiatry. *American Psychologist*, 1960, **15**, 198–200.

Kerlinger, F. N. *Foundations of Behavioral Research*. New York: Holt, Rinehart and Winston, 1965.

Kiesler, D. J. Some myths of psychotherapy research and the search for a paradigm. *Psychological Bulletin*, 1966, **65**, 110–136.

King, P. T. Psychoanalytic adaptations. In B. F. Stefflre (Ed.), *Theories of Counseling*. New York: McGraw-Hill, 1965. Pp. 91–139.

Kintz, B. L., D. J. Delprato, D. R. Mettee, C. E. Persons, and R. H. Schappe. The experimenter effect. *Psychological Bulletin*, 1965, **63**, 223–232.

Kinzer, J. R. The educated counselor. *Journal of Counseling Psychology*, 1961, **8**, 14–16.

Kirk, Barbara. Individualizing of test interpretation. *Occupations*, 1952, **30**, 500–505.

Kirk, Barbara. Extra-measurement use of tests in counseling. *Personnel and Guidance Journal*, 1960, **39**, 658–661.

Kirk, Barbara, and Marjorie Michels. *Occupational Information in Counseling: Use and Classification*. Berkeley, California: Consulting Psychologists Press, 1964.

Kitson, H. D. Psychology in vocational adjustment. *Personnel and Guidance Journal*, 1958, **36**, 314–319.

Kleinmuntz, B., and R. S. McLean. Diagnostic interviewing by digital computer. *Behavioral Science*, 1968, **13**, 75–80.

Koch, E. Disciplinary counseling. In Max Siegel (Ed.), *The Counseling of College Students*. New York: Free Press, 1968. Pp. 337–354.

Koile, E. A. Group guidance—a fringe activity. *School Review*, 1955, **63**, 483–485.

Koile, E. A. Faculty and the university counseling center. *Journal of Counseling Psychology*, 1960, **7**, 293–297.

Koile, E. A., and Dorothy Bird. Preferences for counselor help on freshman problems. *Journal of Counseling Psychology,* 1956, **3,** 97–106.

Kowal, Katherine, D. Kemp, M. Lakin, and S. Wilson. Perception of the helping relationship as a function of age. *Journal of Gerontology,* 1964, **19,** 405–413.

Krasner, L. Studies of the conditioning of verbal behavior. *Psychological Bulletin,* 1958, **55,** 148–170.

Krasner, L. Reinforcement, verbal behavior, and psychotherapy. *American Journal of Orthopsychiatry,* 1963, **33,** 601–613.

Krasner, L. Verbal conditioning and psychotherapy. In L. Krasner and L. P. Ullmann (Eds.), *Research in Behavior Modification.* New York: Holt, Rinehart and Winston, 1965. Pp. 211–228.

Krasner, L., and L. P. Ullmann (Eds.). *Research in Behavior Modification.* New York: Holt, Rinehart and Winston, 1965.

Krause, M. An analysis of Carl Rogers' theory of personality. *Genetic Psychology Monographs,* 1964, **69,** 49–99.

Krauskopf, Joan, and C. Krauskopf. Torts and psychologists. *Journal of Counseling Psychology,* 1965, **12,** 227–237.

Krumboltz, J. D. Behavioral counseling: Rationale and research. *Personnel and Guidance Journal,* 1965, **44,** 383–387.

Krumboltz, J. D. Promoting adaptive behavior. In J. D. Krumboltz (Ed.), *Revolution in Counseling: Implications of Behavioral Science.* Boston: Houghton Mifflin, 1966. Pp. 3–26. (a)

Krumboltz, J. D. (Ed.). *Revolution in Counseling: Implication of Behavioral Science.* Boston: Houghton Mifflin, 1966. (b)

Krumboltz, J. D. Changing the behavior of behavior changers *Counselor Education and Supervision,* 1967, **6,** 222–229.

Krumboltz, J. D., and C. E. Thoreson. The effect of behavioral counseling in groups and individual settings on information-seeking behavior. *Journal of Counseling Psychology,* 1964, **11,** 324–333.

Kuder, G. F. A rationale for evaluating interests. *Educational and Psychological Measurement,* 1963, **23,** 3–12.

Kuder, G. F. *Kuder DD Occupational Interest Survey: General Manual.* Chicago: Science Research Associates, 1966.

Lang, P. J. Experimental studies of desensitization psychotherapy. In J. Wolpe, A. Salter, and L. J. Reyna (Eds.), *The Conditioning Therapies.* New York: Holt, Rinehart and Winston, 1965. Pp. 38–53.

Lang, P. J., and A. D. Lazovik. Experimental desensitization of a phobia. *Journal of Abnormal and Social Psychology,* 1963, **66,** 519–525.

Layton, W. L. *Counseling Use of the Strong Vocational Interest Blank.* Minneapolis: University of Minnesota Press, 1958.

Layton, W. L. (Ed.). *The Strong Vocational Interest Blank: Research and Uses.* Minneapolis: University of Minnesota Press, 1960.

LeMay, M. L. Research on group procedures with college students: A review. *Journal of College Student Personnel,* 1967, **8,** 286–295.

LeMay, M. L., and O. C. Christensen. The uncontrollable nature of control groups. *Journal of Counseling Psychology,* 1968, **15,** 63–67.

Lennard, H. L., and A. Bernstein. Expectations and behavior in therapy. In B. J. Biddle and E. J. Thomas (Eds.), *Role Theory: Concepts and Research.* New York: Wiley, 1966. Pp. 170–185.

Leslie, G. R. Conjoint therapy in marriage counseling. *Journal of Marriage and the Family,* 1964, **26,** 65–71.

Levitt, E. E. The results of psychotherapy with children: An evaluation. *Journal of Consulting Psychology,* 1957, **21,** 189–196.

Levy, L. H. *Psychological Interpretation.* New York: Holt, Rinehart and Winston, 1963.

Lewis, E. C. *Developing Woman's Potential.* Ames, Iowa: Iowa State University Press, 1968.

Liebenson, H. A., and J. M. Wepman. *The Psychologist as a Witness.* Mundelein, Illinois: Callaghan, 1964.

Linden, J., S. Stone, and B. Shertzer. Development and evaluation of an inventory for rating counseling. *Personnel and Guidance Journal,* 1965, **44,** 267–276.

Llewellyn, C., E. Persons, and Caroline Helmick. The mental health program in a college health service. *Mental Hygiene,* 1964, **48,** 93–100.

Loevinger, Jane, and A. Ossorio. Evaluation of therapy by self-report: A paradox. *Journal of Abnormal and Social Psychology,* 1959, **58,** 392–394.

Lofquist, L. H. *Vocational Counseling with the Physically Handicapped.* New York: Appleton-Century-Crofts, 1957.

Longstreth, B. Behavioral research using students: A privacy issue for schools. *School Review,* 1968, **76,** 1–22.

Lorr, M., M. M. Katz, and E. A. Rubenstein. The prediction of length of stay in psychotherapy. *Journal of Consulting Psychology,* 1958, **22,** 321–327.

Loughary, J. (Ed.). *Counseling, a Growing Profession.* Washington: American Personnel and Guidance Association, 1965.

Louisell, D. W. The psychologist in today's legal world. *Minnesota Law Review,* 1957, **41,** 731–750.

McArthur, C. Analyzing the clinical process. *Journal of Counseling Psychology,* 1954, **1,** 203–207.

McCall, J. N., and G. D. Moore. Do interest inventories measure estimated abilities? *Personnel and Guidance Journal,* 1965, **43,** 1034–1037.

McGowan, J. F., and L. D. Schmidt (Eds.). *Counseling: Readings in Theory and Practice.* New York: Holt, Rinehart and Winston, 1962.

McMahon, J. T. The working class psychiatric patient: A clinical view. In F. Riessman, J. Cohen, and A. Pearl (Eds.), *Mental Health of the Poor.* New York: Free Press, 1964. Pp. 283–302.

Magoon, T. M., and S. E. Golann. Nontraditionally trained women as mental health counselors/psychotherapists. *Personnel and Guidance Journal,* 1966, **44,** 788–793.

Mahler, C. A., and D. Caldwell. *Group Counseling in Secondary Schools.* Chicago: Science Research Associates, 1961.

Masia, B. B. What to look for in a review of a personality inventory. *Personnel and Guidance Journal,* 1964, **42,** 1030–1034.

Mayer, G. R., and P. Baker. Group counseling with elementary school children: A look at group size. *Elementary School Guidance and Counseling,* 1967, **1,** 140–143.

Meehl, P. E. *Clinical vs. Statistical Prediction.* Minneapolis: University of Minnesota Press, 1954.

Meehl, P. E. Some ruminations on the validation of clinical procedures. *Canadian Journal of Psychology,* 1959, **13,** 102–128.

Mendelsohn, G., and M. Geller. Structure of client attitudes toward counseling and their relation to client-counselor similarity. *Journal of Consulting Psychology,* 1965, **29,** 63–72.

Menninger, W. W., and J. English. Confidentiality and the request for psychiatric information for nontherapeutic purposes. *American Journal of Psychiatry,* 1965, **122,** 638 645.

Michael, J., and Lee Meyerson. A behavioral approach to counseling and guidance. *Harvard Educational Review,* 1962, **32,** 382–402.

Miller, A. A. A survey of the development and evolution of psychoanalytic treatment. In M. I. Stein (Ed.), *Contemporary Psychotherapies.* New York: Free Press, 1961. Pp. 338–354. (a)

Miller, A. A. A demonstration of psychoanalytic therapy. In M. I. Stein (Ed.), *Contemporary Psychotherapies.* New York: Free Press, 1961. Pp. 355–371. (b)

Miller, C. H. Vocational guidance in the perspective of cultural change. In H. Borow (Ed.), *Man in a World at Work.* Boston: Houghton Mifflin, 1964. Pp. 3–23.

Miller, F. W., and R. J. Simpson. Some legal implications of the counselor-client relationship: A review of the literature. *Counselor Education and Supervision,* 1961, **1,** 19–29.

Mills, D. H., W. Chestnut, and J. P. Hartzell. The needs of counselors: A component analysis. *Journal of Counseling Psychology,* 1966, **13,** 82–84.

Moore, G. D. A negative view toward therapeutic counseling in the public schools. *Counselor Education and Supervision,* 1961, **1,** 60–68.

Mosher, R. L., R. F. Carle, and C. D. Kehas. *Guidance: An Examination.* New York: Harcourt, Brace & World, 1965.

Mullahy, P. Neo-Freudian analytic theory. In B. B. Wolman (Ed.), *Handbook of Clinical Psychology.* New York: McGraw-Hill, 1965. Pp. 341–377.

Munger, P., R. Myers, and Darine Brown. Guidance institutes and the persistence of attitudes: A progress report. *Personnel and Guidance Journal,* 1963, **41,** 415–419.

Murray, E. J. Learning theory and psychotherapy: Biotropic vs. sociotropic approaches. *Journal of Counseling Psychology,* 1963, **10,** 250–255.

Myers, J., and L. Bean. *A Decade Later.* New York: Wiley, 1968.

Nachman, Barbara, E. S. Bordin, and S. J. Segal. Supervision in a university counseling service. *Journal of Counseling Psychology,* 1960, **7,** 229–232.

Neuman, Rebecca. When will the educational needs of women be met? *Journal of Counseling Psychology,* 1963, **10,** 378–383.

Nichols, W., and A. Rutledge. Psychotherapy with teen-agers. *Journal of Marriage and the Family,* 1965, **27,** 166–170.

Norris, Willa. Highlights in the history of the National Vocational Guidance Association. *Personnel and Guidance Journal,* 1954, **33,** 205–208.

Ohlsen, M. M. Counseling children in groups. *School Counselor,* Fall, 1967; reprinted in C. H. Patterson (Ed.), *The Counselor in the School: Selected Readings.* New York: McGraw-Hill, 1967. Pp. 350–357.

Ohlsen, M. M. Standards for the preparation of elementary school counselors. *Counselor Education and Supervision,* 1968, **7,** 172–178.

Olsen, L. C. Success for new counselors. *Journal of Counseling Psychology,* 1963, **10,** 350–355.

O'Sullivan, J. J. Religious counseling. In M. Siegel (Ed.), *The Counseling of College Students.* New York: Free Press, 1968. Pp. 325–335.

Overall, Betty, and H. Aronson. Expectations of psychotherapy in patients of lower socioeconomic class. *American Journal of Orthopsychiatry,* 1963, **33,** 421–430.

Pacella, B. L. A critical appraisal of pastoral counseling. *American Journal of Psychiatry,* 1966, **123,** 646–651.

Parker, C. A. The predictive use of the MMPI in a college counseling center. *Journal of Counseling Psychology,* 1961, **8,** 154–158.

Patterson, C. H. Matching vs. randomization in studies of counseling. *Journal of Counseling Psychology,* 1956, **3,** 262–271.

Patterson, C. H. The use of projective tests in vocational counseling. *Educational and Psychological Measurement,* 1957, **17,** 533–555.

Patterson, C. H. *Counseling and Psychotherapy.* New York: Harper & Row, 1959.

Patterson, C. H. *Counseling and Guidance in Schools.* New York: Harper & Row, 1962.

Patterson, C. H. Control, conditioning, and counseling. *Personnel and Guidance Journal,* 1963, **41,** 680–686.

Patterson, C. H. Supervising students in the counseling practicum. *Journal of Counseling Psychology,* 1964, **11,** 47–53.

Patterson, C. H. Subprofessional functions and short-term training. *Counselor Education and Supervision,* 1965, **4,** 144–146.

Patterson, C. H. *Theories of Counseling and Psychotherapy.* New York: Harper & Row, 1966.

Patterson, C. H. Psychotherapy in the school. In D. Arbuckle (Ed.), *Counseling and Psychotherapy: An Overview.* New York: McGraw-Hill, 1967. Pp. 142–161. (a)

Patterson, C. H. (Ed.). *The Counselor in the School: Selected Readings.* New York: McGraw-Hill, 1967. (b)

Patterson, C. H. Rehabilitation counseling: A profession or a trade? *Personnel and Guidance Journal,* 1968, **46,** 567–571.

Paul, G. L. *Insight vs. Desensitization in Psychotherapy.* Stanford, California: Stanford University Press, 1966.

Paul, G. L. Insight vs. desensitization in psychotherapy two years after termination. *Journal of Consulting Psychology,* 1967, **31,** 333–348.

Pepinsky, H. B. The selection and use of diagnostic categories in clinical counseling. *Applied Psychology Monographs,* 1948, No. 15.

Pepinsky, H. B., E. S. Bordin, M. E. Hahn, D. E. Super, and C. G. Wrenn. Counseling psychology as a specialty. *American Psychologist,* 1956, **11,** 282–285.

Pepinsky, H. B., and Pauline Pepinsky. *Counseling: Theory and Practice.* New York: Ronald Press, 1954.

Peters, H. J. Differential factors between elementary and secondary school counseling. *The School Counselor,* 1959, **7,** 3–11.

Peterson, R. A. Counseling in the rehabilitation process. Unpublished doctoral dissertation, University of Missouri, 1964.

Peterson, R. A., and F. Featherstone. Occupations of counseling psychologists. *Journal of Counseling Psychology,* 1962, **9,** 221–224.

Petras, J. W., and J. E. Curtis. The current literature on social class and mental disease in America: Critique and bibliography. *Behavioral Science,* 1968, **13,** 382–398.

Poser, E. G. The effect of therapists' training on group therapeutic outcome. *Journal of Consulting Psychology,* 1966, **30,** 283–289.

Pronko, N. H., R. Sitterly, and K. Berg. Twenty years of shock therapy in America, 1937–1956: An annotated bibliography. *Genetic Psychology Monographs,* 1960, **62,** 233–329.

Rachman, S. Sexual disorders and behavior therapy. *American Journal of Psychiatry,* 1961, **118,** 235–240.

Rachman, S. (Ed.). *Critical Essays on Psychoanalysis.* Oxford, N.Y.: Pergamon Press, 1963. (a)

Rachman, S. Introduction to behavior therapy. *Behavior Research and Therapy,* 1963, **1,** 1–15. (b)

Rachman, S. Systematic desensitization. *Psychological Bulletin,* 1967, **67,** 93–103.

Rachman, S., and H. J. Eysenck. Reply to a "critique and reformulation" of behavior therapy. *Psychological Bulletin,* 1966, **65,** 165–169.

Rechtschaffen, A. Psychotherapy with geriatric patients: A review of the literature. *Journal of Gerontology,* 1959, **14,** 63–84.

Reisman, J. M. *The Development of Clinical Psychology.* New York: Appleton-Century-Crofts, 1966.

Reyna, L. J. Conditioning therapies, learning theory, and research. In J. Wolpe, A. Salter, and I. J. Reyna (Eds.), *The Conditioning Therapies.* New York: Holt, Rinehart and Winston, 1964. Pp. 169–179.

Rezny, A. A. Inspection and release of records to professional school staff. In Martha Ware (Ed.), *Law of Guidance and Counseling.* Cincinnati: W. H. Anderson, 1964. Pp. 53–64.

Rioch, Margaret. Changing concepts in the training of therapists. *Journal of Consulting Psychology,* 1966, **30,** 290–292.

Rioch, Margaret, and others. National Institute of Mental Health pilot study in training mental health counselors. *American Journal of Orthopsychiatry,* 1963, **33,** 678–689.

Robertson, M. H. A comparison of counselor and student reports of counseling interviews. *Journal of Counseling Psychology,* 1958, **5,** 276–280.

Robinson, F. P. *Principles and Procedures in Student Counseling.* New York: Harper & Row, 1950.

Robinson, F. P. Modern approaches to counseling "diagnosis." *Journal of Counseling Psychology,* 1963, **10,** 325–333.

Roe, Anne, and M. Siegelman. *The Origin of Interests.* Washington: American Personnel and Guidance Association, 1964.

Rogers, C. R. *Counseling and Psychotherapy.* Boston: Houghton Mifflin, 1942.

Rogers, C. R. *Client-Centered Therapy.* Boston: Houghton Mifflin, 1951.

Rogers, C. R. The necessary and sufficient conditions of therapeutic personality change. *Journal of Consulting Psychology,* 1957, **21,** 95–103.

Rogers, C. R. The characteristics of a helping relationship. *Personnel and Guidance Journal,* 1958, **37,** 6–16. (a)

Rogers, C. R. A process conception of psychotherapy. *American Psychologist,* 1958, **13,** 142–149. (b)

Rogers, C. R. A theory of therapy, personality, and interpersonal relationships, as developed in the client-centered framework. In Sigmund Koch (Ed.), *Psychology: A Study of a Science.* New York: McGraw-Hill, 1959. Vol. 3. Pp. 184–256.

Rogers, C. R. *On Becoming a Person.* Boston: Houghton Mifflin, 1961.

Rogers, C. R. The interpersonal relationship: The core of guidance. *Harvard Educational Review,* 1962, **32,** 416–429.

Rogers, C. R. The process of the basic encounter group. In J. F. T. Bugental (Ed.), *Challenges of Humanistic Psychology.* New York: McGraw-Hill, 1967. Pp. 261–276.

Rogers, C. R., and Rosalind Dymond (Eds.). *Psychotherapy and Personality Change.* Chicago: University of Chicago Press, 1954.

Rogers, L. B. A comparison of two kinds of test interpretation interview. *Journal of Counseling Psychology,* 1954, **1,** 224–231.

Rosen, H., and J. Frank. Negroes in psychotherapy. *American Journal of Psychiatry,* 1962, **119,** 456–460.

Rosenbaum, M. Group psychotherapy and psychodrama. In B. B. Wolman (Ed.), *Handbook of Clinical Psychology.* New York: McGraw-Hill, 1965. Pp. 1254–1274.

Rosenthal, R. The effect of the experimenter on the results of psychological research. In Brendan Maher (Ed.), *Progress in Experimental Personality Research.* New York: Academic Press, 1964. Vol. 1. Pp. 79–114.

Rosenthal, R. *Experimenter Effects in Behavioral Research.* New York: Appleton-Century-Crofts, 1966.

Ross, N., and S. Abrahms. Fundamentals of psychoanalytic theory. In B. B. Wolman (Ed.), *Handbook of Clinical Psychology.* New York: McGraw-Hill, 1965. Pp. 303–340.

Rothney, J. W. M. Interpreting test scores to counselees. *Occupations,* 1952, **30,** 320–322.

Rothney, J. W. M. *Guidance Practices and Results.* New York: Harper & Row, 1958.

Rudicoff, L., and Barbara Kirk. Test interpretation in counseling. *Journal of Counseling Psychology,* 1959, **6,** 223–229.

Rutledge, A. L. *Pre-Marital Counseling.* Cambridge, Massachusetts: Schenkman, 1966.

Sager, C. J. The development of marriage therapy: An historical review. *American Journal of Orthopsychiatry,* 1966, **36,** 458–467.

Santostefano, S., and M. Kahn. Clinical psychology in the United States. In J. R. Braun (Ed.), *Clinical Psychology in Transition: Selected Readings.* Rev. Ed. Cleveland: World Publishing Co., 1966. Pp. 1–9.

Sargant, W. Drugs or psychotherapy. *American Journal of Psychiatry,* 1965, **121,** xxvi–xxix.

Sargent, Helen. Methodological problems of follow-up studies in psychotherapy research. *American Journal of Orthopsychiatry,* 1960, **9,** 213–219.

Satir, Virginia. *Conjoint Family Therapy.* Rev. Ed. Palo Alto, California: Science and Behavior Books, 1967.

Saul, L. J., and others. Can one partner be successfully counseled without the other? *Marriage and Family Living,* 1953, **15,** 59–64.

Schmidt, L. D. Some legal considerations for counseling and clinical psychologists. *Journal of Counseling Psychology,* 1962, **9,** 35–44.

Schneiderman, L. Social class, diagnosis and treatment. *American Journal of Orthopsychiatry,* 1965, **35,** 99–105.

Schofield, W. Clinical and counseling psychology. Some perspectives. *American Psychologist,* 1966, **21,** 122–131.

Schonbar, Rosalea. Interpretation and insight in psychotherapy. *Psychotherapy: Theory, Research, and Practice,* 1965, **2,** 78–83.

Schwartz, E. K. Neo-Freudian analytic methods. In B. B. Wolman (Ed.), *Handbook of Clinical Psychology.* New York: McGraw-Hill, 1965. Pp. 1200–1214.

Schwebel, M. Why unethical practice? *Journal of Counseling Psychology,* 1955, **2,** 122–128.

Schwitzgebel, R. I. Survey of electromechanical devices for behavior modification. *Psychological Bulletin,* 1968, **70,** 444–459.

Scott, W. L. Student personnel services in small liberal arts colleges. *Journal of College Student Personnel,* 1961, **2,** 19–22, 31.

Seashore, H. G. (Ed.). Expectancy tables—a way of interpreting test validity. *Test Service Bulletin, Psychological Corporation,* Dec. 1949, No. 38, 11–15.

Seashore, H. G. (Ed.). Methods of expressing test scores. *Test Service Bulletin, Psychological Corporation,* Jan. 1955, No. 48, 7–10.

Seashore, H. G. (Ed.). Aptitude, intelligence, and achievement. *Test Service Bulletin, Psychological Corporation,* Dec. 1956, No. 51, 4–6.

Seeman, J. Perspectives in client-centered therapy. In B. B. Wolman (Ed.), *Handbook of Clinical Psychology.* New York: McGraw-Hill, 1965. Pp. 1215–1229.

Selzer, M. L. Unique aspects of university health service psychiatry. *Mental Hygiene,* 1964, **48,** 288–294.

Shapiro, A. Etiological factors in placebo effect. *Journal of the American Medical Association,* 1964, **187,** 712–714.

Shaw, M., and Rosemary Wursten. Research on group procedures in schools: A review of the literature. *Personnel and Guidance Journal,* 1965, **44,** 27–34.

Shertzer, B., and S. Stone. The school counselor and his publics: A problem in role definition. *Personnel and Guidance Journal,* 1963, **41,** 687–693.

Shneidman, E. S. Projective techniques. In B. B. Wolman (Ed.), *Handbook of Clinical Psychology.* New York: McGraw-Hill, 1965. Pp. 498–521.

Shoben, E. J. Counseling and the learning of integrative behavior. *Journal of Counseling Psychology,* 1954, **1,** 42–48.

Shoben, E. J. The college, psychological clinics, and psychological knowledge. *Journal of Counseling Psychology,* 1956, **3,** 200–205.

Shoben, E. J. The counselor's theory as a personal trait. *Personnel and Guidance Journal,* 1962, **40,** 617–621.

Siegel, Alberta, and Elizabeth Curtis. Familial correlates of orientation toward future employment among college women. *Journal of Educational Psychology,* 1963, **54,** 33–37.

Siegel, M. Group techniques in education, counseling, and psychotherapy. In M. Siegel (Ed.), *The Counseling of College Students.* New York: Free Press, 1968. Pp. 99–113. (a)

Siegel, M. Student services: Administration and structure. In M. Siegel (Ed.), *The Counseling of College Students.* New York: Free Press, 1968. Pp. 419–426. (b)

Siegel, M. (Ed.). *The Counseling of College Students.* New York: Free Press, 1968. (c)

Siegle, Anne. "Graduate" mothers. *SK&F Psychiatric Reporter,* 1968, No. 38, 11–12.

Sinick, D. Ethical and legal implications of the vocational consultant program, *Personnel and Guidance Journal,* 1964, **43,** 355–359.

Skager, R., and C. Weinberg. Relationships between selected social factors and extent of high school counseling. *Personnel and Guidance Journal,* 1967, **45,** 901–906.

Skidmore, R. A., and Hulda Garrett. The joint interview in marriage counseling. *Marriage and Family Living,* 1955, **17,** 349–354.

Slovenko, R. *Psychotherapy, Confidentiality, and Privileged Communication.* Springfield, Illinois: Charles C Thomas, 1966.

Smith, Margaret (Ed.). *Guidance-Personnel Work: Future Tense.* New York: Teachers College Press, Columbia University, 1966.

Smith, V. G., and F. M. Anderson. Conjoint interviews with marital partners. *Marriage and Family Living,* 1963, **25,** 184–188.

Snoxell, L. F. Counseling reluctant and recalcitrant students. *Journal of College Student Personnel,* 1960, **2,** 16–20.

Snyder, W. U. (Ed.). *Casebook of Non-directive Counseling.* Boston: Houghton Mifflin, 1947.

Snyder, W. U. *The Psychotherapy Relationship.* New York: Macmillan, 1961.

Snyder, W. U. Relationship and client-centered therapies. In I. A. Berg and L. A. Pennington (Eds.), *An Introduction to Clinical Psychology.* 3rd edition. New York: Ronald Press, 1966. Pp. 561–590.

Stefflre, B. S. Function and present status of counseling theory. In B. S. Stefflre (Ed.), *Theories of Counseling.* New York: McGraw-Hill, 1965. Pp. 1–29. (a)

Stefflre, B. S. A summing up. In B. S. Stefflre (Ed.), *Theories of Counseling.* New York: McGraw-Hill, 1965. Pp. 257–278. (b)

Stefflre, B. S. (Ed.). *Theories of Counseling.* New York: McGraw-Hill, 1965. (c)

Stefflre, B. S., P. King, and F. Leafgren. Characteristics of counselors judged effective by their peers. *Journal of Counseling Psychology,* 1962, **9,** 335–340.

Stein, M. I. (Ed.). *Contemporary Psychotherapies.* New York: Free Press, 1961.

Stewart, L. H., and C. F. Warnath. *The Counselor and Society: A Cultural Approach.* Boston: Houghton Mifflin, 1965.

Stoughton, R. W. APGA and counselor preparation. In J. W. Loughary (Ed.), *Counseling, a Growing Profession.* Washington: American Personnel and Guidance Association, 1965. Pp. 1–17.

Stripling, R. O. Current and future status of accrediting counselor education. *Counselor Education and Supervision,* 1968, **7,** 200–209.

Stripling, R. O., and others. Standards for counselor education in the preparation of secondary school counselors. *Personnel and Guidance Journal,* 1964, **42,** 1062–1073.

Strong, E. K. *Vocational Interests of Men and Women.* Stanford, California: Stanford University Press, 1943.

Strong, E. K. *Vocational Interests 18 Years after College.* Minneapolis: University of Minnesota Press, 1955.

Strong, E. K. An eighteen-year longitudinal report on interests. In W. L. Layton (Ed.), *The Strong Vocational Interest Blank: Research and Uses.* Minneapolis: University of Minnesota Press, 1960. Pp. 3–17. (a)

Strong, E. K. The Strong Vocational Interest Blank in counseling. In W. L. Layton (Ed.), *The Strong Vocational Interest Blank: Research and Uses.* Minneapolis: University of Minnesota Press, 1960. Pp. 178–191. (b)

Strong, E. K., and D. P. Campbell. *Strong Vocational Interest Blank: Manual.* Stanford, California: Stanford University Press, 1966.

Strong, E. K., D. P. Campbell, R. F. Berdie, and K. E. Clark. *The 1966 Revision of the Strong Vocational Interest Blank for Men.* Stanford, California: Stanford University Press, 1966.

Strong, S. R. Verbal conditioning and counseling research. *Personnel and Guidance Journal,* 1964, **42,** 660–669.

Strong, S. R. Counseling: An interpersonal influence process. *Journal of Counseling Psychology,* 1968, **15,** 215–224.

Strupp, H. H. An objective comparison of Rogerian and psychoanalytic techniques. *Journal of Consulting Psychology,* 1955, **19,** 1–7.

Strupp, H. H. The performance of psychoanalytic and client-centered therapists in an initial interview. *Journal of Consulting Psychology,* 1958, **22,** 265–274.

Strupp, H. H. The outcome problem in psychotherapy revisited. *Psychotherapy,* 1963, **1,** 1–13.

Strupp, H. H. *A Bibliography of Research in Psychotherapy.* Chapel Hill, N.C.: Psychotherapy Research Project, Department of Psychiatry, University of North Carolina School of Medicine, 1964.

Strupp, H. H., and M. Wallach. A further study of psychiatrists' responses in quasi-therapy situations. *Behavioral Science,* 1965, **10,** 113–134.

Strupp, H. H., M. Wallach, and M. Wogan. Psychotherapy experience in retrospect. *Psychological Monographs,* 1964, **78** (11), No. 588.

Sundberg, N., and Leona Tyler. *Clinical Psychology.* New York: Appleton-Century-Crofts, 1962.

Super, D. E. A theory of vocational development. *American Psychologist,* 1953, **8,** 185–190.

Super, D. E. The measurement of interests. *Journal of Counseling Psychology,* 1954, **1,** 168–172.

Super, D. E. Transition: From vocational guidance to counseling psychology. *Journal of Counseling Psychology,* 1955, **2,** 3–9.

Super, D. E. The professional status and affiliations of vocational counselors. In H. Borow (Ed.), *Man in a World at Work.* Boston: Houghton Mifflin, 1964. Pp. 557–585.

Super, D. E., and J. O. Crites. *Appraising Vocational Fitness.* New York: Harper & Row, 1962.

Super, D. E., R. Starishevsky, N. Matlin, and J. P. Jordaan. *Career Development: Self-Concept Theory.* Princeton, New Jersey: College Entrance Examination Board, 1963.

Super, D. E., and others. The practicum training of counseling psychologists. *American Psychologist,* 1952, **7,** 182–188.

Sussman, M. B., and Marie Haug. The practitioners: Rehabilitation counselors in three work settings. Working paper #4, Career Contingencies of the Rehabilitation Counselor. Cleveland, Ohio: Department of Sociology and Anthropology, Western Reserve University, 1967. (a)

Sussman, M. B., and Marie Haug. Rehabilitation counseling leadership: Present and potential. Working paper #5, Career Contingencies of the Rehabilitation Counselor. Cleveland, Ohio: Department of Sociology and Anthropology, Western Reserve University, 1967. (b)

Swain, Emeliza. The standards movement in guidance and its importance to the profession. *Counselor Education and Supervision,* 1968, **7,** 164–171.

Sweeney, T. J. The school counselor as perceived by school counselors and their principals. *Personnel and Guidance Journal,* 1966, **44,** 844–849.

Szasz, T. S. The myth of mental illness. *American Psychologist,* 1960, **15,** 113–118.

Szasz, T. S. *The Myth of Mental Illness.* New York: Harper & Row, 1961.

Tennyson, W. W., D. Blocher, and R. Johnson. Student personnel records: A vital tool but a concern to the public. *Personnel and Guidance Journal,* 1964, **42,** 888–893.

Thompson, A. S. Personality dynamics and vocational counseling. *Personnel and Guidance Journal,* 1960, **38,** 350–357.

Thompson, A. S. School settings for vocational guidance. In H. Borow (Ed.), *Man in a World at Work.* Boston: Houghton Mifflin, 1964. Pp. 487–509.

Thompson, A. S., and D. E. Super (Eds.). *The Professional Preparation of Counseling Psychologists.* New York: Bureau of Publications, Teachers College, Columbia University, 1964.

Thoreson, C. E. Relevance and research in counseling. *Review of Educational Research,* 1969, **39,** 263–281.

Thoroman, E. C. *The Vocational Counseling of Adults and Young Adults.* Boston: Houghton Mifflin, 1968.

Tiedeman, D. V. Decision and vocational development: A paradigm and its implications. *Personnel and Guidance Journal,* 1961, **40,** 15–21.

Tiedeman, D. V., and R. O'Hara. *Career Development: Choice and Adjustment.* New York: College Entrance Examination Board, 1963.

Truax, C. B. Reinforcement and nonreinforcement in Rogerian psychotherapy. *Journal of Abnormal Psychology,* 1966, **71,** 1–9. (a)

Truax, C. B. Some implications of behavior therapy for psychotherapy. *Journal of Counseling Psychology,* 1966, **13,** 160–170. (b)

Truax, C. B., and R. R. Carkhuff. *Toward Effective Counseling and Psychotherapy: Training and Practice.* Chicago: Aldine, 1967.

Truax, C. B., R. R. Carkhuff, and J. Douds. Toward an integration of the didactic and experimental approaches to training in counseling and psychotherapy. *Journal of Counseling Psychology,* 1964, **11,** 240–247.

Tuma, A. H., and J. W. Gustad. The effects of client and counselor personality characteristics on client learning in counseling. *Journal of Counseling Psychology,* 1957, **4,** 136–143.

Tyler, Leona. Theoretical principles underlying the counseling process. *Journal of Counseling Psychology,* 1958, **5,** 3–10.

Tyler, Leona. The development of interests. In W. L. Layton (Ed.), *The Strong Vocational Interest Blank: Research and Uses.* Minneapolis: University of Minnesota Press, 1960. Pp. 62–75. (a)

Tyler, Leona. Minimum change therapy. *Personnel and Guidance Journal,* 1960, **38,** 475–479. (b)

Tyler, Leona. *The Work of the Counselor.* 2nd edition. New York: Appleton-Century-Crofts, 1961.

Tyler, Leona. Research on instruments used by counselors in vocational guidance. *Journal of Counseling Psychology,* 1962, **9,** 99–105.

United States Employment Service. *Counselor's Handbook.* Washington: U.S. Government Printing Office, 1967.

Vance, F., and T. Volsky. Counseling and psychotherapy: Split personality or Siamese twins? *American Psychologist,* 1962, **17,** 565–570.

Van Hoose, W. H. *Counseling in the Elementary School.* Itasca, Illinois: F. E. Peacock, 1968.

Van Hoose, W. H., Mildred Peters, and G. E. Leonard. *The Elementary School Counselor.* Detroit: Wayne State University Press, 1967.

Van Hoose, W. H., and Catherine Vafakas. Status of guidance and counseling in the elementary school. *Personnel and Guidance Journal,* 1968, **46,** 536–539.

Vernon, P. E. *Personality Assessment.* New York: Wiley, 1964.

Vincent, C. E. (Ed.). *Readings in Marriage Counseling.* New York: Thomas Crowell, 1957.

Volsky, T., and Vivian Hewer. A program of group counseling. *Journal of Counseling Psychology,* 1960, **7,** 71–73.

Volsky, T., T. M. Magoon, W. T. Norman, and D. P. Hoyt. *The Outcomes of Counseling and Psychotherapy: Theory and Research.* Minneapolis: University of Minnesota Press, 1965.

Volz, M. M. Law of confidentiality. In Martha Ware (Ed.), *Law of Guidance and Counseling.* Cincinnati: W. H. Anderson, 1964. Pp. 7–17.

Wallin, J. E. W. Some personal comments on the development of clinical psychology. *Exceptional Children,* 1958, **24,** 413–420.

Ware, Martha (Ed.). *Law of Guidance and Counseling.* Cincinnati: W. H. Anderson, 1964.

Warman, R. E. Differential perceptions of counseling role. *Journal of Counseling Psychology,* 1960, **7,** 269–274.

Warman, R. E. The counseling role of college and university counseling centers. *Journal of Counseling Psychology,* 1961, **8,** 231–238.

Warters, Jane. *Group Guidance.* New York: McGraw-Hill, 1960.

Watson, A. S. The conjoint psychotherapy of marriage partners. *American Journal of Orthopsychiatry,* 1963, **33,** 912–922.

Watson, Gladys. An evaluation of counseling with college students. *Journal of Counseling Psychology,* 1961, **8,** 99–104.

Weiner, I. B. The role of diagnosis in a university counseling center. *Journal of Counseling Psychology,* 1959, **6,** 110–115.

Weitz, H. Counseling as a function of the counselor's personality. *Personnel and Guidance Journal,* 1957, **35,** 276–280.

Weitzman, B. Behavior therapy and psychotherapy. *Psychological Review,* 1967, **74,** 300–317.

Wellner, A. M., and R. Simon. A survey of associate-degree programs for mental health technicians. *Hospital and Community Psychiatry,* 1969, **20,** 166–169.

Werry, J. S. The conditioning treatment of enuresis. *American Journal of Psychiatry,* 1966, **123,** 226–229.

Wetzel, R. Use of behavioral techniques in a case of compulsive stealing. *Journal of Consulting Psychology,* 1966, **30,** 367–374.

Wharton, W. The case of Harry and therapist flexibility. *Journal of Counseling Psychology,* 1963, **10,** 179–184.

Whiteley, J. M. Counselor education. *Review of Educational Research,* 1969, **39,** 173–187.

Whiteley, J. M. (Ed.). Vocational development theory. *Counseling Psychologist,* 1969, **1,** 1–36.

Whyte, W. W. The fallacies of "personality" testing. *Fortune,* Sept. 1954, 117–121, 204–208.

Wiener, F. The role of the vocational counselor as an expert witness. *Personnel and Guidance Journal,* 1964, **43,** 348–354.

Williams, Juanita H. Conditioning of verbalization: A review. *Psychological Bulletin,* 1964, **62,** 383–393.

Williamson, E. G. *Student Personnel Services in Colleges and Universities.* New York: McGraw-Hill, 1961.

Williamson, E. G. An historical perspective of the vocational guidance movement. *Personnel and Guidance Journal,* 1964, **42,** 854–859.

Williamson, E. G. *Vocational Counseling.* New York: McGraw-Hill, 1965.

Williamson, E. G., and E. S. Bordin. Evaluating counseling by means of a control-group experiment. *School and Society,* 1940, **52,** 434–440.

Williamson, E. G., and J. G. Darley. *Student Personnel Work.* New York: McGraw-Hill, 1937.

Wiscoff, M. Ethical standards and divided loyalties. *American Psychologist,* 1960, **15,** 656–660.

Wolberg, L. R. *Psychotherapy and the Behavioral Sciences.* New York: Grune & Stratton, 1966.

Wolberg, L. R. *The Technique of Psychotherapy.* 2nd edition. New York: Grune & Stratton, 1967.

Wolman, B. B. (Ed.). *Handbook of Clinical Psychology.* New York: McGraw-Hill, 1965.

Wolpe, J. *Psychotherapy by Reciprocal Inhibition.* Stanford, California: Stanford University Press, 1958.

Wolpe, J. The comparative clinical status of conditioning therapies and psychoanalysis. In J. Wolpe, A. Salter, and L. J. Reyna (Eds.), *The Conditioning Therapies.* New York: Holt, Rinehart and Winston, 1965. Pp. 5–20.

Wolpe, J., A. Salter, and L. J. Reyna (Eds.). *The Conditioning Therapies.* New York: Holt, Rinehart and Winston, 1965.

Womer, F. B., and W. B. Frick. *Personalizing Test Use: A Counselor's Casebook.* Ann Arbor, Michigan: Bureau of School Services, University of Michigan, 1965.

Wrenn, C. G. The ethics of counseling. *Educational and Psychological Measurement,* 1952, **12,** 161–177.

Wrenn, C. G. *The Counselor in a Changing World.* Washington: American Personnel and Guidance Association, 1962.

Wright, E. W. Multiple counseling: Why? when? how? *Personnel and Guidance Journal,* 1959, **37,** 551–557.

Wright, E. W. A comparison of individual and multiple counseling for test interpretation interviews. *Journal of Counseling Psychology,* 1963, **10,** 126–135.

Yamamoto, K. Counseling psychologists—who are they? *Journal of Counseling Psychology,* 1963, **10,** 211–221.

Zapoleon, Marguerite. *Occupational Planning for Women.* New York: Harper & Row, 1961.

Zigler, E., and L. Phillips. Psychiatric diagnosis: A critique. *Journal of Abnormal and Social Psychology,* 1961, **63,** 607–618.

Zubin, J. The measurement of personality. *Journal of Counseling Psychology,* 1954, **1,** 159–164.

Zytowski, D. G. The study of therapy outcomes via experimental analogs: A review. *Journal of Counseling Psychology,* 1966, **13,** 235–240.

Index